HD 62.4 RBS

QM Library

23 1338069 6

KV-637-991

WITHDRAWN
FROM STOCK
QMUL LIBRARY

Resources, Efficiency and Globalization

THE ACADEMY OF INTERNATIONAL BUSINESS

*Published in Association with the UK Chapter of the Academy
of International Business
Titles already published in the series:*

International Business and Europe in Transition
Edited by Fred Burton, Mo Yamin and Stephen Young

Internationalisation Strategies
Edited by George Chryssochoidis, Carla Miller and Jeremy Clegg

The Strategy and Organization of International Business
Edited by Peter Buckley, Fred Burton and Hafiz Mirza

Internationalization: Process, Context and Markets
Edited by Graham Hooley, Ray Loveridge and David Wilson

International Business Organization
Edited by Fred Burton, Malcolm Chapman and Adam Cross

International Business: Emerging Issues and Emerging Markets
Edited by Carla C. J. M Millar, Robert M. Grant and Chong Ju Choi

International Business: European Dimensions
Edited by Michael D. Hughes and James H. Taggart

Multinationals in a New Era: International Strategy and Management
Edited by James H. Taggart, Maureen Berry and Michael McDermott

International Business
Edited by Frank McDonald, Heinz Tusselman and Colin Wheeler

Internationalization: Firm Strategies and Management
Edited by Colin Wheeler, Frank McDonald and Irene Greaves

The Process of Internationalization
Edited by Frank MacDonald, Michael Mayer and Trevor Buck

International Business in an Enlarging Europe
Edited by Trevor Morrow, Sharon Loane, Jim Bell and Colin Wheeler

Managerial Issues in International Business
Edited by Felicia M. Fai and Eleanor J. Morgan

Corporate Governance and International Business
Edited by Roger Strange and Gregory Jackson

Contemporary Challenges to International Business
Edited by Kevin Ibeh and Sheena Davies

Resources, Efficiency and Globalization
Edited By Pavlos Dimitratos and Marian V. Jones

Resources, Efficiency and Globalization

Edited By
Pavlos Dimitratos
Assistant Professor, Athens University of Economics and Business

and

Marian V. Jones
Professor of Internationalisation and Entrepreneurship, University of Glasgow

Selection and editorial content © Pavlos Dimitratos and Marian V. Jones 2010
Individual chapters © contributors 2010
Foreword © Frank McDonald

All rights reserved. No reproduction, copy or transmission of this
publication may be made without written permission.

No portion of this publication may be reproduced, copied or transmitted
save with written permission or in accordance with the provisions of the
Copyright, Designs and Patents Act 1988, or under the terms of any licence
permitting limited copying issued by the Copyright Licensing Agency,
Saffron House, 6-10 Kirby Street, London EC1N 8TS.

Any person who does any unauthorized act in relation to this publication
may be liable to criminal prosecution and civil claims for damages.

The authors have asserted their rights to be identified as the authors of this work
in accordance with the Copyright, Designs and Patents Act 1988.

First published 2010 by
PALGRAVE MACMILLAN

Palgrave Macmillan in the UK is an imprint of Macmillan Publishers Limited,
registered in England, company number 785998, of Houndmills, Basingstoke,
Hampshire RG21 6XS.

Palgrave Macmillan in the US is a division of St Martin's Press LLC,
175 Fifth Avenue, New York, NY 10010.

Palgrave Macmillan is the global academic imprint of the above companies
and has companies and representatives throughout the world.

Palgrave® and Macmillan® are registered trademarks in the United States,
the United Kingdom, Europe and other countries.

ISBN: 978-0-230-23653-0 hardback

This book is printed on paper suitable for recycling and made from fully
managed and sustained forest sources. Logging, pulping and manufacturing
processes are expected to conform to the environmental regulations of the
country of origin.

A catalogue record for this book is available from the British Library.

A catalog record for this book is available from the Library of Congress.

10   9   8   7   6   5   4   3   2
19 18 17 16 15 14 13 12 11 10

Printed and bound in Great Britain by
CPI Antony Rowe, Chippenham and Eastbourne

QM LIBRARY
(MILE END)

In fond memory of Jim Bell (1954–2009)

We would like to dedicate this book to the memory of Professor Jim Bell who was a close friend and colleague of ours and of many in the Academy of International Business (AIB) community. A respected academic, prolific writer and teller of tales from many adventures, Jim will be most remembered for his unique ability to bring people together across borders of all kinds. He was witty, charming and mischievous and made research accessible and fun for those who worked with him or were mentored by him. His research on the internationalisation of the small firm has been central to the development of International Entrepreneurship as a scholarly domain and is widely cited for its insightful approach and eloquent dissemination. He had a wide network of friends and colleagues, was connected internationally and we are lucky to have known him, have worked with him and shared some time with him. His sense of community was and continues to be his contribution to academic life.

Contents

Part III   Subsidiaries and Resource Transfer

Part IV   Internationalized SMEs, Strategies, and Efficiency

Part V   Internationalized SMEs, Resources, and Entrepreneurship

Illustrations

Tables

Figures

Acknowledgements

Many thanks to the Centre for Internationalisation and Enterprise Research (CIER), and the Department of Management of the University of Glasgow for hosting the 36th Annual Conference of the Academy of International Business, United Kingdom and Ireland (UKI) Chapter. Particular thanks to Professors Marian V. Jones and Stephen Young for organizing the conference; the reviewers of the papers of the conference; the associated staff and doctoral students at the University of Glasgow, especially Jane Brittin, Pavlos Dimitratos, Lucrezia Casulli, Margaret Fletcher, Maria Karafyllia, Junzhe Ji, Yee Kwan Tang, Anna Morgan-Thomas, Emmanuella Plakoyiannaki, Shameen Prashantham, Susan Shaw, Emily Stewart, George Vlachos, and Karl Warner for coordinating conference activities and the website, and compiling the proceedings; and Panagiota Sapouna and Emmanouil Sofikitis, doctoral students in the Department of Management Science and Technology of the Athens University of Economics and Business, for helping out in the review process of the chapters in this book.

Foreword

The CIER (Centre for Internationalisation and Enterprise Research) at the University of Glasgow hosted the 36th Annual Conference of the UK and Ireland Chapter of the Academy of International Business on the 2–4 April 2009. This book contains a selection of papers presented at the conference on five major contemporary research areas focusing on the theme of the conference – 'Resources, Efficiency, and Globalization'. The book is the 17th volume in the Palgrave AIB UK and Ireland International Business series.

The plenary session of the conference feature three distinguished figures from parliament, business, and academia, and focussed on contemporary issues that have important implications for research in International Business. The Rt Hon John McFall MP, Chairman of the House of Commons Treasury Select Committee, presented a very informative talk on the implications of the global financial crisis for the global economy and national and local economies. Mr Robin Gordon, Strategy Manager, IBM Greenock Campus, Greenock, Scotland, highlighted a case of the reconstruction of a multinational corporation in response to the growing internationalization of trade, investment, and knowledge flows. The plenary concluded with a stimulating talk by Professor Rod McNaughton, Eyton Chair in Entrepreneurship, Centre for Business, Entrepreneurship & Technology, University of Waterloo, Canada, on the importance of small and new ventures in economic renewal.

The 36th Annual Conference attracted 175 delegates from 26 countries including countries in the Americas, Australia, Africa, Europe, Middle East, Scandinavia, and Russia. The delegates presented 117 papers in the conference tracks and some 50 doctoral students participated in the doctoral colloquium. The colloquium reflects the continuing commitment of the Chapter to promote and develop doctoral work in international business. The work at the annual conference, which is reflected in the papers in this book, confirms the commitment of the Chapter to promote and develop International Business research in the United Kingdom and Ireland. The Chapter is expanding its involvement in the development of international business research by continuing to organize an annual conference and by providing resources and information to enhance the quantity and quality of international business research. Please visit our website (http://www.aib-uki.org) to explore the work of the Chapter and to find out how to become involved with the work of the Chapter.

FRANK MCDONALD
Chair, Academy of International Business,
UK and Ireland Chapter

Contributors

Ulf Andersson is professor of strategy and international management at the Centre for Strategic Management and Globalization, Copenhagen Business School. His research interests reside within the field of knowledge governance in multi-unit firms. In particular, his research has addressed power, control, and knowledge-sharing within the multinational enterprise using external embeddedness as a basis for subsidiary development. Andersson has published articles in several journals, including *Strategic Management Journal, Journal of International Business Studies, Organization Studies,* and *International Business Review.*

Dolores Añón Higón is lecturer in economics at the University of Valencia, Spain, and research associate to the Interdisciplinary Research Network (ERI-CES). Her research interests include the analysis of firms' performance, the role of innovation and information and communication technologies on productivity, and the internationalization of R&D activities. She has published in journals such as *IEEE Transaction on Engineering Management, International Journal of Management Reviews, Research Policy, Review of World Economics,* and *Scottish Journal of Political Economy.*

Luis Bernardino is assistant professor in the Department of Management Science at IBS-ISCTE Business School. He is director of the IBS-ISCTE Business School Executive Doctorate (DBA) Programme. Luis Bernardino has a Ph.D. in management awarded by the University of Glasgow, and a degree in electrical engineering (Electric Power Systems) from IST Engineering School of Lisbon (1978). His research interests reflect his 20 years of experience in industry and encompass the internationalization of SMEs as well as the foreign expansion of multinationals from small and peripheral countries.

Alberto Brugnoli is associate professor of economics at the University of Bergamo and director of Lombardy Regional Institute for Research (IReR).

Gary A. S. Cook is senior lecturer in applied economics at the University of Liverpool Management School, UK. He gained his Ph.D. from Manchester Business School in 1993, where for many years he was Visiting Fellow in Economics. He is the author of numerous journal articles, book chapters, and reports in the areas of industrial clustering, small firm insolvency, entrepreneurship, and vertical integration and vertical restraints. He also writes regularly on the wood, paper, printing, and publishing industries.

Alfredo D'Angelo is a doctoral researcher at the Centre for International Business and the International Economy within the Business Research Department of the University of Pavia (Italy). He obtained a B.A.(Hons) in Economics from the University of Naples 'Federico II' (Italy), an M.Sc.(Distinction) in International Business from the University of Ulster (UK), and an M.Sc.(Distinction) in Management Research from the University of Glasgow (UK). His research interests are focussed on the internationalization, entrepreneurial activities, and innovation of high-technology small firms. He is currently funded through the Ministry for Universities and Scientific Research (Italy). His work has been presented at several international conferences, including the IX Vaasa Conference on International Business 2007 and the AIB-UKI conferences 2007 and 2009. Alfredo has also been involved in consultancy and market research works at both national and international level (among them Euromonitor International, Italian Regional Institute of Research, Irish Food Board, etc.).

Antonio Dal Bianco is research assistant at IReR (Regional Centre of Research of Lombardy) in Milan. At present, he is working on universities' efficiency, small and medium-sized firms' demand of qualified manpower, and cluster policies. He has statistical and econometrics skills, and he is familiar with applied evaluations methods.

Henrik Dellestrand is a Ph.D. candidate at the Department of Business Studies, Uppsala University, Sweden. His research interests include the management of multinational enterprises, more specifically headquarter-subsidiary relationships, subsidiary evolution, and innovation development and transfer.

Pavlos Dimitratos is assistant professor in the Department of Management Science and Technology, Athens University of Economics and Business, Greece, and a Visiting Senior Research Fellow at the Centre of Internationalization and Enterprise Research of the Department of Management, University of Glasgow, UK. His research interests include multinational subsidiary activities, small and medium-sized internationalization, and international entrepreneurship. He has published in journals such as *Journal of Management Studies, British Journal of Management, Entrepreneurship and Regional Development, International Small Business Journal, Journal of World Business,* and *Management International Review.*

Nigel Driffield is professor of international business at Aston Business School, and holds a Ph.D. from Reading University. His main research interests lie in modelling the cause and effect of foreign direct investment, the interactions between multinational firms and goods and factor markets, and the relationship between foreign direct investment and international technology flows.

Mika Gabrielsson, D.Sc. is professor of international business at the Helsinki School of Economics, and adjunct professor of International Marketing, Lappeenranta University of Technology, Finland. His teaching covers areas such as internationalization of the firm and global marketing management, and research interests include, among others, rapid globalization. He has been active in research projects funded by Academy of Finland and Tekes such as the 'Born Globals' and 'Responding to Globalization' projects. He has published over 100 articles in refereed international journals or conference proceedings, and many of them have been included as chapters in international business books. He is a frequent reviewer in many journals and serves, for instance, on the editorial board of *Industrial Marketing Management*. Before joining the academic world, he held several senior positions in purchasing and marketing of global high-tech companies.

Peter Gabrielsson, D.Sc. is professor of international marketing at the University of Vaasa, and adjunct professor of international business, Helsinki School of Economics, Finland. His teaching covers areas such as export and global marketing and his research interests include the globalization process of firms, born globals, globalizing internationals, and global marketing strategies. He is currently leading a large research project investigating born globals funded by Tekes, the Finnish funding agency of technology and innovation. He has published in Journals such as *International Business Review, International Marketing Review,* and *Industrial Marketing Management*. He has a great deal of experience in senior management positions at Nokia and other global information and communication technology firms.

Pervez Ghauri N. is professor of international business at King's College London (UK). He completed his Ph.D. in the Department of Business Studies, Uppsala University, Sweden, where he also taught for several years. He has been working as professor of marketing and international business at the University of Groningen, Netherlands. He has published several books and numerous articles on international business topics, including internationalization process of the firm, entry strategies, globalization and its impact on company strategies, and international business negotiations. He is editor-in-chief for *International Business Review*, the official journal of the European International Business Academy (EIBA). His main areas of interest are local development, regional innovation systems, productivity and competitiveness, regional governance and policy, municipal financing, trade and foreign direct investments, integration of economic systems, and developing countries. He is also member of the scientific committee of foundations, academic journals, nongovernmental organizations, and consultant companies, and author of over 60 books, chapters in books, working papers, and contributions for national and international academic reviews.

Kevin Ibeh, Ph.D. is professor of marketing and international business at the Department of Marketing, University of Strathclyde, where he also serves as director of research. His articles have appeared, or are due to appear, in highly rated outlets such as *Management International Review, Journal of World Business, British Journal of Management, Transnational Corporations Journal, Industrial Marketing Management, Journal of Business Ethics, Small Business Economics, International Small Business Journal, European Journal of Marketing,* and *International Journal of Market Research.* Professor Ibeh recently coedited a new Macmillan book, *Contemporary Challenges to International Business.*

Kiyohiko Ito is Shidler College Distinguished Professor and professor of management at Shidler College of Business, the University of Hawaii at Manoa (USA). He received a Ph.D. from the University of Michigan. His research interests include global strategy, the management of multinational corporations, Japanese spinoff subsidiary management, and millennium companies. He has published in journals such as *Journal of International Business Studies, Management International Review, Management Science,* and *Strategic Management Journal.*

Ruey-Jer (Bryan) Jean is assistant professor in the Department of International Business at National Chengchi University, Taiwan. He received his Ph.D. from Manchester Business School, the University of Manchester (UK), where he also worked as a postdoctoral research fellow. His research focuses on interorganizational relationship management, with particular focus on online and international contexts. His work has appeared in *Critical Perspectives of International Business* and *International Marketing Review.*

Marian V. Jones is professor of internationalization and entrepreneurship and codirector of the Centre for Internationalization and Enterprise Research (CIER) at the University of Glasgow, Scotland (UK). Her research on the internationalization of high-technology small firms has been widely published in internationally recognized journals such as the *Journal of International Business Studies, Journal of Business Venturing,* and *Journal of International Marketing.*

Laila Kasem is Ph.D. researcher in international business at the Strathclyde Business School, Glasgow (UK). She received her M.Sc. degree in international business and emerging markets from the University of Edinburgh Management School, and worked for a few years in the Syrian public sector before commencing her graduate studies.

Tohyun Kim is a Ph.D. candidate in international management at the Shidler College of Business, University of Hawaii at Manoa (USA). His research interests include organizational learning, social networks, and multinational corporations. His dissertation examines the effects of producers' structural positions in the market on their experiential learning and identity exploration in the U.S. feature film industry. His work has recently been published in *Strategic Organization.*

Minnie Kontkanen is a senior assistant of international marketing at the University of Vaasa, Finland. Her research interests include internationalization of SMEs and entry strategy choice.

Jorma Larimo is a professor of international marketing at University of Vaasa, Finland. His research interests include internationalization of SMEs and export performance, foreign direct investment strategies and performance, and entry and marketing strategies in Central and Eastern European countries. He is an active member of several academic associations and has published in several international journals and edited books.

Dimitris Manolopoulos is lecturer in the Department of Business Administration, Athens University of Economics and Business, Greece. His research interests include multinational subsidiary strategies, technology management, and international human resource management. He is the author of a book related to the strategic bases of multinational enterprise expansion in peripheral EU economies. He has published in journals such as the *International Business Review,* the *International Journal of Human Resource Management,* and *Management International Review.*

Anna Morgan-Thomas is a lecturer at the University of Glasgow, United Kingdom. Her research focuses on global impacts of e-commerce, with particular reference to internationalization and export performance of smaller firms. Her articles on e-commerce, internationalization, and global entrepreneurship have been published in *International Marketing Review, International Small Business Journal,* and *European Journal of International Management.*

Naresh R. Pandit is professor of management and Director of Research at Norwich Business School, University of East Anglia. His research focuses on the link between clustering and economic performance and has been funded by grants from the British Academy, the Corporation of London, the DTI, the ESRC, the European Union, and the North West Development Agency.

Magnus Persson received his Ph.D. from Uppsala University and then went on to a job as an analyst at the international construction company Skanska AB. His research interests include knowledge transfer in multinational enterprises and subsidiary strategies and activities in the development and transfer of innovations. Persson has published several chapters in edited books, and his research also appears in among others *International Business Review.*

Noemi Pezderka holds a degree from the Vienna University of Economics and Business (WU-Wien) and is currently a Ph.D. candidate in International Business at Manchester Business School. Her research focuses on international entrepreneurship, information and communication technologies and economic development, and she contributes to research projects in the MBS-CIBER.

Elizabeth L. Rose is visiting professor of international business at the Helsinki School of Economics, Finland, having previously held academic appointments in the United States and New Zealand. Her research interests include global strategy and internationalization, the management of multinational companies, Japanese companies' spinoff subsidiaries, and management of internationalization in the service sector. Her work has appeared in a number of journals, including *Journal of International Business Studies, Management International Review, International Business Review, Asia Pacific Journal of Management,* and *Strategic Management Journal.*

Tomi Seppälä, D.Sc. is professor of quantitative methods in the Department of Business Technology at the Helsinki School of Economics, and adjunct professor at the School of Business, Lappeenranta University of Technology, Finland. His research involves empirical and quantitative studies in the areas of international business, transportation, quality management, accounting, financial management, economics, and medicine. He has published his research in several journals including *European Journal of Operational Research, Journal of Quality Technology, Transport Policy,* and *Population and Environment.* Seppälä is a former resident of the Finnish Operational Research Society. He has also been a consultant for several companies in Finland. Dr. Seppälä is a former sports journalist and still an active soccer and tennis player.

Rudolf R. Sinkovics is professor of international business at Manchester Business School (UK) His research centres on interorganizational governance, the role of information and communication technologies, and research methods in international business. He received his Ph.D. from Vienna University of Economics and Business (WU-Wien), Austria. His work has appeared in international business and international marketing journals such as *Journal of International Business Studies, Management International Review, Journal of World Business, International Business Review,* and *International Marketing Review.*

Yama Temouri holds a Ph.D. in applied industrial economics from Aston Business School, where he is currently a research fellow in the Economics and Strategy Group. His research interests are mainly in the empirical analysis of foreign direct investment on both host and source countries. He is particularly interested in the productivity performance of multinational corporations and their labour market effects in developed and developing countries.

Sigrun M. Wagner is a Teaching Fellow at Royal Holloway, University of London, and completing her PhD at Loughborough University Business School. She holds a B.A. in European Studies from the University of Osnabrück (Germany) and an M.Sc. in International Management from Loughborough University. Her research focusses on corporate political activities of multinational enterprises in the EU, specifically in the area of environmental regulations for the automotive industry. She has presented at various international business conferences (Europe and the United Kingdom), and has won the Neil Hood and Stephen Young Prize for most original new work at the Academy of International Business (UK and Ireland Chapter) conference, in Portsmouth, March 2008, for her doctoral paper presentation.

Karl S. R. Warner is a doctoral researcher at the Centre for Internationalization and Enterprise Research (CIER) within the Department of Management at the University of Glasgow (UK). His research is positioned in the life sciences drawing on dynamic capabilities, networking dynamics, open innovation, and international entrepreneurship. He is currently funded through the Matthew Hudson Scholarship for International Entrepreneurship and is a visiting scholar at the University of Queensland Business School (UQBS) in Brisbane, Australia. His research has been presented to academia and industry, including the Academy of International Business (UK and Ireland Chapter) Chapter 2009 and to Babraham Biosciences Technologies Ltd (BBT), the commercial arm of the internationally regarded Babraham Institute in Cambridge, UK.

Huan Zou is a lecturer in strategic management in the Business School at Loughborough University (UK). She completed her Ph.D. at Manchester Business School (UK). Her research interests include international mergers and acquisitions, growth of entrepreneurial firms in China and knowledge acquisition in high-tech industries. She has published in journals such as the *Journal of World Business, Management International Review, Asia Pacific Journal of Management,* and other economics and marketing journals.

Antonella Zucchella is full professor of international entrepreneurship and marketing at the University of Pavia and invited professor in international marketing at Strasbourg University R.Schuman. She is cofounder and president of the Centre for Research in International Business of the University of Pavia (CIBIE). She authored several articles in international journals, Italian monographies, and a Palgrave book on international entrepreneurship.

Resources, Efficiency, and Globalization: International Business in the Modern Era

Pavlos Dimitratos and Marian V. Jones

Introduction

In the modern interconnected business world, big and small firms strive for efficiency and success over their domestic and foreign rivals. The evolution of modern information and communication technologies and the political democratization in numerous nations has made the marketplace more competitive, albeit with an increasing number of opportunities due the opening of many country-markets. Indeed, globalization presents countervailing forces whereby big global markets and regional/country differences counteract with one another, making the 'rules of the game' for the modern firm much more complex than in the past.

In such an environment, firms seek to nurture and refine the resources that make them different and unique compared with their rivals. This resource-based view has been a significant tool for management theorists and practitioners and its use in international business has been influential (Peng, 2001). Such an important resource can be knowledge from foreign market activities. Big multinational firms look for efficiency through knowledge transfer between other multinational enterprise (MNE) subsidiaries and host market actors. MNEs have to find appropriate systems, motivators, and enablers to facilitate those intraorganizational knowledge transfers (Roth et al. 2009).

Modern MNEs additionally have to identify where and how to source resources and knowledge throughout the globe. Global MNEs resemble the 'global factories' (Buckley, 2007, 2009) that engage in sophisticated sourcing processes in order to maximize their efficiency between MNE headquarters and subsidiaries. Location and geography has been one of the most understudied areas in the international business literature (Buckley and Ghauri, 2004). Significant challenges additionally emerge in the governance mechanisms of these novel organizational forms that include the 'metanational' enterprise (Verbeke and Kenworthy, 2008).

In these competitive circumstances, small and medium-sized enterprises (SMEs) primarily look to hone resources in order to implement their strategies in market niches in the international marketplace. They realize that the efficiency of their activities may often rely on their network partners that may provide access to valuable network resources (Coviello, 2006). Their pursuit for competitiveness and efficiency often relies on the integration and use of an entrepreneurial style that constitutes a proactive, venturesome, and innovative bevaviour in the global marketplace (McDougall and Oviatt, 2000).

Viewed in this light, the edited collection of papers of 'Resources, Efficiency, and Globalization' represents a clear response to these three interrelated themes. The 16 papers included in this text draw from the 36th Academy of International Business (United Kingdom and Ireland Chapter) held at the University of Glasgow in April 2009. This conference was chaired by professors Marian V. Jones and Stephen Young. The chapters are laid out in five parts and deal with MNE strategies, governance, and efficiency; MNE location and human resources; subsidiaries and resource transfer; internationalized SMEs, strategies, and efficiency; and internationalized SMES, resources, and entrepreneurship. Each of these chapters is briefly introduced below.

Part I: MNE strategies, governance, and efficiency

Part I examines strategic aspects, governance mechanisms and related efficiency stemming from MNE activity. Chapter 2 by Ito, Rose, and Kim posits that managers of MNEs have extensive choice with respect to organizing their firms' collections of domestic and foreign subsidiaries. Issues of managerial mind-set and the balance between global integration and local responsiveness have drawn the interest of researchers in management and international business for decades. To date, most of our understanding about how MNEs manage competing tensions at home and abroad is based on in-depth case studies. Ito et al. adopt a different approach. Analyzing observable outcomes of corporate-level strategic decisions regarding organizational configurations, they undertake a large-scale research. They investigate lead-lag relationships in changes in the numbers of domestic and foreign subsidiaries held by Japanese service-sector multinational corporations, during the period following the bursting of the economic bubble in Japan (1991–2005). Traditionally, Japanese MNEs have tended to emphasize global integration over local responsiveness, through the maintenance of strong headquarters control over international subsidiaries. Ito et al.'s analysis suggests that this has not been the typical strategy for Japanese service-sector MNEs in the post-bubble period. They provide evidence of strong bidirectional and contemporaneous lead-lag relationships between changes in the MNEs' numbers of domestic and international subsidiaries. This suggests that a better characterization of the dominant managerial mind-set among these firms may be geocentric, rather than the ethnocentric mind-set traditionally associated with Japanese MNEs.

Chapter 3 by Jean and Sinkovics is based on the idea that in order to enhance local suppliers' responsiveness in international exchange relationships, international MNE customers must work with their local suppliers to create new form of relationship structures. Cultural and country differences may limit the use and effectiveness of traditional relationship governance tools between the international MNE customers and their local suppliers. Drawing on the resource-based view and transaction cost economics, their study uses 219 electronics suppliers from Taiwan to examine the influence of virtual integration, knowledge-sharing, and commitment on their responsiveness in international exchange relationships. Their findings demonstrate that the use of plural forms of governance can enhance interorganizational value creation in terms of supplier responsiveness in international exchange relationships.

Part II: MNE location and human resources

Part II elaborates from different perspectives on MNE location considerations and human resource issues. These two themes can be interrelated, as the opening chapter in this part reveals. In Chapter 4, Temouri, Driffield, and Anon Higón provide firm-level growth-rates of labour of offshore investments using a panel of leading OECD MNEs and their foreign subsidiaries around the world between 1997 and 2006. Their evidence shows that positive growth rates are observed for both the OECD parent and the subsidiaries in various regions across the world. The results hold for both the manufacturing and services sector. This lends some tentative support to the optimistic view that the expansion of employment abroad in search of efficiency gains may not occur at the detriment of employment at home. Given that high-technology industries play an important role in the growth potential for an economy, these findings are somewhat reassuring from a policy point of view.

In Chapter 5, Cook and Pandit address the question of what is the influence of geographic concentration of economic activity on the patterns of foreign direct investment. The case of U.K. financial services is examined as it is home to the world's outstanding internationalized financial services cluster, the City of London. This chapter tests whether the hypothesis that strong clusters are likely to be attractive for inward direct investment is evident in financial services in the United Kingdom using data derived principally from the U.K.'s Annual Foreign Direct Investment survey. Cook and Pandit also distinguish between two different types of agglomeration economy, localization economies based on collocation of firms in related lines of activity, and urbanization economies based on the overall concentration of economic activity in a particular region. A positive influence of cluster strength is found, which again is more strongly related to localization than urbanization economies. There is also evidence from their econometric models that very large and highly dense clusters like the City of London do run into problems of congestion. Two conclusions for practitioners are that the ability to tap into agglomeration economies should feature in strategic thinking, but that discrimination is needed to avoid incurring high costs of location in such clusters for activities unlikely to benefit from such a presence.

In Chapter 6, Wagner investigates the resources used by MNEs in their corporate political activities in the European Union (EU). The research is based on the resource-based theory with a focus on political resources to answer what kind of resources MNEs use in their corporate political activities. Wagner employs a case study methodology based on 70 interviews with stakeholders of the automotive industry in the European Union: companies, trade associations, European Union institutions, and civil society organizations. Findings of the interviews on resources suggest that resources related to human resources (e.g., expertise, reputation, network) are found to be the most important resources in MNE corporate political activities.

In Chapter 7, Manolopoulos and Dimitratos provide insights on career orientations of knowledge professionals. They approach this issue examining two main research objectives: (a) to identify the attractiveness of diverse career routes (managerial, technical, project-based, entrepreneurial and hybrid) offered to R&D employees, and (b) to associate their career preferences with specific demographic variables and organizational characteristics. Based on a questionnaire-based survey that has been addressed to MNE employees of R&D units located in Greece, their findings indicate that though the 'dual ladder' system (promotions to managerial or technical positions) is still prevalent in defining their career orientation, knowledge professionals are no longer restricted to managerial or technical advancement only. Further, R&D professionals are not a homogenous group as one would imagine, given their broad range of career aspirations.

Part III: Subsidiaries and resource transfer

Part III attempts a close look at subsidiary themes and transfer mechanisms and processes. In Chapter 8, Andersson and Persson argue that subsidiaries develop capabilities pertaining to transfer of technological knowledge. The literature suggests that these capabilities may be formed from previous experiences. Two different types of experience may underlie the formation of transfer capabilities, namely general transfer experience and dyadic transfer experience. Andersson and Persson posit that the positive effect of subsidiary transfer capabilities will be most visible when transfer projects are difficult. Using data from 102 intra-MNE transfer projects, hypotheses for direct and moderated relationships of dyadic transfer experience are supported. Their results also indicate that general transfer experience may be negatively related to transfer effectiveness, as the transfer project increases in difficulty.

In Chapter 9, Dellestrand notes that networks and embeddedness can be considered a strategic resource for firms and perhaps even more so in the MNE context. Relationship partners provide subsidiaries with new knowledge, ideas, and opportunities. Dellestrand's research focuses on such subsidiary relational embeddedness during the development of innovations and headquarters involvement in the intra-MNE transfer process of those innovations. Headquarters involvement is seen as a valuable resource allocated to the innovation transfer project. A model based on different dimensions of relational embeddedness is developed and tested on a data set consisting of 169 dyadic, intra-MNE innovation transfer projects. The results reveal that the sending subsidiary's embeddedness, in terms of adaptation and dependence during the development of an innovation, drives headquarters involvement in the transfer phase. Theoretically, the findings offer insights into which subsidiaries are allocated additional resources, in terms of headquarters value-added activity offering the subsidiary favoured for resources a greater possibility of evolving as a unit.

Part IV: Internationalized SMEs, strategies, and efficiency

Part IV deals with SMEs and how their strategies can lead to their enhanced efficiency in the international marketplace. Chapter 10 by Gabrielsson, Seppälä, and Gabrielsson deals with SMEs originating in small and open economies. These firms have faced an ever-increasing industry-level globalization pressure, driven by the reductions of government and other trade restrictions, emergence of global market segments, increased cost efficiencies related to scale, and intensifying global competition. Under these pressures, these firms respond by expanding globally and seeking ways to enhance their competitiveness. Earlier research is, however, indecisive on whether a pure cost or differentiation based strategy or a 'hybrid' competitive strategy should be selected. Gabrielsson et al.'s study is of conceptual nature. They suggest that increased use of 'hybrid' competitive strategies is influenced by the extent of global pressure within the industry, global expansion phases and resources of the firms.

In Chapter 11, Larimo and Kontkanen note that the degree to which firms operating in foreign markets choose standardization in the marketing mix against adaptation has been one of the key research areas in international marketing since the late 1960s. Several authors have presented findings that favoured standardization and several have supported the advantages of adaptation of the marketing mix. As a result, numerous antecedents having an impact on the degree of standardization or adaptation in the international marketing mix strategy have been identified. However, this research area is still lacking a strong underlying theoretical framework. The goal of the study by Larimo and Kontkanen is to use the resource-based view to analyze the impact of selected firm, management, market, and customer factors on the degree of standardization or adaptation applied to the marketing mix elements by SMEs in their foreign sales. Based on research undertaken of 188 Finnish SMEs, the results indicate relatively small differences in the degree of adaptation applied between product, communication, and distribution strategies whereas pricing was more often adapted. When the contingency factors were taken into account, the results showed somewhat more variation, but to a surprisingly limited degree.

In Chapter 12, Zou and Ghauri deal with knowledge management and its impact on growth strategies of knowledge-intensive small firms in an emerging context, China. These authors propose that knowledge is the key element in choosing an international growth strategy of these firms. Zou and Ghauri develop hypotheses from existing literature on entrepreneurship, knowledge-management studies, smaller firms, and studies on internationalization process. Based on a data set from 306 high-tech Chinese new ventures, they adopt logistic regression models to test the hypotheses. The results show that the activities of intrafirm knowledge management are positively but insignificantly related to international growth strategy. Their results also indicate that knowledge-intensive new ventures capable of both internal and external knowledge sharing are more likely to expand businesses internationally. Zou and Ghauri provide an understanding of the impact knowledge management has on the internationalization of high-tech new ventures.

In Chapter 13, Pezderka and Sinkovics posit that the Internet technology sports a massive penetration rate and is deployed as a connectivity enabling technology for small firms, domestically but, more importantly, internationally. Despite this internationalization context, an international business risk framework for the online environment is not yet available. The purpose of their chapter is thus to fill this gap by proposing a multidimensional international e-risk construct as well as to generate propositions for future empirical testing. Key risk dimensions are derived from the extant literatures on international business, risk management, and e-commerce in the context of SME internationalization.

Part V: Internationalized SMES, resources, and entrepreneurship

Part V turns attention to more-resource related themes in SME internationalization and linked entrepreneurial phenomena. Chapter 14 by Bernardino,

Jones, and Morgan-Thomas employs the resource-based view to explore a set of resources affecting international performance of high-technology Portuguese SMEs. Their findings indicate that technological resources, the firms' international orientation and human capital of the CEO are positively and significantly related to performance in the main foreign market as measured by international intensity. While the findings of this preliminary study are interesting in themselves, they raise important questions about the efficacy of survey research in capturing time lags between resource allocations and their effect on performance and whether it is the resources of the strategic utilization of resources to which research should focus attention. Implications from this study are that higher levels of technological capability, CEO capability, and international orientation are associated with higher performance in international markets. The results of this chapter show that firms with higher endowments of technological resources had higher performance through independent entry modes while international orientation as a knowledge resource was important irrespective of entry mode. Financial resources and entrepreneurial orientation were not significant in influencing performance.

In Chapter 15, Kasem and Ibeh draw upon case evidence to explore the relevance of the extant theoretical frameworks in explaining the observed internationalization behaviour of knowledge-based SMEs from Syria. This chapter augments the narrow empirical research base on firm internationalization in the developing world. Analysis results suggest that while each internationalization theory seems partially salient in explaining aspects of the international behaviour observed among Syrian knowledge based SMEs, no one extant theory appears to fully explain the activities of the investigated firms. Although these firms initiated cross-border activities relatively early, they do not possess the threshold attributes and characteristics of born-global firms. They also did not largely follow the evolutionary and unidirectional path described in the stages model, nor could their market selection decisions be comprehensively explained by the psychic distance notion. Certain commonalities observed among the case firms, however, seem to suggest the greater explanatory potential of particular theoretical perspectives, specifically the network perspective and the resource-based view, albeit to a smaller extent. Kasem and Ibeh conclude by reiterating the need for a more holistic platform for explaining firm internationalization that draws upon and integrates aspects of extant theoretical perspectives.

With a view to question an earlier Peng's (2001) prediction of the increasing importance of the resource-based view within the international entrepreneurship literature, in Chapter 16 D'Angelo and Warner review 18 empirical papers during the period from 2001 to the first semester of 2009. Methodologically, they conduct a literature search to understand how international business, entrepreneurship and strategy journals have embraced the resource-based view to advance international entrepreneurship research. D'Angelo and Warner analyze the chosen articles with particular emphasis on the following issues: (1) main research objectives; (2) application and conceptualization of the RBV; and (3) the key findings and conclusions. Among others, the authors conclude that the resource-based view has advanced the discipline of international entrepreneurship since Peng's (2001) prediction.

The final chapter, by Zucchella, Brugnoli, and Dal Bianco, examines the internationalization process of small firms and suggests that this is influenced by a number of barriers. Studies on export barriers for SMEs have usually been approached from the perspective of the firm, but have rarely taken into consideration the perspective of support service providers. Their analysis aims to fill this gap in the literature available through an analysis of the barriers to the internationalization of small firms from the perspective of export promotion organizations. Based on case studies and qualitative information from in-depth interviews, the findings show that soft barriers are the most important ones in influencing the readiness of the small firm to start exporting and the effectiveness of the internationalization process within the firm. In particular, the interviews to service providers highlight the issue of the small firm's human capital and the organization's absorption capacity as predecessors of an appropriate and effective utilization of export promotion programmes and services.

Conclusion

While not exhaustive, this book provides some evidence on the theme of 'Resources, Efficiency, and Globalization'. This collection includes interesting conceptual and empirical work from colleagues affiliated with universities and organizations in numerous countries, primarily the United Kingdom and Europe, but also the United States and Asia. We hope that this edited text will provide useful ideas for further research that seeks to investigate the challenges that modern big and small internationalized firms face nowadays.

References

Buckley, P.J. (2007). 'The strategy of multinational enterprises in the light of the rise of China' *Scandinavian Journal of Management*, 23, 107–26.

Buckley, P.J. (2009). 'The impact of the global factory on economic development' *Journal of World Business*, 44(2), 131–43.

Buckley, P.J. and Ghauri, P.N. (2004). 'Globalisation, economic geography and the strategy of multinational enterprises' *Journal of International Business Studies*, 35, 81–98.

Coviello, N.E. (2006). 'The network dynamics of international new ventures' *Journal of International Business Studies*, 37, 713–31.

McDougall, P.P. and Oviatt, B.M. (2000). 'International entrepreneurship: The intersection of two research paths' *Academy of Management Journal*, 43, 902–06.

Peng, M.W. (2001) 'The resource-based view and international business' *Journal of Management*, 27, 803–29.

Roth, M.S., Jayachandran, S., Dakhil, M. and Colton, Deborah, A. (2009) 'Subsidiary use of foreign marketing knowledge' *Journal of International Marketing*, 17(1), 1–29.

Verbeke, A. and Kenworthy, T.P. (2008) 'Multidivisional vs metanational governance of the multinational enterprise' *Journal of International Business Studies*, 39, 940–56.

Part I

MNE Strategies, Governance, and Efficiency

1

Which Comes First: Domestic or Foreign Subsidiaries? Analysis of Global Integration and Local Responsiveness among Japanese Service Companies

Kiyohiko Ito, Elizabeth L. Rose, and Tohyun Kim

Introduction

Multinational corporations (MNCs), by definition, operate across different markets. Unlike portfolio investment, foreign direct investment (FDI) involves exercising substantial control over foreign assets and operations, making the manner in which firms manage their foreign operations very important. The creation of a subsidiary, either domestic or foreign, represents a major commitment. However, as Bethel and Liebeskind (1998) noted, the legal structure of firms – the configuration of their incorporated subsidiaries – has not received much attention in the organizational literature. While many researchers have studied FDI and MNC governance structures, little work has been done on analyzing the makeup of MNCs, in terms of the mix between numbers of domestic and foreign subsidiaries. We still have a great deal to learn about corporate configuration and implications of MNCs' strategic actions, as they relate to managerial control.

The competitive global business environment pushes firms to provide more high-technology, low-cost, and value-adding products and services. As MNCs seek to improve the ways in which they manage their operations, aspects of the organizations' legal structures, including domestic and foreign subsidiaries assume considerable importance. The strong influence that large MNCs may exert over economies means that their operational decisions have important impacts on both home and host countries. Thus, the complexity of the MNC's legal structure makes it a particularly rich context for theory building and empirical testing.

In this chapter, we extend the literature related to the mind-sets of MNC managers, through an examination of strategic outcomes related to domestic and foreign subsidiaries. Specifically, we investigate lead-lag relationships in the numbers of domestic and foreign subsidiaries held by Japanese service-sector MNCs in the post-bubble period. Using the concept of Granger causality (Granger, 1969), we aim to reveal managers' relative emphases on different markets. Is there empirical evidence that managers in the Japanese service sector have tended to focus primarily on domestic operations or foreign operations? The time period of our study is particularly relevant, as the prolonged environment of slow or nonexistent economic growth in Japan has raised some fundamental questions regarding the export-led strategies that have been dominant among Japanese MNCs after World War II.

Of course, strict causality is effectively impossible to demonstrate using sample data. Granger causality pertains to temporal precedence – for example, when one event consistently precedes another event of interest, based on statistical evidence using accepted levels of confidence. While not providing proof of a causal relationship in a classical sense, Granger causality offers a statistically justifiable approach to establishing precedence relationships using time-series data. To date, this methodological approach has not received wide application in the international business literature.

This chapter is organized as follows. In the next section, we review applicable literature on the management of MNCs, including organizational structure, managerial mindset, and the global integration-local responsiveness framework, and introduce aspects of MNCs in the Japanese service sector. The third section describes our analytical approach and data. We then report the results of regression analysis used to assess Granger causality between numbers of domestic and foreign subsidiary among Japanese MNCs, and conclude the chapter with a summary and discussion of our findings.

Literature review

Managing MNCs

There is a considerable body of research pertaining to the management systems of international operations, including the important aspect of organizational structure. Based on data from large U.S. MNCs, Stopford and Wells (1972) suggested a 'stages model' of international operational structure, based on two dimensions: foreign product diversity and foreign sales as percentage of total sales. Linking organizational structure and international strategy, they argued that an MNC's location in the geometric space defined by level of foreign product diversity and proportion of foreign sales offers insight into its selection of structure, among international divisional, area-based, product divisional, and global matrix. Building on this foundation, researchers, including Bartlett (1983), Daniels, Pitts, and Tretter (1984), Egelhoff (1988), and Hedlund (1993), have studied various aspects of the interaction between structure and management processes in MNCs.

Focusing more on the nature of foreign operations and the relationship between an MNC's headquarters and its international subsidiaries, Perlmutter (1969) defined multinationality in terms of managers' mind-sets, identifying three orientations: ethnocentric (home country focus), polycentric (host country focus), and geocentric (integrated world perspective).

An ethnocentric orientation is essentially a home country-based mentality. In ethnocentric MNCs, products, capital, human resources, and knowledge flow from headquarters to foreign subsidiaries, effectively giving headquarters the primary authority with respect to key aspects of the company's foreign operations, ranging from decision making and control to communication processes. MNCs operating under an ethnocentric mind-set use strategies and managerial approaches, worldwide, that have been developed at home, so that the policies and practices implemented by foreign subsidiaries are dictated by the values, attitudes, practices, and priorities of headquarters.

A polycentric attitude, on the other hand, is based on an assumption that host country cultures are different, and that these differences are important to how business is conducted in various locations. As a result, the company is managed as a loosely connected group – a confederation of foreign and domestic subsidiaries, each of which operates with considerable autonomy. In polycentric MNCs, vital resources, such as products, capital, human resources, and knowledge flows, may remain within each market, with local managers accountable for the bulk of decision making, control, and processes. MNCs characterized by polycentric mind-sets generally focus on specific attributes and needs of each local market when formulating strategies and practices, and devolve key operational decisions, policies, and practices to the level of the local subsidiary. Thus, the values, attitudes, and priorities of the foreign subsidiary are emphasized in the development of local policies and practices, with less influence from headquarters, relative to the ethnocentric situation.

Finally, the geocentric orientation aims for integration and collaboration among headquarters and the MNC's collection of foreign subsidiaries (Perlmutter, 1969). Managers of geocentric organizations recognize the importance of achieving the companies' worldwide objectives, while simultaneously responding to local needs and accounting for location-specific differences. This balance is achieved through a complex, multidirectional flow of products, capital, human resources, and knowledge among the company's various units. Decision making and control are undertaken using collaborative processes that involve headquarters and foreign subsidiaries. In this way, an MNC that operates with a geocentric mind-set has the potential to make particularly effective use of its resources. With the priority of optimizing its resource deployment from the perspective of the entire company, local- and region-specific concerns are subordinate to the success of the broader organization.

Reality, of course, is more complicated than this discrete categorization of MNC operational philosophies. In practice, most companies exhibit aspects of each of the three mind-sets in their international management, and there are many other factors that affect the ways in which headquarters and foreign subsidiaries interact. Still, Perlmutter's (1969) classification remains an important foundation for research pertaining to MNC management.

Moving from discrete states to a continuum, the global integration/local responsiveness framework (Prahalad, 1975; Prahalad and Doz, 1987) allows for more subtlety in accounting for the relative importance of the two often-conflicting demands faced by MNCs. This framework acknowledges the tension between the MNC's need to customize its processes to individual markets and globalizing forces that advance the need for centralized control from headquarters. MNCs faced with high needs for global integration and low pressures for local responsiveness may be compatible with an ethnocentric managerial mind-set. On the other hand, firms that have low needs for global integration and strong pressures to be locally responsive may find a polycentric approach to be a more logical fit. An MNC with strong needs for both global integration and local responsiveness would be expected to manage using a geocentric approach. The global integration/local responsiveness framework advanced the concept of managerial mind-set, progressing from one dimension to two, and offering considerably more flexibility with respect to understanding managerial approaches employed by MNCs.

Bartlett and Ghoshal (1989) extended the global integration/local responsiveness framework, using in-depth case analysis to demonstrate its applicability to MNCs, along with functions and tasks within business units. They suggested four archetypes: international (low global integration, low local responsiveness), global (high global integration, low local responsiveness), multinational (low global integration, high local responsiveness), and transnational (high global integration, high local responsiveness).

Researchers have since investigated particular aspects of the relationship between managerial mind-set and international strategy. For example, Gupta and Govindarajan (1991) analyzed the complexities associated with control in MNCs, examining how corporate control over subsidiaries differs within MNCs, with a focus on knowledge flows among different units. Working with survey data from large US MNCs, Kobrin (1994) studied the relationship between geocentric managerial mind-set and MNC strategy and structure.

Much of the existing research in this area has posited that strategic mind-set is related to country of origin and that MNCs from different home countries tend to have different strategies. For example, traditional European MNCs are said to have polycentric ('multinational', in the Bartlett and Ghoshal framework) approaches, and export-oriented Japanese MNCs are viewed as being more ethnocentric (global) in nature; few MNCs have been classified as geocentric (transnational).

Foreign direct investment and divestment

Foreign direct investment (FDI) has long been a focus of research into the MNC. Dunning's (1979) OLI (ownership, location, internalization) framework integrated previous explanations of FDI, based on the concepts of the investing firm's ownership advantages, the host country's location factors, and the internalization of operations. The issue of divestment of foreign subsidiaries has also received some attention. MNCs have many reasons to opt for retreat from existing investments in international markets, including poor performance of the subsidiary (Boddewyn, 1979a), the desire to streamline operations or exit from a noncore business (Owen and Yawson, 2006), low economic growth in the host country (Boddewyn, 1979b; Benito, 1997), and changes in strategic direction on the part of the parent company (Benito, 2005). Boddewyn (1983) suggested that divestment decision processes are different for foreign and domestic subsidiaries.

Previous studies of FDI and foreign divestment have expanded our knowledge about how MNCs operate. However, we still know remarkably little about issues of the relative timings of investment and divestment for domestic and foreign subsidiaries. This broader perspective seems important, given the interaction between corporate strategy and the configuration of a firm's organization structure.

Observable outcomes pertaining to an MNC's foreign and domestic subsidiaries, including the creation of new subsidiaries and the demise of existing ones, may provide clues to managerial mind-sets with respect to worldwide strategies. An MNC that consistently effects change in its domestic subsidiaries before its foreign subsidiaries may place primary importance on its on domestic operations. This approach to the strategic management of its organizational form would be consistent with an ethnocentric mind-set. On the other hand, if change to the portfolio of foreign subsidiaries systematically precedes change to domestic subsidiaries, it may be that international operations are generally given priority over domestic ones. This emphasis on local (foreign) market responsiveness is consistent with a polycentric mind-set. Finally, the lack of a systematic order of change, between an MNC's domestic and foreign subsidiaries, may reflect a global operation that is integrated, consistent with a geocentric mind-set.

Service-sector MNCs in Japan

Japan's service sector, which is understudied in the international business and management literature, accounts for approximately 70% of the country's economy. While much of the sector is domestic in its orientation, it also boasts a substantial international component. In addition to the inherently multinational trading companies (*sogo shosha*), which include globally familiar names such as Mitubishi, Mitsui, and Sumitomo, Japanese service-sector MNCs have widespread international activity in a variety of industries, including banking, finance (e.g., Nomura Securities), and retailing. Many Japanese financial MNCs (e.g., insurance) have expanded internationally by following Japanese manufacturers into new markets. Currently, there is broad policy interest in expanding the Japanese service sector's international presence.

The period following World War II represented several decades of explosive growth in worldwide FDI. However, the macro trends mask subtleties in country-level patterns. For example, since the early 1990s, many Japanese companies reduced the scale of their international operations; this is probably the result of the challenging domestic economic environment, following the bursting of the bubble economy. The critical importance of maintaining domestic employment in Japan (Yoshino, 1968), means that recession at home provides strong incentive for Japanese MNCs to maintain their domestic operations, at the expense of their international ones, leading to foreign divestment. (This pressure may be particularly strong for Japanese MNCs, which tend to make extensive use of home-country expatriates in their foreign subsidiaries, given the typically high costs associated with maintaining expatriates.)

However, such retrenchment from foreign markets may not be consistent with long-run profit maximization. Many Japanese MNCs generate more of their profits internationally than domestically (e.g., Ito and Rose, 1999), making such a strategy unsustainable in a long-lasting economic downturn. In the post-bubble economy since the early 1990s, several of the industries in which Japan's service sector MNCs operate (e.g., banking, finance, high-end retail) have faced serious domestic difficulties. As a result, wholesale shifting of resources from more profitable international markets could have been extremely detrimental to their overall performance. Rather, it may be that Japanese service-sector MNCs will have sought to achieve a more delicate balance in their legal structures, regularly adjusting their numbers of domestic and foreign subsidiaries in order to maximize returns for the entire organization. Such a strategy would be consistent with a geocentric mind-set.

Method and data

To date, most of the research pertaining to the balance between global integration and local responsiveness has been based on case analysis. We take a different approach in this chapter, considering a collection of MNCs, and undertaking empirical analysis based on measurable outcomes of the firms' managerial mind-sets. Our approach is based on the assumption that an MNC's

configuration of foreign and domestic subsidiaries is a reflection of its position in the global integration/local responsiveness framework, and provides an
identifiable result of its strategic actions.

Granger causality

Most associative modelling (e.g., regression) provides information about relationships among variables, but not causality. Making statistically justifiable
inferences about causal relations is virtually impossible outside the context of
a carefully constructed experimental design, which is effectively precluded in
firm-level studies. Granger (1969) defined a limited form of causality that can
be assessed in a statistical manner. Granger causality is based on analyzing
whether one time-series variable contains information that is both useful for
forecasting future values of another time series variable and not accounted for
by a specified group of other variables (Granger, 1969). A finding of Granger
causality demonstrates temporal precedence relationships among time series
variables, but does not constitute 'causality' in the dictionary sense (Kennedy,
2003). Although the definition of Granger causality is limited, it can be tested
in a statistically reliable manner.

Granger causality can be assessed using regression modelling to examine
whether lagged information on one variable provides significantly predictive
power for the current value of another variable, after controlling for lagged values of the dependent variable. Given the frequent presence of multicollinearity
when using multiple lags, the standard *t*-tests for the significance of individual
coefficients may not be particularly useful, so *F*-tests are employed to assess the
significance of collections of coefficients. Three types of Granger causality can be
entertained: unidirectional, bidirectional, and contemporaneous (Berndt, 1991).

Modelling year-to-year changes in the numbers of domestic and international subsidiaries, we estimate the following models to assess unidirectional
and bidirectional Granger causality:

$$\Delta D_t = a + \sum_{i=1}^{4} b_i \Delta D_{t-i} + \sum_{i=1}^{4} c_i \Delta I_{t-i} + e_t \tag{1}$$

$$\Delta I_t = a + \sum_{i=1}^{4} b_i \Delta I_{t-i} + \sum_{i=1}^{4} c_i \Delta D_{t-i} + e_t. \tag{2}$$

Contemporaneous determination, in the Granger causality sense, is assessed
by estimating the following models:

$$\Delta D_t = a + \sum_{i=1}^{4} b_i \Delta D_{t-i} + \sum_{i=1}^{4} c_i \Delta I_{t-i} + g \Delta I_t + e_t \tag{3}$$

$$\Delta I_t = a + \sum_{i=1}^{4} b_i \Delta I_{t-i} + \sum_{i=1}^{4} c_i \Delta D_{t-i} + g \Delta D_t + e_t. \tag{4}$$

In equations (1) – (4), the following notion applies:

ΔD_{t-i} = the change in the number of domestic subsidiaries from year t-i to year t,

ΔI_{t-i} = the change in the number of international subsidiaries from year t-i to year t,

a = intercept parameter,

b_i, c_i, and g = coefficient parameters,

e_t = random disturbance.

Unidirectional Granger causality occurs when past values of one group of variables explain present values of the other group, but not *vice versa*. For example, considering annual changes in subsidiary numbers, Granger causality from international to domestic can be inferred when the estimated coefficients for the lagged ΔI_{t-i} variables, c_i, in equation (1) are, as a group, significantly different to zero, while those for the lagged ΔD_{t-i} variables in equation (2) are not. Such a result may suggest that MNCs are consistently undertaking strategic changes pertaining to their organizational forms in foreign markets first, ahead of the domestic market. This relative focus on foreign markets could be consistent with a polycentric mind-set, with low emphasis on global integration and high emphasis on local responsiveness. Conversely, unidirectional Granger causality from domestic to international (where the set of c_i coefficients is significant in equation (2), but not in equation (1)) suggests a relative emphasis on the domestic market that would be consistent with an ethnocentric mind-set, high on global integration and low on local responsiveness.

A finding that the c_i coefficients associated with the lagged variables are not significant in equations (1) and (2) suggests relatively independent decision making with respect to the numbers of domestic and international subsidiaries, potentially signifying low levels of both global integration and local responsiveness. The opposite scenario is that of contemporaneous Granger causality, which is indicated if, in equations (3) and (4), the g coefficients, associated with current-year changes in domestic and international subsidiaries, respectively, are significant. This result implies relatively integrated management of the configuration of domestic and international subsidiaries, suggesting high levels of both global integration and local responsiveness, or a geocentric managerial mind-set.

We estimate equations (1)–(4) using multiyear panel data. The fixed effects estimation procedure, which employs firm dummy variables, is selected over ordinary least squares and random effects alternatives, based on Lagrange multiplier and Hausman tests (Greene, 1993).

Data

Our data set consists of the numbers of domestic and foreign subsidiaries for Japanese service sector MNCs, measured each year from 1991 to 2005; the data are sourced from Toyokeizai, which publishes annual lists of domestic (Toyokeizai, various issues a) and foreign subsidiaries (Toyokeizai, various issues b) for firms that are listed on Japan's stock markets. The service sector is of particular interest, given its higher growth, relative to the manufacturing sector, following the bursting of the economic bubble. In total, 1,181 publicly traded service-sector parent firms report having domestic and/or foreign subsidiaries in the Toyokeizai lists between 1991 and 2005. (Our 1991 start date is dictated by the fact that Toyokeizai did not publish 1990 data for foreign subsidiaries.) This period is of particular interest, as it is one in which many Japanese MNCs undertook substantial reductions in both their domestic and foreign operations. Because we incorporate four-year lags, in order to assess Granger causality, our dependent variables are modelled for 1996 through 2005.

Many companies do not report data for both domestic and foreign subsidiaries in each of the years we are considering. The missing data, which may be due to business failure, liquidation, merger or acquisition, or failure to report, means that our models have varying numbers of observations. Therefore, we estimate each model twice: once using all of the available data and then using data from the 86 companies without any missing data for the full period.

Empirical analysis

Results

Table 1.1 shows the estimation results for modelling annual changes in the numbers of domestic subsidiaries (ΔD_t); these changes represent both investment and divestment. Results are shown for four models: equations (1) and (3), using the full data set and the subset of MNCs with complete data for 1991–2005. Comparable results for models of the change in international subsidiary numbers, ΔI_t, comprise Table 1.2. All of the models are characterized by low collinearity among the explanatory variables and no serial correlation in the residuals; both would, if present, have hampered interpretation of the estimated coefficients.

From Table 1.1, the four lagged dependent variables all contribute explanatory power (at least $p < 0.05$), suggesting that past changes in the numbers of domestic subsidiaries are useful for predicting future values. This result is consistent across all four models. While not all of the estimated coefficients associated with ΔI_{t-i} ($i = 1, 2, 3, 4$) differ significantly from zero, the F-tests for

Table 1.1   Regression analysis for domestic subsidiary changes

Dependent Variable: ΔD_t = annual change in the number of domestic subsidiaries

Variables	All data		Complete-data MNCs	
	Equation (1)	Equation (3)	Equation (1)	Equation (3)
ΔD_{t-1}	−0.19**	−0.23**	−0.15**	−0.22**
	(0.03)	(0.03)	(0.04)	(0.04)
ΔD_{t-2}	−0.25**	−0.28**	−0.31**	−0.30**
	(0.03)	(0.03)	(0.04)	(0.04)
ΔD_{t-3}	−0.11**	−0.13**	−0.08*	−0.10**
	(0.03)	(0.03)	(0.04)	(0.04)
ΔD_{t-4}	−0.13**	−0.13**	−0.17**	−0.16**
	(0.03)	(0.03)	(0.04)	(0.03)
ΔI_{t-1}	0.25**	0.31**	0.29**	0.35**
	(0.03)	(0.03)	(0.04)	(0.04)
ΔI_{t-2}	0.16**	0.21**	0.17**	0.20**
	(0.03)	(0.03)	(0.04)	(0.04)
ΔI_{t-3}	0.02	0.10**	0.00	0.07†
	(0.03)	(0.03)	(0.04)	(0.04)
ΔI_{t-4}	0.05	0.10	0.06	0.04
	(0.03)	(0.03)	(0.04)	(0.04)
ΔI_t		0.30**		0.30**
		(0.03)		(0.03)
R^2	0.19	0.26	0.19	0.27
F-statistic for lagged ΔI	23.18**	48.86**	15.43**	30.09**
[df]	[4, 1668]	[5, 1557]	[5, 765]	[5, 765]
N	1991	1872	860	860

†$p \le 0.10$; *$p \le 0.05$; **$p \le 0.01$

Standard errors are in parentheses; tests are two-tailed

each of the four models provide strong evidence ($p < 0.01$) that past changes in the numbers of international subsidiaries have predictive power for ΔD_t. In addition, for both the full data set and the subset of complete-data MNCs, the coefficient associated with ΔI_t is strongly significant ($p < 0.01$).

The results for models of changes in the numbers of international subsidiaries are remarkably similar to those for domestic subsidiaries; see Table 1.2. Past own lags contribute significant (at least $p < 0.10$) predictive ability for current changes in foreign subsidiary numbers, and all four *F*-tests indicate that lagged changes in the numbers of domestic subsidiaries are significantly ($p < 0.01$) related to ΔI_t. The strongly significant ($p < 0.01$) estimated coefficients associated with ΔD_t again suggest a contemporaneous relationship between changes in domestic and international subsidiary numbers.

Table 1.2 Regression analysis for international subsidiary changes

Dependent Variable: ΔI_t = annual change in the number of international subsidiaries

Variables	All data		Complete-data MNCs	
	Equation (2)	Equation (4)	Equation (2)	Equation (4)
ΔI_{t-1}	−0.13**	−0.21**	−0.19**	−0.29**
	(0.03)	(0.03)	(0.04)	(0.04)
ΔI_{t-2}	−0.14**	−0.19**	−0.12**	−0.18**
	(0.03)	(0.03)	(0.04)	(0.04)
ΔI_{t-3}	−0.24**	−0.24**	−0.22**	−0.23**
	(0.03)	(0.03)	(0.04)	(0.04)
ΔI_{t-4}	0.09**	0.07*	−0.09*	0.07†
	(0.03)	(0.03)	(0.04)	(0.04)
ΔD_{t-1}	0.17**	0.22**	0.24**	0.28**
	(0.03)	(0.03)	(0.04)	(0.04)
ΔD_{t-2}	0.00	0.08**	−0.01	0.09*
	(0.03)	(0.03)	(0.04)	(0.04)
ΔD_{t-3}	0.05†	0.08**	0.05	0.08*
	(0.03)	(0.03)	(0.04)	(0.04)
ΔD_{t-4}	0.02	0.02	−0.04	0.01
	(0.03)	(0.03)	(0.04)	(0.04)
ΔD_t		0.27**		0.32**
		(0.02)		(0.04)
R^2	0.16	0.23	0.17	0.25
F-statistic for lagged ΔD	12.05**	37.68**	9.62**	24.95**
[df]	[4, 1570]	[5, 1557]	[5, 765]	[5, 765]
N	1884	1872	860	860

†$p \leq 0.10$; *$p \leq 0.05$; **$p \leq 0.01$
Standard errors are in parentheses; tests are two-tailed

Considering the results in Tables 1.1 and 1.2 together, our modeling demonstrates bidirectional and contemporaneous Granger causality between changes in the numbers of domestic and foreign subsidiaries for Japanese MNCs in the service sector during the post-bubble economy. Bidirectionality is inferred from the fact that past values of domestic and international changes provide predictive power from each other, as demonstrated by the F-tests. The finding of a contemporaneous Granger causality is based on the significance of the estimated coefficients associated with ΔI_t in Table 1.1 and ΔD_t in Table 1.2, providing evidence that, marginal to past values of subsidiary numbers both at home and overseas, a significant relationship exists between the changes in the numbers of domestic and international subsidiaries in a given year.

These findings suggest that the Japanese MNCs in our sample have demonstrated high levels of both global integration and local responsiveness, with respect to the management of their organizational structures during the period of our study. The results of the analysis support our expectation that Japanese MNCs in the service sector have tended to manage their subsidiaries based on an integrated, geocentric approach in the post-bubble economy.

Discussion

We have analyzed observable linkages between the management of domestic and foreign subsidiaries, in the context of Japanese service-sector MNCs, with the goal of understanding more about the managerial mind-sets that drive strategic decision making. Based on assessments of Granger causality, we find evidence that annual changes of the numbers of the organizations' domestic and international subsidiaries have been bidirectional and contemporaneously managed following the bursting of the bubble economy in Japan.

These empirical results provide some evidence that, in the post-bubble economy, Japanese MNCs in the service sector are tending to manage their worldwide organizational form in an integrated manner, akin to a geocentric (Perlmutter, 1989) or transnational (Bartlett and Ghoshal, 1998) strategy. The lack of support for unidirectional Granger causality, either from domestic to international or *vice versa*, suggests that these organizations are not being managed based on polycentric managerial mind-sets or the more ethnocentric approach that is generally associated with firms from Japan. This finding may be related to the stronger focus on customization in the service sector, relative to manufacturing. It may also signal a shift in mind-set among the top managers of large Japanese firms. While ethnocentric mind-sets and strategies were very effective during the expansive period between World War II and the 1990s, the severity of the low-growth domestic economy in more recent times may have forced Japanese MNCs to review their operations in the light of a harsh economic logic, in which profitability depends on the rationalization of worldwide operations – both domestic and foreign – rather than blindly prioritizing domestic employment.

Conclusions

The global integration/local responsiveness framework has considerable appeal to researchers and managers. Most of the literature pertaining to the framework has been based on case analysis. In this work, we have adopted a different approach, undertaking quantitative analysis, with corporate-level data. Using the notion of Granger causality, we have investigated adaptations in organizational structure over time, studying precedence relationships in observable outcomes of strategic mind-sets: annual changes in the numbers of domestic and foreign subsidiaries held by Japanese service-sector MNCs. By introducing this analytical approach, we aim to extend the application of the framework to groups of MNCs, in order to enable more generalizable observations.

Historically, Japanese MNCs' organizational structures have relied on strong control by headquarters, leading to worldwide operations characterized as having high global integration and low local responsiveness (Bartlett and Ghoshal, 1989). Our study of Japanese service-sector MNCs in the post-bubble economy tells a different story. The finding of significant bidirectional and contemporaneous lead-lag relationships suggests that, from the early 1990s, the dominant behaviour has been more consistent with a geocentric managerial mind-set – high in both global integration and local responsiveness – than the traditional ethnocentric one. It may be that the slow-growth domestic economy has provided managers with strong incentives to adapt their international strategies, to provide continuing opportunities for growth and profitability.

The consideration of Granger causality presents a different analytical approach for understanding the balance between global integration and local responsiveness. However, as with all quantitative approaches, there are some caveats to consider. Testing for Granger causality can be sensitive to the sampling period and the specification of the regression models. For example, the use of overly long sampling periods may mask evidence of Granger-causal relationships (Granger, 1969); the fact that we are only able to access annual data is, thus, a limitation. The use of different numbers of lags in the models may also affect findings pertaining to Granger causality.

The autoregressive models do not provide for explicit consideration of exogenous factors, which means that we are not fully capturing external events or conditions that may affect decisions regarding subsidiary numbers. In addition, we are using a simplified application of the global integration/local responsiveness framework, by not making any distinctions among foreign markets. In fact, some markets are critical to individual MNCs, while others may be treated as peripheral; including such distinctions would be a fruitful avenue for future inquiry. Future research may also benefit from separating aspects of investment and divestment, and search for similarities and distinctions.

Our study, while showing highly significant results, probably raises more questions than it answers. We hope that this work will provide a basis for research that develops new insights into the complex decisions associated with the management of MNCs' collections of foreign and domestic subsidiaries.

References

Bartlett, C.A. (1983) 'MNCs: Get off the reorganization merry-round', *Harvard Business Review*, 61(2), 138–46.

Bartlett, C.A. and Ghoshal, S. (1989) *Managing across Borders: The Transnational Solution*, 2nd ed. (Boston: Harvard Business School Press).

Benito, G.R.G. (1997) 'Divestment of foreign production operations', *Applied Economics*, 29(10), 1365–77.

Benito, G.R.G. (2005) 'Divestment and international business strategy,' *Journal of Economic Geography*, 5(2), 235–51.

Berndt, E.R. (1991) *The Practice of Econometrics: Classic and Contemporary* (Reading, MA: Addison-Wesley).

Bethel, J.E. and Liebeskind , J.P. (1998) 'Diversification and the legal organization of the firm', *Organization Science*, 9, 49–67.

Boddewyn, J.J. (1979a) 'Foreign divestment: magnitude and factors', *Journal of International Business Studies*, 10(1), 21–26.

Boddewyn, J.J. (1979b) 'Divestment: local vs. foreign, and U.S. vs. European approaches', *Management International Review*, 19(1), 21–27.

Boddewyn, J.J. (1983) 'Foreign and domestic divestment and investment decisions: like or unlike?', *Journal of International Business Studies*, 14(3), 23–35.

Daniels, J.D., Pitts, R.A. and Tretter, M.J. (1984) 'Strategy and structure of U.S. multinationals: an exploratory study', *Academy of Management Journal*, 27(2), 292–307.

Dunning, J.H. (1979) 'Explaining changing patterns of international production: in defense of the eclectic theory', *Oxford Bulletin of Economics and Statistics*, 41(4), 269–96.

Egelhoff, W.G. (1988) 'Strategy and structure in multinational corporations: A revision of the Stopford and Wells model,' *Strategic Management Journal*, 9(1), 1–14.

Granger, C.W.J. (1969) 'Investigating causal relations by econometric models and cross-spectral methods', *Econometrica*, 37(3), 424–38.

Greene, W.H. (1993) *Econometric Analysis*, 2nd ed. (New York: Macmillan).

Gupta, A.K. and Govindarajan, V. (1991) 'Knowledge flows and the structure of control within multinational corporations,' *Academy of Management Review*, 16(4), 768–92.

Hedlund, G. (1993) 'Assumptions of hierarchy and heterarchy, with applications to the management of the multinational corporation', in S. Ghoshal and D.E Westney, *Organization Theory and the Multinational Corporation*, 1st ed., 211–236 (New York: St. Martin's Press).

Ito, K. and Rose, E.L. (1999) 'The implicit return on domestic and international sales: An empirical analysis of cross-subsidization', Association of Japanese Business Studies Best Papers Proceedings.

Kennedy, P. (2003) *A Guide to Econometrics*, 5th ed. (Cambridge, MA: MIT Press).

Kobrin, S.J. (1994) 'Is there a relationship between a geocentric mind-set and multinational strategy?', *Journal of International Business Studies*, 25 (3), 493–511.

Owen, S. and Yawson, A. (2006), 'Domestic or international: Divestitures in Australian multinational corporations', *Global Finance Journal*, 17(2), 282–93.

Perlmutter, H.V. (1969) 'The tortuous evolution of the multinational corporation', *Columbia Journal of World Business*, 4(1), 9–18.

Prahalad, C.K. (1975) 'The strategic process in a multinational corporation'. Doctoral Dissertation, Harvard Business School: Boston.

Prahalad, C.K. and Doz, Y.L. (1987) *The Multinational Mission: Balancing Local Demands and Global Vision* (New York: Free Press).

Stopford, J.M. and Wells Jr, L.T. (1972) *Managing the Multinational Enterprise* (New York: Basic Books).

Toyokeizai (various issues a) *Nihon no Kigyo Group* (Tokyo: Toyokeizai Shimposha).

Toyokeizai (various issues b) *Kaigai Shinshutsu Kigyo Soran: Kaishabetsu Hen* (Tokyo: Toyokeizai Shimposha).

Yoshino, M.Y. (1968) *Japan's Managerial System: Tradition and Innovation* (Cambridge: MIT Press).

2
The Role of Virtual Integration, Commitment, and Knowledge-Sharing in Improving International Supplier Responsiveness

Ruey-Jer 'Bryan' Jean and Rudolf R. Sinkovics

Introduction and motivation

Globalization has triggered significant structural strategy shifts of multinational enterprises (MNEs). With increasing global competition, MNEs have disintegrated their value-adding activities with their suppliers or subcontractors around the world (Buckley and Ghauri, 2004; Sturgeon, 2002). As a function of this mega-trend, the issue of how MNEs can effectively coordinate and control their global supply chain relationships with local suppliers becomes a critical task for MNE efficiency and competiveness.

In the supply chain literature, responsiveness has become one of the most important performance metrics for managers in today's time-based competition era (Handfield and Bechtel, 2002; Hult, Ketchen, and Slater, 2004). With increasing demands from global customers, industrial suppliers or contract manufacturers have been pushed to respond more quickly and effectively to their international MNE customers. Interestingly, despite the overarching importance of supply chain responsiveness, the issue of how international supply chain partners can govern their transactions to enhance supplier responsiveness has not received widespread recognition in the literature (Hult et al. 2004). To this end, the main question of this research is 'What is the impact of specific governance mechanisms on supplier responsiveness in international customer-supplier relationships?'

Previously, several governance mechanisms have been identified that drive value creation in international channel relationships, such as, for example, relational norms, contracts, and knowledge-sharing (Cavusgil, Deligonul, and Zhang, 2004; Wu et al. 2007). Additionally, supply chain partners have embraced information technologies (IT) and adopted these with a view to enhance supply chain performance through higher levels of process and information integration. Virtual integration of supply chain partners via IT has been considered a structural dimension of governance which can help control and relationship building in exchange relationships (Wang and Hsiao-Lan, 2007; Wang, Tai, and Wei, 2006). Therefore, improved understanding of how IT can impact on vertical governance mechanisms and generate interorganizational governance value is essential for firms. This study seeks to develop and test a model to explore the effects of three forms of governance that may be employed to generate higher supplier responsiveness in international customer-supplier relationships: virtual integration, commitment, and knowledge-sharing. In doing so, we aim to contribute to relevant literature in two ways: first, rather than focusing on cost-minimization of governance which transactional cost economics (TCE) proposed (Williamson, 1975), drawing from resource-based view (RBV) (Barney, 1991), this study focuses on the value and performance effect of governance, which is still limited in the extant literature. Second, we advance out knowledge on the effectiveness of plural forms of governance to realize the full potential of vale creation in international channel relationships.

The context in which we investigate this issue is that of upstream supply chain relationships between MNEs and their contracting suppliers. Specifically, the relationship between international MNE customers and their OEM suppliers in Taiwan is used. This context helps to elucidate key managerial in the globally dispersed supply and value chain (Choe, 2008; Handfield and Nichols, 2004; Myers and Cheung, 2008). Survey methodology was pursued and structural equation modelling was employed to analyze the data.

The paper will be structured as follows. We start with a conceptual framework, where we define supply chain responsiveness and develop hypotheses relating the interrelationships between three different forms of governance mechanisms including virtual integration, commitment, and knowledge-sharing. Moreover, we also develop hypotheses which address the impact of different governance mechanisms on value creation in terms of supplier responsiveness in international customer-supplier relationships. We then follow with an empirical study that tests the framework and its hypotheses. We report the findings and discuss the implications for theory and managers. We conclude by outlining this study's limitation and areas for future research.

Conceptual framework

As shown in Figure 2.1, drawing from resource-based view and transaction cost economic (TCE) and following the emerging view of governance value analysis, we propose that three different governance mechanisms – virtual integration, commitment, and knowledge-sharing – can stimulate interorganizational

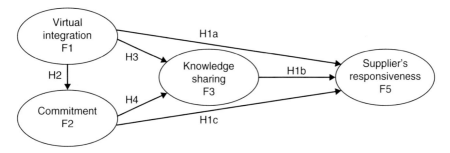

Figure 2.1   Conceptual framework

value in terms of supply chain responsiveness. Various governance mecha-nisms have been proposed for minimizing the cost of transactions in inter-firm relationships (Cavusgil et al. 2004; Wu et al. 2007). We select these three governance mechanisms because they represent a wider spectrum of govern-ance modes that capture technological, sociological, and information aspects of relationship management, respectively. We also argue that different govern-ance mechanisms can complement and reinforce each other in the process of interorganizational value creation.

Responsiveness

Supplier responsiveness, the ultimate outcome variable in this study, is defined as the extent to which suppliers are effective in marshalling and redeploying resources in their attempt to respond quickly to environmental changes (Fang et al. 2008; Handfield and Bechtel, 2002). In supply chain relationships, cycle time reduction has been regarded as one of the most important outcome vari-ables (Hult, Ketchen, and Arrfelt, 2007; Hult et al. 2004). Today's complicated and dynamic business environment requires suppliers to develop cycle time-based capability to deal with competitive and changing situations to satisfied demanding global customers. Parallel with dynamic capability theory, respon-siveness can be one of the most important dynamic capabilities which help firms to achieve greater competiveness ahead of others. Researchers have dem-onstrated that higher supplier responsiveness links contribute to improving customer satisfaction (Handfield and Bechtel, 2002) and enhancing market performance (Kim, Cavusgil, and Calantone, 2006).

Governance mechanisms

Researchers have explored governance mechanisms that exist between organ-izations (Heide, 1994; Weitz and Jap, 1995) and within organizations (Ouchi

1980). Traditional TCE proposed that governance decisions of firms are based on either pure market or hierarchy. More recently, researchers have examined the effectiveness of hybrid governance mechanisms, which are between pure market and hierarchy, for governing interfirm relationships as the transactional context becomes increasingly complex. In the international context, particularly, scholars highlighted that relational governance dimensions such as trust and commitment are important hybrid structures that allow international exchange partners to cope with uncertainty including cultural and geographical distance (Skarmeas, Katsikeas, and Schlegelmilch, 2002). Moreover, Wu et al. (2007) hold that knowledge-sharing can also serve as a relational governance mechanism between exchange partners in which the partners coordinate their activities to increase the potential for higher performance. Recent work suggests that IT can reduce transaction cost and create hybrid governance forms between markets and hierarchies (Jean, Sinkovics, and Kim, 2008; Kim and Mahoney, 2006). Therefore, this study focuses on commitment, knowledge-sharing, and virtual integration as three important hybrid governance mechanisms for governing international customer-supplier relationships.

Research hypotheses

The impact of different governance mechanisms on supplier responsiveness

Virtual integration

The advancement of Internet and B2B technology has changed and restructured interfirm relationships. Virtual integration in this study refers to the extent to which firms conduct supply chain activities via virtual interconnectivity through Internet and B2B technology with their exchange partners (Jean et al. 2008; Wang and Hsiao-Lan, 2007; Wang et al. 2006). These virtual integrations involve activities ranging from online billing, checking ordering status, inventory levels etc. in supply chain relationships. It is one type of quasi-integration and is considered as part of governance structures in many studies (Wang et al. 2006; Zaheer and Venkatraman, 1994).

Because virtual integration can enhance information processing capabilities and reduces transaction cost, a higher level of virtual integration allows exchange parties to share more timely and more accurate information. Moreover, because all the joint actions between channel partners are information-intensive, online virtual integration can increase information visibility within supply chain relationships and thus improve all relevant coordination activities (Kim et al. 2006; Wang et al. 2006). Both coordination and information visibility-enhancing effects of virtual integration

(Yamin and Sinkovics, 2007) can help suppliers to achieve more adaptive and flexible relationships with their international customers. Thus,

Hypothesis 1a: The greater the virtual integration in international customer-supplier relationships, the greater the supplier responsiveness.

Knowledge-sharing

In this study, knowledge-sharing is defined as the extent to which the supplier and its international customer work together in joint exchange of information and know-how, analyzing and solving operational and strategic issues and problems to facilitate communication about the relationship (Wu et al. 2007). This reflects a process dimension of bilateral governance that involves the parties carrying out joint cooperative efforts which can help reduce transaction costs and deter opportunistic behaviours in the relationships (Cavusgil et al. 2004; Chang and Gotcher, 2007), which follows the transaction cost perspective (TCE) (Williamson, 1979).

The process of knowledge-sharing can result in the formation of relationship norms that help to reduce the need for and cost of monitoring in the exchange process (Wu et al. 2007). Thus, knowledge-sharing can serve as relational governance mechanism between channel partners which enhances confidence to cooperate and coordination efforts. Building on RBV's notion of value, rarity, and inimitability, the knowledge-based view argues that unique abilities to create and exploit knowledge can deliver competitive advantage and thereby enhance outcomes. In the supply chain context, Hult et al. (2007) find that knowledge development has a positive effect on supply chain responsiveness. Hence,

Hypothesis 1b: The greater the knowledge-sharing in international customer-supplier relationships, the greater the supplier responsiveness.

Commitment

Commitment in this study refers to an exchange partner belief that an ongoing relationship with another party is important and thus a maximum effort in terms of maintaining it is warranted (Morgan and Hunt, 1994). Studies have shown that relationship commitment represents an essential part of successful long-term business relationships. It facilitates the smooth organization and coordination of economic activates between trading parties (Morgan and Hunt, 1994). In international customer-supplier relationships, a supplier that is committed to its overseas customer can serve a mechanism for reducing transaction cost also promote the willingness of partners to perform recurrent transactions and thus permit flexibility when a trading partner introduces extra requirement. Such flexibility allows efficient interfirm coordination and adaptation to environment changes. Commitment was regarded as a relational governance mechanism which is manifested in its flexibilities-enabling feature as a form of cooperative behaviour (Skarmeas et al. 2002). Empirical studies also find that commitment is a critically important element for improving international channel performance (Skarmeas et al. 2002). Therefore,

> *Hypothesis 1c: The greater the supplier commitment in international customer-supplier relationships, the greater the supplier responsiveness.*

Interrelationships between different governance mechanisms

The relationship between virtual integration and commitment

Virtual integration in international customer-supplier relationships requires both suppliers and their international customer to invest a lot of fiscal and nonfiscal investments including systems, personnel, and knowledge which are specific to the exchange relationships. Such relationship assets are highly specialized and impossible or difficult to redeploy to an alternative exchange arrangement. This specificity forces firms to try their best to maintain the relationship in order to keep and enhance the value of their investments in the relationships (Wang and Hsiao-Lan, 2007). Previous research showed that transactional specific investment can create a lock-in effect and bind firms together constructively in exchange relationships (Anderson and Weitz, 1992). Accordingly, virtual integration was regarded as a relationship-specific investment which can enhance mutual commitment in business exchange relationships (Kim and Mahoney, 2006). Hence, it is hypothesized that:

> *Hypothesis 2: The greater the virtual integration in the international customer-supplier relationship, the greater the supplier commitment to the relationship.*

The relationship between virtual integration and knowledge-sharing

Some researchers have linked the impact of IT to knowledge-sharing (Kane and Alavi, 2007; Real, Leal, and Roldán, 2006; Tippins and Sohi, 2003). Most of them argue that IT can enhance the quality and quantity of information exchange within and between firm boundaries (Kim et al. 2006) and thus can facilitate greater knowledge-sharing. In the context of supply chains and buyer-seller relationships, electronic integration is expected to assist joint learning activities like information exchange and joint sense making. Unlike traditional Electronic Data Interchange (EDI), new formats of Internet-based IT systems in SCMs allows firms to link up with a large number of supply chain partners and exchange rich information that goes beyond day-to-day operational levels. Moreover, advanced IT in SCMs like collaborative planning, forecasting, and replenishment (CPFR) can help uncover patterns in data and help in the processing of large quantities of raw data. Such IT-based systems can help interpret information in a timely and accurate way for the whole supply chain members (Malhotra, Gosain, and Sawy, 2005). Further, enterprise resource planning (ERP) systems, include advanced databases which allows firms to tap into previously stored information received from external sources in order to create new knowledge in exchange relationships (Malhotra et al. 2005). Building on the above arguments, we posit:

> *Hypothesis 3: The greater the virtual integration in the international customer-supplier relationship, the greater the knowledge-sharing in the relationship.*

The relationship between supplier commitment and knowledge-sharing

High levels of commitment can encourage suppliers to become more deeply involved in interactions with international customers by devoting additional resources to their international exchange relationships, which, in turn, are expected in enhanced knowledge-sharing activities. It has been suggested that partner commitment and shared vision is related to collaborative learning activities (Dyer and Singh, 1998). Recent studies also find that commitment has a positive effect on relationships learning (Selnes and Sallis, 2003). Therefore,

> *Hypothesis 4: The greater the supplier's commitment to the international customer-supplier relationships, the greater the knowledge-sharing in the relationship.*

Methodology

Empirical context and data collection

The empirical context of this paper is international customer-supplier relationships between Taiwanese OEM/ODM suppliers and their international buyers in the electronics industry, a type of international subcontracting relationship. Our focus is on a particular OEM/ODM supplier's action, in the form of their responsiveness, to the form of exchange relationships with their international customers with regard to international governance strategy including coordination efforts, control, trust and virtual integration. We deliberately focus on the electronics industry in Taiwan as empirical context because members in electronics industry are firms that pioneer the development of information technology and make great IT investments in supply chain management. Moreover, the structure of the ODM/ODM electronics supplying network is characterized by significant asymmetric bargaining relationships between international customers and their local suppliers (Kang, Mahoney, and Tan, 2009).

We collected data through a cross-sectional survey. The sampling frame for the survey comprised of all electronic companies from the year 2007 directory of the Top 5000 Largest Firms in Taiwan, published by China Credit Information Service Ltd (a total of 1069 companies). This database covers a range of electronics companies including communication products, semiconductors, computer components, and peripherals, and so on. All 1069 firms were contacted to assess their eligibility and locate appropriate informants for the study.

Data was obtained through a key informant technique, which has been deployed in prior studies on interorganizational issues (Kumar, Stern, and Anderson, 1993). Key informants in this study are senior account managers and marketing managers who are in charge of maintaining relationship with international customers and have knowledge about IT investment in supply chain relationships. We also assessed their familiarity with the themes raised in the questionnaire to ascertain appropriate responses.

The survey was conducted in two waves. Four weeks after the first mailing of questionnaires and introductory letter, reminder letters and questionnaires were sent out to no respondents. As result, 219 useable questionnaires were received, for a response rate of 20%.

Nonresponse bias was assessed by a comparison of (1) sample statistics to known values of the population, such as annual sales volume and number of employees, and (2) firs and second wave data (Armstrong and Overton, 1977). Neither procedure revealed significant different between sampled and target populations.

Descriptive information about of the respondents is shown in Table 2.1.

Table 2.1 Characteristics of responding firms

Product distribution	Percentage	Sales revenue	Percentage
Communication products	12.2	NT100M-NT500M (US $3M)	19.1
Systems	6.5	NT501-NT1B	15.9
Computer peripherals	14.2	NT1B-NT5B	39.0
Optoelectronics	14.6	NT5B-NT10B	7.3
Semiconductors	15.9	More than NT10B (US $300M)	18.7
Computer components	36.6	Total	100
Total	100		
Employee numbers		**Length of international partnerships**	
Less than 100	20.3	Less than 1 year	4.5
100–199	21.1	1–2 years	8.9
200–499	26.4	3–5 years	39
500–999	13	6–10 years	35
1000–4999	14.6	11 years and above	12
5000–9999	1.6		
10000 and above	2.8	**Country of origin of international customers**	
Total	100		
		America	43.5
		Asia	34.6
		Europe	22.9

Questionnaire development and measures

Global supply chain management research is relatively new in terms of theoretical development (Samiee, 2008). Therefore, to create the survey items, 15 in-depth interviews were conducted with 15 senior OEM/ODM account or marketing managers or directors. Additionally, to balance the dyadic point of view in international subcontracting, we also conducted two interviews with branded electronics international buyers. These interviews, along with and extensive review of the literature, were used to develop the questionnaire.

Overall, all constructs in the model were measured with multiple-item reflective scales. In general, well-validated measures reported in previous top marketing, international business and strategic management journal were used. We also followed Churchill's (1979) multiple-steps and multi-validation methods to modify and develop the items for key construct in the conceptual framework. For all scales, each item was measured using a 7-point Likert scale (7 = strongly agree, 1 = strongly disagree).

As shown in Table 2.2, virtual integration was measure by four items, building on the work by Wang et al. (2006) and adapted to the cross-border context in the study. A 4-item scale was used to measure trust. It was taken from Morgan and Hunt (1994) and adapted to our context. Knowledge-sharing was measured by four items assessing the joint activities between exchange partners in which the partners share information that is jointly interpreted to generate mutually shared behaviour. The items were adapted from Chen et al. (2009) work. Finally, supplier's responsiveness was measured by four items which modified from Kim et al (2006) and Handfield and Bechtel's (2002) work. The items were used to capture suppliers' capability to quickly respond's to their international customers' need.

Reliability and validity

A confirmatory factor analysis was carried out to investigate the convergent and discriminant validity of each construct in the proposed conceptual model (Bentler, 2005). The measurement model including all constructs was fitted by the estimated procedure of the EQS program (Bentler, 2005).The results of the analysis are shown in Table 2.2. The model provides a good fit given the complex nature of the second-order confirmatory factor analysis (CHI-SQUARE = 282.866 with degree of freedom (d.f.) = 137; CFI = 0.945; NFI = 0.945; NNFI = 0.931; RMSEA = 0.071). Moreover, all items loaded on their respective constructs are statistically significant. Further, the composite reliability for all constructs was above the 0.7 level (shown in Table 2.2) suggested by Hair et al. (2006), indicating adequate reliability for each construct.

Moreover, all factors loadings were statistically significant at the 5% level, and all of the factor loadings exceed the arbitrary 0.5 standard (Fornell and Larcker, 1981a), as shown in Table 2.2. Thus, these measures demonstrate

Table 2.2   Results of CFA

Construct and measures	Std. factor loadings	Composite reliability (α) (Average Variance Extraction)
Virtual integration		0.865(0.570)
Our international customer accesses or traces our shipping/delivery schedule electronically.	0.598	
Our international customer monitors our quality of product electronically.	0.680	
We exchange product price and market information with our international customer electronically.	0.645	
We and our international customer coordinate production plans with each other electronically.	0.899	
Commitment		0.885(0.658)
We believe the information that our international customer provides us.	0.765	
Our international customer is genuinely concerned that our business succeeds.	0.882	
We trust our international customer keeps our best interests in mind.	0.765	
Our international customer is trustworthy.	0.827	
Knowledge-sharing		0.768(0.530)
It is common to establish joint teams to analyze and discuss strategic issues.	0.579	
The atmosphere in the relationship stimulates productive discussion encompassing a variety of opinions.	0.771	
We have a lot of face-to-face communication in this relationship.	0.812	
In this relationship, we frequently adjust our common understanding of trends in technology related to our business.	0.703	
Supplier's responsiveness		0.893(0.676)
Compared to our competitors, our supply chain responds more quickly and effectively to changing major international customer needs.	0.838	

Continued

Table 2.2 Continued

Construct and measures	Std. factor loadings	Composite reliability (α) (Average Variance Extraction)
Compared to our competitors, our supply chain develops and markets new products more quickly and effectively.	0.783	
We have the ability to deal with orders for our international customer in a short lead time.	0.870	
We have the ability to be outstanding in on time delivery for our international customer.	0.794	

CFA Model Goodness of Fit Indexes: CHI-SQUARE = 282.866 and with degree of freedom(d.f.) = 137; Comparative Fit Index (CFI) = 0.945 ; Bollen Fit Index = 0.945; Bentler-Bonett Non-Normed Fit Index (BBNNFI) = 0.931; root mean square of approximation (RMSEA) = 0.071; 90% confidence of RMSEA (0.059; 0.082).

Table 2.3 Mean, SD, inter-construct correlations, and average variance extracted (n = 219)

	Mean (S.D.)	F1	F2	F3	F4
F1 Virtual integration	4.560 (1.032)	**0.754**			
F2 Commitment	5.560 (1.107)	0.054	**0.811**		
F3 Knowledge-sharing	5.236 (0.928)	0.239**	0.432**	**0.728**	
F4 Responsiveness	5.675 (1.124)	0.254**	0.495**	0.602**	**0.904**

Note: Numbers in bold denote the square root of the average Variance extracted (AVE), **=p < 0.01

adequate convergent validity. In terms of discriminant validity, this study assessed the discriminant validity of each construct in two ways (Wu et al. 2007). First, a procedure recommended by Bagozzi, Yi, and Phillips (1991) was adopted. We examined pairs of related constructs in a two-factor CFA, once constraining the correlations between two constructs to unity and once freeing this parameter. Then a chi-square difference test was conducted. The results indicated that the chi-square values were significantly lower for the unstrained models at the 5% level, which suggest that the constructs exhibit discriminant validity. This study also checked the methods suggested by Fornell and Larcker (1981b). As shown in Table 2.3, the square root of the average variance extracted is greater that all corresponding correlations, which indicates adequate discriminant validity.

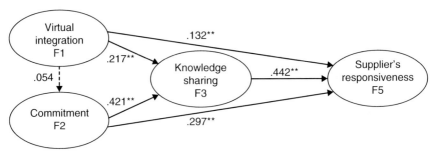

Chi-square: 247.615, df = 97, NNFI: 0.918, IFI: 0.935, CFI: 0.934, RMSEA:0.081
*p < 0.05; **p < 0.01, Dashed line indicates insignificant paths.

Figure 2.2   Structural model

Table 2.4   Summary of hypothesis test results

Hypothesis	Results
H1a: The greater the virtual integration in international customer-supplier relationships, the greater the supplier responsiveness.	Supported
H1b: The greater the knowledge-sharing in international customer-supplier relationships, the greater the supplier responsiveness.	Supported
H1c: The greater the supplier commitment in international customer-supplier relationships, the greater the supplier responsiveness.	Supported
H2: The greater the virtual integration in the international customer-supplier relationship, the greater the supplier commitment to the relationship.	Not supported
H3: The greater the virtual integration in the international customer-supplier relationship, the greater the knowledge-sharing in the relationship.	Supported
H4: The greater the supplier commitment in the international customer-supplier relationship, the greater the knowledge-sharing in the relationship.	Supported

Structural model test results

Figure 2.2 presents results of the structural tested evaluating overall model fit. The overall fit statistics indicate a very good fit for the full model (Chi-square: 257.615, df = 97, NNFI: 0.918, IFI: 0.935, CFI: 0.934, RMSEA: 0.081). Regarding the hypothesis relationships, consistent with the claim of Hypothesis 1a, 1b, and 1c, virtual integration, knowledge-sharing, and commitment have positive and significant impacts on supplier responsiveness.

(t = 4.323, *p* < 0.1), (t = 6.379, *p* < 0.1), (t = 2.142, *p* < 0.05), respectively. Thus, the results suggest that Hypothesis 1a, 1b, and 1c are all supported. The path coefficient from virtual integration to commitment is .045 (t = .730; *p* > 0.1), which does not support Hypothesis 2. We will provide possible explanation for this result in the next section. The path coefficient from virtual integration to knowledge-sharing is 0.2197 (t = 2.978, *p* < 0.01), which supports Hypothesis 3. We tested a positive effect of supplier commitment on knowledge-sharing with Hypothesis 4. According to the result, supplier commitment facilitates knowledge-sharing in international customer-supplier relationships (*p* < 0.01), as expected in Hypothesis 4. All the summary of hypotheses test results was shown in Table 2.4.

Discussion and implications

Although different governance mechanisms and their impacts on cost minimization in interfirm relationships has been examined by previous studies, which based on TCE, there is limited understanding the roles of that governance mechanisms play in interorganizational value creation in international exchange relationships. This study adds to the contemporary knowledge based RBV by providing an explanation of how different governance mechanisms including virtual integration, knowledge-sharing and commitment impact on supplier responsiveness in international customer-supplier relationships. The model was tested using data collected from Taiwanese electronics suppliers in relationships with international customers. The results support most hypotheses but fail to support the link between virtual integration and commitment. Based on the findings, a number of guidelines can be offered to both scholars and practitioners regarding the theoretical and managerial implications.

Interorganizational governance value creation through effective governance mechanism

First of all, we postulated that different governance mechanisms including virtual integration, knowledge-sharing, and commitment will facilitate supplier responsiveness in international customer-supplier relationships. The hypotheses are all supported. The results suggest that different governance mechanisms including relational, technology, and information aspects of governance can contribute to supplier responsiveness in the exchange relationships. This is consistent with the view of plural forms of governance in the value creation process in the exchange relationships (Wu et al. 2007). Firms can simultaneously use different governance approaches to create value in terms enhancing supplier responsiveness in international exchange relationships. Moreover, among different hybrid governance mechanisms, we find that knowledge-sharing has the strongest positive effect on supplier responsiveness, following by commitment and virtual integration. The results indicated that knowledge-sharing play the most effective role in interorganizational governance value creation in international exchange relationships. This is consistent with Myer and Cheung's (2008) recent findings that the crucial role of knowledge-sharing plays in creating vale in global supply chain relationships. Moreover, the results show that relational governance such as relationship commitment is also crucial in facilitating suppler responsiveness. This contributes the emerging stream of research highlighting the importance and the performance enhancement of relational norm in governing international exchange relationships (Cavusgil et al. 2004). In additional, the findings also indicate that virtual integration can facilitate supplier responsiveness in the international customer-supplier relationships. This sheds some lights on the debate and inconsistent findings on performance implications of IT investment in supply chain relationships (Kim et al. 2006).

Interrelationships between different governance mechanisms

In addition to a direct impact of three different governance mechanisms including virtual integration, knowledge-sharing, and commitment on value creation in international customer-supplier relationships, this study investigates the interrelationships between different governance. Whether different governance mechanisms function as complements or substitutes can be an intriguing research question. The findings of this study reveal that virtual integration and commitment can facilitate knowledge-sharing in international customer-supplier relationships, which in turn, can lead to greater supplier responsiveness. Knowledge-sharing not only has the strongest direct impact on supplier responsiveness, but it also plays a key mediating role for technology and relationship aspect of governance mechanism. The findings contribute to the emerging stream of research on the interacting and mediating effect of knowledge management with other capabilities in supply chain relationships.

In terms of the relationships between virtual integration and commitment, the empirical findings do not support the positive link. One line of speculation for the lack of positive link between virtual integration and commitment pertains to the firm's potential lock in risk of virtual integration in the exchange relationship (Saraf, Langdon, and Gosain, 2007). Virtual integration can reduce firm's flexibility, make firms change partners more difficult and costly, and limit the specificity facilitating capability of virtual integration in international customer-supplier relationships. Therefore, virtual integration may not be able to serve as an effective mechanism in enhancing relationship commitment in the exchange relationships.

Limitations and future research

As research is always messy and never perfect, several limitations of this study have to be acknowledged. Firstly, this study only adopted one perspective in the dyadic supply chain relationship, focusing on perceptual data from a supplier's perspective. This raises a potential bias and future research may complement this research by examining our proposed model from the international customers' perspectives. Secondly, this study is based on cross-sectional data. Given significant advantages of longitudinal data over cross-sectional data (Rindfleisch et al. 2008) future longitudinal research is encouraged, as it may provide valuable insight into the dynamic nature of IT, commitment, and knowledge-sharing facilitated responsiveness in international channel relationships. Finally, this study only examines commitment and virtual integration as antecedents of knowledge-sharing and determinants of supplier's responsiveness. Other potential variables such as contracts or dependence (Handfield and Bechtel, 2002) should be examined in the future.

References

Anderson, E. and Weitz, B. (1992) 'The use of pledges to build and sustain commitment in distribution channels', *Journal of Marketing Research*, 29(1), 18–43.

Armstrong, J.S. and Overton, T. S. (1977) 'Estimating nonresponse bias in mail surveys', *Journal of Marketing Research*, 14(3), 396–402.

Bagozzi, R.P., Yi, Y. and Phillips, L.W. (1991) 'Assessing construct validity in organizational research', *Administrative Science Quarterly*, 36(3), 421–58.

Barney, J. (1991) 'Firm resources and sustained competitive advantage', *Journal of Management*, 17(1), 99–120.

Bentler, P.M. (2005) *EQS 6 Structural Equations Program Manual.* Encino, CA: Multivariate Software Inc.

Buckley, P.J. and Ghauri, P.N. (2004) 'Globalisation, economic geography and the strategy of multinational enterprises', *Journal of International Business Studies*, 35(2), 81–98.

Cavusgil, S.T., Deligonul, S. and Zhang, C. (2004) 'Curbing foreign distributor opportunism: An examination of trust, contracts, and the legal environment in international channel relationships', *Journal of International Marketing*, 12(2), 7–27.

Chang, K.-H. and Gotcher, D.F. (2007) 'Safeguarding investments and creation of transaction value in asymmetric international subcontracting relationships: The role of relationship learning and relational capital', *Journal of World Business*, 42(4), 477–88.

Chen, Y.-S., Lin, M.-J. J. and Chang, C.-H. (2009) 'The positive effects of relationship learning and absorptive capacity on innovation performance and competitive advantage in industrial markets', *Industrial Marketing Management*, 38(2), 152–58.

Choe, J.-M. (2008) 'Inter-organizational relationships and the flow of information through value chains', *Information & Management*, 45(7), 444–50.

Churchill, G.A. (1979) 'A paradigm for developing better measures of marketing constructs', *Journal of Marketing Research*, 16(1), 64–73.

Dyer, J.H. and Singh, H. (1998) 'The relational view: Cooperative strategy and sources of interorganizational competitive advantage', *Academy of Management Review*, 23(4), 660–79.

Fang, E., Palmatier, R.W., Scheer, L.K. and Li, N. (2008) 'Trust at different organizational levels', *Journal of Marketing*, 72(2), 80–98.

Fornell, C. and Larcker, D.F. (1981a) 'Structural equation models with unobservable variables and measurement error: Algebra and statistics', *Journal of Marketing Research*, 18(3), 382–88.

Fornell, C. and Larcker, D.F. (1981b) 'Evaluating structural equation models with unobservable variables and measurement error', *Journal of Marketing Research*, 18(1), 39–50.

Hair, J. F., Black, W.C., Babin, B.J., Anderson, R.E. and Tatham, R.L. (2006) *Multivariate Data Analysis*, 6th ed. Upper Saddle River, NJ: Prentice Hall.

Handfield, R.B. and Bechtel, C. (2002) 'The role of trust and relationship structure in improving supply chain responsiveness', *Industrial Marketing Management*, 31(4), 367–82.

Handfield, R.B. and Nichols, E.L. Jr (2004) 'Key issues in global supply base management', *Industrial Marketing Management*, 33(1), 29–35.

Heide, J.B. (1994) 'Interorganizational governance in marketing channels', *Journal of Marketing*, 58(1), 71–85.

Hult, G.T.M., Ketchen, D.J. and Slater, S.F. (2004) 'Information processing, knowledge development, and strategic supply chain performance', *Academy of Management Journal*, 47(2), 241–53.

Hult, G.T.M., Ketchen, D.J. and Arrfelt, M. (2007) 'Strategic supply chain management: Improving performance through a culture of competitiveness and knowledge development', *Strategic Management Journal*, 28(10), 1035–52.

Jean, R.-J. 'Bryan', Sinkovics, R.R. and Kim, D. (2008) 'Information technology and organizational performance within international business to business relationships: A review and an integrated conceptual framework', *International Marketing Review* 25(5), 563–83.

Kane, G.C. and Alavi, M. (2007) 'Information technology and organizational learning: An investigation of exploration and exploitation processes', *Organization Science*, 18(5), 796–812.

Kang, M.-P., Mahoney, J.T. and Tan, D. (2009) 'Why firms make unilateral investments specific to other firms: The case of OEM suppliers', *Strategic Management Journal*, 30(2), 117–35.

Kim, D., Cavusgil, S.T. and Calantone, R.J. (2006) 'Information system innovations and supply chain management: Channel relationships and firm performance', *Journal of the Academy of Marketing Science*, 34(1), 40–54.

Kim, S.M. and Mahoney, J.T. (2006) 'Mutual commitment to support exchange: Relation-specific it system as a substitute for managerial hierarchy', *Strategic Management Journal*, 27(5), 401–23.

Kumar, N., Stern, L.W. and Anderson, J.C. (1993) 'Conducting interorganizational research using key informants', *Academy of Management Journal*, 36(6), 1633–51.

Malhotra, A., Gosain, S. and Sawy, O.A. El (2005) 'Absorptive capacity configurations in supply chains: Gearing for partner-enabled market knowledge creation', *MIS Quarterly*, 29(1), 145–87.

Morgan, R.M. and Hunt, S.D. (1994) 'The commitment-trust theory of relationship marketing', *Journal of Marketing*, 58(3), 20–38.

Myers, M.B. and Cheung, M.-S. (2008) 'Sharing global supply chain knowledge', *MIT Sloan Management Review*, 49(4), 67–73.

Real, J.C., Leal, A. and Roldán, J.L. (2006) 'Information technology as a determinant of organizational learning and technological distinctive competencies', *Industrial Marketing Management*, 35(4), 505–21.

Rindfleisch, A., Malter, A. J., Ganesan, S. and Moorman, C. (2008) 'Cross-sectional versus longitudinal survey research: Concepts, findings, and guidelines', *Journal of Marketing Research*, 45(3), 261–79.

Samiee, S. (2008) 'Global marketing effectiveness via alliances and electronic commerce in business-to-business markets', *Industrial Marketing Management*, 37(1), 3–8.

Saraf, N., Langdon, C.S. and Gosain, S. (2007) 'Is application capabilities and relational value in interfirm partnerships', *Information Systems Research*, 18(3), 320–39.

Selnes, F. and Sallis, J. (2003) 'Promoting relationship learning', *Journal of Marketing*, 67(3), 80–95.

Skarmeas, D., Katsikeas, C. S. and Schlegelmilch, B.B. (2002) 'Drivers of commitment and its impact on performance in cross-cultural buyer-seller relationships: The importers perspective', *Journal of International Business Studies*, 33(4), 757–83.

Sturgeon, T. J (2002) 'Modular production networks: A new American model of industrial organization', *Industrial and Corporate Change*, 11(3), 451–96.

Tippins, M. J and Sohi, R.S (2003) 'IT competency and firm performance: Is organizational learning a missing link?', *Strategic Management Journal*, 24(8), 745–61.

Wang, E.T.G., Tai, J.C.F. and Wei, H.-L. (2006) 'A virtual integration theory of improved supply-chain performance', *Journal of Management Information Systems*, 23(2), 41–64.

Wang, Eric T.G. and Hsiao-Lan, Wei (2007) 'Interorganizational governance value creation: Coordinating for information visibility and flexibility in supply chains', *Decision Sciences*, 38(4), 647–74.

Weitz, B.A. and Jap, S.D. (1995) 'Relationship marketing and distribution channels', *Journal of the Academy of Marketing Science*, 23(4), 305–20.

Williamson, O.E. (1975) *Markets and Hierarchies: Analysis and Antitrust Implications*. New York: Free Press.

Williamson, O.E. (1979) 'Transaction-cost economics: The governance of contractual relations', *Journal of Law and Economics*, October, 233–61.

Wu, F., Sinkovics, R.R., Cavusgil, S.T. and Roath, A.S. (2007) 'Overcoming export manufacturer's dilemma in international expansion', *Journal of International Business Studies*, 38(2), 283–302.

Yamin, M. and Sinkovics, R.R. (2007) 'ICT and MNE reorganisation – the paradox of control', *Critical Perspectives on International Business*, 3(4), 322–36.

Zaheer, A. and Venkatraman, N. (1994) 'Determinants of electronic integration in the insurance industry: An empirical test', *Management Science*, 40(5), 549–57.

PART II

MNE Location and Human Resources

3
The Importance of Location: Does Outward FDI lead to Unemployment?

Yama Temouri, Nigel L. Driffield, and Dolores Añón Higón

Introduction

The purpose of this chapter is to examine the spread of high-tech manufacturing and services away from the West, and the subsequent impact on output and employment in the home country. There is a large amount of work that seeks to examine the extent to which low skill workers in high-income countries are vulnerable to competition from workers in developing countries. Initially, this literature focussed on trade as the mechanism of reallocation, assuming that firms from the developing world compete with western firms through exports. However, the focus has since moved to the relocation of activities by Western firms, to more low-cost locations. This literature is discussed in detail in Driffield and Chiang (2009), for example, who also show that countries such as Taiwan are not immune to this. However, the focus of this literature has been on the low-tech firms, seeking to relocate low-skill, low-productivity activities to low-cost locations. The purpose of this chapter is to examine the extent to which other parts of a developed economy are also vulnerable to the attractions of relocation. To this end we focus on high-tech firms, and on services as well as manufacturing.

As is well known, governments around the world have offered various investment incentives to attract internationally mobile capital, though with few exceptions these have been based on employment or export growth and import substitution. Crucially, the introduction of technology that is new to the country is seen as a bonus. However, with the number of locations offering the potential of supporting the development or exploitation of frontier technology ever increasing, attention is focussed on the relocation of knowledge intensive manufacturing and services to such locations. Equally, the impact on the home country is also attracting a good deal of policy debate; see, for example, BERR (2008). Such analysis is an extension of the policy stance of multilateral development agencies, such as the World Bank, the International

Monetary Fund (IMF), and the United Nations (UN). Indeed, it is a long-held view that one of the major benefits from FDI to a host economy is the superior foreign technology that accompanies the investment (Caves, 1974). In other words, MNEs are assumed to be more technologically advanced than their purely domestic counterparts, and consequently some of this superior technology may spill over and be assimilated by domestic firms. For this reason, instruments of domestic regional and industrial policy as well as EU structural funds are often directed, at a national and subnational level, towards attracting internationally mobile investment, through various subsidies, capital grants, and tax holidays.

On the other hand, heated debates about low competitiveness at home, outsourcing, and job exporting have sparked widespread concern among policy makers and the media in many developed countries (Amiti and Wei, 2005). The fear is that direct investments abroad replace home country production and exports which as a consequence increases unemployment at home. Such views are heard especially across Europe and North America in the face of the economic threat from China, India, and other low-wage countries.

Whether outward FDI substitutes or complements domestic employment has been the subject of a large number of empirical studies, particularly in the United States (Mankiw 2004; Mankiw and Swagel 2006). In fact, recent empirical evidence for the United States is not conclusive, which in turn makes it difficult for policy makers to devise any type of response to the growing phenomenon of internationalization (Harrison and McMillan 2007). Given the widespread national media coverage and public debate, which is focussed largely on the negative effects of outsourcing and offshoring, the question of whether MNEs relocate employment abroad at the detriment of employment at home is an important political issue and high on the policy agenda (German Federal Ministry of Economics and Technology 2007).

This chapter therefore provides firm-level growth-rates of labour of offshore investments using a panel of MNEs based in the leading OECD countries and their foreign subsidiaries around the world between 1997 and 2006. Given that high-technology industries play an important role in terms of growth potential for any advanced economy, it is thus imperative from an OECD perspective to see whether outward FDI from these sectors is occurring at the detriment of home employment and the possible erosion of the skill base at home.

Hence, the contribution to the existing literature is threefold. Firstly, this is an attempt to analyze the growth rates of outward FDI using a firm level data set which allows cross-country comparisons, in this case advanced OECD countries over a 10-year period. Secondly, in line with the theoretical literature, an important contribution of this chapter is the classification of outward FDI flows. We group outward investments in several distinct ways. The reason for doing this is to ascertain whether certain effects are driven by location or type of investments. It particularly highlights the differences between low- versus high-cost destinations and whether the type of investment is of a manufacturing or services nature. This is a unique feature of our data set in that it allows us to link a parent firm's domestic operations with its subsidiaries across the world including whether the investment is of a manufacturing or services nature. Thirdly, most of the previous studies focus on the manufacturing sector, either on aggregate or at the firm level. However, the services sector includes knowledge-intensive industries which play an ever more important role in the structure and volume of outward FDI in advanced economies. To this end, this chapter contributes further by incorporating the high-technology service sector in the analysis.

The rest of the chapter is organized as follows. The second section gives an overview of the arguments in previous empirical studies on the relationship between outward FDI and labour demand. The third section offers a description on how the data set is constructed and descriptive statistics. The fourth section presents the results, and the last section concludes.

Previous empirical evidence

The empirical work which has investigated the role of FDI on labour demand has until recently only considered inward FDI (see Conyon et al. 2004 for effects on overall U.K. wage rates; Driffield et al. 2009; Blonigen and Slaughter 2001, for the impact of FDI on wage inequality in the United Kingdom and the United States, respectively). Indeed, in recent years various aspects of outward FDI have been discussed in the academic literature. This section will focus on the firm-level studies that analyze the labour demand effects of outward FDI.

Outsourcing of intermediate inputs, in particular the production tasks performed by lower skilled workers, to foreign countries which offer lower wages compared to the home country is likely to impact on labour demand by reducing the demand for lower skilled labour (Feenstra and Hanson 1999). However, the demand for skilled labour is enhanced by any increase in technological capability of the firm at the expense of less skilled workers. Recently, Hijzen et al. (2005) estimating a system of variable factor demands have reported evidence for the United Kingdom showing that over the period 1982 to 1996 outsourcing has had a detrimental impact upon unskilled labour (see also Taylor and Driffield 2005 for the United Kingdom and Machin and Van Reenen 1998).

Brainard and Riker (2001) use matched U.S. parent-subsidiary data for 1983–1992 and find small substitution effects between parent and subsidiary employment. Subsidiary employment in both high and low income countries substitute for employment in the United States. Blomström et al. (1997) find that U.S. MNEs relocate their labour-intensive activities to subsidiaries in developing countries which are not found in the activities of Swedish MNEs. However, Braconier and Ekholm (2000) find some evidence that home country employment in Swedish MNEs is a substitute for employment in subsidiaries in other high-income host countries for the period 1970–1994.

Barba Navaretti et al. (2009) examine how outward FDI to cheap labour countries affect home activities for a sample of French and Italian firms that turn multinational between the years 1993 to 2000. They use propensity score matching and find no evidence of a negative effect for both countries of outward investments to cheap labour countries. Italian MNEs enhance their efficiency and show a positive effect on output and employment. For France, they find a positive effect on the size of domestic activity. The same methodology is used on employer-employee data by Becker and Muendler (2007) in the case of Germany. They show that German MNEs would shed more labour if it was prevented from internationalizing compared to national rival firms.

Marin (2004) uses Austrian and German firm-level data from 1997 to 2001, collected through surveys, and finds that Eastern Enlargement leads to small job losses in both cases. The argument put forward is that jobs in Eastern Europe do not compete with jobs in Austria and Germany in the case of vertical investments. Low-cost jobs in subsidiaries in Eastern Europe reduce production costs and induce Austrian and German MNEs to produce more and demand more labour which in turn makes them stay competitive.

Marin (2006) also examines what factors influence the outsourcing decision of German and Austrian firms, in particular considering the impacts from Eastern European countries. The more labour-intensive the production process, the higher the probability of outsourcing occurring outside the firm to an independent input supplier from Eastern Europe, suggesting that labour costs matter.

Konings and Murphy (2006) match MNEs with their subsidiaries, both located in Europe, to test for employment substitution in response to wage differentials. Their findings are surprising in that they suggest substitutability only for North European MNEs and their subsidiaries which are also located in North Europe. No significant effects are found for subsidiaries located in South or Central and Eastern Europe from which they conclude that competition from low-wage countries does not represent a threat to parent firm employment. This latter result confirms findings presented by Barba Navaretti et al. (2009).

Previous available evidence is mostly country specific, using different econometric specifications and results are generated from various data sources. This makes it difficult to identify whether conflicting results stem from different models, samples, data sets, and/or time periods. An exception is Konings and Murphy's (2006) study, and although our analysis is similar to it, this chapter is significantly different in a number of ways. First, this chapter tests whether outward FDI for a sample of leading OECD countries, either across or within industries, leads to a reduction or expansion in home employment. Using a cross-country comparable data set, the analysis uses the number of employees rather than wage rates, for both the parent and the subsidiaries and differentiates the latter by destination country (low- or high-income country) and type of investment (manufacturing or services). Secondly, it extends the panel period from 5 to 10 years and includes subsidiaries which are located beyond Europe. This is possible because the data set used in this chapter has grown extensively in the last few years and thus one can analyze a broader set of issues with a larger panel. To our knowledge, very little work has been done with this dataset using a panel of more than 5 years.

Data and descriptive statistics

The focus in this chapter is on manufacturing and service firms from the OECD which operate in high-technology sectors. A feature of 'high-tech' industries is that they possess high levels of identifiable technology in the form of R&D and tacit knowledge which is intangible in nature. Such industries are seen as engines for growth in any economy and thus the threat of relocation of employment from high-tech industries make it a highly sensitive issue, both in a political and economic sense. The analysis is then contrasted to industries which are considered low-technology industries.

Our data is taken from *Orbis*, a rich firm-level data set, provided by Bureau van Dijk, which is an electronic publishing and consultancy firm. It offers detailed financial and other operational information on private and public companies around the world. The data set in this chapter covers the period 1997–2006. Table 3.1 shows the number of OECD MNEs and their network of subsidiaries across the world, while Table 3.2 lists our sample of countries and industries by level of technology intensity used in the subsequent analysis.

Table 3.3 shows the distribution of parent firms and their subsidiaries across the various countries and regions. The United States, France, Germany, and the United Kingdom combined host 75.9% of the parent firms in the sample. While Sweden, the Netherlands, Belgium and Japan each host from 3.3 to 8.5% of the parent firms. With regard to the subsidiaries, the EU-15 region holds the

Table 3.1 OECD MNEs and their subsidiaries

Sector	Manufacturing	Service	Parent firms (Total)	Subsidiaries (Total)
High-tech	2,594	2,575	5,169	9,055
Low-tech	6,375	15,232	21,607	56,737

Source: Authors' calculations using Orbis database.

Table 3.2   Sample of countries and industries

Country	Level of technology intensity	
	Manufacturing – High tech	*Manufacturing – Low tech*
Belgium Germany France Sweden Netherlands United Kingdom Japan United States	Chemicals and chemical products Machinery and equipment Office machinery and computers Electrical machinery and apparatus n.e.c. Radio, television and communication equipment and apparatus Manufacture of medical, precision and optical instruments, watches and clocks Motor vehicles, trailers Other transport equipment	Food products and beverages Tobacco products Textiles Wearing apparel; dressing and dyeing of fur Tanning and dressing of leather; manufacture of luggage, handbags, saddlery, harness and footwear Wood and of products of wood, cork, except furniture; straw and plaiting materials Pulp, paper and paper products Publishing, printing and reproduction of recorded media Coke, refined petroleum products and nuclear fuel Rubber and plastic products Other non-metallic mineral products Basic metals Fabricated metal products, except machinery and equipment Furniture; manufacturing n.e.c. Recycling
	Services – High tech	*Services – Low tech*
	Water transport Air transport Post and telecommunications Financial intermediation, except insurance and pension funding Insurance and pension funding, except compulsory social security Activities auxiliary to financial intermediation Real estate activities Renting of machinery and equipment without operator and of personal and household goods Computer and related activities Research and Development Other business activities	Sale, maintenance and repair of motor vehicles and motorcycles; retail sale of automotive fuel Wholesale trade Retail trade Hotels and restaurants Land transport; transport via pipelines Supporting and auxiliary transport activities; activities of travel agencies

Note: Classification based on Eurostat.

Table 3.3 Distribution of MNEs and subsidiaries by country and sector (in %)

Parent firms	Frequency	Subsidiaries	Frequency
Belgium	5.5	EU 15	67.1
Germany	15.9	Other Europe	3.5
France	11.6	Eastern Europe	6.4
Sweden	6.8	North America	13.6
Netherlands	8.5	Latin America	5.7
United Kingdom	14.8	Asia	2.3
United States	33.6	Africa & Middle East	1
Japan	3.3	Oceania	0.4
Total	100		100

Sector distribution of parent and subsidiary firms

Parent firms	MFG	SERV	Subsidiaries	MFG	SERV
Belgium	6.2	4.9	EU 15	50.0	71.4
Germany	18.5	13.4	Other Europe	2.9	3.9
France	13.7	9.5	Eastern Europe	8.6	6.0
Sweden	5.1	8.5	North America	20.5	12.2
Netherlands	7.5	9.6	Latin America	12.0	4.1
United Kingdom	10.8	18.8	Asia	3.9	1.8
United States	33.3	34.0	Africa & Middle East	1.4	0.4
Japan	4.9	1.3	Oceania	0.7	0.2
Total	100	100		100	100

Parent	Subsidiary		
	MFG	SERV	Both
MFG	23.4	40.6	36.0
SERV	4.2	68.9	26.9

Note: MFG – manufacturing; SERV – service sector. Other Europe = Norway and Switzerland.
Source: Authors' calculations using Orbis database.

majority of subsidiaries at 67% followed by North America and Eastern Europe at 13.6 and 6.4%, respectively. Locations least attractive are Latin America, Asia, Africa, the Middle East, and Oceania, ranging from 0.4% to 5.7% of all subsidiaries. The lower panel of Table 3.2 illustrates the sector distribution of parent and subsidiary firms across the manufacturing and services sectors. Of all manufacturing firms in the sample, Germany, France, the United Kingdom, and the United States host the majority of parent firms (76%) which is followed by the Netherlands, Sweden, Belgium, and Japan. In terms of service firms, parent firms are mostly located in Germany, the United Kingdom, France, and the United States. With regard to the distribution of subsidiaries, the majority is located in the EU and North America. The EU-15 and Other Europe (i.e., Switzerland and Norway) have a lower percentage of manufacturing parent firms compared with service parent firms whereas for the other regions the opposite is true. On the bottom of the table, one can see that around a quarter (23.4%) of the manufacturing parent firms have subsidiaries in only the manufacturing sector, 40.6% in only the services sector and 36% have subsidiaries in both the manufacturing and services sector. The majority of services parent firms have their subsidiaries in the services sector only, 4.2% in the manufacturing sector only and 26.9% in both the manufacturing and services sector.

Table 3.4 presents some statistics for firm-level performance of MNEs by technological classification. One of the interesting results from this is that high-tech firms on average are less capital intensive than low-tech manufacturing firms. Equally, while average wages are higher for high-tech manufacturing firms, the average earnings per employee of high-tech manufacturing firms are only $5000 more than for low-tech firms. This suggests that high-tech firms still employ a large number of relatively lowly paid employees, who may be vulnerable to relocation of activity.

Table 3.4   Characteristics of OECD MNEs

Variable	Manufacturing		Services	
	High-tech	Low-tech	High-tech	Low-tech
Output	1,538,475	1,167,622	846,230	1,041,009
	(8,110,907)	(8,383,803)	(5,281,893)	(6,836,943)
No of Employees	5,050	3,024	3,568	3,845
	(22,503)	(12,639)	(22885.66)	(34,098.5)
Capital	356,277	334,274	371,305	222,240
	(2,246,376)	(2,879,664)	(3,951,128)	(1,829,196)
Intermediate inputs	227,141	195,403	114,718	208,664
	(1,855,492)	(1,111,635)	(1,262,037)	(1,308,643)
Intangible fixed assets	195,235	167,488	333,907	66,786
	(1,810,194)	(1,331,187)	(4,345,040)	(611,319)
Profits	100,382	100,662	66,151	43,535
	(776,848)	(1,097,752)	(892,367)	(355,729)
Wage bill	147,906	75,349	150,816	68,015
	(1,064,856)	(453,222)	(1,051,414)	(491,655)
Cash flow	138,847	104,341	138,453	52,185
	(921,187)	(1,003,663)	(1,397,082)	(385,188)
Long term debt	342,646	206,930	321,176	184,150
	(4,658,308)	(1,047,782)	(2,765,319)	(1,424,877)

Note: Mean and standard deviations in parenthesis.

Source: Authors' calculations using Orbis database.

This contrasts with the service sector, where the high-tech firms are far more capital intensive and have much higher average wages. It is interesting to note, however, that profitability is higher for manufacturing firms than for service firms. The group of firms overall with the highest profitability is the low-tech manufacturing firms. For a sample of large Italian firms, Zeli and Mariani (2009) find also that low-tech manufacturing firms have higher profitability rates and a good financial situation. This group however also has the greatest variability, suggesting that low performers in this sector are still the most likely to relocate to reduce costs.

High-tech service firms have by far the greatest levels of intangible assets. These are notoriously the most difficult form of firm specific asset to manage across national boundaries. As Temouri et al. (2010) show, the desire by firms to relocate such activities to developing or transition countries, with weaker IPR protection, makes relocation of these firms the least likely, with Western countries showing the highest growth in these sectors, as we discuss below.

Evidence of OECD firm internalization

The main form of analysis employed in this chapter will focus on growth rates of outward FDI along regional and industry lines. The trend in employment growth of the parent and subsidiary firms is described in an attempt to identify whether outward FDI stimulates or hinders employment at home.

Figure 3.1 shows the average annual growth rate of the labour force employed in the parent firm. It indicates that growth rates were considerably higher

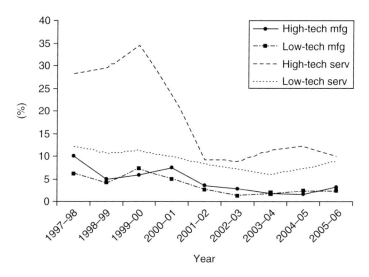

Figure 3.1   Growth rate of labour force (1997–2006)

during the late 1990s. For example, in high-tech services MNEs employment growth was above 25%, whereas they were between 5 and 15% for the other technology groups. Since then, employment growth has fallen to around 10% and between 1 and 5%, respectively.

Figure 3.2, however, highlights the significant differences between countries. While the average annual figures reveal that high-tech services industries have grown the fastest over the period 1997–2006 in most countries, low-tech services industries have grown half as fast. However, they also highlight the differences in growth between countries. The United Kingdom, for example, with the most flexible labour market of the countries listed (see Sapir 2005), experienced one of the greatest relative growth in low-tech manufacturing, and with the exception of Japan, the lowest growth in high-tech manufacturing. In the United States, both low- and high-tech services industries have grown at an average of around 12%. Interestingly, the fastest growing service firms on average were in Belgium. In manufacturing, employment growth has been much slower compared with the service sector. The highest percentage growth rates were found for Belgium and Sweden in the high-tech manufacturing industries (6%). The least performing manufacturing firms regardless of technological intensity were especially in Japan and the United Kingdom, followed by Germany, France, and The Netherlands.

The reason for this heterogeneity in employment growth across countries and industries may lie in the type of outward investment that is undertaken. One can group outward investments in several distinct ways. The reason for doing this is to ascertain whether certain effects are driven by location or type of investments. The literature on FDI makes a distinction between horizontal and vertical FDI. Horizontal FDI is likely to have a negative impact on

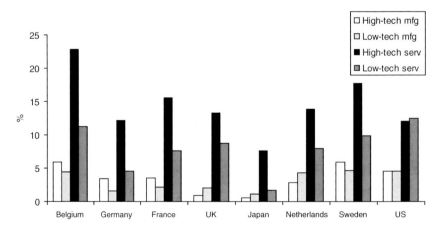

Figure 3.2   Labour force growth of parent firm by country (1997–2006)

home employment as domestic production for exports is replaced by affiliate production in foreign host countries. However, in the case of so-called *export platform FDI,* which is closely related to horizontal FDI, the employment effects for the home country are less clear (Braconier and Ekholm 2002). According to the theory of vertical FDI, firms take advantage of factor price differentials between countries in an effort to reduce costs and become more efficient. In this case, increased investment abroad is less likely to have a negative effect on home employment. The reason is that gains in overall productivity due to lower costs make firms more competitive, which in turn may lead firms to expand total employment within the MNE and the home country.

Distinguishing between type of investments and location (e.g., high- vs. low-income countries), our preliminary results show that at least for the high-tech industries in the OECD countries, the expansion of employment abroad does not occur at the detriment of employment at home. The following two tables show average growth rates of subsidiary employment across a number of dimensions. Subsidiaries which belong to manufacturing parent firms are shown in Table 3.5, whereas subsidiaries belonging to service parent firms are shown in Table 3.6. The tables include a lot of information, which is best described by drawing a number of common features.

Firstly, albeit considerable heterogeneity, it shows that the highest rates of employment growth are found among subsidiaries in Eastern Europe and Asia. This is true for subsidiaries belonging to high-tech European manufacturing MNEs (18.8% and 13.7%) and low-tech Japanese manufacturing MNEs (20.3% and 12.0%). For high-tech U.S. manufacturing MNEs, their fastest growing subsidiaries in Eastern Europe (8.2%) and Asia (3.4 %), but Europe is still a very important location (6.0%). For low-tech U.S. manufacturing MNEs, locations such as Latin America and Africa/Middle East show growth rates of 9.5% and 8.1%, respectively. Subsidiaries in other regions of the world have more modest employment growth rates as shown in the table and the only negative growth rate of –3.4% is for subsidiaries in Africa/ Middle East belonging to low-tech Japanese manufacturing MNEs. The situation is very similar for the services sector. Again, subsidiaries located in Eastern Europe and Asia show the highest growth rates, followed by Europe, North America, and other developing regions.

Secondly, when grouping manufacturing/services subsidiaries in either developed (DC) or less developed countries (LDC), the larger growth rates are to be found in LDC, regardless of technological intensity, compared with DC. For example, Table 3.5 shows that subsidiaries in LDC belonging to manufacturing MNEs have growth rates up to four times as high as their counterparts in DC. The gap in growth rates between LCD and DC is somewhat less pronounced for subsidiaries belonging to services MNEs (see Table 3.6).

Table 3.5   Average growth rate of the labour force in subsidiaries (Average over 1997–2006 in %)

	European MNEs	Japanese MNEs	US MNEs
*Subsidiaries of **High**-tech **manuf'** Parent firms*			
Of which located in EU 15	5.4	6.8	6.0
Other Europe	1.9	–	4.4
Eastern Europe	18.8	–	8.2
North America	8.1	9.1	2.2
Latin America	7.0	6.8	0.2
Asia	13.7	12.8	3.4
Africa & M.E.	3.8	–	–
Oceania	3.1	3.8	–
Of which Manufacturing in DC	4.3	6.7	1.8
Manufacturing in LDC	16.2	5.7	2.9
Services in DC	6.2	8.0	7.9
Services in LDC	19.7	–	4.0
*Subsidiaries of **Low**-tech **manuf'** Parent firms*			
Of which located in EU 15	5.0	5.8	3.7
Other Europe	3.1	1.4	1.1
Eastern Europe	13.4	20.3	10.4
North America	7.2	7.7	1.4
Latin America	8.9	9.8	9.5
Asia	12.5	12.0	7.2
Africa & M.E.	10.3	–3.4	8.1
Oceania	4.7	–	–
Of which Manufacturing in DC	3.9	5.9	2.1
Manufacturing in LDC	13.0	22.2	11.0
Services in DC	6.1	6.3	5.1
Services in LDC	13.0	10.4	6.1

Note: – represents some parent firm that do not have a presence in certain regions or subsidiaries with observation of only 1 year.

Source: Authors' calculation using the Orbis data.

Conclusion

This chapter investigates the growth rates of labour using a panel of OECD MNEs and their foreign subsidiaries around the world between 1997 and 2006. Our results show that for both the manufacturing and services sectors the absence of any pervasive negative growth rates is to be noted. At least for the industries in the advanced OECD countries, the expansion of employment

Table 3.6 Average growth rate of the labour force in the services sector (Average over 1997–2006 in %)

	European MNEs	Japanese MNEs	US MNEs
*Subsidiaries of **High**-tech service Parent firms*			
Of which located in EU 15	10.8	10.2	12.6
Other Europe	8.3	–	0.5
Eastern Europe	24.3	–	20.4
North America	13.4	–3.3	7.4
Latin America	2.0	11.3	–0.6
Asia	12.7	–	33.8
Africa & M.E.	–	–	–
Oceania	0.4	–	13.1
Of which Manufacturing in DC	7.1	–	12.4
Manufacturing in LDC	9.9	–	19.2
Services in DC	11.1	6.5	11.3
Services in LDC	24.4	11.3	13.4
*Subsidiaries of **Low**-tech service Parent firms*			
Of which located in EU 15	8.1	6.2	9.8
Other Europe	6.5	4.4	6.9
Eastern Europe	16.2	11.1	11.7
North America	9.4	8.2	4.3
Latin America	8.3	17.8	6.9
Asia	9.5	12.4	13.5
Africa & M.E.	10.1	–	–1.1
Oceania	5.8	–	0.4
Of which Manufacturing in DC	4.9	5.8	3.5
Manufacturing in LDC	13.8	23.7	8.4
Services in DC	8.9	6.9	9.6
Services in LDC	16.8	12.4	10.1

Note: – represents some parent firm that do not have a presence in certain regions or subsidiaries with observation of only 1 year.

Source: Authors' calculation using the Orbis data.

abroad does not seem to occur at the detriment of employment at home. Given that high-technology industries play an important role in terms of growth potential for an economy, these findings are somewhat reassuring from a policy point of view.

Overall, our results thus far suggest that employment growth rates for both OECD parent firms and their subsidiaries are on average positive over the sample period. However, it is important to note a number of significant limitations of the analysis in this chapter. One limitation of the data is that it does not allow us to distinguish between the skill composition of the labour force (i.e., whether skilled or unskilled) which would certainly have a consequence on the skill-mix employed by the firm. Thus, any growth trends can be the result of a number of factors. Firstly, efficiency gained from locating low-skilled workers abroad would certainly make the firm more competitive; but would only have a positive effect on labour demand if the firm decides to employ more high-skilled workers at home. If however, the percentage increase in additional high-skilled workers at home is smaller than the increase in low-skilled workers abroad, the result may be negative. Thus, the net effect on labour demand at home is a combination of labour elasticities in both locations. The issue may become more complex in case of MNEs which have more than one subsidiary located in a number of countries.

Secondly, firms often undertake both types of investments simultaneously in a number of locations which may have opposing effects. For example, firms which increase their productivity due to cost-savings in low-income countries may expand production and employ more labour not at home but in another high-skilled country. Another possibility is that firms may only increase R&D-related activity at home complemented with high-skilled workers in a third country. There are a multitude of possibilities for firms in deciding the skill-mix of workers they wish to employ and in what locations. Therefore, in this regard our results are merely an indication of labour demand effects and are likely to be driven by the above-mentioned forces.

Given the limitations of this research and mixed findings by previous studies and it is our view that the jury is still out on the impact that outward FDI may have on employment, both at the aggregate and at the firm level. Thus, it is imperative that future research may combine the various investment opportunities by MNEs on a country by country analysis with the skill composition of the labour force to enrich the analysis. It would also be of interest to see whether effects are any different for MNEs from transition and developing countries. This seems to be an important avenue of further research to assess the heterogeneous employment effects induced by the expansion and relocation of MNEs around the world.

The findings presented here, and indeed the statistics discussed, highlight a good deal of heterogeneity at the firm level, that previous analysis of offshoring/outsourcing has not explored. For example, the data reveal lot of labour intensive activity in 'high-tech' sectors. As such, these activities should be analyzed in the same way as low tech firms when evaluating the threats or potential of offshoring/outsourcing. This requires more firm level analysis, and on a larger scale than has been carried out hitherto. In the service sector, the pattern is perhaps more straightforward, though still warranting further examination. High-tech service firms are found highly capital-intensive and, particularly, with large levels of intangible assets. As a result, we observe that regions with weak IPR systems, such as Africa, the Middle East, and Latin America, have experienced low growth rates of employment of MNEs subsidiaries in the high-tech service industries.

Overall, we postulate that a large proportion of the activity in high-tech manufacturing is vulnerable to offshoring/outsourcing to low-cost locations. However, a further avenue for investigation is the long-run impact of this. In the widest sense, FDI, and indeed other measures of globalization are assumed to benefit the owners of capital, and those in possession of human capital. Attempts have been made to measure this in the short run, and studies of the employment effects of offshoring/outsourcing are a case in point. However, it should also be recognized that in the long term, the transformational impacts of offshoring/outsourcing may be more beneficial. As low-skill activities are relocated, resources become allocated to more productive activities, in the long run boosting aggregate productivity, and generating more high skilled employment. This however requires a longer time frame of data in order to be effectively tested.

References

Amiti, M. and Wei, S-J. (2005) 'Fear of service outsourcing: Is it justified?', *Economic Policy*, 20(42), 308–347.

Barba Navaretti, G., Castellani, D. and Disdier, A. (2009) 'How does investing in cheap labour countries affect performance at home? Firm-level evidence from France and Italy', *Oxford Economic Papers*.

Becker, S. and Muendler, M.A. (2007) 'The effect of FDI on job separation', Discussion Paper Series 1, Economic Studies, Bundesbank, Germany.

BERR (2008) 'Five dynamics of change in global manufacturing: Supporting analysis for manufacturing strategy: New challenges, new opportunities', Economics Paper 2.

Blomström, M., Fors, G., and Lipsey, R.E. (1997) 'Foreign direct investment and employment: Home country experience in the United States and Sweden', *Economic Journal*, 107(445), 1787–97.

Blonigen, B. and Slaughter, M. (2001) 'Foreign-subsidiary activity and U.S. skill upgrading', *Review of Economics and Statistics*, 83(2), 362–79.

Braconier, H., and Ekholm, K. (2000) 'Swedish multinationals and competition from high- and low-wage locations', *Review of International Economics*, 8(3), 448–61.

Braconier, H. and Ekholm, K. (2002) 'Locating foreign subsidiaries in Germany: The case of Swedish multinational enterprises', in R. Jungnickel (ed.), *Foreign-Owned Firms: Are They Different?* (London: Palgrave Publishers Ltd).

Brainard, L. and Riker, D. (2001) 'Are US multinationals exporting US jobs?', in D. Greenaway and D.R. Nelson (eds), *Globalization and Labour Markets* (Cheltenham, UK, and Northampton, MA: Elgar).

Caves, R. E. (1974) 'Multinational firms, competition, and productivity in host-Country markets', *Economica*, 41(162), 176–193.

Conyon, M., Girma, S., Thompson, S. and Wright, P. (2004) 'Do wages rise or fall following merger?', *Oxford Bulletin of Economics and Statistics*, 66(5), 847–62.

Driffield, N. and Chiang. P.C. (2009) 'The effects outsourcing to China. Reallocation, employment and productivity in Taiwan', *International Journal of the Economics of Business*, 16(1), 19–38.

Driffield, N. and Love, J.H., and Taylor, K. (2009) 'Productivity and labour demand effects of outward and inward FDI on UK industry', *Manchester School*, 77(2), 171–203.

Federal Ministry of Economics and Technology (2007) Press release given by Michael Glos and Wolfgang Tiefensee http://www.bmvbs.de/en/Federal-Government-Commissione/Economy-and-investments-,2575.985440/Tiefensee-and-Glos-Activities-.htm.

Feenstra, R. and Hanson, G. (1999) 'The impact of outsourcing and high-technology capital on wages: Estimates for the U.S., 1979–1990', *Quarterly Journal of Economics*, 114(3), 907–40.

Harrison, A. and McMillan, M. (2007) 'On the links between globalization and poverty,' *Journal of Economic Inequality*, 5(1), 123–34.

Hijzen A., Görg, H. and Hine, R. (2005) 'International outsourcing and the skill structure of labour demand in the United Kingdom', *Economic Journal*, 115(506), 860–78.

Konings, J. and Murphy, A. (2006) 'Do multinational enterprises relocate employment to low-wage regions? Evidence from European multinationals', *The Review of World Economics*, 142(1), 1–20.

Machin, S. and Van Reenen, J. (1998) 'Technology and changes in skill structure: Evidence from seven OECD countries', *Quarterly Journal of Economics*, 113(4), 1215–44.

Mankiw, N. (2004) 'The economic report of the President', Council of Economic Advisors, Washington, D.C., February 2004.

Mankiw, N.G., Swagel P. (2006) 'The politics and economics of offshore utsourcing', NBER Working Paper 12398.

Marin, D. (2004) 'A nation of poets and thinkers: Less so with eastern enlargement? Austria and Germany', CEPR Discussion Paper 4358.

Marin, D. (2006) 'A new international division of labor in Europe: Outsourcing and offshoring to Eastern Europe', *Journal of the European Economic Association*, 4(2–3), 612–22.

Sapir, A. (2005) 'Globalisation and the reform of european social models' background document for the presentation at ECOFIN informal meeting in Manchester', available at http://www.brugel.org.

Taylor, K. and Driffield, N. (2005) 'Wage inequality and the role of multinationals: evidence from UK panel data', *Labour Economics*, 12(2), 223–49.

Temouri, Y., Driffield, N. and Añón Higón, D. (2010) 'The future of offshoring FDI in high-tech sectors', *Futures*, forthcoming.

Zeli, A. and Mariani, P. (2009) 'Productivity and profitability analysis of large Italian companies: 1998–2002', *International Review of Economics*, 56(2), 175–88.

4
Agglomeration and Flows of Inward and Outward Direct Investment: An Analysis of Financial Services in the United Kingdom

Gary A. S. Cook and Naresh R. Pandit

Introduction

Research on the foreign direct investment (FDI) activities of multinational enterprises (MNEs) has a long and rich tradition (Dunning, 2001). Research on the advantages, disadvantages and processes that arise in business clusters has a similar tradition (Marshall, 1890; Porter, 1998). Whilst it is clear that there is a considerable amount of MNE FDI in clusters (Kozul-Wright and Rowthorn, 1998), that FDI is relatively highly concentrated geographically (Shatz and Venables, 2000) and that this activity is increasing (Nachum, 2003), the body of research on this interface is small (Birkinshaw and Solvell, 2000). However, it is growing fast in the face of increased globalization, deregulation, and advances in information and communication technology all of which have begun to prompt a reevaluation of the spatial organization of MNE activity (Buckley and Ghauri, 2004). Much of the work on FDI location has focussed on where firms will choose to invest overseas at a macro level, with broad geo-political regions or nations being the unit of analysis. Work done at the sub-national level has tended to focus on broad variables relating to either costs or demand. This paper adds to the growing numbers of studies which focusses on agglomeration effects at the subnational scale. The paper further addresses the neglected question of whether agglomeration promotes outward direct investment (ODI) as well as attracting inward direct investment (IDI). This neglect is somewhat surprising, given that a central proposition of Porter (1990), which spurred strong academic and policy interest in clusters, was that location in clusters should promote international competitiveness.

The U.K. financial services industry is a good case for exploring these issues, displaying a high degree of agglomeration and high levels of MNE activity, involving both inward and outward direct investment flows. It is also home to one of the world's major financial services clusters, London. This study asks two related questions:

1. What theoretical reasons have been advanced that might explain the high level of MNE activity in strong clusters?
2. To what extent do strong clusters promote both IDI and ODI?

The paper is structured as follows. The second section reviews the literature on the MNE FDI/Clusters interface. The third section details the methodology of the study. The fourth section presents the findings and discusses these in relation to the literature on the MNE FDI/Clusters interface. A final section concludes.

Literature on the MNE FDI/clusters interface

Firm performance may improve if certain activities are located in clusters where higher levels of productivity (Henderson, 1986; Porter, 1998) and innovation (Baptista and Swann, 1998; Porter, 1998) may be achievable. In addition, clusters may be a focus for demand. The idea that firm-specific advantages might be developed in strong clusters has been a mainstay of Porter's work and that such advantages developed in home markets can be leveraged into overseas markets has a long tradition in theories of the MNE (Dunning, 2001). Since clusters are usually expensive and congested locations (Swann et al. 1998), unless an activity needs to be located in a cluster, it will pay the MNE to move it elsewhere. These reasons, coupled with the trends of increased globalization, deregulation and advances in information and communication technologies, mean that MNEs are increasingly employing cluster-based thinking to inform their investment and location decisions (Enright, 1998, 2000). This relates to what Porter (1998) has dubbed the 'globalization paradox', that easier movement of goods and people has increased the importance of hard-to-copy local advantages, which may exist in clusters, thus promoting an increased geographic concentration of activity.

There is a growing body of more specific evidence that shows that MNEs are attracted to clusters (Gong, 1995; Head et al. 1999; Wheeler and Mody, 1992) and that MNE FDI in clusters is increasing (Nachum, 2003). This evidence suggests that 'liability of foreignness' (Zaheer, 1995) is being compensated by the advantages of cluster location. Beyond so-called fixed effects (Swann et al. 1998) – advantages that exist at a location that are not a function of the co-presence of related firms and institutions (for example, climate, time-zone, and cultural capital) – there are advantages that are directly related the co-presence of other firms that exists within a cluster which are referred to as economies of agglomeration. These can emanate on the demand or supply side and are extensively detailed in Porter (1998) and Swann et al. (1998). As articulated by Porter (1990), these advantages may provide the basis for firms to succeed in international competition by promoting the development of firm-specific advantages. This may be a foundation for ODI and also, as argued below, the reason why IDI is attracted to a particular location.

The majority of the literature acknowledges and builds on the classic insights of Marshall (1890) into the sources of superior performance in clusters (industrial districts in Marshall's terms): labour market pooling, which in part brings benefits of a deeper division of labour and more highly specialized skills; the emergence of specialized input suppliers; and technological and knowledge spill-overs. A distinction has long been made in the literature (Hoover, 1948) between two potential sources of dynamism: urbanization economies, which refer to the benefits of size and diversity of economic activity within an agglomeration; and localization economies which refer to the benefits of large scale *in a particular industry*, essentially related to the classic Marshallian externalities. Jacobs (1985) lays particular emphasis on size and diversity as being critical to dynamism and innovation, ascribed to the free interchange of different ideas and the abundance and variety of resources.

What particular advantages which might attract inward direct investment? There is a large literature that attempts to explain MNE FDI in terms of the benefits that certain locations provide for investing MNEs. Dunning (1993) presents an FDI typology differentiating between investments that are 'natural-resource seeking', 'market-seeking', 'efficiency-seeking', and 'strategic-asset seeking'. More recently, he has drawn from economic geography (Dunning, 1998) to elaborate the location element of his 'OLI' framework by incorporating clusters thinking. The idea that strategic-asset seeking and competence building are seen as being important influences on location decisions is consistent with this cluster thinking (Chen and Chen, 1998; Makino et al. 2002; Rugman and Verbeke, 2007; Sethi et al. 2003). The importance of location in major nodes is that much of the strategically important knowledge is tacit (Chung and Alcacer, 2002; Nachum and Keeble, 2003), and access to this knowledge is of paramount importance in high technology industries and complex service industries, of which financial services is a major example (Storper, 2000). Another important asset which firms may seek is highly skilled labour (Makino et al. 2002; Sethi et al. 2003). It should be noted that agglomeration economies will not be equally relevant to all forms of FDI and may not be the reason why MNEs collocate (McCann and Mudambi, 2005). Pelegrin and Bolance (2008) find that FDI is attracted to agglomerations where there is high R&D intensity or where interfirm linkages are an important characteristic of the industry, but not where cost-reduction is the primary objective of the FDI. In the latter case, favourable factor endowments are more important.

On the subject of MNE location in *clusters*, Birkinshaw and Hood (2000) find such activity to be rational as subsidiaries located in clusters make greater strategic contributions to parent companies than subsidiaries that are not located in clusters. Enright (1998) elaborates a typology of such contributions. 'Listening posts' aim to absorb knowledge from the cluster and then disseminate it within the wider enterprise (Dupuy and Gilly, 1999). 'Stand-alone corporate portfolio investments' serve as centres for particular business activities perhaps benefiting from the reputation spill-over of a particular location. Another type is the subsidiary that 'supplies products and activities' for the MNE's other activities and finally there is the subsidiary which absorbs 'skills and capabilities' from the cluster and then transfers these to the wider enterprise. Beaverstock's (1994) study of multinational banks elaborates this type of MNE FDI by finding that such firms benefit from the ability to transfer skills and capabilities between subsidiaries in their worldwide operations through international personnel movements. The ability of MNEs to leverage knowledge and skills in this way may not be straightforward, however (Cohendet et al. 1999).

Although this typology encourages us to think of MNEs 'taking' from clusters, we should guard against such a conclusion. Studies by Birkinshaw and Hood (2000), Head et al. (1999), Nachum (2000) and Wheeler and Mody (1992) show that MNEs can play a major role in cluster development and evolution. Much emphasis is placed in Pred's (1977) seminal analysis of dynamic cities on the importance of multilocational organizations (which may or may not be multinationals) as they will tend to be particularly wide conduits through which flows of goods, services, capital, and information may flow. Amin and Thrift (1992) likewise argue persuasively that models which are just locally based do not recognize the importance of emerging global corporate networks and interconnected global city regions (Scott, 2001). There is, moreover, a self-reinforcing process whereby the more high level corporate activity a metropolis has, the more specialized services, labour, and infrastructure it attracts. The fact that others are operating successfully in a given location may be taken as a credible signal of favourable demand and/or cost conditions, leading to imitation and herd behaviour (Henisz and Delios, 2001; Knickerbocker, 1973).

In addition to the influence of factors which permit development or exploitation of firm-specific advantages, it is important to acknowledge the importance of institutional factors in location decisions. Cultural factors include the notion of 'psychic distance', where the ability of firm-specific advantages to carry over to different cultural contexts, be it on the demand side with acceptability of products and services, or on the cost side in terms of the ability to establish efficient operations, may be imperfect. This implies increasing 'psychic distance' will deter direct investment. Institutional influences such as political stability and security of property rights are also generally held to be influential. In taking a single country context, this paper abstracts from many of the influences which are more relevant to choice of location among countries, to focus more narrowly on what influences location within one country. Institutional and economic factors are not unrelated, however. As Porter (1990) himself has argued, dynamic clusters are more likely to flourish in countries which are stable economically and politically and which have a sound institutional infrastructure. Such locations are apt to be favoured sites for IDI (Globerman and Shapiro, 2003). Moreover, firms based in more dynamic clusters may be able to develop greater firm-specific advantages, leaving them better placed to overcome greater 'psychic distance'.

The preceding literature review suggests three testable hypotheses, which this study will examine:

1. Firms located in stronger clusters are more likely to engage in ODI
2. Cluster strength is positively related to the extent of ODI
3. Cluster strength is positively related to the extent of IDI

Methodology

The basic data set on which this analysis was conducted is the U.K.'s Annual Foreign Direct Investment (AFDI) Survey. The survey examines outward and inward direct investment flows at the firm level. The outward direct investment database is particularly useful in that it breaks down by country the outward investment flows of each firm. In order to produce meaningful analysis of the pattern and extent of outward and inward investment flows, the AFDI data was merged with a variety of additional databases maintained by the U.K.'s Office for National Statistics, although gaps in the matching fields used to merge databases did reduce the number of usable observations. Skeleton information was obtained from the ARD Regional Panel Database, comprising number of employees, five-digit SIC code and region of operation. Information on year of formation and ultimate country of foreign ownership, where applicable, was obtained from a further database, the Business Structure Database. Where the HQ could not be identified, the observations were dropped. Likewise, firms not actively trading were removed from the data set.

Some limitations of the AFDI database must be acknowledged. Firstly, the identity of the firms in the database is not disclosed, each being assigned a unique identifier. This prevented firm-level data derived from other sources being introduced into the analysis. A second major disadvantage of the AFDI database as far as the study of financial services is concerned is that it has very limited coverage of banks (the rationale for this is unclear). The third major limitation is that in a small number of cases, the data on FDI flows was imputed from other sources. Given the relatively small number of observations available for firms engaging in FDI, these observations were retained at the cost of some noise in the measurement of the dependent variable.

Participating in ODI

The first set of models estimated were logistic regressions based on a 1,0 dependent variable depending on whether the firm was engaged in outward direct investment or not. This analysis could not be performed for inward direct investment as data was not available on firms in other countries which do not direct investment flows to the UK. The basic model had the form:

$$L_i = \beta_1 Size_i + \beta_2 Size_i^2 + \beta_3 Age_i + \beta_4 Age_i^2 + \beta_5 Locquo_i + \beta_6 Locquo_i^2 + \beta_7 Totemp_i + \beta_8 Totemp_i^2 + \beta_9 Banks_i + \beta_{10} Lifeins_i + \beta_{11} Nonlifeins_i + \beta_{12} Auxfi_i + \beta_{13} Netprofit_i$$

where L_i is the log of the odds ratio $Ln\left(\frac{P_i}{1-P_i}\right)$ and P_i is the probability that the firm engages in ODI. The coefficients reported for the logistic regression show the change in the log-odds ratio for a 1-unit change in the independent variable, therefore a coefficient less than 1 indicates an increase in the independent variable made ODI less likely and *vice versa* where the coefficient exceeded one.

- Size was measured by the natural log of numbers of employees, due to the strong positive skew. This is *a priori* expected to be positive as larger firms are likely to have greater resources which will enable international activity. In the case of U.K. subsidiaries of overseas MNEs, size has had to be based on the size of the subsidiary as this was the only data available. As for Age and Locquo below, a squared term was included to allow for either the possibility of exponential increase beyond some critical mass, or possibly diminishing returns.
- Age is the age in years of the firm since first registration, sign expected positive. For subsidiaries of overseas MNEs, this is based on the age of the subsidiary.
- Locquo is the location quotient of the region in which the firm is located. The location quotient is constructed as the ratio of total financial services employment in the region to that of all financial services employment in Britain *divided by* the ratio of total employment in the region to all employment in Britain. The location quotient thus represents the extent of localization economies in the region. A quotient above 1 indicates that the region has a disproportionate share of financial services employment relative to its

total employment. The prior expectation is that the coefficient will be positive, representing the effect of stronger clusters.

- Totemp is total employment in the region. This crudely represents the extent of urbanization economies in the region. It also acts as a proxy for market size. Again the prior expectation is that this variable will have a positive sign.
- A set dummies was included to control for principal line of activity, Banks (SIC651), Lifeins (SIC 6601 life insurance), Nonlifeins (SIC6603 non-life insurance), Auxfi (SIC671, activities auxiliary to financial intermediation).
- Net profit. The sign is expected to be positive.

The magnitude of ODI and IDI flows

A set of models were run to examine the principal influences on the volume of inward and outward direct investment. This was measured as the net investment flow in 2005 (the most recent year for which data was available). Some additional regressions (not reported) using FDI capital stock as the dependent variable were run as a robustness check, important given that a range of idiosyncratic factors might have influenced the net investment flows in one particular year. These yielded qualitatively similar results. The Heckman (1979) two-step procedure is the preferred method as observations of ODI and IDI are censored, arising only for firms which actually undertake such investments. Failing to take into account the fact that firms have made this prior choice leads to biased estimates. Unfortunately, lacking data on overseas firms which chose not to invest in the United Kingdom meant that the Heckman two-step could not be used in the IDI analysis, therefore the simple OLS results reported need to be treated with caution.

The IDI and ODI equations were as follows, with a full and a restricted model being separately estimated (in the case of the ODI equations these were the second step in the Heckman two-step, the selection equation taking a very similar form). All models were estimated using robust standard errors.

Restricted model

$$Y_i = \beta_0 + \beta_1 \text{Size}_i + \beta_2 \text{Size}_i^2 + \beta_3 \text{Age}_i + \beta_4 \text{Age}_i^2 + \beta_5 \text{Locquo}_i + \beta_6 \text{Locquo}_i^2 + \beta_7 \text{Totemp}_i + \beta_8 \text{Totemp}_i^2 + \beta_9 \text{Banks}_i + \beta_{10} \text{Lifeins}_i + \beta_{11} \text{Nonlifeins}_i + \beta_{12} \text{Auxfi}_i + \beta_{13} \text{Netprofit}_i$$

Variables were measured identically as for the logistic regressions above. Dummies was included in the IDI equation to control for the home country of the MNE parent, USA, EUROPE and JAPAN, the default being any other country.

Full model

A more extensive model was estimated in cases where additional financial information for a subset of firms was available, in order to control for firm-specific advantages as an influence on FDI flows.

$$Y_i = \beta_0 + \beta_1 Size_i + \beta_2 Size_i^2 + \beta_3 Age_i + \beta_4 Age_i^2 + \beta_5 Locquo_i + \beta_6 Locquo_i^2 + \beta_7 Totemp_i + \beta_8 Totemp_i^2 + \beta_9 Banks_i + \beta_{10} Lifeins_i + \beta_{11} Nonlifeins_i + \beta_{12} Auxfi_i + \beta_{13} Netprofit_i + \beta_{14} Productivity_i + \beta_{15} Advertising/sales_i + \beta_{16} R\&D/sales_i + \beta_{17} Meanwage_i + \beta_{18} Investment\ intensity_i$$

- Productivity is measured as gross value-added per head. The expected sign is positive as greater productivity implies greater cost competitiveness.
- Advertising/sales is a standard proxy for a resource strength in product differentiation. The expected sign is positive.
- R&D/sales is a standard proxy for resource strength in innovation. The expected sign is positive.
- Mean wage. The expected sign here is ambiguous. A high value might imply resource strength in terms of a labour force skewed towards more highly skilled employees. Alternatively it may represent a disadvantage of relatively high costs.
- Investment intensity is measured as net capital expenditure/sales. The expected sign is positive as a high investment intensity implies a progressive company.

Geographic extent and diversity of ODI flows

The final set of models estimated explores the propensity to send outward direct investment to more heterogeneous markets. These were based on the count of the number of separate markets each firm was engaged in. The appropriate modelling technique was negative binomial regression as the presence of a small number of firms investing in a very large number of countries meant that the over-dispersion test of Cameron & Trivedi (1990) rejected the restriction implicit in the Poisson model that mean and variance be equal. The dependent variable is the count of the number of markets to which the firm sends outward direct investment and the independent variables are the same as in the logistic regressions described above.

Results

Engaging or not in outward direct investment

This model includes a dummy for foreign ownership of the firm engaging in outward direct investment (Table 4.1). This is positive and strongly significant which is intuitively reasonable, given that the subsidiary is already part of an MNE; therefore it is more likely to have the competence, strategic orientation, and resources to engage in outward investment. This dummy for foreign ownership was entered in all the other outward direct investment models reported in the paper but was never close to significance, and therefore is not reported. This indicates that foreign ownership makes it more likely a firm will engage in outward direct investment, but beyond that does not influence the size of such flows. Again this is plausible. Those domestically controlled firms which cross the threshold of becoming multinational will exhibit a similar propensity to invest overseas as foreign multinationals.

The results indicate that the location quotient is positively and significantly associated with the probability of engaging in outward direct investment. The result is robust to alternative specifications of the model (not reported), with the exception of including a dummy variable for location in London, which indicates that the positive effect of clustering is essentially a London phenomenon. In this quadratic form, the positive marginal effect of the square of the location quotient indicates increasing returns to cluster size, subject to the obvious *caveat* that such increasing returns would probably eventually peter out as a cluster ran into worsening problems of congestion. This result

Table 4.1 Logistic regression for probability of engaging in outward direct investment

Variable	Outward direct investment		
	Coefficient	Z	Marginal effect
Size	2.166	2.65	0.0001***
Size squared	0.969	−0.99	−0.000002
Age	1.128	1.56	0.00001
Age squared	0.997	−1.55	−0.0000002
Location quotient	0.002	−2.07	−0.0005**
Location quotient squared	16.362	2.43	0.0002**
Total regional employment	0.997	−2.21	−0.0000002**
Total regional employment squared	1.000	2.09	0.000000**
Banks	0.915	−0.15	−0.00001
Life insurance	2.898	2.19	0.00014**
Non-life insurance	1.541	1.01	0.00004
Auxiliary to financial intermediation	0.407	−1.90	−0.00007*
Foreign	43.088	3.59	0.0014***
N observations	24196	–	–
Wald χ^2	263.07***	–	–
Pseudo-R^2	0.2835	–	–

*** significant at 1% ** significant at 5% * significant at 10%

provides strong support for Hypothesis 1. Urbanization economies, as proxied by total regional employment, have only a very small, almost negligible, positive influence. The positive coefficient on firm size and negative coefficient on firm size squared indicates that initially it has a positive influence but that eventually the influence of greater size will become negative, although this effect is weak. Much the same may be said of age.

The extent of inward and outward direct investment flows

These results show a general lack of significance which reflects a lack of degrees of freedom due to the small number of observations with full data for firms engaged in outward direct investment. (Table 4.2). This is above all true in the

Table 4.2   Heckman two-step model of outward direct investment flows

Variable	Restricted model		Full model	
	coefficient	Z	coefficient	Z
Net profit	2.778	15.85***	2.324	7.00***
Size	−4.953	−0.54	−0.914	−0.14
Size squared	0.042	0.09	–	–
Age	−0.957	−0.59	1.328	1.26
Age squared	0.022	0.51	–	–
Location quotient	−99.853	−0.97	−205.985	−1.43
Location quotient squared	33.163	0.83	62.868	1.10
Total regional employment	0.049	1.31	−0.103	−0.91
Total regional employment squared	−0.00001	−1.02	0.00003	1.13
Banks	5.324	0.66	–	–
Life insurance	−7.212	−0.56	–	–
Non-life insurance	15.484	1.61	–	–
Auxiliary to financial intermediation	9.251	0.88	–	–
Productivity	–	–	0.004	0.43
Advertising/sales	–	–	458.870	2.43**
Mean wage	–	–	−0.001	−0.00
Investment intensity	–	–	−209.234	−1.23
Constant	44.917	0.70	184.564	1.68*
Rho	−0.740	–	−0.823	–
Sigma	20.024	–	29.457	–
Lambda	−14.827	–	−24.253	–
N observations	24196	–	979	–
Censored obs.	24146	–	958	–
Uncensored obs.	50	–	21	–
Wald χ^2	430.31***	–	208.75***	–

*** significant at 1% ** significant at 5% * significant at 10%

'full' model, where only a very small number of firms had a complete range of financial data available. For this reason, the squares of size and age and the industry dummies were dropped from the full model, which was data admissible on a variable deletion test, in order to conserve degrees of freedom and produce more accurate estimates of the remaining coefficients.

Clearly the rate of profit earned is strongly associated with the volume of outward direct investment, as would be expected. The coefficients on the location quotient indicate an exponential increase in the rate of investment as cluster strength increases, supporting Hypothesis 2. A similar exponential rise is indicated by the coefficients on size and age, where again the coefficient on the squared term is positive. This is suggestive of some notion of critical mass beyond which investment increases sharply. The coefficients on total regional employment, however, indicate an inverted-U, with investment slowing down and diminishing as total employment rises, which is indicative of a congestion effect. Non-life insurance and banks emerge as tending to invest overseas more heavily than other lines of activity, although the coefficients are outside conventional significance. With regard to the variables measuring firm strength, the positive and significant coefficient on advertising intensity is consistent with the received wisdom in the field; however, the negative coefficient on investment intensity is more difficult to interpret. R&D intensity had to be dropped from the module due to multicollinearity.

The results from the IDI models in Table 4.3 need to be treated with caution, as they were based on ordinary least squares because information was not available on overseas firms that did not invest in the United Kingdom, precluding use of the Heckman two-step. Clearly, they suffer from low R-squares, although did pass Ramsey's RESET test for model specification. Nevertheless, the evidence regarding the central variable of interest, the location quotient, is robust. It shows a positive exponential relationship with IDI flows, which is close to significance in the restricted model. This provides support for Hypothesis 3. Total regional employment has an inverted-U relationship with inward direct investment, as indicated by the positive coefficient on the variable and a negative coefficient on its square. This relationship is generally close to significance.

Taken together, these results suggest some tentative conclusions. Firstly, there is evidence consistent with positive agglomeration spillovers. Secondly, these appear to derive principally from localization economies of being located close to other firms in financial services. Here it is important to state the *caveat* that in the models using the capital stock rather than investment flows, urbanization economies as proxied by total regional employment featured more prominently, but did not dominate localization economies. Thirdly, the positive coefficients indicate that the positive spill-overs outweigh any congestion effects, most apparent in London, by far the largest and densest cluster. The inverted-U relationship with total regional employment implies a positive

Table 4.3   OLS model of inward direct investment flows

Variable	Restricted model		Full model	
	Coefficient	t	coefficient	T
Net profit	0.261	0.41	0.843	2.40**
Size	−0.160	−0.11	0.373	0.22
Size squared	0.210	0.85	–	–
Age	0.312	0.97	−0.043	−0.07
Age squared	−0.009	−0.83	–	–
Location quotient	−39.737	−1.43	−30.899	−0.72
Location quotient squared	14.500	1.53	13.344	0.89
Total regional employment	0.017	1.43	0.002	0.09
Total regional employment squared	−0.000002	−1.28	0.000001	0.17
Banks	2.262	1.20	−1.033	−0.17
Life insurance	−4.162	−0.76	8.827	0.94
Non-life insurance	0.117	0.11	−2.296	−0.35
Auxiliary to financial intermediation	−0.549	−0.28	5.389	0.54
USA	0.847	0.54	−12.387	−1.44
Europe	0.005	0.00	3.386	0.28
Japan	−2.02	−1.77*	−6.291	−0.74
Productivity	–	–	0.001	0.61
Advertising/sales	–	–	−6.929	−1.02
R&D/sales	–	–	−1005.221	−0.56
Mean wage	–	–	0.007	0.66
Constant	−11.040	−1.24	0.873	0.09
N observations	315	–	55	–
F	2.51***	–	2.18**	–
R-square	0.0482	–	0.1369	–

*** significant at 1% ** significant at 5% * significant at 10%

influence of urbanization economies at first, which may be undermined by congestion effects as cluster scale increases. The positive and generally significant coefficient on firm size is intuitively reasonable, as is the positive coefficient on subsidiary profit rate. The insignificant effect of age, and its occasional negative coefficient, probably reflects the weakness of only having subsidiary age to work with.

The industry dummies are never close to significance. The coefficients on the home country dummies are generally reasonable. The negative coefficient for Japan in the IDI flow models reflects the continued weakened state of the Japanese financial services sector (the coefficient was positive in the unreported capital stock model). The firm strength variables are somewhat problematic, the negative coefficients on R&D and advertising intensity possibly reflecting the imprecision of the estimation.

Geographic and psychic distance

A final set of models examined another dimension of the extent of overseas direct investment, which is the geographic scope of the investment measured as the number of countries ODI was sent to (Table 4.4). Localization economies as proxied by the location quotient are a significant influence. The positive coefficient on the location quotient and the negative coefficient on location quotient squared imply an inverted-U relationship with cluster strength at first promoting a greater scope of investment, but at a diminishing rate which would eventually lead to an absolute decline (rather implausible if interpreted literally). The coefficients on total regional employment lie just outside conventional significance and imply and exponential relationship. The positive and significant coefficients on age and size are intuitively reasonable (the squares of both variables were omitted to conserve degrees of freedom, which was data admissible based on a variable deletion test).

As a robustness check, a set of ordered logit models were run based on a crude qualitative ranking of the degree of 'psychic distance' of the most 'distant' market to which ODI was made (not reported). The results obtained were qualitatively similar to those using the more objective measure of number of countries served. These results provide further clear support for Hypothesis 2.

Table 4.4 Negative binomial regressions of number of countries invested in

Variable	Number of countries invested in		
	coefficient	Z	Marginal effect
Size	0.120	1.77	0.275*
Age	0.085	5.90	0.194***
Location quotient	6.709	1.80	15.359*
Location quotient squared	−2.167	−1.72	−4.960*
Total regional employment	−0.003	−1.46	−0.006
Total regional employment squared	0.0000006	1.41	0.000001
Banks	0.075	0.25	0.178
Life insurance	−0.240	−0.41	−0.502
Non-life insurance	−0.584	−1.36	−1.093
Auxiliary to financial intermediation	0.065	0.33	0.151
Constant	−1.813	−1.21	–
N observations	46	–	–
Wald χ^2	188.95***	–	–

*** significant at 1% ** significant at 5% * significant at 10%

Discussion

The results obtained are broadly consistent with the thrust of the literature on the FDI/clusters interface. Stronger clusters do appear to promote ODI, with firms being more likely to engage in FDI, to engage in a higher volume of ODI and to send ODI to a wider array of countries. These findings support Porter's (1990) contention about the positive effects of location in a strong cluster for success in international competition. Porter emphasizes the positive effect on domestic firms. Results here add some nuance to that proposition in so far as subsidiaries of overseas MNEs, all else equal, are more likely to be a source of ODI from London than are domestic firms. This fits with the general tenor of the results in the IB literature which have tended to focus on the benefits for overseas MNEs of locating in a strong overseas cluster (principally London in the context of this paper) and support's Enright's (2000) position that domestic clusters do not uniquely privilege domestic firms. Once domestic firms take the step of becoming MNEs, then they appear to be neither advantaged nor disadvantaged by their location relative to the subsidiaries of overseas MNEs. Stronger clusters attract higher volumes of IDI. These relationships imply a positive feedback loop, consistent with the literature (Sethi et al. 2003), whereby cluster strength attracts inward investment and promotes outward investment, both of which further strengthen the cluster.

The generally positive coefficients on size and age are intuitively reasonable, both in terms of the IB literature and the broader literature of economics and strategy. Size may be associated with the possession of resource strengths (Barney, 1991) which enable the firm to grow. This sits comfortably with the increasing importance of the resource-based view for explaining firm success in the IB literature (Peng, 2001), albeit that a lot is being read into weak proxies for resource strength here. Size may also be associated with the ability to realize economies of scale and scope, though there is no direct evidence for either of these two effects. Similarly age may proxy accumulated experience and therefore, up to a point, increase the chances of becoming multinational. Longer established firms will acquire greater experience in conducting overseas business, specifically cited by Dunning (1993) as an important ownership advantage.

To what extent is there a genuine cluster in London, as opposed to it being simply a convenient entrepot where firms have the same reason for locating but do not directly benefit from the co-presence of other firms? Taylor et al. (2003) present detailed evidence that the City exhibits all the hallmarks of a highly developed, dynamic cluster. Dense and flexible vertical and horizontal interlinkages between firms, a balance of competition and cooperation, a strong emphasis on the importance of face-to-face contact and personal relationships, exchange of tacit knowledge and the ability to tap into a highly skilled and deep labour pool feature prominently in the advantages firms perceive of their location in the City. Location in the City is also important for being seen as a credible player in the industry and to gain access to the highest level and most demanding customers. Together with the econometric results, this is consistent with the emerging consensus in the IB literature that MNEs place a premium on locating complex service activities in strategically important and information and resource-rich clusters. Taylor et al. also detail the very real concern of incumbents in the City regarding high and rising levels of congestion, effects hinted at in these results.

The broader discourse within which the paper is situated is the regionalization versus globalization debate (Clark and Knowles, 2003; Flores and Aguilera, 2007). Whilst not gainsaying the claims of Bird and Stevens (2003) and Stevens and Bird (2004) that in some respects there is a growing emergence of elements of global culture, one implication of the evidence presented in the paper is to reinforce the general point made by Rugman and Verbeke (2004, 2007) that the geographic pattern of multinational activity is very unevenly spread. The essential point about increasing volumes of FDI in the context of this paper is that its effects are disproportionately concentrated on certain locations, a point acknowledged by Rugman and Verbeke (2004), leaving what Jane Jacobs (1985) dubbed 'bypassed places'. Rugman and Verbeke (2004), in common with much of the IB literature, acknowledge the importance of the subnational scale when considering where MNEs will choose to locate overseas. This paper indicates the subnational scale is also highly relevant in explaining the source of FDI.

Conclusions

This paper has answered the two questions posed in the introduction in the affirmative. There is a growing body of theory which articulates why location in strong agglomerations may be especially beneficial for MNEs. It has also provided evidence that agglomeration economies are important in both promoting ODI and attracting IDI. The logit model clearly demonstrated that firms located in stronger clusters are significantly more likely to engage in ODI, supporting hypothesis one. What is more, the Heckman two-step model showed, rather weakly, that the volume of ODI flows if higher, controlling for a range of firm-specific characteristics, from firm located in stronger clusters. Stronger evidence was provided in the negative binomial models that, all else equal, firms located in stronger clusters tended to send ODI to a greater variety of locations. Taken together these results support Hypothesis 2. Finally, the OLS model of IDI flows demonstrated that stronger clusters attract a higher volume of investment, supporting Hypothesis 3. The evidence indicates that the agglomeration economies principally relate to localization economies based on collocation with firms in the same and related lines of activity to a greater extent than to urbanization economies based on the scale and diversity of the region's economic base. This concords with Bronzini's (2007) similar finding for Italy. The IB literature needs to be more careful to distinguish between these two regional effects, which imply different processes whereby firms build capabilities and resource strengths. Size and age were also found to be positively related to FDI, as would be expected. These findings accord with the emerging theoretical and empirical work on the clusters/FDI interface.

The current study suffers from some important limitations. There was only a limited number of observations available for firms engaging in FDI with full financial information, which undermined the precision of the econometric estimation. In addition, it would be desirable to incorporate a wider range of controls for differences in regional characteristics. That said, the lack of control for regional costs should, if anything, have confounded the positive effect of geographic concentration in London. The econometrics afford no insight into the strategic orientation of firms, nor how firms create and leverage advantages from locating within strong clusters and the empirical proxies for resource strength were weak.

Implications for practitioners and policy makers

Some basic practitioner and policy implications flow, although given the limitations of the study they are expressed with due caution. The importance of agglomeration effects as an influence on international activity is supportive of the idea in policy circles that cluster promotion may be a fruitful strategy. Policy thinking has lighted upon two particular ideas about clusters. The first is the ideal type exemplified by Silicon Valley (Saxenian, 1994) and the idea of flexible specialization where clusters are composed of agile and highly networked small and medium-sized enterprises, exemplified by the Third Italy and Baden Wurttemberg. The second is the cluster concept developed and popularized by Porter (1990). There have been two general criticisms of the flexible specialization model. Firstly, that it is not an accurate representation even of Silicon Valley, Baden Wurttemberg, and the Third Italy (Malmberg & Maskell, 2002). Secondly, that this type of concentration is not the most common and that other types exist which also have a distinct rationale (Gordon & McCann, 2000; Markusen, 1996). In the case of financial services, multinationals, both domestic and overseas, are important hub firms which are central to the dynamism of London above all, but absent from the prevalent policy view of clusters.

A particularly trenchant critique of Porter has been advanced by Martin and Sunley (2003), who argue among other things that Porter's concept is devoid of empirical operationalization because he is utterly vague concerning the geographic boundaries of a cluster, how many firms ought to exist there and how (strongly) they ought to be related to each other and at what stage in the evolution of an industry at a particular location it merits being called a cluster. They claim the *reduction ad absurdum* is that almost anything could be delineated as a cluster. In this light, it is instructive to consider the following quotation from the Department of Trade and Industry's (DTI) *A Practical Guide to Cluster Development* (Ecotech, 2005, p4).

This guide starts from the perspective that policy intervention cannot create cluster from scratch but that it can help existing clusters to develop. It also starts from the proposition that the cluster being considered by practitioners have already been identified. Consequently, it does not dwell on the question of `what is a cluster'.

There are two immediate objections. Firstly, the distinctive nature of a particular geographical concentration of activity will have a bearing on what policy measures are appropriate to support it. Secondly, it assumes practitioners can unproblemtically identify clusters, which is at odds with the weight of evidence and argument in the literature. The emphasis in the *Guide* is on dense linkages in geographical propinquity; therefore, it is relatively blind to processes operating at wider spatial scales, in which the core literature in economic geography asserts that MNEs will be particularly strongly implicated. The *Guide* proceeds to rank order critical success factors based on the number of times particular factors are mentioned in the articles reviewed in the process of writing the guide. In common with other official documents preaching the text of regional competitiveness, there is no underlying theoretical rationale for the particular set of drivers advanced (Kitson et al. 2004). In respect of large firms, whereas the *Guide* makes many valid points regarding the positive influence that they may exert on local agglomerations, it says almost nothing about the particular role of multinational enterprises. What the evidence in this paper suggests is that there is an important relationship between clusters and MNE activity which warrants more attention in policy thinking.

For practitioners there are two simple implications. Firstly, access to agglomeration economies is a relevant element in the location decision, although benefitting from such economies is not automatic and requires competence and effort. Secondly, the problems of congestion in major clusters like the City mean a critical view needs to be taken of which activities are best placed or retained within a particular cluster.

Directions for future research

The limitations identified above give some clues as to directions for future research. The extension to a wider range of industries is a priority, being easily achievable using the databases employed in the current study. It is also relatively straightforward to introduce additional regional controls, particularly given that looking at a wider range of industries would create far more degrees of freedom. Such straightforward extensions would evaluate how robust and general the findings for financial services are. Another obvious extension is to extend the analysis to other countries. Building on one of the central findings of the paper, that agglomeration economies are important foundations of FDI, greater attention might be paid in the literature to the more fine-grained analysis of the geographic dispersion of the sources of FDI at the subnational level. This might include an assessment of how choice of subnational location relates to choice between countries. What is also required is deeper theoretical and empirical work to enhance our understanding of both how agglomeration economies arise, how and why some firms capitalize on them more than others, supporting their global strategies, what, if anything, differentiates MNEs and non-MNEs as actors in clusters and how agglomerations are interconnected across space.

References

Amin, A. and Thrift, N. (1992) 'Neo-marshallian nodes in global networks', *International Journal of Urban and Regional Research*, XVI, 571–87.

Baptista, R.M.L.N. and Swann, G.M.P. (1998) 'Do firms in clusters innovate more?', *Research Policy*, XXVII, 527–42.

Barney, J.B. (1991) 'Firm resources and sustained competitive advantage', *Journal of Management*, XVII, 99–120.

Beaverstock, J.V. (1994) 'Re-thinking skilled international labour migration: World cities and banking organizations', *Geoforum*, XXV, 323–38.

Bird, A. and Stevens, M.J. (2003) 'Toward an emergent global culture and the effects of globalization on obsolescing national cultures', *Journal of International Management*, IX, 395–407.

Birkinshaw, J.M. and Hood, N. (2000) 'Characteristics of foreign subsidiaries in industry clusters', *Journal of International Business Studies*, XXXI, 141–54.

Birkinshaw, J.M. and Solvell, O. (2000) 'Preface', *International Studies of Management and Organization*, XXX, 3–9.

Bronzini, R. (2007), 'FDI flows, agglomeration and host country firms' size: Evidence for Italy', *Regional Studies*, XLI, 963–78.

Buckley, P.J. and Ghauri, P.N. (2004) 'Globalization, economic geography and the strategy of multinational enterprises', *Journal of International Business Studies*, XXXV, 81–98.

Cameron, A. and. Trivedi, P.K. (1990) 'Regression-based tests for over-dispersion in the poisson model', *Journal of Econometrics*, XLVI, 347–64.

Chen, H. and Chen, T.-J. (1998) 'Network linkages and location choice in foreign direct investment', *Journal of International Business Studies*, XXXIX, 445–68.

Chung, W. and Alcacer, J. (2002) 'Knowledge seeking and location choice of foreign direct investment in the United States', *Management Science*, XLVIII, 1534–54.

Clark, T. and Knowles, L.L. (2003) 'Global myopia: Globalization theory in international business', *Journal of International Management*, IX, 361–72.

Cohendet, P., Kern, F., Mehmanpazir, B. and Munier, F.(1999) 'Knowledge coordination, competence creation and integrated networks in globalised firms', *Cambridge Journal of Economics*, XXIII, 225–41.

Dunning, J.H., (2001) 'The key literature on IB activities: 1960–2000', in A.M. Rugman and T.L. Brewer (eds), *The Oxford Handbook of International Business*, 36–68 (Oxford: Oxford University Press).

Dunning, J.H. (1998) 'Location and the multinational enterprise: A neglected factor?', *Journal of International Business Studies*, XXIX, 45–66.

Dunning, J.H. (1993) *Multinational Enterprises and the Global Economy* (Reading: Addison-Wesley).

Dupuy, C. and Gilly, J.-P. (1999) 'Industrial groups and territories: The case of Matra-Marconi-Space in Toulouse', *Cambridge Journal of Economics*, XXIII, 207–25.

Ecotec (2005) *Criteria for Success in Cluster Development*. Report commissioned by Department of Trade and Industry (London: DTI).

Enright, M.J. (2000), 'Regional clusters and multinational enterprises', *International Studies of Management and Organization*, XXX, 114–38.

Enright, M.J. (1998) 'Regional clusters and firm strategy', in A.D. Chandler, O. Solvell and P. Hagstrom (eds), *The Dynamic Firm: The Role of Technology, Strategy, and Regions* 315–342 (Oxford: Oxford University Press).

Flores, R.G. and Aguilera, R.V. (2007) 'Globalization and location choice: An analysis of US multinational firms in 1980 and 2000', *Journal of International Business Studies*, XXXVIII, 1187–1210.

Globerman, S. and Shapiro, D. (2003) 'Governance infrastructure and US foreign direct investment', *Journal of International Business Studies*, XXIV, 19–39.

Gong, H. (1995) 'Spatial patterns of foreign investment in China's cities, 1980–1989', *Urban Geography*, XVI, 198–209.

Gordon, I.R. and McCann, P. (2000) 'Industrial clusters, complexes, agglomeration and/or social networks?', *Urban Studies*, XXVII, 513–32.

Head, K., Ries, J.C. and Swenson, D.L. (1999) 'Attracting foreign manufacturing: investment promotion and agglomeration', *Regional Science and Urban Economics*, XXIX, 197–218.

Heckman, J.J. (1979) 'Sample selection bias as a specification error', *Econometrica*, XLVII, 153–61.

Henderson, J.V. (1986) 'Efficiency of resource usage and city size', *Journal of Urban Economics*, XIX, 47–70.

Henisz, W.J. and Delios, A. (2001) 'Uncertainty, imitation and plant location: Japanese multinational corporations 1990–1996', *Administrative Science Quarterly*, XLVI, 443–75.

Hoover, E.M. (1948) *The Location of Economic Activity* (New York: McGraw-Hill).

Jacobs, J. (1985) *Cities and the Wealth of Nations. Principles of Economic Life* (Harmondsworth: Penguin).

Kitson, M., Martin, R. and Tyler, P. (2004) 'Regional competitiveness: An elusive yet key concept?', *Regional Studies*, XXXVIII, 991–99.

Kozul-Wright, R. and Rowthorn, R. (1998) 'Spoilt for choice? Multinational corporations and the geography of international production', *Oxford Review of Economic Policy*, XIV, 74–92.

Knickerbocker, F.T. (1973) *Oligopolistic Reaction and the Multinational Enterprise* (Cambridge, Mass.: Harvard University Press).

Makino, S., Lau, C.M. and Yeh, R.-S. (2002) 'Asset exploitation versus asset-seeking: Implications for location choice of foreign direct investment from newly industrialized countries', *Journal of International Business Studies*, XXXIII, 403–21.

Malmberg, A. and Maskell, P. (2002) 'The elusive concept of localisation economies: Towards a knowledge-based theory of spatial clustering', *Environment and Planning A*, XXXIV, 429–49.

Markusen, A. (1996) 'Sticky places in slippery space: A typology of industrial Districts', *Economic Geography*, LXXII, 293–313.

Marshall, A. (1890) *Principles of Economics* (London: Macmillan).

Martin, R. and Sunley, P. (2003) 'Deconstructing clusters: Chaotic concept or policy panacea?', *Journal of Economic Geography*, III, 5–35.

McCann, P. and Mudambi, R. (2005) 'Analytical differences in the economics of geography: The case of the multinational firm', *Environment and Planning A*, XXXVII, 1857–76.

Nachum, L. (2000) 'Economic geography and the location of TNCs: Financial and professional service FDI to the USA', *Journal of International Business Studies*, XXXI, 367–85.

Nachum, L. (2003) 'Liability of foreignness in global competition? Financial service affiliates in the city of London', *Strategic Management Journal*, XXIV, 1187–1208.

Nachum, L. and Keeble, D. (2003) 'Neo-marshallian clusters and global networks: The linkages of media firms in central London', *Long Range Planning*, XXXVI, 459–80.

Pelegrin, A. and Bolance, C. (2008) 'Regional foreign direct investment in manufacturing. Do agglomeration economies matter?', *Regional Studies*, XLII, 505–22.

Peng, M.W. (2001) 'The resource-based view and international business', *Journal of Management*, XXVII, 803–829.

Porter, M.E. (1998) *On Competition* (Cambridge, Mass.: HBS Press).

Porter, M.E. (1990) *The Competitive Advantage of Nations* (London: Macmillan).

Pred, A. (1977) *City-Systems in Advanced Economies: Past Growth, Present Processes and Future Development Options* (London: Hutchinson).

Rugman, A.M. and Verbeke, A. (2007) 'Liabilities of regional foreignness and the use of firm-level versus country-level data: A response to Dunning *et al*', *Journal of International Business Studies*, XXXVIII, 200–05.

Rugman, A.M. and Verbeke, A. (2004) 'A perspective on regional and global strategies of multinational enterprises', *Journal of International Business Studies*, XXXV, 3–18.

Saxenian, A. (1994) *Regional Advantage: Culture and Competition in Silicon Valley and Route 128* (Cambridge, Mass.: Harvard University Press).

Scott, A.J. (2001) *Global City-Regions* (Oxford: Oxford University Press).

Sethi, D., Guisinger, S.E., Phelan, S.E. and Berg, D.M. (2003) 'Trends in foreign direct investment flows: a theoretical and empirical analysis', *Journal of International Business Studies*, XXXIV, 315–26.

Shatz, H.J. and Venables, A.J. (2000) 'The Geography of International Investment', in G. L. Clark, M. P. Feldmann and M. S. Gertler (eds), *The Oxford Handbook of Economic Geography*, 125–45 (Oxford: Oxford University Press).

Stevens, M. J. and Bird, A. (2004) 'On the myth of believing that globalization is a Myth: or the effects of misdirected responses on obsolescing an emergent substantive discourse', *Journal of International Management*, X, 501–10.

Storper, M. (2000) 'Globalization, localization and trade', in G.L. Clark, M.P Feldmann and M.S. Gertler (eds), *The Oxford Handbook of Economic Geography*, 146–65 (Oxford: Oxford University Press).

Swann, G.M.P., Prevezer, M. and Stout, D. (1998) *The Dynamics of Industrial Clustering: International Comparisons in Computing and Biotechnology* (Oxford: Oxford University Press).

Taylor, P. , Beaverstock, J.V. Cook, G. and Pandit, N.R. (2003) *Financial Services Clustering and its Significance for London* (London: Corporation of London).

Wheeler, D. and Mody, A. (1992) 'International investment location decisions', *Journal of International Economics*, XXXIII, 57–76.

Zaheer, S. (1995) 'Overcoming the liability of foreignness', *Academy of Management Journal*, XXXVIII, 341–63.

This work contains statistical data from ONS which is Crown copyright and reproduced with the permission of the controller of HMSO and Queen's Printer for Scotland. The use of the ONS statistical data in this work does not imply the endorsement of the ONS in relation to the interpretation or analysis of the statistical data. This work uses research datasets which may not exactly reproduce National Statistics aggregates.

5
Resources of Multinational Enterprises Used for Corporate Political Activities in the European Union

Sigrun M. Wagner

Introduction and literature background

The following chapter deals with the resources used by multinational companies from the automotive industry in their corporate political activities in the European Union regarding environmental regulations. It investigates the research questions what kind of resources and competences MNEs use in their CPA and whether these resources fit the typology of political resources suggested by Dahan (2005a).

This section introduces the relevant literature before the next section discusses the theoretical underpinning – resource-based theories (RBT/RBV). This is followed by methods, presentation and discussion of results, and conclusion with an outlook.

The justification for lobbying and corporate political activities lies in the influences and effects that government decisions and policies may have on business enterprises and their competitive environment (Keim and Hillman 2008). These effects vary according to the issue area and the type of policy.

The study of corporate political activities (or public affairs) is naturally an interdisciplinary subject and draws from the literatures in political sciences, economics, and management. The various terms used for business-government relations (such as political behaviour, lobbying, corporate affairs, external relations, public affairs, business-government interaction) vary slightly in their definitions, but they all have in common that they refer to the function of

> enlisting the support and/or negating the opposition of non-market and non-economic players in a firm's environment. (Griffin et al. 2001a: 11)

For the specific context of this research, three different perspectives on business-government relations have been chosen: MNE-host government relations from the International Business literature; Corporate Political Activities (CPA) from publications on Strategic Management, interest representation and lobbying from Political Science perspectives. The strategic management literature related to CPA focuses mostly on American corporations, whereas the political science literature focuses on the European Union perspective and interest groups in general, and the international business literature focusses on MNE-host government relations. These three areas all contribute to a better understanding of the context of this research on the resources used by automotive MNEs in their political activities in the EU regarding environmental regulations.

According to Boddewyn and Brewer (1994: 137), political behaviour is intrinsic to international business as crossing borders means introducing companies into other sovereignties. The authors assert that International Business (IB) research is much more concerned with political factors than research in domestic business (ibid.). Governmental policies differ from country to country and thus distinguish international from domestic business (Boddewyn and Brewer 1994: 123–25, see also Grosse and Behrman 1992: 119 as well as Toyne and Nigh 1998). Boddewyn (1988) anticipates this notion in claiming that the distinction between international and domestic business is fundamentally political (see also Boddewyn 1997). This is echoed by Grosse (2005). Grosse implicitly defines international business-government relations as the relations between national governments and multinational firms (ibid.). For Meznar and Johnson (2005: 119) business-government relations include 'all manner of interactions between a firm and its political stakeholders'.

Moon and Lado (2000) confirm that an important issue in IB is the interaction between multinationals and host governments, between which often strategic interdependence exists (Ring et al. 1990). Blumentritt and Nigh (2002) argue for more integration between MNE literature and literature on international business-government interactions. Also Dunning (2002) stresses the need for a reappraisal of the significance of governments for MNE activities.

The resources of a firm and its ownership-specific advantages (see Dunning's OLI paradigm, Dunning 1981) have an effect on its overall bargaining power vis-à-vis its host government (Fagre and Wells 1982, see also Luo 2001, Moon and Lado 2000 as well as Capron and Chatain 2008). Similarly, Boddewyn and Brewer (1994) propose that the intensity of political behaviour is greater when a firm's political competences are more developed – enterprises in a stronger market, or financial, position will be in a better position to engage in political activities (Keillor and Hult 2004, Gladwin and Walter 1980). Also Eden et al. (2005) discuss the influence of resources on bargaining power and use insights of the resource-based theory in their elaboration (see next section for the RBT).

Until the mid-1980s, political decision making had received little attention in the (strategic) management literature dealing with the political environment of the enterprise (Keim and Zeithaml 1986, Epstein 1980). Gale and Buchholz (1987) point out that since the 1960s public policy has become an influential determinant of firm behaviour and Mahon (1989) stresses that corporations expanded their political-action activity immensely in the 1980s. In Griffin et al.'s (2001a, 2001b) extensive bibliography of public affairs and corporate political activity it can be seen how the field developed and grew from only some individual contributions in the 1960s and start of the 1970s to a whole host of publications in the 1980s and 1990s. In the last decade, studies have become more systematically theoretical as opposed to prior decades when research in the area was conducted in a more ad hoc manner (Griffin et al. 2001a).

Baysinger (1984) identifies corporate political activities (CPA) as corporate attempts to shape government policy in ways favourable to the firm and Getz defines CPA as 'any deliberate firm action intended to influence governmental policy or process' (Getz 1997).

Keim and Hillman (2008) point out that it is mostly larger firms that are more international in scope that are most active in the political arena (see also Lenway and Rehbein 1991). Keim and Hillman (2008) also point to the likely results of inaction (e.g., potential costs, competitors' actions) that determine how active businesses are in the public policy process.

Rehbein and Schuler (1995) state that the structures, routines, resources, issue salience, and stakeholder dependencies determine why and how a firm responds to its external environment. In line with Yoffie (1987), Hillman et al. (2004) argue that the level of CPA is dependent on resources. This is an important commonality the CPA literature shares with the previous IB discussion. The authors (ibid.) furthermore point out that research into firm political resources can be greatly aided by the RBV, which is echoed by Bonardi et al. (2005). Also Keim (2001a) points to the importance of resources that need to be valuable, rare, inimitable and not readily substitutable in order to be sources of competitive advantage for firms' CPA. These resource characteristics will be further discussed in the next section. Schuler et al. (2002) relate resources used in CPA to the size of the firm, with larger firms possessing more clout to influence public policy according to their complex needs.

Epstein (1969) used the term 'corporate political resources or assets' as early as 1969, but not within the context of the RBT (next section) (see also Mitnick 1993). Corporate resources yield corporate political power, according to Schuler (2008); scarce resources are deployed to politically relevant activities in order to influence public policy (Windsor 2007). Political resources can be defined as those 'assets and skills utilized in the implementation of corporate political strategies' (Jacomet 2005: 83). Both Jacomet (2005) and Dahan (2005a, 2005b) point out that these political resources are traditionally of individual corporate nature but can also be of collective nature (genuine collective resources or pooled individual resources; see also Oberman (1993) and Salorio et al. (2005) for political resources).

In the context of firm-specific political resources, Frynas et al. (2006) point out that research has mostly been conducted on the domestic political process in the United States without a regard for the international dimension. This is where this chapter will contribute to research in CPA and political resources by focusing on the political process in the European Union.

Lobbying as a political science term originates from the hotel lobby where U.S. President Ulysses Grant (1869–77) met waiting interest representatives (Köppl 2005), although Mack (2005) points to the lobby of the Palace of Westminster in London as origin of the term and Buholzer (1997) states that lobbying is as old as politics itself. Either way, lobbying as a term is firmly rooted in the Anglo-Saxon political world while being regarded as suspicious in other languages (e.g., McGrath 2005, Gardner 1991).

The European Union presents a very unique context for lobbying which is different from any national policy-making context (Greenwood 2007). In the wake of the Single European Act (1986) and the single market (1993), individual firm lobbying increased – Coen (1997) states the figure of over 200 large firms setting up direct lobbying capabilities in Brussels[1] between 1985 and 1993.[2] Broscheid and Coen (2003: 166) call this a 'lobbying boom'. Before the Act, interest representation was in the form of European-wide federations of national association, so-called Euro-groups (Mazey and Richardson 1993b). As European law takes precedence over national law in many areas (Van Schendelen 1993), firms have needed to move their business-government relations from a national to a European level.

Business groups predominate in the EU, accounting for nearly two-thirds of interest groups (Aspinwall and Greenwood 1998, Greenwood 2007). Business belongs to the more powerful lobbies, although it does not always get what it wants (Grant 1993: 44); business is indeed recognized as a 'special' interest group because of its key role in organizing the economy and the considerable amount of resources that business interests possess (Lindeque 2007: 564, John 2002). The amount of resources a firm controls can be linked to its size, and the size of a firm influences whether businesses lobby individually in Brussels[3] (Bennett 1999). Woll (2007) indicates financial resources, social capital, legal, or technical expertise as well as other information as resources that are used by lobbyists. Similarly, Van Schendelen (2002) lists expertise, networks, positions, and financial means as the most frequently used resources, but does not relate them to any theoretical concept. This will be done in the next section.

What binds all three areas of literature on business-government relations (International Business, Strategic Management, and Political Science) together is that individual corporate political activities are only pursued if sufficient resources are available (e.g., Boddewyn and Brewer 1994 on political competences, see also Keillor and Hult 2004, based on Gladwin and Walter 1980, see also Lenway and Rehbein 1991, Schuler and Rehbein 1997). The size of firms serves as a proxy for resources and political clout which determine benefits from pursuing political activities (Wan and Hillman 2005). The automotive industry as one of the world's biggest industries contains large multinational firms, and thus a resource-based approach to its lobbying activities is appropriate.

Regarding the terminology, 'corporate political activities' will be the main term used, but 'government relations' or 'interest representation' and 'lobbying' will also be used. Corporate Political Activities is an academic term very specific to a certain type of literature that could be misunderstood by laymen because of the 'political' connotation, while lobbying is used by practitioners and in everyday language, despite its negative connotations. Government relations and interest representation seem to have more neutral connotations than the other two terms.

In this research, all of these terms will be understood to:

- Include any intended firm action with the purpose of influencing governmental policy or processes (based on discussions of the term corporate political activities)
- Include an aspect of communication (based on the definition of lobbying)
- Include activities that are specifically influencing governmental policies but also activities that keep relations with governments on an ongoing basis as a pre-condition for influence (based on the relational aspect of business-government relations).

The rest of the chapter is structured in the following way: conceptual framework, methods, presentation and discussion of results, and conclusion with an outlook.

Conceptual framework

All three discussed areas of literature share an underlying resource-based assumption: only firms with a sufficient resource base will engage in business-government relations (e.g., Boddewyn and Brewer 1994; Hillman and Hitt 1999; Bennett 1999; Luo 2001). The main theory that will be used as a conceptual framework for this research will therefore be the resource-based view or theory (RBV/RBT[4]).

Unlike the interest representation literature from political science which takes a government or state perspective on lobbying, the RBV enables a firm perspective on corporate political activities as the following quote demonstrates:

> The Resource-Based View is an inside-out perspective on organizations that seeks to identify the characteristics of firms with superior performance. Unlike outside-in approaches which begin with the external environment

explanations of sustained superior performance, the Resource-Based View posits that we look inside organizations and more explicitly holds a place for managers and what they do as important to organizational outcome. (Rouse and Daellenbach 2002: 966)

Capron and Chatain (2008) encourage research that links CPA and firm resources. Also, Moon and Lado (2000) encourage the use of the RBV for IB research on MNE-host government relations. Furthermore, Hart (1995) promotes the inclusion of the environmental aspect into the RBV. Although the RBV already has been used in analyses of CPA, this has only been in a U.S. domestic context, and therefore there is a need for international extension of the RBV (Frynas et al. 2006; McWilliams et al. 2002), especially with regard to the European (Union) setting. This research thus closes these gaps by using the RBV as a conceptual framework to investigate how MNEs in the EU influence environmental policies.

The emergence of the resource-based theory of the firm has been one of the main developments in recent international business and strategic management research, with Wernerfelt (1984) and Barney (1991) at the forefront (Peng 2001). In the strategy literature it has served as the dominant explanation for firm differences (Hoopes, Madsen, and Walker 2003; Gibbert 2006; see also Wernerfelt 2003).

The principle focus in the theory is on firm resources contributing to sustainable competitive advantage. In order to be a basis for sustainable competitive advantage, resources need the following characteristics (Barney 1991; Moon and Lado 2000): valuable, rare, imperfectly imitable, and nonsubstitutable.

Furthermore, an elemental assumption of the theory is that resources need to meet the conditions of heterogeneity and immobility to exhibit the mentioned characteristics. Penrose (1959: 75) – an important precursor of the theory – points out that '[I]t is the heterogeneity, and not the homogeneity, of the productive services available or potentially available from its resources that gives each firm its unique character' (1959: 75). Among the required resource characteristics leading to uniqueness and competitive advantage, inimitability is a crucial factor, as it inhibits other firms from obtaining valuable and rare resources.

Boddewyn and Brewer (1994) criticize the resource-based theory for only looking at economic and organizational competences of firms, not at political capabilities. Moon and Lado (2000) point out that research of the MNE-Host government relationship has not used insights of the RBT: resource-based academics have primarily used a 'domestic' context in theorizing about the links between corporate resources and capabilities, and economic rent. Furthermore, resource-based-view-oriented strategists take the nonmarket environment as exogenous and neutral (Boddewyn 2003), whereas this research questions the

exogenous nature of the nonmarket environment. By taking into account corporate actions towards its environment and questioning this environment as
endogenous, the understanding between a firm's resources and its competitive
advantage will be increased (Capron and Chatain 2008).

Frynas, Mellahi and Pigman (2006: 325) point out that

> [A]ccess to key government minister, experience in dealing with corrupt
> officials and other political resources, which result in a firm's advantageous
> treatment by political decision-makers, are frequently in scarce supply and
> difficult to obtain.

As a corollary, political resources can be aligned to Barney's (1991) framework
where critical resources need to be valuable, rare, imperfectly imitable and
imperfectly substitutable in order to be advantageous (see also Keillor and Hult
2004 on distinctive nonmarket competencies used for competitive advantage).
As political resources can be difficult for competitors to equalize, they may
be a source of competitive advantage (Frynas et al. 2006). McWilliams et al.
(2002) extend the RBT to political strategies where it can be applied to raising
rivals' costs by blocking the use of substitute resources for competitors through
regulation.

Boddewyn and Brewer (1994: 137) assert that competitive advantages do
have an 'unavoidable political dimension' that must be factored into strategy
and IB research. A more favourable political-legal environment is the goal of
corporate political strategies, that is, of political activities for which political
resources are used:

> The favourable application or a change in a current public policy is thus the
> final goal to be achieved through the implementation of a political strategy
> that requires specific resources, which some have called 'political resources'.
> (Dahan 2005b: 11)

Frynas et al. (2006) remark that the literature has defined the terms 'political
capital', 'political resources' or 'political competences' variously. The authors
broadly define political resources as

> any firm attributes, assets, human resources, or any other resources that
> allow the firm to use the political process to improve its efficiency and prof-
> itability. (ibid. 324)

Similarly, Dahan (2005a) restricts the use of the term 'political resource' to the
assets and skills that are utilized in the political arena. In terms of advantages
for firms, he uses the term 'regulatory advantage' to describe a 'favourable state

of public policies for a given firm' (2005a: 43). As with other resources, political resources are not necessarily owned by a firm, but are under its control (Dahan 2005b). Other terms also include nonmarket resources or assets (Dahan 2005a; Baron 1995).

Resources can generally be categorized as follows: financial resources, physical resources, human resources, technological resources, and organizational resources (Grant 1991). Dahan's (2005a) typology of political firm resources consists of the following: expertise, financial resource, relational resource, organizational resource, reputation with other nonmarket actors, public image, support of stakeholders, recreational skills. This typology forms part of the basis for the interview guide as discussed in the next section. Dahan's political resources will be discussed in turn.

Expertise: According to Dahan (2005a) expertise can be gained in various areas such as technical/technological, economic/managerial, social, environmental, legal, and political/administrative fields. Boddewyn (1988) points out political knowledge and expertise as resource that can lead to firm-specific advantages and political advantages in the form of better intelligence, readier access, and superior influence skills (see also Boddewyn and Brewer 1994). Technological know-how is also pointed out by Moon and Lado (2000). Attarça (2002) distinguishes among economic, technical, scientific, and legal expertise. Although not using a resource-based approach, Woll (2007) mentions legal or technical expertise or other information as resources which can be placed in this typology. Van Schendelen (2002: 177) even considers political expertise as a meta-resource which is the 'single most important variable asset' a lobby group may have.

Financial resource: This can be both a direct resource (e.g., through campaign contributions) and an indirect resource (financing other political resources) (Dahan 2005a). Van Schendelen (2002) emphasizes financial resources as important resources due to the costs of lobbying and political action which includes for example the setting up of structures, communication campaigns, public relations, information acquisition, for example, through studies, participation in coalitions, and associations (Attarça 2002). Also Newell and Paterson (1998) and Woll (2007) underline financial resources while Salorio et al. (2005) point out that although money is commonly listed as a 'political' resource, it is really an economic asset.

Relational resource: This includes formal relations (e.g., membership in a committee) and informal relations (interpersonal contacts) (Dahan 2005a). Schuler (2008) uses the terms political connections and networks (see also Van Schendelen 2002 for the latter). Li and Zhang (2007) point out managerial resources as social capital which is gained by political networking, indicated by ties with government officials. Also Woll (2007) and Oliver and Holzinger (2008) use the term social capital, while Yoffie and Bergenstein (1985) use the term political capital for these relational resources. Moon and Lado (2000) see social relationships as relationship-based resources. Such relational resources lead to access to decision and policy makers (Attarça 2005).

Organizational resource: This resource can be either internal such as a permanent representation and public affairs office or external such as a consultancy and trade association offices (Dahan 2005a). Attarça (2002 and 2005) includes human resources, public affairs structures and procedures in organizational resources. Managerial resources are widely accepted as being a critical resource for SCA (Moon and Lado 2000; see also Castanias and Helfat 1991/2001; Fiol 1991; Reed and DeFillippi 1990). Moon and Lado (2000) point to managers' ability to enact beneficial firm-environment relationships and to mange the 'political imperative' (see also Ring et al. 1990).

Reputation with other nonmarket actors: this resource is built up over time and thus relates to the concept of political capital (Dahan 2005a; Yoffie and Bergenstein 1985; see also Yoffie 1987) and corporate social capital (Preston 2004). Moon and Lado (2000) set reputation in relation to trust(worthiness) and legitimacy (similarly, Salorio et al. 2005), while Dahan (2005a) points out credibility in connection with reputation. There is a distinction between individual and corporate reputation of firm representatives and the company (Dahan 2005a). Also Boddewyn and Brewer (1994) mention reputation as a political capability. Attarça (2002 and 2005) calls reputation and public image together symbolic resources.

Public image: This resource is the perception of the firm's political action by public opinion (Dahan 2005a and 2005b). The difference between reputation and public image, according to Dahan (2005a), is that reputation builds up over time while public image varies in the short run. Van Schendelen (2002) does not list public image in his discussion of resources for lobbying but brings up a good image as a requirement for a successful lobby group.

Support of stakeholders: This resource adds weight and legitimacy to a firm's position and can be formal or informal and of temporary or permanent nature (Dahan 2005a and 2005b). Van Schendelen (2002) mentions external positions as a link between one's own group and the networks of stakeholders – in this context, a network of different stakeholders could also be seen a resource in the form of support. In Boddewyn and Brewer's (1994) terms, this is coalition-building ability.

Recreational skill: This resource creates opportunities for more informal and personal contacts with decision makers and journalists and includes recreational services such as wining and dining, plant visits, and so on (Dahan 2005a). Dahan (2005b: 16) remarks on the rivalry in Brussels to 'come up with the most original public relations event to attract influential public decision makers who are oversolicited'. While being very common in practice, this resource has not been acknowledged in the literature, according to Dahan (2005a).

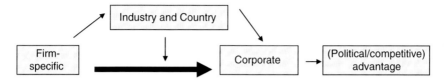

Figure 5.1   Resource-based determinants of MNE political activities (author graph, modified from Moon and Lado 2000: 101)

The author therefore suggests that this conceptualization be empirically validated through in-depth case studies or large-scale surveys (Dahan 2005a). This research will take Dahan's typology of political resources as a basis for investigating, through case studies, which resources MNEs use in their CPA in the EU. This research could therefore validate or explore/test his typology.

Figure 5.1 illustrates the focus of the research, which is how firm-specific political resources are directed into corporate political activities. Other moderating influences on political activities are the context of the industry, and the context of country or region. In the RBT, the main objective of companies is to attain (sustainable) competitive advantage. As political activities might not necessarily lead to competitive (market) benefits, but to legislative advantages, the chapter also uses the term political (nonmarket) advantage, thus illustrating the RBT's application in a different context. One example of political advantage is the reputation a firm has or enjoys among policy makers, which makes it more likely for decision makers to trust the firm's expertise and information provided through its interest representation.

Methodology

This research has employed a case study approach to explore the corporate political activities of the major automobile manufacturers active in the European Union. The case study methodology is most appropriate as the relations among the actors and their context is complex. Case studies can offer the breadth and depth of information for descriptive, causative, and inductive analysis to be performed (Eisenhardt 1989; Miles and Huberman 1984; Yin 1994; cf. Levy and Rothenberg 1999). Shaffer (1995) emphasizes the strength of case study approaches to the investigation of corporate political activity, which comes from their potential qualitative nature, and the use of longitudinal designs. In particular, case studies, he argues, account better for political behaviour on specific policy issues. He also acknowledges the classic limiting problem of generalizability.

Corporate political activities are a contemporary phenomenon in a real-life context, where a case study strategy can offer benefits (Yin 1994). One of the strengths of the case study approach is to handle a variety of evidence (Yin 1994): as corporate political activities are often seen in a critical light because of 'lobbying scandals', it is important to not only collect data from companies but also from other stakeholders (the 'lobbied' European institutions and other stakeholders and observers like nongovernmental organizations and supplying industries). This is only possible with a case study, which allows for a multi-method approach that uses triangulation.

The chosen organizations and interview partners were selected according to their role as stakeholders in the policy-making process of EU environmental regulations for the automobile industry. These organizations have an interest in this process and try to influence it. They were identified as stakeholders by investigating the contributions to the consultation process of EU legislation as well as by following up references in organizational documents, and academic and professional publications related to the cases. Furthermore, this author was given recommendations by interviewees and by contacted interview partners who were not available for interviews.

Three cases were chosen as a basis for comparison: CO_2 emissions, pollutant emissions, and end-of-life vehicles (ELVs). A 'strategy of diverse sampling' (Eisenhardt 1989: 537) was followed to cover a broad range of environmental regulations for the automotive industry: the ELV directive is the first case of its kind, the CO_2 case serves as the only voluntary agreement in the automotive sector, and the Euro Norms on pollutant emissions consist of a series of directives that were successively tightened. These exploratory cases are all particular examples of environmental regulations and are therefore expected to show some similarities, but they may also have differences in view of their varying environmental objectives.

In total, 73 interviews were conducted for this research as part of a doctoral research project. Between 130 and 140 potential interviewees were contacted, resulting in a response rate above 50%. Considering the contentious nature of the subject, this is considered a very high response rate. In the following all interviewees and companies that were interviewed have been anonymized. Greek letters are used for the companies that were interviewed (ALPHA through to LAMBDA, plus compounds for country-specific subsidiaries, e.g., ETA-ALPHA), while interview quotes are attributed by showing the date, order (A, B, C) and what kind of stakeholder of the automotive industry they are (the following abbreviations are used: AA – Market side, Automotive Association; AC – Market side, Automotive Company; CS – Civil Society; OSH – Other stakeholder or not readily classifiable; SOSH – state side other stakeholder; RA – Market side, Related Industry, Association; RC – Market side, Related Industry, Company; SEC – State side, European Commission; SEP – State side, European Parliament). Interview quotes have not been rectified

Figure 5.2 Overview of distribution of interview partners

Organization/Interview partner	Number of interviews	Total
Market side	(14 + 5)	36
Corporate public affairs offices (automotive industry – other stakeholder industry)	(7 + 10)	
Business associations (automotive industry – other stakeholder industry)		
State side (EU Institutions)	13	27
European parliament	12	
Commission	2	
Council		
Civil society side	7	8
Environmental NGOs	1	
Consumer organizations		
Others and informal meetings	2	2
Total		73

for grammatical correctness in order to preserve the original nature of the interviewees, often not native speakers.

Figure 5.2 displays the distribution of interviewees among the stakeholder organizations. In the interviews, respondents were asked what kind of resources and competences companies and the associations use in their interest representation and which role they play. The question was asked openly; prompts that were given to interviewees were based on Dahan's (2005a) typology of political firm resources (see above). Other resources that came up as a result of the interviews were continuity, time, and studies. These resources constituted the basic structure for coding relevant interview sections. The resources will now be discussed in turn.

Results and discussion

Human resources and expertise
Broadly speaking, staff involved in CPA come from two different backgrounds:

- Political world: background in politics, government, public affairs, European institutions, as well as the 'Brussels world', and
- Industrial world: company, industry and technical background, sometimes legal or management background.

There seemed to be no clear profile of people employed in this area and a mixed background was emphasized by interviewees and applies in two different ways:

Teams of mixed people: this is the case where staff employed have a mixed background, for example, trained engineers who have developed into lobbyists or government affairs specialists who have expanded their expertise to technical areas. This also concerns the nationalities of employees.

Mixed teams of people: this is the case where human resources with a technical background work alongside those with a political background; these could also be called specialists (engineers) and generalists (public affairs practitioners).

This mix is captured in the following quotes:

> Yes, that is an area of tension between an understanding of Brussels and of the automobile industry. With a mix you are on the right way. The one who is only an expert doesn't get anywhere. But on the other hand you are not credible either if you only work with experts on Brussels here. (16.03.07 B, AA)

> You need both I think. Sometimes I would say the communications people are passing businesses to commercial people, the door openers, and the technical people need to come with the more complex arguments, and the communications people are important to reduce the technical stories to simple communication language. So it is a kind of tandem I think, it is important. (19.03.07 B, RA)

In terms of the nationalities of people involved in CPA it can be stated that most companies employ a mixed approach, also in order to cover a range of languages (04.03.08 AC) for the linguistic complexity of Brussels. Exceptions from this case were ALPHA, GAMMA, and DELTA, who only seemed to employ home country nationals in their Brussels offices.

Furthermore, organizations differed in what they viewed as relevant backgrounds. Whereas most companies had a combination of backgrounds, two companies, incidentally from the same country, are at either end of the extreme as highlighted in the next two quotes:

> (...) people who have worked either previously in other departments at ZETA, because it's very important to know the company from the inside, I think it's really impossible to push interests of a company you don't know from the inside, and when I say knowing from the inside, not just 3 months as a trainee, so for instance J. joined the team last year and previously she has worked 7 years for ZETA, so she knows the company, you know when we talk about our competitiveness, we have visited many plants, we know people from the engineering department, we really know exactly how big

projects are being managed, all that. So it's very important, important background from the inside, knowing the different departments, the constraints and so on. (04.03.08 AC)

For ZETA, company background is crucial – knowledge of the firm's issues and of what drives the corporation, whereas for EPSILON, it is crucial for staff to have a background in EU institutions and lobbying:

> (...) it's a priority for us also to have the good expertise but also representative of different nationalities, all those people were in the past linked to the European institutions, they were trainees or they have studied, I would say, the European law or European economy, so they have all a background, myself also, I was a trainee but a long time ago, unfortunately, in DG Trade in the beginning of the 80s and I spent 4 years in DG Enterprise as 'agent temporaire', before joining the automotive association. So we have 5 persons here and all of them have a background of Europe, have a background also of lobbying, in some respects. (12.03.08 AC)

This is a very interesting finding and could possibly be explained that organizations place different significance on the input and output of the process of interest representation where the input stands for the company and industrial background and the output stands for the interaction with policy makers. The other companies tend to move in between those two extremes and have a mix of company-own experts and people coming from a political or lobbying background as well as people who have experience in both areas. Especially for human resources coming to Brussels from industry, adjustment can be a difficult process and involves getting to know how the EU functions.

These *learning processes* that are involved differ thus according to the background of human resources. As there is no clear-cut profile of human resources involved in CPA there are no tailored degrees or courses as for example in the case of engineers.[5] Consequently, important learning processes are involved when people take up public affairs functions: 'learning by doing/experience' was a recurrent theme among interviewees. These are especially difficult for engineers-turned-lobbyists compared with lobbyists who are switching from one industry to another within the 'Brussels Spaceship' (term used by Oldag and Tillack 2004), often being able to keep their established network. For such engineers, coming from the industry and firms, learning to communicate their expertise to politicians and civil servants – technical laymen – is a demanding task. Also, getting to know 'how Brussels works' creates additional challenges. Some corporate offices and associations send their new assignments to short training courses on the institutions, but for the majority of people there has been no training involved. People are thrown into cold water (12.03.07 A, AC) and are possibly accompanied by more experienced colleagues to guide them in the beginning (ibid., 07.03.07 A, AC) as illustrated in the following quote:

> Until recently I had a colleague from England here who was an engineer, who was an excellent technical expert but who had to learn lobbying basically and I took him to many meetings, and within meetings he was responsible for partial areas which he was to present and so on and to build up own trust in principle so that after 3 years, well, I mean after 1.5 years, I can let him go on his own with certain topics and I would say that today he is a fully-fledged lobbyist who can communicate excellently in addition to the fact that he brings his engineering knowledge with him. (07.03.07 A, AC)

This quote shows the importance of the learning process as well as expertise needed to execute CPA. The expertise is either developed through learning processes in the beginning or has been acquired from before. As with the background, perspectives on what kind of expertise is needed for successful CPA differ, and there is a mixed picture:

Technical expertise: A basic technical understanding is necessary, but apart from that, it is more important to know where expertise can be found, either in the firm or in the association. If necessary, experts from headquarters are flown in; this was frequently mentioned in interviews. Again, while dealing with laymen it is critical to translate technical language or jargon into laymen's terms. This is possibly a reason why some interviewees viewed technical expertise as less important than communication, which is vital for 'getting your message across' to politicians.

Institutional expertise: Michalowitz (2004: 128) terms this 'specific Brussels knowledge'. This learning process results in vital knowledge which can be summarized in 'to know the right moment to contact decision-makers and to know which decision makers to contact' (06.03.07 A, SEP). Because of the way the European institutions work, timing is crucial – the Commission prepares and publishes legislative proposals whereas the Council and the Parliament decide upon it. This decision-making process determines the right moments of when to talk to whom in which institution. A precondition for being able to talk to decision makers is getting to know them prior to legislative processes. Other resources closely connected to human resources apart from relational resources (network aspect) include resources like image, reputation, and continuity.

A European Commission employee involved in the Euro 5 discussions pointed out that the kind of expertise also depends on the topic that is being legislated:

> Lots of the people I have direct contact with have engineering backgrounds and because of the vehicle type approval system background so that is fairly,

emission, development engineers. But there are some people who have specialized in government relations but often have a very technical background as well. It then depends, it changes, if you move over to a CO2 agenda you get more, much more of this sort of standard government relations type people. (14.03.07 A, SEC)

Some interviewees pointed out the roles of personalities in the case of human resources – these play a role as the people represent their companies externally. They have to be able to communicate and work well in a team (07.03.07 A, AC), be credible (ibid; 21.03.07 C, SEP), polite (16.03.07 B, AA) and benefit from a 'friendly outgoing personality' (12.03.07 D, AA). Two former MEPs recounted the behaviour of two separate incidents where lobbyists had been a negative example in terms of rudeness and arrogance which did not help the case of their companies (20.10.06 SEP and 24.10.06 SEP). Thus, this is an aspect not to be neglected among background and expertise, and it is certainly an area where a company can distinguish itself from others.

Independent of what kind of knowledge corporate representatives possess, be it technical or political, it will only be useful for interest representation when the expertise and information provided are trusted by policy-makers. The provision of credible and reliable data build up a firm's or an individual's reputation, which is another resource for political corporate success in the long term.

Reputation and public image

According to Dahan (2005a), public image could be a moderating factor in policy makers' reactions to corporate political activities. Reputation relates to the long-term perception of a firm by policy makers; it is accumulated over time (Dahan 2005b; see also Yoffie and Bergenstein 1985). Of these two related resources, reputation was given more weight among interviewees. The image of companies was either seen as consistent with their public image (e.g., marketing) or as less important than reputation. Reputation was very much linked to the individuals rather than to the organizations they were representing:

> So reputation of the company doesn't matter. Reputation of the individual who is doing the lobbying does, because lobbying is a social activity as well as a political activity. (09.05.07 SEP)

Discussions regarding reputation hinged around the notions of being credible and reliable – both are characteristics that need to be accumulated over time and are based on the information given by firms to policy makers. As one interviewee remarked, expertise is more important than reputation (23.03.07 B, RA), which confirms that reputation is based on the expertise and information given and, thus, as an asset it approximates what Yoffie and Bergenstein (1985) call 'political capital' which takes time to build up.

Relational resources

Relational resources include formal relations such as membership in a committee and informal relationships through interpersonal contacts; both serve access functions in corporate political activities, that is, gaining entrance to either institutions or people working there (Dahan 2005a and 2005b). Luo (2004) points out that whether at the individual or organizational level, relationships are firm-specific assets that are not transferable to other firms. Relational resources seem to touch the very core or essence of CPA and interest representation, as very clearly demonstrated by the following two interviewees:

> It's the heart of our work. (04.03.08 AC)

> Absolutely important, that is THE thing. Well, without it, forget it, that's why entrance as a newcomer or as new director of office, well, it's very very difficult because you can't fall back on existing networks. (23.10.06 AC)

The importance of such a network of people and information was underlined by a number of interviewees (06.03.07 B, SEP; 25.10.06 AC; 07.11.06 AC; 09.05.07 SEP; 07.03.07 C, RA, 13.07.07 SOSH; 19.03.07 A, AC; 28.060.6 B, AC, and so on), exemplified by the following interview extract:

> (...) [T]he influence of a political process or of political decisions is only then successful if you network continually, not according to the motto 'oh well something is being discussed in Brussels at the moment, get a meeting in Brussels and we will talk'. In the end, something is only successful if you are continuously present here, if you network regularly and exchange regularly and get to know what's going on, who are the decision-makers and the players. (21.03.07 C, SEP)

Like reputation and image, relational resources are also emphasized as being inextricably linked to individual representatives and the interpersonal aspect of corporate political activities was repeatedly remarked upon. Personal chemistry between market and non-market actors is thus an important factor. This was highlighted by an otherwise very matter-of-fact, down-to-earth Scandinavian interviewee favouring a scientific, fact-based approach to legislation, thus showing the significance of relations within interest representation:

> (...) [W]hen it comes to the actually developing of regulations it is more a matter of the personal chemistry. It is a very small unit you know in our

case within DG Enterprise that deal with the directives. It is a handful of people which are replaced on perhaps a 3-year basis or sometimes a little bit longer. The way of working is actually very much connected to the personal characteristics of the people in charge, not necessarily the recognition of the kind of expertise that one individual or one association can provide. (16.03.07 B, AA)

Being connected, knowing people (and thus knowing whom to talk to when it matters) creates social capital (Althaus 2005b), and thus relational resources provide real value for companies. They create advantage as it is easier to find open ears when you know the relevant people already (30.03.07 RC). For company representatives and association personnel, this means getting to know policy makers before critical legislative processes (09.05.07 SEP). Networks take time to build (this also links in with continuity – see below) and the time needed to do this is taken away from being effective in CPA:

Yes, the disadvantage can be huge. In the association and in the firm. You can't work effectively in the first six months. (16.03.07 B, AA)

One respondent who had been seconded to the Commission and had worked on the issue in a national administration before being recruited by an industry association pointed to the advantage of already having an established network in place when starting his new role:

It plays a strong role, because, and, since I know most of the people, it has made my job a bit easier in being able to communicate with them without having to introduce myself and get to know them. So from my time here in [Association] since September, I have been lucky in hitting the ground running in terms of networking out there. (12.03.07 D, AA)

Although the overwhelming majority of respondents emphasized the positive and crucial aspects of relational resources, there were two instances in which interviewees were critical in this respect and they should also be mentioned:

(...) [N]owadays it's more important that you put yourself quickly into the position, to build up contacts again and again. The business is different than what it used to be. It used to be... old boys' network and so on who had known each other for decades. It might partly still be like this, but with the fluctuation we have today on the European level, on the global level, on the political level, the civil servants change every 5 to 7 years in Brussels, here in Germany this hasn't really arrived yet. (...) So the ideal case I would say, no longer exists. Today you have to manage through training and other approaches to be able to establish contacts, to take care of them. But it will be less and less the case to have a relational network that has grown over decades. (01.11.06 AC)

The interviewee had been in Brussels for seven years before moving to a national capital for his company to perform a similar function. The following respondent had been in Brussels for many years as well before moving back to his home country:

(...) Brussels has an enormous turnover. Brussels is constructed as a permanent socialising. A continuous getting to know each other, building new alliances, one issue after the other is being pushed through Brussels and with every topic, alliances and enmities are formed anew. (...) I think the *rapid* ability to build networks is more important. (17.07.07 CS, emphasis added)

These were also the two interviewees who did not view continuity as an essential resource as many others did. Continuity emerged from the interviews as a resource and is very much connected to relational resources. This is discussed below. Keeping the concerns of these two respondents in mind, the main thrust is still that relational resources are of immense significance to corporate political activities.

Financial resources

Unlike the previous resources who all share personal aspects, this resource is of impersonal nature. Although financial resources can be used directly through campaign contributions or other financial incentives (Dahan 2005a; Hillman and Hitt 1999), this is a rare case in the European Union compared to the United States and thus the chapter views financial resources as indirect resources, that is, as financing other resources (e.g., human resources, offices, events). This distinction is supported by the data: Financial resources only seem to play a role as basis for setting up offices for being 'on the ground', that is, gaining access and maintaining lobbying operations. This is in stark contrast to the United States, where financial contributions from firms through Political Action Committees (PACs) are very common (12.03.07 B, AC). One interviewee actually replied when asked about resources used in CPA, possibly reflecting the so-called Abramoff lobbying scandal in the United States that happened that year and involved corrupt practices:

What shall I say? Well, I can say this much, we are not using money. (07.11.06 AC)

Financial resources can also be used for events which are discussed in the next section on recreational skills.

Recreational skills

Recreational skills set up opportunities for more informal and personal contacts and create access and contacts to decision makers (Dahan 2005a, 20.06.06 A). These include the organization of various events in order to network, for example, receptions and 'wining and dining' (09.03.07 CS).

> What comes to mind is the annual ALPHA summer fete. (24.10.06 SEP)

> There are lavish receptions, nearly every day there is some function going on by some company. Food and drink, they think it's important, but in terms of effects it's not very successful. It creates moments of contacts, you also need that. (20.06.06 A, CS)

Furthermore, interviewees (from companies and institutions, 28.06.06 B, AC, 15.08.06 SEP) mention invitations and visits to plants, which give politicians and civil servants practical insights into the day-to-day operations of businesses as well as into the direct effects of legislation.

The support of stakeholders

The support of other stakeholders adds legitimacy and political weight to the representation of a firm's interests (Dahan 2005b). As this strongly depends on the topic, support arrangements can be more or less durable (Dahan 2005a). Other stakeholders include suppliers, customers, other industries, NGOs, trade unions, academia, and national and local governments (all mentioned by various interviewees). Such support does not seem to play a big role for companies, although there is a growing tendency for firms to work with environmental organizations. Traditionally, trade unions (social partners) play a role as a supporting voice, but as the following interviewee pointed out, the automotive industry is a very strong industry:

> What is of course going on is that they bring the trade unions on line with the job argument and partly the trade unions join in. And through that they manage to get the civil parties who are traditionally industry friendly as well as the social democratic parties behind them, the industry friendly and industry political ones. And they achieve that relatively often. And apart from that I think the automobile industry is economically such a strong sector that it doesn't need any broader alliances. (17.07.07 CS)

Suppliers as a supportive resource seem to be a double-edged sword and, dependent on the topic, can either be helpful when interests are aligned or rather divisive when interests and technology developments differ. This was pointed out for the case of Euro norms by two interviewees: suppliers had developed relevant technologies and were pushing for these while the OEMs contended that those technologies were not fully developed for being fitted and aligned to a car except at great costs (07.03.07 A, AC; 29.06.06 AA).

This issue is more important for policy makers, especially in the European Parliament where coalition partners are needed to pass legislation:

> The support through other stakeholders is very very important, the more interest, the more pressure and influence you have on politics. (21.03.07 D, SEP)

If politicians see that a company's or association's case has support by other stakeholders, then this piece of legislation is more likely to be passed.

Other resources

In terms of *organizational resources* which refer to how CPA are organized, Dahan (2005b) distinguishes between internal resources such as an in-house unit and external ones such as hiring a consultancy or using an industry association (see also De Figuerido and Tiller 2001). All companies where interviews took place have their own in-house units in Brussels and their home country capitals (and possibly host country capitals). All of these are also members of either ACEA or JAMA (European and Japanese Association of Automobile Manufacturers), thus they all use a mix of external and internal resources (and thus a mix of collective and individual resources).

The use of consultants by both companies and the European association was noted by one Commission official regarding the Auto Oil programme and Euro norms (22.03.07 B, SEC). Apart from that, the use of consultants seems to be rather the exception than the norm since both the BARs (Brussels Automotive Representatives) and the association are in place. One interviewee was outright when he stated:

> We don't work with consultants. (12.03.08 AC)

A former association and company representative also stressed that

> Consultants – they're in it for themselves (15.03.07 A, RC),

thus pointing towards potential difficulties or tensions for companies when using consultants who often work for several clients simultaneously.

Companies and associations have certainly more credibility when they are using their own (internal) resources, especially when dealing with MEPs as pointed out by the following delegate:

> The most awkward form of lobbying is, while I also have to say that is rather not the case for the automotive industry, when consultants are mandated. I mean here in Brussels, there is a great networking of lobbyists, a gigantic consultancy industry where you have consultants in the wild receiving fees only for having meetings. And there I can in fact advise every company that this is of no use at all, unless they have a really good name that have a foot on the ground here in the longer term. (21.03.07 C)

Other resources that emerged from the interviews were continuity, studies, and time. *Time* was indicated in two different ways. First of all,

> Time as a resource is a constraint for everybody. (07.03.07 C, RA)

Secondly, the aspect of time was emphasized in terms of the timing of legislation, for example when will a directive come into force? This is a crucial issue for car producers as one interviewee in a related industry remarked:

> (...) The main concern of the car manufacturers is the timing. (13.03.07 B, RC)

A respondent directly from the industry confirmed this:

> I often mention the word timing, often it's the case that it's totally clear to us that some legislative rules will come in any case and they have to come; which goes back to these societal trends, that's why it's often the case for us, i.e., that our approach is, 'doesn't work' is not an option but it's always a question of when, i.e., that we talk about timing. (07.03.07 A, AC)

The issue of timing was also confirmed by sources in the Commission and the Parliament (14.03.07 A, SEC; 15.08.06 SEP). A related aspect of timing that was already referred to above (regarding expertise) is to know when to intervene and to talk to which persons in which institution.

Studies were also among the resources that were pointed out by interviewees; these may serve as a tool for industry to their advantage, an interesting point raised by a civil servant in the Commission:

> (...) through studies you can steer the kind of the debate, you establish a nomenclature, you establish ideas that can't be debated away, that can only be taken away with great difficulties again. You can influence the debate to your advantage. (07.03.07 B, SEC)

Studies also came up in interviews with civil society (09.03.07 16.03.07 C, both CS) and an MEP (06.03.07 B, SEP).

The most significant other resource that was brought to the discussion by an interviewee was *Continuity*, who introduced it as follows:

> I think also to some extent the one factor that you have not put in there, which in my view is by far the most important one, is actually a level of continuity. (15.08.06 SEP)

As a result, this resource was incorporated into the list of resources asked of interviewees in subsequent interviews and the responses received supported/confirmed this decision. It is very much connected to relational resources, stressing the interpersonal aspect of continuous relationships.

Overwhelmingly interviewees viewed continuity as positive (16.03.07 B, AA; 14.03.07 A, SEC; 04.09.07 A, CS):

> If I have cooperated with someone with whom I got along well, where the exchange of information was very fruitful, then of course it's a pity when this person has to leave again and is replaced by someone else. (13.07.07 SOSH)

However, one interviewee pointed out that it can be seen negatively and that in today's fast changing policy environment it can almost amount to a disadvantage:

> Oh well, you know, continuity means also, not only positively trust, but also negatively convenience/laziness and I think nowadays it's more important that you put yourself quickly into the position to build up contacts again and again. The business is different than what it used to be. (01.11.06 AC)

From a legislator's viewpoint, continuity is especially important for policy makers who deal with many different issues during a legislative period value having the same corporate contacts over a period of time:

> Continuity is very important. Absolutely, you need a certain mutual trust in order to be able to develop an idea really confidentially and you have to be able to come back to that half a year later. If there's annual change then it is of course difficult to talk about a strategy. (20.10.06 SEP)

The value of continuity can often be seen when there is disruption and new people starting to work:

> The disadvantage can be immense, in the association and in the company; you cannot work effectively in the first half year. (16.03.07 B, AA)

Companies may pass on contacts for continuity when people shift positions (04.03.08 AC), but this is not necessarily the case (23.10.06 AC).

Continuity can thus be a significant resource for companies in providing policy-makers with trusted people that have established networks. However, these advantages have to be carefully balanced against possible side-effects such as convenience (01.11.06 AC) and people staying too long and missing opportunities back home in their firms (30.03.07 RC). When human resources leave, care has to be taken that not all bridges are being burnt (16.03.07 B, AA). It is vital to continue providing good information in such a dynamic environment, as one respondent put it:

Continuity is important, but dynamics [is] as important. (22.03.07 A, RA)

Thus, companies need to strike a balance between continuity and dynamism.

Conclusion and outlook

Although there was an existing structure of *resources* that was asked of respondents, new resources emerged as a result from the interviews. Resources such as continuity served to pinpoint the significance that human resources play as the main competence for CPA including assets such as expertise, reputation, and networking contacts. Dahan's (2005a and 2005b) typology of political resources is thus confirmed and expanded.

The importance of human resources as found in this research confirms what Bartlett and Ghoshal (2002) write on building competitive advantage through people – they are crucial in corporate strategy. Furthermore, as human resources are intangible resources, the findings confirm that the most influential resources in the RBV (which *per se* does not distinguish between tangibles and intangibles) are intangible resources (Kristandl and Bontis 2007).

While human resources could possibly be imitated or hired away, a firm's reputation and long-term dealings with decision makers cannot easily be duplicated or substituted (Keim 2001b). Even though human resources may change jobs from one company to another, this is rarely the case in Brussels – the one time it happened it cause huge uproar, when an ACEA employee left to start LAMBDA's public affairs office in Brussels (Spell 2000).

This chapter has presented a general discussion of resources used by MNEs in their CPA. In a next step, this author wants to look at resources more specifically. Firstly, resources of individual companies will be investigated to find out whether companies use different resources and approaches in their CPA. Secondly, resources will be investigated according to the three cases of environmental regulations (pollutant and CO_2 emissions, end-of-life vehicles).

Limitations of this research include the focus on one single industry and a single location. Future research could compare the automotive industry's CO_2 voluntary agreement and ELV directive to the electronics and electrical goods industry and its voluntary agreement over energy use and its so-called WEEE directive (Waste of Electrical and Electronic Equipment). The research could also be expanded to include Washington, D.C., and Tokyo as two centres of regulation for the automotive industry.

As a possible recommendation for companies engaged in corporate political activities, it could be advised that great care needs to be taken in the recruitment and selection of human resources for corporate political activities if companies want to benefit from all possibilities in speaking for their interests at the institutions of the European Union. The research has shown that human resources are the most important resource in business-government relations.

Acknowledgements

The author would like to thank all interviewees for their valuable contribution to this research.

Notes

1. Although not all EU institutions are based in Brussels all the time, the European Parliament and the Commission have their main base there, and therefore 'Brussels' is used here as shorthand for the capital of Europe (see also Mack 2005).
2. Coen (1997) does not give a baseline number, but the number of individual firms represented in Brussels before 1986 can be assumed to be very low.
3. See Dür and de Bièvre (2007) for a similar argument for interest groups as opposed to individual firm activities.
4. These two terms will be used interchangeably.
5. This situation is slowly changing as tailor-made post- and undergraduate programmes are being introduced in this area and as the field is increasingly professionalized (Althaus 2005a).

References

Althaus, M. (2005a) 'Professionalisierung', in M. Althaus, M. Geffken, and S. Rave (eds), *Handlexikon Public Affairs*, 258–62 (Münster: LIT Verlag).

Althaus, M. (2005b) 'Netzwerk', in M. Althaus, M. Geffken, and S. Rave (eds), *Handlexikon Public Affairs*, 196–99 (Münster: LIT Verlag).

Aspinwall, M. and Greenwood, J. (1998) 'Conceptualising collective action in the European Union: an introduction', in J. Greenwood and M. Aspinwall (eds), *Collective Action in the European Union: Interests and the New Politics of Associability*, 1–30 (London: Routledge).

Attarça, M. (2002) 'Les ressources politiques de l'entreprise : proposition d'une typologie', XI Conférence Internationale de Management Stratégique, Paris ESCP-EAP, 5–7 June.

Attarça, M. (2005) 'A Contribution to the modeling of corporate political environment dynamics', *International Studies of Management and Organization*, 35(3), 25–49.

Barney, J.B. (1991) 'Firm resources and sustained competitive advantage', *Journal of Management*, 17, 99–120.

Baron, D.P. (1995) 'Integrated strategy: Market and nonmarket components', *California Management Review*, 37(2), 47–66.

Bartlett, C.A. and Ghoshal, S. (2002) 'Building competitive advantage through people', *MIT Sloan Management Review*, 43(2), 34–41.

Baysinger, B.D. (1984) 'Domain maintenance as an objective of business political activity: An expanded typology', *Academy of Management Review*, 9(2), 248–58.

Bennett, R.J. (1999) 'Business routes of influence in Brussels: Exploring the choice of direct representation', *Political Studies*, XLVII, 240–57.

Blumentritt, T.P. and Nigh, D. (2002) 'The integration of subsidiary political activities in multinational corporations', *Journal of International Business Studies*, 33(1), 57–77.

Boddewyn, J.J. and Brewer, T.L. (1994) 'International-business political behavior: New theoretical directions', *Academy of Management Review*, 19(1), 119–43.

Boddewyn, J.J. (1988) 'Political aspects of MNE Theory', *Journal of International Business Studies*, 19(3), 341–63.

Boddewyn, J.J. (1997) 'The Conceptual domain of international business: Territory, boundaries, and levels', in B. Toyne and D. Nigh (eds), *International Business: An Emerging Vision*, 50–61 (Colombia, S.C.: University of South Carolina Press).

Boddewyn, J. J. (2003) 'Understanding and advancing the concept of "nonmarket"', *Business and Society*, 42(3), 297–327.

Bonardi, J.-P., Hillman, A.J. and Keim, G.D. (2005) 'The Attractiveness of political markets: Implications for firm strategy', *Academy of Management Review*, 30(2), 397–413.

Broscheid, A. and Coen, D. (2003) 'Insider and outsider lobbying of the European Commission: An informational model of forum politics', *European Union Politics*, 4(2), 165–89.

Buholzer, R. (1997) 'Taming the Lobbies in Brussels', Paper 266, available at www.ipw. unisg.ch/org/ipw/web.nsf/SysWebRessources/266_1997/$FILE/266.pdf (06.11.2008).

Capron, L. and Chatain, O. (2008) 'Competitors' resource-oriented strategies: Acting on competitors' resources through interventions in factor markets and political markets', *Academy of Management Review*, 33(1), 97–121.

Castanias, R.P. and Helfat, C.E (1991) 'Managerial resources and rents', *Journal of Management*, 17(1), 155–71.

Castanias, R.P. and Helfat, C.E. (2001) 'The managerial rents model: Theory and empirical analysis', *Journal of Management*, 27(6), 661–78.

Coen, D. (1997) 'The European business lobby', *Business Strategy Review*, 8(4), 17–25.

Dahan, N. (2005a) 'A contribution to the conceptualization of political resources utilized in corporate political action', *Journal of Public Affairs*, 5(1), 43–54.

Dahan, N. (2005b) 'Can there be a resource-based view of politics?', *International Studies of Management and Organization*, 35(2), 8–27.

De Figueiredo, J.M.and Tiller, E.H. (2001) 'The structure and conduct of corporate lobbying: How firms lobby the federal communications commission', *Journal of Economics and Management Strategy*, 10(1), 91–122.

Dunning, J.H. (1981) International Production and the Multinational Enterprise (London: Allen & Unwin).

Dunning, J.H. (2002) 'Perspectives on international business research: A professional autobiography, fifty years researching and teaching international business', *Journal of International Business Studies*, 33(4), 817–35.

Dür, A. and de Bièvre, D. (2007) 'The question of interest group influence', *Journal of Public Policy*, 27(1), 1–12.

Eden, L., Lenway, S. and Schuler, D.A. (2005) 'From the obsolescing bargain to the political bargaining model', in R. Grosse (ed.), *International Business and Government Relations in the 21st Century*, 251–269 (Cambridge: Cambridge University Press).

Eisenhardt, K.M. (1989) 'Building theories from case study research', *Academy of Management Review*, 14(4), 532–50.

Epstein, E.M. (1969) *The Corporation in American Politics* (Englewood Cliff, N.J.: Prentice Hall).

Epstein, E.M. (1980) 'Business political activity: Research approaches and analytical issues', in L.E. Preston (ed.), *Research in Corporate Social Performance and Policy*, 2, 1–55 (Greenwich, Conn.: JAI Press).

Fagre, N. and Wells, L.T.JR (1982) 'Bargaining power of multinationals and host governments', *Journal of International Business Studies*, 13(2), 9–23.

Fiol, C.M. (1991) 'Managing culture as a competitive resource: An identity-based view of sustainable competitive advantage', *Journal of Management,* 17(1), 191–211.

Frynas, J.G., Mellahi, K. and Pigman, G.A. (2006) 'First mover advantages in international business and firm-specific political resources', *Strategic Management Journal*, 27(4), 321–45.

Gale, J. and Buchholz, R.A. (1987) 'The political pursuit of competitive advantage: What business can gain from government', in A.A. Marcus, A.M. Kaufman, and D. R. Beam (eds), *Business Strategy and Public Policy: Perspectives from Industry and Academia*, 31–41 (New York: Quorum Books).

Gardner, J.N. (1991) *Effective Lobbying in the European Community* (Deventer: Kluwer).

Getz, K.A. (1997) 'Research in corporate political action: Integration and assessment', *Business and Society,* 36(1), 32–72.

Gibbert, M. (2006) 'Generalizing about uniqueness, an essay on an apparent paradox in the resource-based view', *Journal of Management Inquiry*, 15(2), 124–34.

Gladwin, T.N. and Walter, I. (1980) 'How multinationals can manage social and political forces', *Journal of Business Strategy*, 1(1), 54–68.

Grant, R.M. (1991) 'The resource-based theory of competitive advantage: Implications for strategy formulation', *California Management Review*, 33(3), 114–35.

Grant, W. (1993) 'Pressure groups and the European Community', in S. Mazey and J.J. Richardson (eds), *Lobbying in the European Community*, 27–46 (Oxford: Oxford University Press).

Greenwood, J. (2007) '*Interest Representation in the European Union*', 2nd ed. (Basingstoke: Palgrave Macmillan).

Griffin, J.J., Fleisher, C.S., Brenner, S.N. and Boddewyn, J.J (2001a) 'Corporate public affairs research: Chronological reference list, part 1: 1985–2000', *Journal of Public Affairs*, 1(1), 9–32.

Griffin, J.J., Fleisher,C.S, Brenner, S.N. and Boddewyn, J.J. (2001b) 'Corporate public affairs research: Chronological reference list, part 2: 1958–84', *Journal of Public Affairs,* 1(2), 169–86.

Grosse, R. (2005) 'Introduction', in: ibid. (ed.), *International Business and Government Relations in the 21st Century*, 1–21 (Cambridge: Cambridge University Press).

Grosse, R. and Behrman, J.N. (1992) 'Theory in international business', *Transnational Corporations*, 1(1), 93–126.

Hart, S.L. (1995) 'A natural-resource-based view of the firm', *Academy of Management Review*, 20(4), 986–1014.

Hillman, A.J. and Hitt, M.A. (1999) 'Corporate political strategy formulation: A model of approach, participation, and strategy decisions', *Academy of Management Review*, 24(4), 825–42.

Hillman, A.J., Keim, G.D. and Schuler, D. (2004) 'Corporate political activity: A review and research agenda', *Journal of Management*, 30(6), 837–57.

Hoopes, D.G., Madsen, G.L. and Walker, G. (2003) 'Guest editors' introduction to the special issue: Why is there a resource-based view? Toward a theory of competitive heterogeneity', *Strategic Management Journal*, (special issue), 24(10), 889–902.

Jacomet, D. (2005) 'The collective aspect of corporate political strategies: The case of U.S. and European business participation in textile international trade negotiations', *International Studies of Management and Organization*, 35(2), 78–93.

John, S. (2002) *The Persuaders – When Lobbyists Matter* (Basingstoke: Palgrave Macmillan).

Keillor, B.D. and Hult, G.T.M. (2004) 'Predictors of firm-level political behavior in the global business environment: an investigation of specific activities employed by US firms', *International Business Review*, 13(3), 309–29.

Keim, G.D. (2001a) 'Managing business political activities in the USA: Bridging between theory and practice', *Journal of Public Affairs*, 1–2/4–1, 362–75.

Keim, G.D. (2001b) 'Business and public policy: Competing in the political marketplace', in M.A. Hitt, R.E. Freeman and J. Harrison (eds), *The Blackwell Handbook of Strategic Management*, 583–601 (Oxford: Blackwell).

Keim, G.D. and Hillman, A.J. (2008) 'Political environments and business strategy: Implications for managers', *Business Horizons*, 51, 47–53.

Keim, G. and Zeithaml, C.P. (1986) 'Corporate political strategy and legislative decision making: A review and contingency approach', *Academy of Management Review*, 11(4), 828–43.

Köppl, P.(2005) 'Lobbying', in M. Althaus, M. Geffken, and S. Rave (eds), *Handlexikon Public Affairs*, 191–95 (Münster: LIT Verlag).

Kristandl, G. and Bontis, N. (2007) 'Constructing a definition for intangibles using the resource based view of the firm', *Management Decision*, 45(9), 1510–24.

Lenway, S.A. and Rehbein, K. (1991) 'Leaders, followers, and free-riders: an empirical test of variation in corporate political involvement', *Academy of Management Journal*, 34(4), 893–905.

Levy, D.L. and Rothenberg, S. (1999) 'Corporate strategy and climate change: Heterogeneity and change in the global automobile industry', ENRP Discussion Paper E-99–13, Kennedy School of Government, Harvard University.

Li, H. and Zhang, Y. (2007) 'The role of managers' political networking and functional experience in new venture performance: Evidence from China's transition economy', *Strategic Management Journal*, 28, 791–804.

Lindeque, P. (2007) 'A firm perspective of anti-dumping and countervailing duty cases in the United States', *Journal of World Trade*, 41(3), 559–79.

Luo, Y. (2001) 'Toward a cooperative view of MNC-host government relations: Building blocks and performance implications', *Journal of International Business Studies*, 32(1), 401–19.

Luo, Y. (2004) *Coopetition in International Business* (Copenhagen: Copenhagen Business School Press).

Mack, R. (2005) 'Lobbying effectively in Brussels and Washington – Getting the right result', *Journal of Communication Management*, 9(4), 339–47.

Mahon, J.F. (1989) 'Corporate political strategy', *Business in the Contemporary World*, 2(1), 50–62.

Mazey, S. and Richardson, J.J. (1993) 'Introduction: Transference of power, decision rules, and rules of the game', in ibid (eds), *Lobbying in the European Community*, 3–26 (Oxford: Oxford University Press).

McGrath, C. (2005) Lobbying in Washington, London, and Brussels: The Persuasive Communication of Political Issues (Lewiston, N.Y.: Edwin Mellen Press).

McWilliams, A., Van Fleet, D.D. and Cory, K.D. (2002) 'Raising rivals' costs through political strategy: An extension of resource-based theory', *Journal of Management Studies*, 39(5), 707–23.

Meznar, M.B. and Johnson, J.H. (2005) 'Business-government relations within a contingency theory framework: Strategy, structure, fit, and performance', *Business and Society*, 44(2), 119–43.

Michalowitz, I. (2004) EU Lobbying – Principals, Agents and Targets: Strategic Interest Intermediation in EU Policy-Making (Münster: LIT Verlag).

Miles, M.B. and Huberman, A.M. (1984) *Qualitative Data Analysis: A Source Book of New Methods* (Newbury Park, Calif.: Sage).

Mitnick, B.M. (1993) Corporate Political Agency: The Construction of Competition in Public Affairs (Newbury Park, Calif.: Sage).

Moon, C.W. and Lado, A.A. (2000) 'MNC-host government bargaining power relationship: A critique and extension within the resource-based view', *Journal of Management*, 26(1), 85–117.

Newell, P. and Paterson, M. (1998) 'A climate for business: global warming, the state and capital', *Review of International Political Economy*, 5(4), 679–703.

Oberman, W.D. (1993) 'Strategy and tactic choice in an institutional resource context', in B.M. Mitnick (ed.), *Corporate Political Agency: The Construction of Competition in Public Affairs*, 213–241 (Newbury Park, Calif.: Sage).

Oldag, A. and Tillack, H.-M. (2004) *Raumschiff Brüssel: Wie die Demokratie in Europa scheitert* (Frankfurt: Fischer).

Oliver, C. and Holzinger, I. (2008) 'The effectiveness of strategic political management: A dynamic capabilities framework', *Academy of Management Review*, 33(2), 496–520.

Peng, M.W. (2001) 'The resource-based view and international business', *Journal of Management*, 27, 803–29.

Penrose, E.T. (1959) *The Theory of the Growth of the Firm* (Oxford: Blackwell).

Preston, L.E. (2004) 'Reputation as a source of corporate social capital', *Journal of General Management*, 30(2), 43–49.

Reed, R. and DeFillippi, R.J. (1990) 'Causal ambiguity, barriers to imitation, and sustainable competitive advantage', *Academy of Management Review*, 15(1), 88–102.

Rehbein, K. and Schuler, D.A. (1995) 'The firm as a filter: A conceptual framework for corporate political strategies', *Academy of Management Best Paper Proceedings*, 406–10.

Ring, P.S., Lenway, S.A. and Govekar, M. (1990) 'Management of the political imperative in international business', *Strategic Management Journal*, 11(2), 141–51.

Rouse, M.J. and Daellenbach, U.S. (2002) 'More thinking on research methods for the resource-based perspective', *Strategic Management Journal*, 23, 963–67.

Salorio, E.M., Boddewyn, J.J. and Dahan, N. (2005) 'Integrating business political behavior with economic and organizational strategies', *International Studies of Management and Organization*, 35(2), 28–55.

Schuler, D.A. (2008) 'Peering in from corporate political activity', *Journal of Management Inquiry*, 17(3), 162–67.

Schuler, D.A. and Rehbein, K. (1997) 'The filtering role of the firm in corporate political involvement', *Business and Society*, 362, 116–39.

Schuler, D.A., Rehbein, K. and Cramer, R.D. (2002) 'Pursuing strategic advantage through political means: A multivariate approach', *Academy of Management Journal*, 45(4), 659–72.

Shaffer, B. (1995) 'Firm-level responses to government regulation: Theoretical and research approaches', *Journal of Management*, 21(3), 495–514.

Spell, S. (2000) *Japanese Automobile Lobbying in Brussels: The Role of the Japanese Motor Car Industry in EU Policy Networks*, Ph.D. Thesis, University of Stirling, Stirling, Scottish Centre for Japanese Studies, United Kingdom.

Toyne, B. and Nigh, D. (1998) 'A more expansive view of international business', *Journal of International Business Studies*, 29(4), 863–76.

Van Schendelen, M. (1993) *National Public and Private EC Lobbying* (Aldershot: Dartmouth).

Van Schendelen, R. (2002) *Machiavelli in Brussels: The Art of Lobbying the EU* (Amsterdam: Amsterdam University Press).

Wan, W.P. and Hillman, A.J. (2005) 'One of these things is not like the others: What contributes to dissimilarity among MNE subsidiaries' political strategies', *Management International Review*, 46(1), 85–107.

Wernerfelt, B. (1984) 'The resource-based view of the firm', *Strategic Management Journal*, 5, 171–80.

Wernerfelt, B. (2003) 'Why do firms tend to become different', in C.E. Helfat (ed.), *The SMS Blackwell Handbook of Organizational Capabilities: Emergence, Development, and Change*, 121–33 (Malden, Mass.: Blackwell).

Windsor, D. (2007) 'Toward a global theory of cross-border and multilevel corporate political activity', *Business and Society*, 46(2), 253–78.

Woll, C. (2007) 'Leading the dance? Power and political resources of business lobbyists', *Journal of Public Policy*, 27(1), 57–78.

Yin, R.K. (1989/1994) *Case Study Research: Design and Methods*, 2nd edn (Thousand Oaks, Calif.: Sage Publications).

Yoffie, D. (1987) 'Corporate strategies for political action: A rational model', in A.A. Marcus, A.M. Kaufman, and D.R. Beam (eds), *Business Strategy and Public Policy: Perspectives from Industry and Academia*, 43–60 (New York: Quorum Books).

Yoffie, D.B. and Bergenstein, S. (1985) 'Creating political advantage: The rise of the corporate political entrepreneur', *California Management Review*, 28(1), 124–39.

6
Career Orientations of the 21st-Century Knowledge Professionals

Dimitris Manolopoulos and Pavlos Dimitratos

Introduction

Early perceptions of human resource management conceived careers as a progression up an ordered hierarchy within an organization/corporation. In recent years, though, this has been changed, since employees' career development is seen not as being chosen based on a 'linear model' but, rather, as carefully constructed through a series of planned (and maybe asymmetric) choices that people make throughout their employment. This is especially the case for the main implementers of corporate knowledge, that is, namely knowledge professionals. The impact of a wide range of transformations that reshaped the modern workplace, and in particular the underlined imperatives of the new knowledge economy (advances in technology, intensification of competition, mobility of the labour force, and changing skill requirements), have totally reformed employment relationships and, as a result, created the need for the highly skilled workforce to revalidate its career perspectives in an environment of shifting priorities.

Following the work of Bryan and Joyce (2005), in our study we use the term knowledge professional in order to describe a new class of employee whose basic means of production is no longer labour or capital, but the productive use of knowledge. It mainly includes researchers, engineers, and scientists involved in the research and development (R&D) activities of a corporation. Though the career development component of a human resource strategy for managing knowledge professionals has been a subject of investigation for several decades (e.g., Badawy, 1988; Greenhaus and Callanan, 1994; Farris and Cordero, 2002), there are still numerous challenges and unresolved research questions of particular importance to academics and technology-related managers. We can summarize our understanding of the work on R&D careers that has emerged through the recent literature as providing two motivations that dictate a reappraisal of this subject. Conceptually, many extant paradigms on R&D career advancement are still constrained by the overly rational, static and traditional 'dual ladder' reward system (that is, promotions to managerial or technical positions). However, its effectiveness has long been debated in the academic field (Allen and Katz, 1986; McKinnon, 1987). In order to keep up with the rapid pace of change, the 21st-century knowledge professionals need to anticipate, recognize, and adapt to the changing dynamics of the market environment prevailing today. As a result, their career development strategy is now centred on challenging posts rather than the dominant perception of life-employment within one single corporation. In practice, the evolving nature of organizational knowledge creation and development (namely the dynamic interaction between the individual and the collective knowledge of social groups) has created diverse R&D career paths (Baugh and Roberts, 1994). However, these changes have not yet been incorporated within firms' career management systems (Bryan and Joyce, 2005). In the work environment, the existing vertically oriented organizational structures still tend to relate knowledge professionals' career development mainly with the achievement of technical outcomes (Biddle and Roberts, 1993; Cordero, 1999). Provided that these career models may be singularly ill-suited to actual professionals' expectations and preferences, the new strands of R&D careers that have emerged (e.g., Bailyn, 1991; Kim and Cha, 2000) should be assessed, scrutinized, and carefully evaluated.

The importance of revalidation of R&D careers in the dawn of the new century is well founded: nowadays, knowledge workers make up a significant fraction of the workforce in the advanced economies and knowledge-related inputs are fundamental to successful companies' competitive advantage (Tanner, 1998). Accordingly, a better understanding of employees' aspirations and the antecedents of career development can help practitioners and managers increase the effectiveness of their human resources and design the most appropriate career management system in order to retain those highly value-added employees within their organizations. Surprisingly, despite that interest in the issues of organizational learning and knowledge in international firms has increased, management theorists paid scant attention to problems unique to the main implementers of corporate knowledge, that is, the engineers and scientists employed in R&D departments (Manolopoulos, 2006).

Based on a questionnaire-based survey that has been addressed to employees in the decentralized R&D units of multinational enterprises (MNEs) located in Greece, the purpose of this research is to complement existing work on career management by surveying the career orientation of knowledge professionals (paths and preferences). We approach this issue through two core research objectives: (a) to identify the attractiveness of five career routes (managerial, technical, project-based, entrepreneurial, and hybrid) for R&D employees, and (b) to associate their career preferences with specific demographic and organizational characteristics.

Our study offers three main contributions. First, while up-to-now there has been a discussion of the appropriate management of R&D employees, according to Farris and Cordero (2002), most of the work cited related to this theme is conceptual or anecdotal. In our investigation, we present empirical evidence on career management issues. Second, there are disproportionly few studies in the literature on the management of human resources in multinational firms (let alone knowledge professionals), since the vast majority of the empirical work done in the field emphasized national corporations (Clark et al. 1999). Third, the limited existing evidence identified in the literature relates to MNEs located in technologically and industrially developed economies (notably the United States). This theme has been only rarely studied in less advanced economies. In our work, we investigate how the generalized perceptions on career management of knowledge professionals are reflected in the peripheral EU advancing economy of Greece, whereby foreign direct investment research activities are less complex than those of more advanced economies. To the best of our knowledge this is the first study investigating such issues for advancing economies.

Theoretical background

The literature (e.g., Badawy, 1988; Petroni, 2000; Farris and Cordero, 2002) suggests that any effective human resource strategy relies upon four distinctive (yet interrelated) dimensions: (i) human resource planning, (ii) performance appraisal, (iii) reward systems, and (iv) career management. Here, we focus on the last component by exploring aspects of the career orientation of knowledge professionals. According to Petroni (2000), the management of employees' careers relate to the simultaneous accomplishment of two objectives: the enhancement of individual career growth and the maximization of their contribution to the organization. Thus, career management can be investigated from both individuals' (internal to the worker) and organizations' (external to the worker) viewpoint. In this research we attempt to combine both perspectives by investigating employees' preferences concerning the sequence of jobs, tasks and positions offered to them throughout their employment.

Early work on R&D careers revealed that the most widespread utilized and assessed career strategy for knowledge professionals is the 'dual ladder'. According to this concept, employees have two main alternatives: career advancement linked to managerial responsibility or promotions to technical positions (Merton, 1957). Promotions to the managerial path mean managing more R&D employees and coordinating their work while promotions to the technical track mean doing technical work (Farris and Cordero, 2002). The dual ladder was conceived as an effective managerial solution in order to link employees' performance with their underlying orientation and preferences. In this regard, it is considered that employees with a more technical background would value freedom for research and *technical* performance (Aryee and Leong, 1991; Womack and Jones, 1996), whereas those with a managerial orientation would value managerial achievements and *organizational* performance. The origins of the dual ladder can be traced to the implicit assumption that productive technical employees should be offered administrative roles in order to attain higher salary levels, power, and organizational status (Allen and Katz, 1986). As pinpointed by Allen and Katz (1992), the assignment of managerial responsibilities is considered to be more attractive than technical careers due to cultural reasons: social members seem to attribute higher prestige to managerial than technical promotions, with the latter being often perceived as 'loyalty' prizes and not true career advancements.

Existing evidence for the effectiveness of dual ladder is controversial and still not conclusive: while many studies have shown that a high proportion of technical employees link their career aspirations with managerial responsibilities (e.g., Ritti, 1971; Bailyn, 1980) and see their career goals in terms of eventual progress in management (Allen and Katz, 1986), others (e.g., Evetts, 1994) suggest that there is an important portion of employees who prefer to remain in full contact with technical problem solving, find no attraction in managerial tasks and view a technical ladder career more rewarding.

While the assignment of managerial responsibilities and the involvement in technical activities remain traditional fixtures in the career development system offered to employees, later work has witnessed that R&D careers could evolve in a variety of different ways. More recent contributions in the field (e.g., Debackere et al. 1997; Hesketh et al. 1992) suggest that scientists and engineers may valorize diverse career aspirations, stressing the importance for firms to adopt alternative modes of career development programmes, which will also depend upon individual-specific job expectations. In this regard, a large portion of engineers and scientists may desire to follow a project-based career path, namely be involved in a succession of technical projects that broaden their technical skills, instead of being specialized in a particular sector (Tremblay et al. 2002). This career choice may provide no direct advancement in the hierarchical ladder of the corporation (i.e., it could be irrespective of promotion); but is usually preferred by those knowledge professionals who find it exciting to be involved in the implementation of challenging and dynamic technical-oriented work. Finally, the entrepreneurial path (McKinnon, 1987; Kim and Cha, 2000) is another alternative route that can suit those professionals that have the desire to develop a new venture. According to evidence reported by Tremblay et al. (2002), with the increasing job insecurity and the massive restructuring of the business environment, the entrepreneurial path has recently gained in popularity.

All these career paths described here are not mutually exclusive. Hybrid career systems have been developed that consider employees' advancement in terms of multiple and simultaneous work assignments and view careers in terms of discontinuous chunks (Petroni, 2000). Indeed, it has been recorded that some employees may experiment with a range of different alternatives (such as the technical path and the involvement in projects outside the corporation) without opting for an irreversibly career direction.

Empirical work in the field indicates that the major determinants of employees' career development preferences can be traced to the impact of the work-related and organizational environments. In addition, evidence (e.g., Badawy, 1971; Petroni, 2000) suggests that the career management of knowledge professionals is also influenced by individual-associated determinants such as age, gender, seniority, educational background, and field of specialization. However, it should be noted that most of the empirical work done addressed relevant issues related to the dual ladder, while the more novel career alternatives (project-based and entrepreneurial routes) have not received much attention.

Research setting, sampling, and methods

Survey instrument and data collection

Against this background, we studied the career orientation of R&D employees in the MNE decentralized R&D laboratories located in Greece. The sampling frame employed in our research was provided by *ICAP Greek Financial Directory*, a standard source for foreign investment in this country. According to Souitaris (2002), this Directory offers the more accurate description of the Greek industry. Our research took place in two phases. The first phase involved a wide survey on the strategic motivations for MNEs' expansion in the country. The response rate was approximately 42% (133 useable responses out of 315 corporations), which is considered to be perfectly acceptable in comparison to similar investigations (Harzing, 1997). By focusing on firms operating in diverse industries/sectors, we minimize a number of sources of extraneous variance and make our results as generalizable as possible. Moreover, by investigating corporations that vary by size, country of origin, year of entrance, and so on, it seems that there is no reason to expect any systematic bias in the forthcoming empirical analysis. Table 6.1 summarizes the response rates and number of respondents by industry and country of headquarters' origin. As presented, among the responding 133 subsidiaries, 70 (52.63 %) were identified to have an R&D department.

The second phase of the research involved a survey on the international human resources practices of MNEs. Once subsidiaries with R&D laboratories

Table 6.1 Sample breakdown by subsidiaries' sector of activity and country of headquarters' origin

Sector	Total sample	Number of respondents	Number of respondents with R&D	Response rate(%)	Rate of R&D subsidiaries in whole data set(%)	Rate of R&D subsidiaries in sample under examination(%)
Automobiles and transport equipment	19	11	0	57.89	0.00	0.00
Chemicals	18	8	5	44.44	27.78	62.50
Electronics and IT	15	7	5	46.67	33.33	71.43
Food and beverages	47	29	19	61.70	40.43	65.52
Manufacturing	62	31	18	50.00	29.03	58.06
Miscellaneous[a]	19	9	4	47.37	21.05	44.44
Other manufacturing[b]	34	8	6	23.53	17.65	75.00
Pharmaceuticals	31	16	12	51.61	38.71	75.00
Services	51	10	0	19.61	0.00	0.00
Textiles	19	4	1	21.05	5.26	25.00
Total	315	133	70	42.22	22.22	52.63

HQz Country of location	Total sample	Number of respondents	Number of respondents with R&D	Response rate(%)	Rate of R&D subsidiaries in whole data set(%)	Rate of R&D subsidiaries in sample under examination(%)
EU Countries	129	57	29	44.19	22.48	50.88
Other European Countries	78	31	18	39.74	23.08	58.06
Asia Pacific Rim	46	17	10	36.96	21.74	58.82
US	62	28	13	45.16	20.97	46.43
Total	315	133	70	42.22	22.22	52.63

Notes:
[a] Miscellaneous in cludes Agribusiness, equipments for bakery, home equipment
[b] Other manufacturing includes tobacco, paper and forest products, heating and air conditioning and office machinery

Source: Auhors' survey

have been identified, R&D professionals were asked to report their preferred career development route. In total, 921 responses have been collected. Of the respondents, 562 (61.02%) are male and 571 (62%) are married; 433 (47.01%) hold a (broadly defined) technical degree, whereas a considerable 43.97% has a managerial educational background. The average age of respondents is 39.8 years, with a standard deviation of seven. The descriptive statistics providing evidence on R&D professionals' demographic characteristics (age, gender, marital status, and educational background) are reported in Table 6.2.

Potential nonresponse bias was evaluated in a number of ways. Firstly, following Harzing and Noorderhaven (2004), we tested whether responses on key variables in the survey differed significantly between early and late respondents. Secondly, we compared respondents and the population on two variables: number of employees and the age of the corporation (cf. Lin, 2003). None of these t-tests examining differences between the sample and the population means was statistically significant at the level of 0.10. To further test nonresponse bias, personal interviews with managers of selected non-respondent firms were arranged. The results were quite similar with those of the sample.

Measures

Following the work of Gardner (1990), career preferences (promotions in the managerial path, advancements in the technical ladder, involvement

Table 6.2 Sample breakdown by respondents' demographic characteristics

Gender			Marital status		
	Nr.	**Percentage(%)**		**Nr.**	**Percentage(%)**
Male	562	61,02	Married	571	62,00
Famale	359	38,98	Single	350	38,00
Total	921	100	Total	921	100
Age of researcher			**Educational background**		
	Nr.	**Percentage(%)**		**Nr.**	**Percentage(%)**
Under 36	319	34,64	Technical Degree	433	47,01
Between 36–45	354	38,44	Managerial Degree	405	43,97
Over 45	248	26,93	Other	83	9,01
Total	921	100	Total	921	100

Source: Auhors' survey

in challenging technical projects and entrepreneurial path) were assessed in two ways: first, R&D employees were asked to report any of the career paths that seemed to be attractive to them. A combination of the above responses would provide us with a proxy of the attractiveness of the hybrid path. We found inter-rater reliability for all respondents to be high (0.85). At a second level, and in order to identify their relative importance, employees were asked to evaluate the most preferred career path through the use of a four-point Likert-type scale (4 = totally desirable; 3 = quite promising; 2 = career path that sounds interesting; and 1 = does not match my objectives).

The set of constructs considered here can be broadly grouped in two groups (individual- and work-related) and three subcategories: the strategic mandates of overseas R&D units, demographic characteristics and organization-related determinants. The classification suggested for the different decentralized R&D roles derives from the works of Haug et al. (1983) and Hood and Young (1982), and identifies three distinctive roles for an overseas R&D laboratory: the first refers to the effective use of the MNE group's well existing technologies. Its main function is, therefore, adaptation development either of the product or the production process. Laboratories that focus on that role are defined as Support Laboratories (SLs) and are considered critical for the successful commercialization of subsidiaries' products in already determined target markets (Papanastassiou and Pearce, 1999). As the limited adaptation role of SLs may decline in relevance, some decentralized R&D units are assigned to develop a distinctive product, which can be supplied to a regional, or even global, market (Pearce, 1999). This type of R&D lab is termed as Locally Integrated Laboratory (LIL). The third possible role that can be distinguished for a laboratory, or the second that plays a part in the longer-term competitiveness and global-innovative strategy, is to provide basic or applied research inputs into a program of precompetitive work organized by the MNE (Papanastassiou and Pearce, 1999). Laboratories that are involved in such tasks are defined as Internationally Interdependent Laboratories (IILs). In order to identify the prevalence of each role, a four-point Likert-type scale was prepared, where the scale value '4' indicates a defining role of the activity and the scale value '1' the opposite case.

Following the research practice of many authors (for example, Allen and Katz, 1992; Petroni, 2000), demographic characteristics include categorical variables, such as age (3 scale points), educational background (3 scale points), gender (binary, 1 = male) and marital status (binary, 1 = married). Finally, building on the works of Gerpott et al. (1988) and Manolopoulos (2006), we included country of MNE origin as another factor that can influence international human resource practices. All constructs are defined and operationalized in Table 6.3.

Table 6.3 Operationalization of constructs

Variables	Type[a]	Operational definition
Laboratory role	L/D	In order to evaluate laboratoriesa roles, respondents were asked to grade each of the following roles in terms of the importance in the operations of the R&D lab as being: (i) not part of their role, (ii) main role, (iii) secondary role and (iv) only role
		(i) Adaptation of existing products and/or processes to make them more suitable to our markets and conditions
		(ii) To play a role in the development of new products for our distinctive markets
		(iii) To carry out basic reseach (not directly related to the current products) as part of a wider MNE group level research program
Support Laboratory (SL)		Laboratory that adapts existing products and/or processes (4=only role, 3=main role, 2=secondary role, 1=not part of role)
Locally Integrated Laboratory(LIL)		Laboratory that has a distinctive role in the development of products (4=only role, 3=main role, 2=secondary role, 1=not part of role)
International Independent Laboratory (IIL)		Laboratory that carries out basic research (4=only role, 3=main role, 2=secondary role, 1=not part of role)
Demographic		
Age of researcher	L/D	According to the date of researchers1 birth, three categories were created: R&D professionals over 45 years old take the value of 3, R&D professionals between 36–45 take the value of 2, under 36 years old take the value of 1.
Educational background	L/D	3=Researcher with a technical background, 2=Researcher with a managerial background, 1=Other
Gender	B/D	1=Male, 0=Female
Marital status	B/D	1=Married, 0=Single
Organization-related		
Country of MNE origin	B/D	1=parent from a European country, 0=otherwise

Notes:
[a] Binary (B); / Likert – Type (L); / Discrete (D)

Results and discussion

In order to provide evidence on the changes that have occurred in the career management of knowledge professionals, in our research we synthesize on existing literature and investigate the prevalence of five career routes (managerial, technical, project-based, entrepreneurial, and hybrid) available to R&D employees. Results are presented in the form of frequencies and average response rates that report the degree of importance of the career advancement alternatives under investigation.

According to our findings, out of the 921 respondents, one of the four career route preferences under investigation unequivocally emerges in 474 cases (51.47%), indicating the considerable straightforward perceptions of R&D professionals concerning their career development (Table 6.4). Thus, it seems that engineers and scientists have clear expectations for the advancement

Table 6.4 Frequency table of career preferences[a]

	Nr of cases	Percentage(%)
Only Choice		
Managerial	379	41,15
Technical	38	4,13
Project based	31	3,37
Entrepreneurial	26	2,82
Average total	474	51,47
Chi-square (degrees of freedom: 3)		7.23
Significance level		*P*=.052
Hybrid: Two (or more) Choices		
Managerial – technical	55	5,97
Managerial – project based	104	11,29
Managerial – entrepreneurial	72	7,82
Technical – project based	89	9,66
Technical – entrepreneurial	82	8,90
Project based – entrepreneurial	45	4,89
Managerial – technial – project based	6	0,65
Managerial – technical – enterpreneurial	11	1,19
Average total	447	48,53
Chi-square (degrees of freedom: 7)		6.45
Significance Level		*P*=.041
Total number of responses	921	100,00

Notes:
[a] Respondents were asked to report any career path that seems to be desired for their career advancement

Source: Authors' survey

route they should follow so as to enhance their individual career growth. The remaining 447 (48.53%) cases are characterized by tied scores (hybrid routes), indicating a propensity towards greater involvement, experimentation and interaction with multiple career alternatives. This could reflect the complexity of modern knowledge marketplaces that require employees' involvement in different aspects of scientific and organizational contribution. Hybrid paths present a wide degree of variation; however some orientations are more common. Among these, the project responsibility together with advancements in the managerial and technical ladder are rated as the most preferable career routes by the majority of participants (capturing 11.29% and 9.66% of respondents, respectively).

Providing support to existing literature (e.g., Katz et al. 1995; Debackere et al. 1996), advancements in both managerial and technical path seem to be mutually exclusive, capturing only 55 responses (5.97%). Our findings further suggest that the proportion of knowledge professionals that identify their career development within the traditional career opportunities (dual ladder, notably managerial or technical) is 45.2% (417 out of 921 participants). This implies that the specific reward system could still serve as an effective managerial solution to motivate employees. Between these two career alternatives, the vast majority of respondents (379 out of 417) report management as the most desirable career goal. Four main explanations can be provided for this tendency: First, there is a general cultural norm that associates high prestige with advancement in the managerial ladder (Petroni, 2000). Second, management career ladder could be a solution for knowledge employees to avoid technological obsolescence (Clarke, 2002). Third, managerial positions may obtain greater autonomy and responsibility compared to technical ones (Allen and Katz, 1986). Fourth, it seems that the work implemented in decentralized R&D units in Greece does not provide for challenging and exciting technical involvement.

A considerable 33.7% of R&D employees (311 out of 921 respondents) have defined their career advancement within the context of promotions in non-managerial career alternatives, showing that there is a portion of engineers and scientists who do not wish to join the ranks of management. By citing the work of Clarke (2002), several reasons can be offered for that: it could be that R&D employees may value research-based activities more highly that management, lack R&D management training, fear to lose technical expertise and become obsolete, or have poor R&D manager role models. Project-oriented knowledge professionals (as the only choice) capture only a 3.37% of responses, whereas, surprisingly enough, entrepreneurial career path only is also at almost insignificant levels (2.82%). This could be partially explained by taking into consideration some structural characteristics of the Greek economic environment, such as inefficient bureaucratic institutional and regulative framework, inflexibility in the labour market, and a lack of access to entrepreneurial funding (EIU, 2007).

Some further insights on the career preferences of knowledge professionals are provided by the calculation of the average response (AR) of each career path. Results are displayed in Table 6.5. Our findings indicate the existence of a multifaceted context of career aspirations which is differentiated among

Table 6.5 Career preferences of knowledge professionals (average responses)[a]

	Managerial path (a)	Technical path (b)	Project-based path (c)	Entrpreneurial path (d)
Role of laboratory[b]				
SL	3.11	2.48	2.18	2.11
LIL	3.01	2.61	2.39	2.06
IIL	1.85	3.40	3.50	1.77
Average total	3.02	2.56	2.30	2.08
Gender				
Males	2.87	2.61	2.39	2.21
Females	3.27	2.47	2.15	1.86
Average total	3.02	2.56	2.30	2.08
Marital status				
Married	3.11	2.44	2.32	2.10
Single	2.89	2.74	2.27	2.05
Average total	3.02	2.56	2.30	2.08
Age of researcher				
Under 36	2.89	2.74	2.28	2.11
Between 36–45	3.04	2.60	2.31	2.09
Over 45	3.15	2.31	2.31	2.03
Average total	3.02	2.56	2.30	2.08
Educational background				
Technical	2.98	2.64	2.30	2.11
Managerial	3.01	2.57	2.33	2.07
Other	3.40	1.90	2.04	1.95
Average total	3.02	2.56	2.30	2.08
Country of origin				
European	3.03	2.57	2.28	2.07
Rest of World	2.99	2.53	2.35	2.11
Average total	3.02	2.56	2.30	2.08

Notes:
[a] Respondents were asked to evaluate each career path as (i) totally desirable, (ii) very promising, (iii) intresting, and (iv) exceeds my aspirations being the only influence. The average response was calculated by allocating the value of 4 to totally desirable, 3 to very promising, 2 to interesting and 1 to exceeds employees' aspirations
[b] For the operationalization of laboratory roles, see Table 3
Source: Authors' survey

the different types of laboratories. In particular, a generalized preference for the managerial ladder (AR of 3.11) is clearly emphasized for those knowledge professionals who are assigned with the reapplication of MNEs' technological competencies (SL role). On the contrary, scientists involved in pre-competitive R&D activities (IIL role) prefer advancement in the technical ladder (AR of 3.40) and show a surprising high preference for having the opportunity to engage in research projects (AR of 3.50). Following the work of Manolopoulos (2006), this could be an indicator that researchers in laboratories where basic research is the main priority derive more satisfaction and utility from the actual performance of 'mainstream' scientific activities that are not directly allied to financial rewards or other status-carrying symbols. It seems that this category of knowledge professionals represent the perception of Jain and Triandis (1990) for R&D employees who are characterized as independent, intellectual and curious; and, have a tendency to be involved in technical research projects. As far as LIL employees are concerned, average responses reveal a comparatively different pattern, since the managerial route is rated as the most preferable career pattern (AR of 3.01), followed by the technical path and the project career route (ARs of 2.61 and 2.39 respectively). Despite the fact that the development of new products requires career opportunities that advance new knowledge and skills, it seems that LIL employees value more the security, prestige and rewards provided by managerial advancement.

Career preferences are also related to age. In relative terms, younger knowledge professionals favour the technical ladder progression and the entrepreneurial path more strongly than older ones, who see managerial advancement as the most likely form of career development. These results partially overlap with those provided by earlier studies. In an investigation of the career route preferences of 442 engineers, Petroni (2000) found marked age-dependent differences in responses and argued for the attractiveness of advancement opportunities in the technical ladder for younger scientists. To corroborate, Allen and Katz (1992) argue that the advancement opportunities along the technical ladder are diminishing with age. Moreover, Biddle and Roberts (1993) have shown that as knowledge professionals get older they are increasingly likely to hold managerial positions, whereas younger scientists tend to be employed in technical capacities.

Female participants report a distinct preference for managerial careers (AR of 3.27), while male respondents tend to deviate from the traditional practice of preferring rigid career routes within the career ladder and indicate a relatively high preference for interesting projects (AR of 2.39) and the entrepreneurial route (2.21). Single employees show a desire to work in the technical field, whereas, surprisingly, married employees are more willing to take the risk to start their own business. Finally, the proportion of knowledge professionals citing a preference for the entrepreneurial path seems to be linearly related with a technical educational background. No significant differences in respondents' preferences have been observed in relation to MNE country of origin. This could be justified by arguing that despite the fact that subsidiaries belong to MNE groups of diverse locations and one could expect differentiated human resource management practices, respondents are locals and share similar cultural characteristics.

Conclusions

The purpose of this survey was to provide some further insights into the career orientation of knowledge professionals. Despite the fact that the importance of effective utilization of highly value-added employees has gained increased recognition in recent years, our knowledge of their career development perceptions is neither complete, nor conclusive. Thus, there are valuable insights for research and management that can be drawn from our findings. With regard to the implications for research, this present work is, to our knowledge, the sole empirical study examining career development issues of MNE R&D employees based in an advancing economy. Moreover, it is one of the few studies that provide empirical evidence on career preferences of R&D professionals. But, even more importantly, the present research empirically shows that the roles of decentralized R&D labs seem to be influential along with other demographic characteristics in determining the desired career path of R&D employees. Finally, our findings reappraise the prevalence of the dual career ladder system as a device for managing knowledge professionals. Despite recent theoretical research strands that have widely challenged its effectiveness, the respondents in this study score highly in this reward system, indicating the attractiveness and popularity of the managerial (mainly) career route.

With regard to implications for MNE managers, the evidence of our work adds further insights to the long-lasting debate concerning the most efficient system of managing R&D employees. Given the results reported here, subsidiary managers need to identify that a formalized career ladder system may be an oversimplified approach in order to capture the full spectrum of the desired career development paths of knowledge workers. On the contrary, organizations need to evaluate and carefully assess this diversity and provide the career opportunities that match the intended orientation of their employees, since it is well understood that career opportunities suitable for a group of R&D employees may be irrelevant or even inappropriate for another (Petroni, 2000). In this regard, our findings indicate that the scientific involvement in adaptations of MNEs' technological heritage attracts R&D professionals that wish to advance in the managerial field, while the expansion of MNEs' technological trajectory seems to be interesting for those employees that valorize cross-functional transfers and promotions in the technical domain of a corporation. Corporate career development systems may be structured accordingly.

Our research has certain limitations. First, our findings concerning the career preferences of knowledge professionals could be more solid and accurate if we also consider the desired career paths of R&D workers employed in domestic firms and public research institutions. Further, we address the concept of geographic scope as a unidimensional construct, not taking into account for the environmental, social, and cultural diversities between countries. Being focussed on a specific country (Greece) we minimize a number of sources of extraneous variance. However, employees' career preferences are definitely influenced by local socioeconomic and labour conditions, as well as industry determinants. It is impossible to tell how much this variance affects the results but we should recognize that this must have an influence.

The limitations of this study guide suggestions for future research. The generalizability of the findings of the current research would be strengthened if similar studies were carried out in domestic firms and public research institutions. Further, comparison of datasets involving human resource issues of knowledge professionals in countries with different levels of technological development would illuminate whether the two country categories indeed produce different results. Similarly, extensions of the research reported in this chapter could include examination of other variables likely to affect the career preferences of employees, such as organizational size and pay plateau. Finally, a comprehensive study of the reward systems provided by corporations could provide valuable further insights on the career preferences of knowledge professionals.

References

Allen, T.J. and Katz, R. (1992) 'Age, education and the technical ladder', *IEEE Transactions on Engineering Management*, 39, 237–45.
Allen, T.J. and Katz, R. (1986) 'The dual ladder: Motivational solution or managerial delusion?', *R&D Management*, 16(2), 185–97.
Aryee, S. and Leong, C.G. (1991) 'Career orientations and work outcomes among industrial R&D professionals', *Group and Organizational Studies*, 16(2), 193–205.
Badawy, M.K. (1988) 'Managing human resources: What we have learned', *Research-Technology Management*, 31(5), 19–35.
Badawy, M.K. (1971) 'Understanding the role orientations of scientists and engineers', *Personnel Journal*, 50(6), 449–54.
Bailyn, L. (1991) 'The hybrid career: An explanatory study of career routes in R&D', *Journal of Engineering and Technology Management*, 8, 1–14.
Bailyn, L. (1980) *Living with Technology: Issues at Mid Career* (Cambridge, Mass.: MIT Press).
Baugh, S.G. and Roberts, R.M. (1994) 'Professional and organizational commitment among engineers: Conflicting or contradictory?', *IEEE Transactions on Engineering Management*, 42(2), 108–14.
Biddle, J. and Roberts, K. (1993) 'Private sector scientists and engineers and the transition to management', *Journal of Human Resources*, 29(1), 82–107.

Bryan, L.L. and Joyce, C. (2005) 'The 21st-century organization', *McKinsey Quarterly*, 3, 25–33.

Clark, T.E., Gospel, H. and Montgomery, J. (1999) 'Running on the spot? A review of twenty years of research on the management of human resources in comparative and international perspective', *International Journal of Human Resource Management*, 10 (3), 520–44.

Clarke, T.E. (2002) 'Why do we still not apply what we know about managing R&D personnel?', *Research-Technology Management*, 45(2), 9–11.

Cordero, R. (1999) 'Developing the knowledge and skills of R&D professionals to achieve process outcomes in cross-functional teams', *Journal of High Technology Management Research*, 10(1), 61–78.

Debackere, K., Buyens, D. and Vandenbossche, T. (1997) 'Strategic career development for R&D professionals: Lessons from field research', *Technovation*, 17(2), 53–62.

EIU (Economist Intelligence Unit) (August 2007) *Country Report – Greece* (London).

Evetts, J. (1994) 'Notes and issues – women and career in engineering: The 'Glass Ceiling' for women's careers', *Women in Management Review*, 8(7), 19–25.

Farris, G.F. and Cordero, R. (2002) *What Do we Know about Managing Scientists and Engineers: A Review of Recent Literature* (New Brunswick, N.J.: Rutgers University Press).

Gardner, A.M. (1990) 'Career orientations of software developers in a sample of high tech companies', *R&D Management*, 20(4), 337–52.

Gerpott, T.J., Domsch, M. and Keller, R.T. (1988) 'Career orientations in different countries and companies: An empirical investigation of West German, British and US industrial R&D professionals', *Journal of Management Studies*, 25(5), 439–62.

Greenhaus, W. and Callanan, G. (1994) *Career Management* (Orlando, Fla.: Dryden Press).

Harzing, A.W. (1997) 'Response rates in international mail surveys', *International Business Review*, 6(6), 641–65.

Harzing, A.W. and Noorderhaven, N.G. (2004) 'Knowledge flows in MNCs: An empirical test and extension of Gupta & Govindarajan's typology of subsidiary roles', *International Business Review*, 15(3), 195–214.

Haug, P., Hood, N. and Young, S. (1983) 'R&D intensity in the affiliates of US-owned electronics companies manufacturing in Scotland', *Regional Studies*, 17, 383–92.

Hesketh, B., Gardner, D. and Lissner, D. (1992) 'Technical and managerial career paths: An unresolved dilemma', *International Journal of Career Management*, 4(3), 9–16.

Hood, N. and Young, S. (1982) 'US multinational R&D: Corporate strategies and policy implications for the UK', *Multinational Business*, 2, 10–23.

Jain, R.K. and Triandis, H.C. (1990) *Management of Research and Development Organizations: Managing the Unmanageable* (New York: Wiley).

Katz, R., Tushman, M. and Allen, T. (1995) 'The influence of supervisory promotion and network location on subordinate careers in a dual ladder R&D setting', *Management Science*, 41(5), 848–63.

Kim, Y. and Cha, J. (2000) 'Career orientations of R&D professionals in Korea', *R&D Management*, 30(2), 121–37.

Lin, B.W. (2003) 'Technology transfer as technological learning: A source of competitive advantage for firms with limited R&D resources', *R&D Management*, 33(3), 327–41.

Manolopoulos, D. (2006) 'Motivating R&D professionals: Evidence from MNEs decentralized laboratories in Greece', *International Journal of Human Resource Management*, 17(4), 616–46.

McKinnon, P.D. (1987) 'Steady-state people: A third orientation', *Research Management*, 30, 26–32.

Merton, R.K. (1957) *Social theory and Social Structure* (New York: The Free Press).

Papanastassiou, M. and Pearce, R. (1999) *Multinationals, Technology and National Competitiveness* (Cheltenham: Edward Elgar).

Pearce, R. (1999) 'Decentralized R&D and strategic competitiveness: Globalized approaches to generation and use of technology in multinational enterprises', *Research Policy*, 28(2–3), 157–78.

Petroni, A. (2000) 'Career route preferences of design engineers: An empirical research', *Career Development International*, 5/6, 288–94.

Ritti, R.R. (1971) *The Engineer in the Industrial Corporation* (New York: Columbia University Press).

Souitaris, V. (2002) 'Firm specific competences determining technological innovation: A survey in Greece', *R&D Management*, 32(1), 61–76.

Tanner, D. (1998) *Total Creativity in Business and Industry: Road Map to Building a More Innovative Organization* (New York: John Wiley & Sons).

Tremblay, M., Wils, T. and Proulx, C. (2002) 'Determinants of career path preferences among Canadian engineers', *Journal of Engineering and Technology Management*, 19(1), 1–23.

Womack, J.P. and Jones, D.T. (1996) 'From lean production to the lean enterprise', *IEEE Management Review*, Winter, 38–48.

Part III
Subsidiaries and Resource Transfer

7
Experience and Performance in Interunit Knowledge Transfer

Ulf Andersson and Magnus Persson

Introduction

In the wake of the expansion of resource- and knowledge-based perspectives, knowledge has moved to the forefront as the strategically most important resource for organizations (Grant, 1996). From these perspectives, sustained competitive advantage is achieved by a superior organizational capability to coordinate heterogeneous knowledge resources in the firm (Grant, 1996; Kogut and Zander, 1992, 1996). This has directed a vast amount of research to deal with factors affecting the transfer of knowledge across subsidiaries, that is, how the gap between what is known and what is put to use in the organization is closed (Hansen and Løvås, 2004; McEvily et al. 2004; Pfeffer and Sutton, 2000).

Literature has primarily focused on three sets of factors influencing knowledge transfer between subsidiaries. First, heavily influenced by the resource-based view, a significant amount of literature has emerged that portrays knowledge attributes, such as tacitness, complexity, and ambiguity, as important sources both of sustainable competitive advantage (Lippman and Rumelt, 1982) and of potential impediments to knowledge transfer (Szulanski, 1996). Externalization of knowledge may be difficult due to the ambiguity of cause-effect relationships (Reed and Defillippi, 1990; Wilcox King and Zeithaml, 2001) or because knowledge is embedded in social and institutional contexts (Galunic and Rodan, 1998; Zander and Kogut, 1995). Second, different features of the subsidiaries themselves affect outbound and inbound knowledge transfer. This include the absorptive capacity of the recipient unit (Cohen and Levinthal, 1990; Lane and Lubatkin, 1998; Tsai, 2004), and the level of communication (Ghoshal et al. 1994; Tushman and Scanlan, 1981), and usage of lateral integrative mechanisms (Galbraith, 1973; Gupta and Govindarajan, 2000) between the source and recipient unit. Third, the structural context of subsidiaries may influence knowledge transfer. The formal structure, including coordination mechanisms, control, incentive programs, and centralization have been shown to influence knowledge transfer (e.g., Björkman et al. 2004; Gupta and Govindarajan, 1991; Gupta and Govindarajan, 1994; Roth and O'Donnell, 1996; Tsai, 2002). Furthermore, some source-recipient units may have common goals, for instance when in an internal buying-selling relationship; others may be in a relationship characterized by competitive behaviour, such as when performing similar activities in the organization (see Birkinshaw et al. 2005; Birkinshaw and Lingblad, 2005). The nature of the source-recipient relationship, as determined by the relation between the activities of these units, may influence knowledge transfer (Gupta and Govindarajan, 2000; Mudambi, 2002).

Taken together, these research efforts have provided significant insights into the determinants that increase or decrease interunit knowledge transfer. However, even if knowledge transfer between a source and recipient unit is initiated, such transfers are often incomplete (Argote and Ingram, 2000), they may not be easily implemented (Kostova, 1999), and they may require changes in the technology as well as in the organization of the recipient (Leonard-Barton, 1988). It is hence imperative to understand not only what organizational levers to pull to increase/decrease knowledge transfer, but also what factors that underlie *successful* knowledge transfer. Despite some noteworthy exceptions concerning the transfer of best practices in multiunit organizations (Kostova, 1999; Kostova and Roth, 2002; Szulanski, 1996; Szulanski et al. 2004), literature has remained rather silent on this matter.

In the present study we take a first step towards examining this gap in the empirical context of multinational corporations (MNCs). To do this, we conceive of knowledge transfer as distinct and purposeful projects. This view differs from the conceptualization of knowledge transfer as flows between subsidiaries in the MNC organization (Gupta and Govindarajan, 2000). By studying transfer at a project level, this allows us to attribute each transfer project with a performance level. We suggest that the extent to which the transferred knowledge is adopted and used with the recipient unit is an important dimension of transfer performance, and label this dimension the *effectiveness* of the transfer project.

We advance the view that capabilities to transfer knowledge successfully may exist at the subsidiary level. We focus on one particular antecedent to such capabilities, namely experience. That experience in conducting an activity leads to enhanced capabilities is well established in theory and research (Cyert and March, 1963; Eisenhardt and Martin, 2000; Helfat, 2000; Winter, 2003; Yelle, 1979; Zollo and Winter, 2002). It is argued that source subsidiaries can learn how to organize and execute interunit knowledge transfers by drawing inference from past transfer activities. Subsidiaries that repeatedly use their existing routines relating to knowledge transfer activities will, over time, refine and adjust these routines, keeping those that are feasible and changing inadequate ones.

We further distinguish in our framework between experience that is specific to a certain source-recipient dyad and such experience that is general across many recipient units, in the build-up of transfer capabilities (Ethiraj et al. 2005). Moreover, we argue that transfer capabilities will be increasingly beneficial to transfer effectiveness as the transfer project increases in difficulty. Drawing on organizational learning theory, we suggest that technological dissimilarity between the source and recipient unit is a potential barrier to transfer effectiveness (Cohen and Levinthal, 1990; Lane and Lubatkin, 1998). We examine the moderating effects of technological dissimilarity on the relationship between subsidiary transfer experience and performance of the knowledge transfer. What we basically argue for is that experience in knowledge transfer becomes increasingly important for achieving effectiveness in complex transfer situations, for example, where there is technological dissimilarity between the sending and receiving units. Knowledge transfer situations of low complexity can often be handled effectively by, relatively speaking, inexperienced senders while experience will be instrumental to achieve effective transfers in complex transfer situations between technologically dissimilar units. Four hypotheses are developed and tested using data on 102 transfer projects.

Theoretical model

Capabilities are most often conceptualized and tested as a firm level phenomenon, but as recently pointed out by Ray et al. (2004), there may also be reason to study the subprocesses that, on an aggregated level, constitute what the organization actually accomplishes or fails to accomplish. In this sense, organizational capabilities refer not to one, but to several different but related ones. Eisenhardt and Martin (2000) suggested three such distinct capabilities, relating to the integration, reconfiguration and the gain and release of resources. We posit here that one such important capability is the transfer of technological knowledge between subsidiaries, since this represents a fundamental way of reconfiguring organizational resources to improve performance. Transfer of knowledge is often undertaken because superior performance is observed elsewhere in the organization (Szulanski et al. 2004). By engaging in transfer of knowledge, organizations attempt to close existing gaps between what is known and what is put to use (Cool et al. 1997; Pfeffer and Salancik, 1978; Pfeffer and Sutton, 2000; Repenning, 2002).

Knowledge transfer performance

While there is a growing body of research addressing factors that predict the levels of outbound and inbound knowledge transfer from subsidiaries, much less attention has been brought to how this process could be conceptualized as successful. Despite some notable exceptions (see Kostova, 1999; Szulanski, 1996), research has to date examined a relatively limited amount of potential outcomes of knowledge transfer between subsidiaries. This is particularly evident within the "knowledge flow" perspective (Björkman et al. 2004; Gupta and Govindarajan, 2000; Schulz, 2001, 2003). Haas and Hansen (2005) noted that '...research on knowledge flows between task units in firms tends to emphasize the processes of knowledge sharing without explicitly considering whether the potential difficulties and drawbacks of knowledge sharing could outweigh the potential benefits' (p. 3). Furthermore, these studies seldom speak of the outcomes of transfer, that is, the performance of the transfer projects. Here, it is argued that knowledge transfer *per se* cannot automatically be considered to pertain to organizational performance at any level. Rather, it is the outcomes of knowledge transfer projects that may affect organizational performance. The outcome of knowledge transfer is a crucial objective of study.

We define transfer as a discrete event (the 'transfer project') with which a source unit shares its technological knowledge with a recipient unit. This conceptualization of knowledge transfer differs from knowledge transfer as flows between a subsidiary and other units (see Gupta and Govindarajan, 2000; Haas and Hansen, 2005). These transfer projects can be seen as the discrete elements building up the knowledge flows within a firm. This way of disaggregating flows into its constituent parts makes it possible to attribute a performance to individual transfer projects.

Daft (1992) and Pfeffer and Salancik (1978) suggested *effectiveness* as a term with which one could compare achievement to goals in organizational processes. For the purpose of this chapter, we define the goal of knowledge transfer projects as the recipient's adoption and usage of the new knowledge. By prescribing each transfer project a specific goal we can examine the extent to which each project could be regarded as successful. Effectiveness of the knowledge transfer project is seen as the extent to which the transferred knowledge has been adopted and used by the receiving unit. Reaching effectiveness is a fundamental dimension of transfer outcome; if transferred knowledge is not implemented and used, it cannot have any implications for the behaviour of the recipient unit.

Experience and capabilities

Stating that organizations may own capabilities begs the question how they are acquired or developed. One important source to current capabilities is the past activities of organizations, that is, they may 'learn' through earlier experiences. By repetition, certain processes and causal relationships will be more fully understood by actors inside the organization. The best-known manifest of the beneficial effects of experience is perhaps the learning curve (see Argote,

1999; Epple et al. 1991; Yelle, 1979). This postulates that the performance of an actor increases at a decreasing rate with the frequency of the task. These learning effects of experience have so far primarily been documented as efficiency gains through repetition of well-defined production tasks, but also at other levels such as the individual level as an effect of learning-by-doing, at the organizational level in terms of organizational improvements, and as technological development at the industrial level (Devinney, 1987). Recently, experience has also been appreciated as an important source of capabilities also to far more complex and strategic tasks. The relevance of prior experience has been studied in the context of firm alliances (Sampson, 2005), acquisitions (Haleblian and Finkelstein, 1999; Zollo and Singh, 2004), software development projects (Ethiraj et al. 2005) and has been suggested to influence the formation of wider dynamic capabilities (Zollo and Winter, 2002).

Learning through direct experience includes drawing inferences from history to create and adapt routines that guide future behaviour (Levitt and March, 1988). Fiol and Lyles (1985) identified two types of organizational learning, differentiated by their cognitive impact – higher-level learning and lower-level learning. The former is characterized by changes in heuristics and insights, and manifests in, for instance, the development of myths, organizational values, and mission. The latter occurs within a given organizational structure, and includes, for instance, issues such as routines and specific tasks. Lower-level learning is thus more pertinent in lower levels of the organization, but as noted by Fiol and Lyles (1985), this need not always be true. Further, lower-level organizational learning takes place as a result of repetition and routinized action, involving association building, and has the desired consequence of affecting the level of performance of certain tasks in the organization (Fiol and Lyles, 1985). This agrees with Cyert and March (1963), who proposed that unsatisfactory performance of procedures will lead to a problem-driven search process, through which feasible routines are kept intact, while those leading to unsatisfactory outcomes are altered or replaced.

Development of subsidiary knowledge transfer capabilities

Albeit empirical research on the link between experience and outcomes in knowledge transfer processes is currently lacking, there are indications that it might be fruitful to connect these issues. In analyzing results put forward by Davidson and McFetridge (1984), Kogut and Zander (1993) came to the conclusion that '... experience in internal transfers is codified in a way idiosyncratic to the firm ...' (p. 632). This appeals much to the notion of a build-up process of capabilities to transfer knowledge inside the organization. Extensive experience on knowledge transfer is likely to enhance the transferring unit's ability to organize, coordinate, and execute the task of transferring knowledge.

All knowledge transfer projects differ in important respects. They differ in complexity of the underlying knowledge, such as level of perceived ambiguity (Szulanski et al. 2004), size and scope (some may concern minor improvements to existing processes, others may concern the change of the process in its totality), duration (some take months – some are rather quick), and the perceived strategic importance. Due to these interproject differences, each transfer project requires different planning, set of mechanisms, level of communication and interaction between the source and recipient unit, level and type of governance, engagement, project control, and so on. We argue that for each transfer project, there are specific set-ups, ways of communicating, planning, and executing this project that are better than others.

As a source unit repeatedly engages in knowledge transfer projects, it will also repeatedly try to match the project-specific requirements as outlined above, with an appropriate design of the planning, executing, personnel, and interaction level. On some occasions, this will be a good fit, leading to a high transfer performance. On some occasions, this fit will be poor – leading to less satisfactory results. Over time, as this process of evaluating the requirements of the project, adapting the set-up and design of the project to those requirements, and observing the outcome, reoccurs, the source subsidiary will accumulate experience of how to organize transfer projects. Through feedback in the means-ends framework, the source unit learns how to manage knowledge transfer in a better way. In other words, the subsidiary learns from its transfer experience and develops capabilities to transfer technological knowledge.

Given that organizational learning takes place at several different levels in the organization (Huber, 1991; Levitt and March, 1988), it seems reasonable to expect that firm subsidiaries differ in their skills with which they manage the transfer process. Units that repeatedly engage in knowledge transfer activities have a significant experience base of these activities; these experiences can add to the development of specific capabilities in executing knowledge transfers, and these capabilities then to some extent reside at the subsidiary level. From the literature, we can derive two different types of transfer capabilities, residing in subsidiaries, which are derived from experience – *general transfer capabilities* and *dyadic-specific transfer capabilities*.

General transfer capabilities

Subsidiaries hold different strategic roles in the organization (Birkinshaw, 1996; Pearce, 1999; Roth and Morrison, 1992). Some subsidiaries might be unique inside the organization due to their specific competences. Such units may come to hold a central role in the organizational knowledge processes, for instance, as a centre of excellence (Forsgren et al. 2000; Forsgren and Pedersen, 2000; Frost et al. 2002; Holm and Pedersen, 2002). These have a more encompassing role in terms of creating and sharing knowledge with other organizational units. In such cases, experience is accumulated from a wide variety of transfer projects with a number of different recipient counterparts. In such cases, capabilities are formed from a broad spectrum of experiences relating to many different source-recipient dyads. Thus, the transfer capabilities serving (and being developed from experience in) such units must be flexible enough to balance between simultaneous transfer projects, and also to work iteratively between different recipient units. These transfer capabilities are *general,* meaning that they are independent of the specific dyadic context of the source and recipient unit.

Following the definition of lower-level learning in organizations, extended operational scope, in terms of providing other parts of the corporation with knowledge, is likely to lead to the development of certain skills and capabilities relating to this task. Others have developed similar views; Grant (1996) sees the frequency of knowledge management processes as positively influencing the integration of knowledge; Gold et al. (2001) noted that: '[T]he more frequently a company carries out its knowledge management processes, the more routine the norms and more efficient the integration process.' Subsidiaries that on a regular basis share internal developments with other parts of the firm are thus likely to learn from past behaviour and over time improve the procedures of knowledge transfer. Hypothesis 1 follows from the above arguments:

Hypothesis 1: Development of transfer capabilities through accumulation of general transfer experience is positively related to the transfer process effectiveness.

Dyadic-specific capabilities

Recent research has provided evidence that repeated interaction between two specific counterparts pertains to the development of capabilities to handle this interaction (Ethiraj et al. 2005). This finding relates to the current study, in that some subsidiaries exchange knowledge between each other more frequently than others. For instance, Hansen and Løvås (2004) recently found that the existence of informal social relationships between subsidiaries moderated the effects of other determinants such as the relatedness of competences residing within units. This implies that subsidiaries are more likely to turn repeatedly to specific counterparts when transferring knowledge, and that sources and recipients in knowledge exchanges are not only determined by the potential value of specific combinations of knowledge. In effect, some units will be more familiar with each other within the context of knowledge transfer activities. Capabilities developing as a response to this recurrent interaction between two specific subsidiaries may therefore to a large extent be *dyadic-specific,* and not necessarily beneficial if the recipient units differ between transfer projects.

Kogut and Zander (1993) pointed out that firms out-compete markets as coordinating mechanisms for knowledge transfer since participants of a firm, to a greater extent than participants of a particular market, will share identities and coding schemes, and enjoy easier and less cumbersome communication and interaction. This, then, makes firms more efficient than markets in transferring complex and tacit knowledge. Hence firms are communities that share common knowledge on how to cooperate and communicate, making them efficient relative to markets in transferring knowledge. However, Kogut and Zander (1993) also note: 'Through repeated interaction, individuals and groups in a firm develop a common understanding by which to transfer knowledge from ideas into production and markets.' Explaining this argument, capabilities to transfer knowledge might not only reside at firm (or subsidiary) level (although this is enough to provide support for the argument of firm superiority to markets) – but also at a dyadic level. Following this, we would expect that the more the source and recipient unit have interacted and shared knowledge previously, the greater the effectiveness with which this can be done. To summarize the arguments, it is posited that:

Hypothesis 2: Development of transfer capabilities through accumulation of dyad-specific transfer experience is positively related to the transfer process effectiveness.

Technological dissimilarity as a moderator variable

The value of experience to the performance of future tasks depends on certain characteristics of this task. For example, Sampson (2005) found that prior alliance experience has greater impact on the collaborative benefits from new alliances, if the activities in the alliance are uncertain and complex. We expect a similar effect on the value of earlier transfer experience on the effectiveness of transfer projects.

It is commonly accepted that organizations more easily learn such knowledge as bears similarities to what is previously known; that it is imperative that the 'student' firm understands the relevant basic knowledge and thereby the assumptions that underlie and shape the 'teachers' knowledge (Lane and Lubatkin, 1998). The importance of such common basic knowledge in knowledge transfer activities has also been emphasized within the knowledge-based view (Kogut and Zander, 1992; Spender, 1994). Sharing basic knowledge is important, since it facilitates communication by usage of common codes and shared coding schemes, or interpretive schemes (Dougherty, 1992).

Technological understanding and shared basic knowledge about how to transform input into valuable output are especially critical when attempting to transfer technological knowledge. If both units operate with similar technologies, the individuals in these units will share common knowledge about how to organize and execute tasks in this environment. They will be better able to understand each other, given that they have similar reference points from which to draw

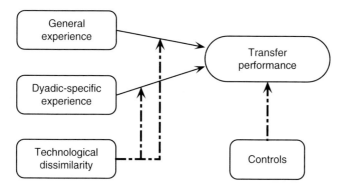

Figure 7.1 The hypothesized model

inferences in communication. Likewise, lack of such common knowledge and understanding will yield more difficulties in the transfer process. We suggest that because of this, high technological dissimilarity between the source and recipient unit would increase the difficulty of the transfer project.

We expect that the link between experience and transfer effectiveness is moderated by the difficulty of the current transfer project. If the transfer project is nonproblematic, even inexperienced source units will be able to handle this with sufficient skill and precision in terms of planning, organizing and execution to reach a satisfactory outcome. However, if the transfer is difficult, the benefits of having accumulated experience from other transfer projects may be great. In other words, we posit that the positive relationship between transfer experience and transfer effectiveness will become stronger as technological dissimilarity increases.

> *Hypothesis 3: Subsidiary general transfer experience will be more positively related to transfer effectiveness under conditions of technological dissimilarity between the source and recipient unit.*

> *Hypothesis 4: Subsidiary dyadic transfer experience will be more positively related to transfer effectiveness under conditions of technological dissimilarity between the source and recipient unit.*

In Figure 7.1, the hypothesis are displayed graphically.

Data collection and sampling methods

While knowledge may be conceptualized in a number of different ways (and indeed no coherent view has emerged on how to do this), we believe that one potential viable way of conceiving technological knowledge in organizations is by its innovations. Innovations consist of technological knowledge of how to do things better than the current state of the art (Teece, 1986, p. 288), and they are frequently subjected to transfer attempts. Innovations are often characterized in terms of the novelty of their constituent knowledge, ranging from being radical to incremental (Dewar and Dutton, 1986). Within the frame of this study, innovation is defined as new to the organization as a whole (Downs and Mohr, 1976), albeit it is recognized that the degree of novelty, as perceived by the source and recipient unit, does not have to correspond perfectly. However, even less radical innovations may have significant effects on competition (Henderson and Clark, 1990), and thus be important to organizations. In line with this, the present study captures technological knowledge by focusing on subsidiary product and process innovations. In this sense, we also depart from other attempts towards empirically assessing knowledge transfer success, which mostly have dealt with the transfer of best practices (Kostova and Roth, 2002; Szulanski, 1996).

The data for this study were collected from subsidiaries of 25 international divisions belonging to 14 MNCs. The sampling procedure was done in cooperation with firm managers, with whom innovations were jointly identified. In total, the transfer of 67 different innovations from 47 locations yielded (N) 139 studied transfer projects, comprising the sample. The overall aim of the project was to collect data on the development, transfer, and commercialization of subsidiary innovations. Due to missing values in the data covering innovation transfer, the sample was reduced to an effective size of (n) 102 transfer projects in the subsequent statistical analysis. All in all, this means that every innovation has been transferred 102/67 = 1.52 times. The highest number of transfers of one specific innovation is 4 times. The characteristics measured regarding the specific transfers vary to a large extent even between the transfers of the same innovation why we have little reason to believe that this has any major effects on the results received.

In the investigation, the sampling was done in cooperation with top-level managers (CEOs, heads of Divisions, and RandD Directors) in the MNCs. While this permitted access to lower-level managers, it also directed the sampling towards specific innovations to which access was granted by these top-level managers. The alternative would be to survey technological development in each firm and based on this choose a suitable sample; however, this would raise immense and likely insurmountable problems relating to access and the legitimacy of the research project. Because of this, the present sample is admittedly biased as there possibly is an overrepresentation of successful innovations, that is, undersampling of failure (Denrell, 2003). It is important to note that the selective criterion for transfer observations was that the innovation had the potential to be transferred, rather than having been successfully transferred. Accordingly, there is considerable variance in the dimensions of transfer performance. Furthermore, recognizing this problem, this method of tracking innovations through their development, transfer, and commercialization provided high-quality data, even though generalization of the results has to be done with care.

The data were collected using a standardized questionnaire administered through face-to-face interviews. We interviewed key personnel in the source unit, who had been involved in the processes of development and transfer of the investigated innovations. The informants were usually one or more of the CEO, R&D managers, or project managers of the subsidiary. We invited the informants to freely discuss and describe the innovation processes, before introducing them to the standardized questionnaire. This approach often gave us a valuable descriptive background against which our questions concerning the transfer process could be posed.

Dependent variable

Three indicators were used to create the dependent variable, transfer effectiveness. First, respondents were asked to evaluate the *<Level of completed innovation transfer>*. Answers could be indicated on a scale from 1 (not at all) to 7 (very high). Given that all transfer projects were completed, that is, not ongoing, at the time of the interviews, this question targeted the extent to which the innovation was actually adopted into the operations of the recipient unit at the time of the interview. The respondents were then asked to indicate the extent to which they agreed to the following statements: *<The counterpart adopted the innovation very quickly>* and *<The innovation has been very easy to adopt by this counterpart>*. Here again, it is crucial to understand the difference between the transfer process and the adoption of the innovation. The transfer process may be quick but the recipient unit's adoption of the innovation into its operation may still be cumbersome and time-consuming. These indicators target the friction associated with the adoption of the innovation into the operations of the recipient unit. Answers could be indicated on a scale from 1 (totally agree) to 7 (totally disagree). The indicators were summed and averaged to form a construct measuring transfer effectiveness. The internal reliability of the construct was within acceptable limits (coefficient alpha: 0.7955).

Independent variables

Two indicators were used to measure the construct 'dyadic transfer experience'. Respondents were asked to indicate, on a scale from 1 (not at all) to 7 (very much) the extent to which the source and recipient unit had interacted previously, in addition to this innovation. The indicators were obtained by asking *<what is the level of knowledge shared previously with the recipient unit>* and *<what is the level of previous cooperation between your unit and the recipient unit>*. The indicators were summed and averaged to form the construct. Internal reliability of the construct was within acceptable limits (coefficient alpha: 0.7411).

To measure a subsidiary's general experience of knowledge transfer, respondents were faced with four questions regarding the extent to which the unit had transferred core technology and product innovations to other units in the MNC. The questions were posed with consideration as to the formal organizational structure on which the units operated, and were thus divided into (1) extent to which the unit had transferred innovations to other units within the same division, and (2) extent to which the unit had transferred innovations to other units outside their division/business area. The indicators were formulated as follows: <*to what extent have innovations released by your unit during the past five years been transferred to other units within your division/business area*> and <*to what extent have innovations released by your unit been transferred to other units within the MNC external to your division/business area*>. For each question, the respondent answered with respect to (1) core technology innovations, and (2) product innovations. This yielded a total of four indicators. Answers could be given on a scale from 1 (not at all) to 7 (very much). The four indicators were summed and then averaged to form the construct. Internal reliability of the construct was within acceptable limits (coefficient alpha: 0.7181).

Moderator variable

To create the construct 'technological dissimilarity', two indicators were used. The respondents were asked to indicate, on a scale from 1 (not similar at all) to 7 (very similar), the <*unit's technical similarity with other MNC/divisional units*>. For this question, the respondents answered with respect to (1) product technology knowledge, and (2) production technology knowledge. This yielded a total of two indicators in this construct. These indicators were then reverse scored, summed, and averaged to create the construct. Internal reliability of the construct was within acceptable limits (coefficient alpha: 0.8651). We acknowledge that this measure might not be optimally suited to determine the technological dissimilarity specifically between the source and the recipient unit. It does, though, give an indication about how similar/dissimilar the respondent perceives the focal unit to be with respect to technology, compared to other units in the firm.

Control variables

To finalize the specification of the model, five variables were used to control for unobserved heterogeneity. First, one of the factors most emphasized as influential in knowledge transfer is the character of the knowledge in question (Subramaniam and Venkatarman, 2001; Szulanski, 1996; Zander and Kogut, 1995). Albeit there are many different suggestions for how to conceptualize knowledge characteristics, we chose to focus on knowledge tacitness, as it is arguably the characteristic that has received the most attention as an impediment to knowledge transfer. To control for this, we used two indicators to create a construct of 'knowledge tacitness'. The respondents were asked to indicate, on a scale from 1 (strongly disagree) to 7 (strongly agree), their opinion of two statements concerning the nature of the innovation knowledge. *<The innovation technology/process know-how is easily codifiable (in blueprints, instructions, formulas, etc.)>*, and *<The innovation technology/process know-how is more explicit (i.e., easily transferable) than tacit>*. The indicators were summed and averaged to form a construct of tacitness of the innovation knowledge (coefficient alpha: 0.6219). Although the alpha value is slightly under the commonly used threshold of 0.7, we find it important to keep both items in the construct as they reflect different facets of the taciteness construct not necessarily captured by each of them alone.

Second, the age of the subsidiary can be influential. Older subsidiaries may be may be more autonomous (Forsgren, 1990; Foss and Pedersen, 2002); and they may have accumulated considerably more experience in knowledge transfer activities than younger units. To control for this, age was included in the regression equation as the logarithm of the number of years the subsidiary had been operating on the market.

Further, the structure of the organization may influence the ease with which knowledge is transferred. It is reasonable to believe that transfers that take place within a divisional structure will be subject to fewer difficulties than those projects that extend across different divisional structures. Units operating in different divisions are likely to have less communication and interaction with each-other than those that operate within the same divisional structure. They will also respond to different divisional headquarter organizations, making cross-divisional coordination potentially more difficult. Further, divisionalization may represent a natural distinction between technologies employed in the operations of units. To control for the effects of divisionalization, a dummy variable coded with the value 1 if the transfer took place between units belonging to the same division, and 0 otherwise, was included in the regression equation.

Research has on several occasions indicated that denser communication and interaction between units facilitates knowledge transfer; especially if the transfer is difficult and involves, for instance, tacit and un-codified knowledge (Galbraith, 1973; Gupta and Govindarajan, 2000). To control for this, we used four indicators to target the usage of mechanisms of interaction during the transfer process. The respondents were asked *<With regard to the transfer of the innovation, what was the level of use of a) face-to-face meetings, b) exchange of employees, c) temporary training at partner sites d) cross-unit teams, project groups etc>*. Answers could be given on a scale from 1 (not at all) to 7 (very much). The indicators were added up and averaged to form the variable lateral mechanisms. Internal reliability of the scale was within acceptable limits (coefficient alpha: 0.7414).

Finally, previous research has also indicated that motivational issues may be influential in interunit knowledge transfer (Szulanski, 1996). We believe that if the locus of initiative to the transfer is found at subsidiary level, there is considerably less risk that lack of motivation in the source unit will impede the transfer process. To control for this, a construct containing two indicators was formed and included in the regression equation. The respondents were asked to indicate *<to what extent is the transfer of the innovation driven by benefits to your own business from transfer of knowledge to this counterpart>*, and *<to what extent is the transfer of the innovation driven by high dependence on this counterpart>*. In both cases, answers could be given on a scale from 1 (not at all) to 7 (very much). Internal reliability of this construct was not reaching the usual rule of thumb of 0.7, but could be considered sufficient as the construct is only used to control for otherwise unexplained heterogeneity in the estimation of the model and is built on only two items (coefficient alpha: 0.6283).

Common method bias

Studies employing a methodology of using self-reported data are always at risk of common method bias. To check for this, we used Harman's one-factor test, as suggested by Podsakoff and Organ (1986). All indicators used in the relevant constructs were included in a principal component factor analysis. In the case of high common method variance, only one factor will emerge with an eigen-value above 1, or alternatively one factor will be dominant in terms of account-ing for a majority of the total explained variance. In this case, four factors were extracted, corresponding to the dependent, independent, and moderator variables. Further, none of the factors explained a majority of the variance; the highest amount explained by one factor was 24% and the lowest was 11%. Although we cannot exclude the presence of common method bias based on this result, it will likely not be a serious problem in analyzing the data.

Descriptive statistics on all variables in the model are presented in Table 7.1. The values for the two independent variables and the moderator variables are

Table 7.1   Correlations and descriptive statistics[a]

Variable	Mean	S.d.	1	2	3	4	5	6	7	8
1. Effec.	5.12	1.42	–							
2. Tacitness	2.72	1.49	−0.014	–						
3. Unit Age	1.56	0.38	0.257	0.042	–					
4. Intra-div.	0.53	0.50	0.320	−0.196	−0.173	–				
5. Lat. Mech.	3.55	1.51	−0.032	−0.043	0.063	0.017	–			
6. Subs. Driv.	4.05	1.95	0.071	−0.054	0.053	0.119	0.446	–		
7. Tech. Diss.	3.68	1.79	−0.142	−0.045	−0.254	0.179	0.107	0.165	–	
8. Dyadic Exp.	4.91	1.54	0.299	−0.086	0.212	0.089	0.199	0.284	0.174	–
9. Gen. Exp.	4.11	1.31	0.096	0.158	−0.083	−0.125	0.035	−0.156	−0.001	0.210

[a] Values are standardized parameter estimates.

given before standardization. Overall, the correlation between the variables is low; only between the control variables 'subsidiary driver' and 'lateral mechanisms' does the correlation exceed 0.4.

Results

In total, three different models were estimated. The models were estimated using Ordinary Least Squares (OLS) regression. The results are presented in Table 7.2. Model 1 examines only the control variables. Only two control variables show significant coefficients – unit age and intra-divisional transfer. Overall, Model 1 is significant with an F-value of 5.13 ($p < 0.001$). About 17% of the variance in the dependent variable is explained by the control variables. Model 2 examines the control variables, along with the independent variables (dyadic transfer experience and general transfer experience) and the moderator variable (technological dissimilarity). The amount of explained variance increases from 17% to about 24%. Both the coefficients for 'technological dissimilarity' and 'dyadic transfer experience' are significant ($p < 0.05$) with the expected signs. Model 2 is significant overall with an F-value of 5.04 ($p < 0.001$). The significance of the independent and moderator variables is further confirmed by the partial F-test.

Finally, Model 3 introduces the interaction term between the two types of experience and technological dissimilarity. Hypothesis 1 states that subsidiaries' general experience is positively related to transfer effectiveness. In

Table 7.2 Results of multiple regression for transfer success[a]

Variable	Model 1	Model 2	Model 3
Tacitness	0.045	0.043	0.018
Unit Age	1.279**	0.955*	1.147**
Intra-div.	1.121***	1.161***	1.098***
Lateral Mech.	−0.074	0.098	−0.099
Subs. Driv.	0.036	0.034	−0.011
Tech. Dissimilarity		−0.293*	−0.356*
Dyadic Exp.		0.396*	0.488**
General Exp.		0.176	0.207
Dyad. Exp.*Tech. Diss.			0.401*
Gen. Exp.*Tech Diss.			−0.427**
F-value	5.13***	5.04***	5.38***
ΔF(partial)	–	4.06**	5.03**
R^2	0.211	0.302	0.371
Adj. R^2	0.169	0.242	0.302
df.	5, 96	8, 93	10, 91

[a] Values are standardized parameter estimates.
† $p < 0.1$, * $p < 0.05$, ** $p < 0.01$, *** $p < 0.001$, N = 102

Table 7.2, it can be seen that the coefficient for general experience does not reach any significant level; accordingly, Hypothesis 1 is unsupported. This means that accumulation of experience of transferring innovations to other subsidiaries in general does not lead to higher transfer effectiveness. Hypothesis 2 states that subsidiaries' dyadic transfer experience is positively related to transfer effectiveness. In contrast to Hypothesis 1, Hypothesis 2 is only concerned with the experience of transferring knowledge to the specific counterpart. The coefficient for dyadic transfer experience is positive and significant ($p < 0.01$), indicating that transfer experience specific to the source-recipient dyad is directly and positively related to effectiveness of the transfer. Hypothesis 3 states that technological dissimilarity will moderate the relationship between general transfer experience and transfer effectiveness, so that general transfer experience will be more positively related to transfer effectiveness as technological dissimilarity increases (Baron and Kenny, 1986; Sharma et al. 1981). To test this hypothesis, we created an interaction term by multiplying general experience by technological dissimilarity and then included this interaction term in the regression equation. Given the risk of introducing multicollinearity when including a product term of component variables already in the model, we followed the procedure suggested by Marquardt (1980) and Cronbach (1987) and standardized the variables (see also Jaccard et al. 1990a; Jaccard et al. 1990b). This reduces the risk of multicollinearity and 'inflated' error terms in estimating the model. The coefficient for this interaction term is significant ($p < 0.01$) but has a negative sign, meaning that Hypothesis 3 is not supported. Hypothesis 4 states that technological dissimilarity moderates the relationship between dyadic transfer experience and transfer effectiveness, so that the positive effect of dyadic experience of transfer effectiveness will increase as technological dissimilarity increases. The coefficient for this interaction term is significant ($p < 0.05$) and has a positive sign. This indicates that as the difficulty of the transfer project increases, so does the positive impact of earlier experience of transferring knowledge to this recipient unit. Accordingly, Hypothesis 4 is supported. When introducing the two interaction terms, the adjusted R^2 increases from 0.242 to 0.302, that is, Model 3 explains an additional 6% of the variance compared to Model 2 (without the interaction terms). The significance of the interaction terms is also shown by the partial F-test ($F = 5.03$, $p < 0.01$).

To check for multicollinearity among the predictor variables, the variance inflation factor (VIF) was calculated. Different acceptable sizes of VIF have been proposed, but 10 seems to be a generally agreed cut-off value (see for instance Hair et al. 1998; see, for instance, Marquardt, 1970). The values returned between 1 and 2 for all predictors in Model 3, which could be considered very low, given that there are interaction factors in the model. The conclusion is that multicollinearity will not constitute a problem to the interpretation of results for the predictors.

Discussion of results

At the beginning of this chapter, we pointed out a lack of concern in current research with the actual outcomes of knowledge transfer projects. To address this, the current chapter sought to examine the question of what determines effectiveness of knowledge transfer between MNC subsidiaries. We conceptualized knowledge transfer as specific, discrete projects, argued that no two transfer projects are identical, and that every transfer project is unique in terms of suitable transfer mechanisms, ways of organizing, and ways of executing the process. We also briefly outlined the learning dynamics of the development of knowledge transfer capabilities. Therefore, rather than focussing on specific transfer mechanisms, the ability to match the demands given by the knowledge and context of the transfer with the appropriate methods – that is, knowledge transfer capabilities – would be an important determinant to the transfer effectiveness. We further posited that one important antecedent to these transfer capabilities would be subsidiaries' earlier experience in knowledge transfer activities. To empirically examine our arguments, we used data on 102 specific inter subsidiary transfer projects.

The results reported in this chapter indicate both that subsidiaries may benefit from past transfer experiences in future transfer projects – that is, experience from earlier transfer projects assist in the formation of subsidiary 'transfer capabilities' – as well as indicate restrictions to this logic. Two out of four hypotheses were supported. It was shown that dyadic-specific experience has a direct and positive impact on knowledge transfer effectiveness, and further, that the level of technological dissimilarity between the source and recipient unit moderates this relationship. In other words, the effects of dyadic-specific experience on transfer effectiveness increases with the technological dissimilarity between the source and receiving unit. On the other hand, the statistical analysis failed to support the hypothesis pertaining to general transfer experience. In fact, general experience seemed to have no direct effect on transfer effectiveness. Further, as the technological dissimilarity between the source and recipient unit increases, general experience becomes negatively related to transfer effectiveness.

The interpretation of the results suggests that while experience of transferring knowledge may be beneficial to transfer effectiveness, this effect is specific to dyadic conditions. Subsidiaries do learn how to organize and execute transfer projects from earlier experiences, but the actual effects of this experience are contextually bound to each transfer dyad. In other words, the possibilities to generalize experiences from one recipient unit to another are very limited. This seems to confirm the notion that capabilities induced by experiential learning are largely of a tacit nature (Nelson and Winter, 1982) and consist of 'social knowledge' rather than explicit rules of organizing (Kogut and Zander, 1992).

Furthermore, we found statistical support for the interaction term between technological dissimilarity and dyadic transfer experience. The interpretation of this is that the effect of dyadic-specific experience increases as the source and recipient unit become increasingly technologically dissimilar. In other words, the ability to draw inferences from earlier transfer projects pays off more when new transfer projects are difficult. When the transfer project is easy, the relative value of dyadic-specific experience declines but is still present. This result underlines the importance of forming strong interunit linkages inside the organization in order to utilize knowledge effectively.

Concerning the effects of general experience, the direct effect was insignificant, and furthermore, the interaction term was statistically significant and the coefficient had an unexpected negative sign. This means that as the source and recipient unit become increasingly technologically dissimilar, general transfer experience has a negative impact on transfer effectiveness. Research has earlier suggested that experience under certain circumstances is not necessarily beneficial to performance through, for instance, myopic learning (Levinthal and March, 1993), and this result seem to confirm this suspicion. This effect may be because experience is overvalued In certain situations, rather than because experience does not lead to learning. Earlier experience can be detrimental because it may induce the use of already developed solutions and procedures, even in cases when a more specialized set-up is required to reach effectiveness. Thus, managers may generalize too quickly, and use previous set-ups instead of examining the specific problem at hand and designing a suitable method of execution (see Eisenhardt and Martin, 2000). In this way, actors can become overconfident in their capabilities as their experience increases, and because of this apply solutions that earlier were appropriate but do not fit the current circumstances.

Based on the results presented here, one could severely question the benefit of aiming at inducing high levels of outbound knowledge flows from subsidiaries. Rather, as argued by Doz, Santos, and Williamson (2001), effective knowledge management seems not to be about everyone knowing everything or creating a mass of internal linkages between competences and knowledge. Instead, it is most important to hone specific, carefully chosen connections and relationships between different operating units. Not merely a matter of 'more is better', transfer of technological knowledge is a difficult activity that should be driven with care.

Albeit our chapter contributes in several areas, we would like to be open about certain limitations of this study. First and foremost, had we had alternatives, we would have chosen to use data also from the recipient unit. While we believe that our current data are reliable, it is always preferable to attempt to triangulate data during collection – it provides higher data quality and there is less risk of being subject to individual biases. Such a methodological design could increase the precision of the measurements used in the study. Second, the study took place in a sample of MNCs that is by no means representative for the entire global population of MNCs. The sample firms are all large corporations with a long history of multinational business activity in different production industries. Our results may therefore neither be possible to generalize to other types of industries (such as service industries) nor to smaller firms or 'born-global' firms. Third, knowledge transfer involves the ability, as well as the willingness, of subsidiaries to share their knowledge. Here, our model is explicitly conditional on motivational aspects. One important determinant here can be how the activities of the source and recipient unit are related to each other, if they have 'natural' incentives to cooperate or compete (cf. Mudambi, 2002). A similar point was made by Gupta and Govindarajan (2000). This is something that is likely to be a fruitful area of future investigations.

We believe that this chapter raises important questions that future research in this area should consider addressing. First, being that this is to our knowledge one of the few attempts to investigate different dimensions of performance of interunit transfer of technological knowledge, there is plenty of room for additional and more fine-grained approaches to this. In particular, one may contrast between effectiveness and efficiency dimensions of the transfer performance – the extent to which the process reaches the goal set, and the cost of doing so (Daft, 1992). This would allow for a more holistic understanding of how different determinants work to influence knowledge transfer, and also, an insight into the resource cost side of transferring knowledge which up until now have been sparsely addressed (however, see Teece, 1977; Zander and Kogut, 1995) and always considered in isolation. Particularly, by avoiding subsuming different dimensions of transfer outcome under one conceptual umbrella, research may get closer to the actual logic underlying knowledge flows in organizations. Second, we believe that a fruitful area of study would be the underlying antecedents to the formation of knowledge transfer capabilities. This chapter dealt with but one – direct experience – and research should in the future also appreciate the managerial aspect of this important issue, and investigate how different support structures and processes can be deliberately put in place to facilitate effective knowledge transfer.

References

Argote, L. (1999) *Organizational Learning: Creating, Retaining and Transferring Knowledge* (Norwell, Mass.: Kluwer Academic Publishers).
Argote, L. and Ingram, P. (2000) 'Knowledge transfer: a basis for competitive advantage', *Organizational Behavior and Human Decision Processes,* 82(1), 150–69.
Baron, R.M. and Kenny, D.A. (1986) 'The moderator-mediator variable distinction in social psychological research: conceptual, strategic, and statistical considerations', *Journal of Personality and Social Psychology,* 51(6), 1173–82.

Birkinshaw, J. (1996) 'How multinational subsidiary mandates are gained and lost', *Journal of International Business Studies*, 27(3), 467–95.

Birkinshaw, J., Hood, N. and Young, S. (2005) 'Subsidiary entrepreneurship, internal and external competitive forces, and subsidiary performance', *International Business Review*, 14, 227–48.

Birkinshaw, J. and Lingblad, M. (2005) 'Intrafirm competition and charter evolution in the multibusiness firm', *Organization Science*, 16(6), 674–86.

Björkman, I., Barner-Rasmussen, W. and Li, L. (2004) 'Managing knowledge transfers in MNCs: the impact of headquarters control mechanisms', *Journal of International Business Studies*, 35(5), 443–55.

Cohen, W.M. and Levinthal, D.A. (1990) 'Absorptive capacity: A new perspective on learning and innovation', *Administrative Science Quarterly*, 35(1), 128–52.

Cool, K.O., Dierickx, I. and Szulanski, G. (1997) 'Diffusion of innovations within organizations: Electronic switching in the bell system, 1971–1982', *Organization Science*, 8(5), 543–59.

Cronbach, L.J. (1987) 'Statistical tests for moderator variables: Flaws in analyses recently proposed', *Psychological Bullentin*, 102(3), 414–17.

Cyert, R. and March, J.G. (1963) *A Behavioural Theory of the Firm* (Cambridge, Mass.: MIT Press).

Daft, R.L. (1992) *Organization theory and design*, 4th ed. (St. Paul, Minn.: West Publishing Company).

Davidson, W.H. and McFetridge, D.G. (1984) 'International technology transactions and the theory of the firm', *The Journal of Industrial Economics*, 32(3), 253–64.

Denrell, J. (2003) 'Vicarious learning, undersampling of failure, and the myths of management', *Organization Science*, 14(3), 227–43.

Devinney, T.M. (1987) 'Entry and learning', *Management Science*, 33(6), 706–24.

Dewar, R.D and Dutton, J.E. (1986) 'The adoption of radical and incremental innovations: an empirical analysis', *Management Science*, 32(11), 1422–33.

Dougherty, D. (1992) 'Interpretive barriers to successful product innovation in large firms', *Organization Science*, 3(2), 179–202.

Downs, G.W.J. and Mohr, L.B. (1976) 'Conceptual issues in the study of innovation', *Administrative Science Quarterly*, 21(4), 700–14.

Doz, Y., Santos, J. and Williamson, P. (2001) *From Global to Metanational – How Companies Win in the Knowledge Economy* (Boston, Mass.: Harvard Business School Press).

Eisenhardt, K.M. and Martin, J.A. (2000) 'Dynamic capabilities: What are they?', *Strategic Management Journal*, 21, 1105–21.

Epple, D., Argote, L. and Rukmini, D. (1991) 'Organizational learning curves: a method for investigating intra-plant transfer of knowledge acquired through learning by doing', *Organization Science*, 2(1), 58–70.

Ethiraj, S.K., Kale, P., Krishnan, M.S. and Singh, J.V. (2005) 'Where do capabilities come from and how do they matter? A study in the software services industry', *Strategic Management Journal*, 26, 25–45.

Fiol, C.M. and Lyles, M.A. (1985) 'Organizational learning', *Academy of Management Review*, 10(4), 803–813.

Forsgren, M. (1990) 'Managing the international multi-centre firm: Case studies from Sweden', *European Management Journal*, 8(2), 261–67.

Forsgren, M., Johanson, J. and Sharma, D. (2000) 'Development of MNC centers of excellence', in U. Holm and T. Pedersen (eds), *The Emergence and Impact of MNC Centers of Excellence – a Subsidiary Pespective*, 45–67 (London: Macmillan).

Forsgren, M. and Pedersen, T. (2000) 'Subsidiary influence and corporate learning – centres of excellence in Danish foreign-owned firms', in U. Holm and T. Pedersen (eds), *The Emergence and Impact of MNC Centers of Excellence – a Subsidiary Pespective*, 68–78 (London: Macmillan).

Foss, N.J. and Pedersen, T. (2002) 'Transferring knowledge in MNC´s: The role of sources of subsidiary knowledge and organizational context', *Journal of International Management*, 8(1), 49–67.

Frost, T.S., Birkinshaw, J. and Ensign, P.C. (2002) 'Centers of excellence in multinational corporations', *Strategic Management Journal*, 23, 997–1018.

Galbraith, J. (1973) *Designing Complex Organizations* (Reading, Mass.: Addison-Wesley Publishing Company).

Galunic, C.D. and Rodan, S. (1998) 'Resource recombinations in the firm: Knowledge structures and the potential for schumpeterian innovation', *Strategic Management Journal*, 19, 1193–201.

Ghoshal, S., Korine, H. and Szulanski, G. (1994) 'Interunit communication in multinational corporations', *Management Science*, 40, 96–110.

Gold, A.H., Malhotra, A. and Segars, A.H. (2001) 'Knowledge management: An organizational capabilities perspective', *Journal of Management Information Systems*, 18(1), 185–214.

Grant, R.M. (1996) 'Towards a knowledge-based theory of the firm', *Strategic Management Journal*, 17, 109–22.

Gupta, A.K. and Govindarajan, V. (1991) 'Knowledge flows and the structure of control within multinational corporations', *Academy of Management Review*, 16(4), 768–92.

Gupta, A.K. and Govindarajan, V. (1994) 'Organizing for knowledge flows within MNCs', *International Business Review*, 3(4), 443–57.

Gupta, A.K. and Govindarajan, V. (2000) 'Knowledge flows within the multinational corporation', *Strategic Management Journal*, 21, 473–96.

Haas, M.R. and Hansen, M.T. (2005) 'When using knowledge can hurt performance: the value of organizational capabilities in a management consulting company', *Strategic Management Journal*, 26, 1–24.

Hair, J.F., Anderson, R.E., Tatham, R.L. and Black, W.C. (1998) *Multivariate data analysis*, 5th edn (Upper Saddle River, N.J.: Prentice Hall).

Haleblian, J. and Finkelstein, S. (1999) 'The influence of organizational acquisition experience on acquisition performance: A behavioral learning perspective', *Administrative Science Quarterly*, 44(1), 29–56.

Hansen, M.T. and Løvås, B. (2004) 'How do multinational companies leverage technological competencies? Moving from single to interdependent explanations', *Strategic Management Journal*, 25, 801–22.

Helfat, C.E. (2000) 'The Evolution of Firm Capabilities', *Strategic Management Journal*, 21, 955–59.

Henderson, R.M. and Clark, K.B. (1990) 'Architectural innovation: the reconfiguration of existing product technologies and the failure of leading firms', *Administrative Science Quarterly*, 35(1), 9–30.

Holm, U. and Pedersen, T. (2002) *The Emergence and Impact of MNC Centres of Excellence. A Subsidiary Perspective* (London: Macmillan Press).

Huber, G.P. (1991) 'Organizational learning: The contributing processes and the literatures', *Organization Science*, 2(1), 88–115.

Jaccard, J., Turrisi, R. and Wan, C.K. (1990a) *Interaction Effects in Multiple Regression* (London: SAGE Publications).

Jaccard, J., Wan, C.K. and Turrisi, R. (1990b) 'The detection and interpretation of inter-action effects between continuous variables in multiple regression', *Multivariate Behavioral Research*, 25(4), 467–78.

Kogut, B. and Zander, U. (1992) 'Knowledge of the firm, combinative capabilities, and the replication of technology', *Organization Science*, 3, 383–97.

Kogut, B. and Zander, U. (1993) 'Knowledge of the firm and the evolutionary theory of the multinational corporation', *Journal of International Business Studies*, 24(4), 625–45.

Kogut, B. and Zander, U. (1996) 'What firms do? Coordination, identity, and learning', *Organization Science*, 7(5), 502–18.

Kostova, T. (1999) 'Transnational transfer of strategic organizational practices: A contextual perspective', *Academy of Management Review*, 24(2), 308–24.

Kostova, T. and Roth, K. (2002) 'Adoption of an organizational practice by subsidiaries of multinational corporations: institutional and relational effects', *Academy of Management Journal*, 45(1), 215–33.

Lane, P.J. and Lubatkin, M. (1998) 'Relative absorptive capacity and interorganizational Learning', *Strategic Management Journal*, 19, 461–77.

Leonard-Barton, D. (1988) 'Implementation as mutual adaptation of technology and organization', *Research Policy*, 17(5), 251–67.

Levinthal, D.A. and March, J.G. (1993) 'The Myopia of Learning', *Strategic Management Journal*, 14, 95–112.

Levitt, B. and March, J.G. (1988) 'Organizational learning', *Annual Review of Sociology*, 14, 319–40.

Lippman, S. and Rumelt, R. (1982) 'Uncertain imitability; an analysis of interfirm differences in efficiency under uncertainty', *Bell Journal of Economics*, 13(2), 418–38.

Marquardt, D.W. (1970) 'Generalized inverses, ridge regression and biased linear estimation', *Technometrics*, 12(3), 591–612.

Marquardt, D. W. (1980) 'A critique of some ridge regression methods: Comment', *Journal of the American Statistical Association*, 75(369), 87–91.

McEvily, S.K., Eisenhardt, K.M. and Prescott, J.E. (2004) 'The global acquisition, leverage, and protection of technological competencies', *Strategic Management Journal*, 25, 713–22.

Mudambi, R. (2002) 'Knowledge management in multinational firms,' *Journal of International Management*, 8(1), 1–9.

Nelson, R.R. and Winter, S.G. (1982) *An Evolutionary Theory of Economic Change* (Cambridge, Mass.: The Belknap Press of Harvard University Press).

Pearce, R. (1999) 'The evolution of technology in multinational enterprises: The role of creative subsidiaries', *International Business Review*, 8(2), 125–48.

Pfeffer, J. and Salancik, G.R. (1978) *The External Control of Organizations: A Resource Dependence Perspective* (New York: Harper & Row).

Pfeffer, J. and Sutton, R. I. (2000) *The Knowing-Doing Gap: How Smart Companies Turn Knowledge into Action* (Boston: Harvard Business School Press).

Podsakoff, P.M. and Organ, D. (1986) 'Self-Reports in organizational research: Problems and Prospects', *Journal of Management*, 12(4), 531–44.

Ray, G., Barney, J.B. and Muhanna, W.A. (2004) 'Capabilities, business processes, and competitive advantage: Choosing the dependent variable in empirical tests of the resource-based view', *Strategic Management Journal*, 25, 23–37.

Reed, R. and Defillippi, R.J. (1990) 'Causal ambiguity, barriers to imitation, and sustainable competitive advantage', *Academy of Management Review*, 15(1), 88–102.

Repenning, N.P. (2002) 'A simulation-based approach to understanding the dynamics of innovation implementation', *Organization Science*, 13(2), 109–27.

Roth, K. and Morrison, A.J. (1992) 'Implementing global strategy: Characteristics of global Subsidiary Mandates', *Journal of International Business Studies*, 23(4), 715–35.

Roth, K. and O´Donnell, S. (1996) 'Foreign subsidiary compensation strategy: an agency theory perspective', *Academy of Management Journal*, 39(3), 678–703.

Sampson, R. (2005) 'Experience effects and collaborative returns in R&D alliances', *Strategic Management Journal*, 26, 1009–31.

Schulz, M. (2001) 'The uncertain relevance of newness: Organizational learning and knowledge flows', *Academy of Management Journal*, 44(4), 661–81.

Schulz, M. (2003) 'Pathways of relevance: Exploring inflow of knowledge into subunits of multinational corporations. *Organization Science*, 14(4), 440–59.

Sharma, S., Durand, R.M. and Gur-Arie, O. (1981) 'Identification and analysis of moderator variables', *Journal of Marketing Research*, 18(August), 291–300.

Spender, J.-C. (1994) 'Organizational knowledge, collective practice and Penrose rents', *International Business Review*, 3(4), 353–67.

Subramaniam, M. and Venkatarman, N. (2001) 'Determinants of transnational new product development capability: Testing the influence of transferring and deploying tacit overseas knowledge', *Strategic Management Journal*, 22, 359–78.

Szulanski, G. (1996) 'Exploring internal stickiness: impediments to the transfer of best practice within the firm', *Strategic Management Journal*, 17, 27–43.

Szulanski, G., Cappetta, R. and Jensen, R.J. (2004) 'When and how trustworthiness matters: knowledge transfer and the moderating effect of causal ambiguity', *Organization Science*, 15(5), 600–13.

Teece, D.J. (1977) 'Technology transfer by multinational firms: the resource cost of transferring technological know-how', *Economic* Journal, 87(346), 242–61.

Teece, D.J. (1986) 'Profiting from technological innovation: implications for integration, collaboration, licensing and public policy', *Research* Policy, 15(6), 285–305.

Tsai, W. (2002) 'Social structure of "coopetition" within a multiunit organization: coordination, competition, and intraorganizational knowledge sharing', *Organization Science*, 13(2), 179–90.

Tsai, W. (2004) 'Knowledge transfer in intraorganizational networks: Effects of network position and absorptive capacity on business unit innovation and performance', *Academy of Management Journal*, 44(5), 996–1004.

Tushman, M.L. and Scanlan, T.J. (1981) 'Boundary spanning individuals: Their role in information transfer and their antecedents', *The Academy of Management Journal*, 24(2), 289–305.

Wilcox King, A. and Zeithaml, C.P. (2001) 'Competencies and firm performance: examining the casual ambiguity paradox', *Strategic Management Journal*, 22, 75–99.

Winter, S.G. (2003) 'Understanding dynamic capabilities', *Strategic Management Journal*, 24, 991–95.

Yelle, L. (1979) 'The learning curve: Historical review and comprehensive survey'. *Decision Science*, 10(2), 302–28.

Zander, U. and Kogut, B. (1995) 'Knowledge and the speed of the transfer and imitation of organizational capabilities: an empirical test', *Organization Science*, 6, 76–92.

Zollo, M. and Singh, H. (2004) 'Deliberate learning in corporate acquisitions: Post-acquisition strategies and integration capability in U.S. bank mergers', *Strategic Management Journal*, 25, 1233–56.

Zollo, M. and Winter, S.G. (2002) 'Deliberate learning and the evolution of dynamic capabilities', *Organization Science*, 13(3), 339–51.

8
Embedded Subsidiaries and the Involvement of Headquarters in Innovation Transfer Processes

Henrik Dellestrand

Introduction

In the multinational enterprise (MNE), headquarters possess a special position compared to other units. It has a responsibility for managing the multinational, and this amongst other things entails a responsibility for making sure that activities are integrated and combined throughout the organization. This opens up the possibility of the individual parts adding up to a greater sum compared to the individual parts alone (Andersson, Forsgren, and Holm, 2005). In some cases, headquarters needs to get involved and support promising subsidiary projects through intervention (Rugman and Verbeke, 2001). In other cases, the support of headquarters is sought by the subsidiaries. Key questions are why, when and how should headquarters intervene in subsidiary level activities? This chapter focus on subsidiary business network embeddedness as a driver behind headquarters involvement in innovation transfer projects.

Business network embeddedness implies both an internal and external perspective for the focal subsidiary (Forsgren, Holm, and Johanson, 2005). This in turn presents the MNE, its subsidiaries and headquarters with a multitude of strategic challenges. Embeddedness is important within the network view, where relationships are assumed to affect the behaviour of actors (Gulati, Nohria, and Zaheer, 2000) and to a large extent contribute to the competitive advantage of both the focal units in a MNE and also to the overall competitive advantage of the organization. By being embedded in different business networks, subsidiaries can provide the MNE with knowledge, ideas and opportunities (Andersson, Forsgren, and Holm, 2002). Embeddedness and networks can be viewed as a strategic resource for firms in general and even more so in the MNE context (Andersson et al. 2002). Granovetter's (1985) writings on embeddedness have paved the way for research in international business on this topic. Subsidiary embeddedness has been conceptualized in different ways in the literature, mainly building on Granovetter's (1985, 1992) classification into relational and structural embeddedness. This chapter focuses on subsidiary relational embeddedness during the development of an innovation and head-quarters involvement during the intra-MNE transfer of the innovation between two subsidiaries. This is an important perspective owing to the fact that subsidiaries engaged in innovation development are connected to relationship partners that can add value and novelty to the development process, thus enhancing the business opportunities and performance. A basic assumption is that the more subsidiaries are involved in embedded relationships, the more the reason for headquarters to involve itself in subsidiary level activities, given that headquarters are interested in performance outcomes. Headquarters can involve itself in many different ways in subsidiary activities, directly or indirectly.

Innovation transfer is arguably a key activity in MNEs adding to the competitive advantage of the organization (Argote and Ingram, 2000; Kogut and Zander, 1992; 1993), and by looking at headquarters involvement in innovation transfer, an activity of key strategic importance for MNEs is captured. Innovation transfer needs to be managed and coordinated within the MNE, thus headquarters become a strategically important player because of its holistic responsibility and formal power within the MNE.

Research related to environmental factors and headquarters involvement in innovation transfer has been scarce, that is, the connection between different kinds of subsidiary embeddedness and headquarters has received limited attention in the literature. This chapter is an effort to bridge this gap in the literature by addressing the question of how the embeddedness of subsidiaries drives headquarters involvement in intra-MNE innovation transfer projects between a sending and a receiving subsidiary. Headquarters involvement is also an attempt to address the call for research about specifying the meta-construct of headquarter attention in that 'research investigating the unique qualities of effective global leaders should broaden its focus to include their concrete attention practices, rather than focusing solely on the particular cognitive tendencies they demonstrate in strategic decision-making activities' (Bouquet, Morrison, and Birkinshaw, 2009, p. 124).

This is achieved here by specifically looking at headquarters involvement in innovation transfer, a key strategic activity in the MNE. The current chapter adds insights into what type of embeddedness configurations can drive headquarters involvement, thus increasing our understanding of drivers behind headquarters involvement in subsidiary level activities. The findings are based on data collected through structured interviews with subsidiary managers involved in 169 specific intra-MNE innovation transfer projects. By looking at specific transfer projects a fine grained understanding of both the hierarchical relationships and embeddedness is achieved in every observation.

The remainder of the chapter is structured in the following way. Next, a theoretical background focusing on embeddedness in MNEs is outlined. This is followed by the hypotheses. Data and methods are presented in the subsequent section which is followed by the results from the statistical analysis. The chapter ends with a discussion of the results and concluding remarks.

Theoretical background

Embeddedness

Embeddedness refers to the fact that economic action and outcomes, like all social action and outcomes, are affected by actors' dyadic relations and by the structure of the overall network of relations. (Grabher, 1993, p. 4)

The concept of embeddedness was introduced by Polanyi (1944) and, following a more current stream of literature (Granovetter, 1985; Grabher, 199; Uzzi, 1996), embeddedness is referred to as the process in which social relations shape economic action. As noted by Uzzi (1996), however, the statement that economic action is embedded in social action is a vague one. By disaggregating the concept of embeddedness into subcomponents, it is possible to achieve a better understanding of what forms of embeddedness shape different areas of economic activity. Zukin and DiMaggio (1990) classify embeddedness in four dimensions (1) structural – that is, consisting of both a structural and relational dimension, (2) cognitive, (3) cultural, and (4) political. Here the focus is on the relational aspects of embeddedness.

Not only is embeddedness a general concept, but this is equally true for relational embeddedness. By deconstructing this dimension, a fine-grained conceptualization of relational embeddedness is attained. This builds on the argument that embeddedness consists of different types of relationships and functional areas (Andersson and Forsgren, 1996; Grandori and Soda, 1995). By looking at relationships in different functional areas, the specific attributes of the relationship can be covered, that is, the activities, interdependence, and adaptation of the relationship and the effects these areas have. Embeddedness can be conceptualized as 'degree of embeddedness' which in turn is a function of the relational attributes between subsidiaries and direct and indirect counterparts, that is, the relationship actors. For example, different relationship partners demand adaptation in different dimensions related to the needs of the embedded actors. These dimensions relate differently to management issues in the MNE because of the difference in perceived importance of the various components of embeddedness for different actors in the MNE network.

Embedded multinationals

The management of relationships is mainly an organizational problem, and in the MNE this problem exists at both the subsidiary and headquarters level. Here the notion of embeddedness becomes important and embeddedness in networks is an important explanatory variable not only for performance, but also for competence development within the MNE (Andersson et al. 2002). Furthermore, firms embedded in networks have a higher survival chance than firms maintaining arm's-length market relationships (Uzzi, 1996). Embeddedness and networks are considered to be strategic resources in general and especially in a MNE context (Dacin, Ventresca and Beal, 1999; Gulati, Nohria, and Zaheer, 2000; Tsai and Ghoshal, 1998).

Cooperation between firms takes place in a business relationship consisting of, amongst others, buyers and suppliers without the need to formalize the relationship (Forsgren et al. 2005). Subsidiary knowledge can come from both internal and external sources connected to the focal subsidiary through exchange relationships building on economic activities and every single subsidiary of a MNE has a unique set of embedded relationships that constitutes its business network (Forsgren et al. 2005; Kogut, 2000). These relationships can act as a power base for the subsidiary where it can exert actual influence in the business network and over headquarters. However, headquarters, as the supreme hierarchical unit, still maintain formal power in the MNE, but the embeddedness of MNE subsidiaries can affect headquarters behaviour related to how it manages the MNE network.

Headquarters' role in embedded multinationals

As found by Uzzi (1999) embeddedness can reduce the need to employ formal governance mechanisms and, as a corollary, resources that would have been used for control or monitoring can be put to more productive alternative uses. This turns the role of headquarters, which is often perceived as a negative and detrimental one, away from the negative picture towards a productive and supportive role where MNE subsidiaries, through their embeddedness, can benefit from headquarters. Headquarters needs to be aware of activities at the subsidiary level and of what type of economic activities the subsidiaries are embedded in. Headquarter attention (Bouquet et al. 2009; Ocasio, 1997) can serve as a starting point for untangling how subsidiaries gets noticed and under what conditions headquarters move from governance mechanisms to value adding activities.

Following Bouquet and Birkinshaw (2008, p. 579), headquarter attention is defined as 'the extent to which a parent company recognizes and gives credit to a subsidiary for its contribution to the MNE as a whole'. Attention is a meta-construct and the literature is relatively silent about what factors make headquarters involve itself and participate in subsidiary level activities besides giving recognition and credit (Bouquet et al. 2009). The attention perspective perceives headquarters in a positive way, not employing governance mechanisms but instead supporting the subsidiary.

Headquarters involvement in activities at the subsidiary level is affected by the heterogeneous environment in which the subsidiaries are located. This heterogeneity not only relates to the geographical dispersion of subsidiaries, but also to the embeddedness of subsidiaries. As argued by Andersson and colleagues (2007), a heterogeneity of relationships exists within business networks and this not only affects how knowledge is gained, but should also relate to why and when headquarters gives attention to subsidiaries embedded in various types of relationships and gets involved in their activities. Network theory tells us that the most important resource of a unit is its relationships. Hence, when considering headquarters involvement, a deeper investigation of different aspects of embedded relationships needs to be considered. This builds on the notion that embeddedness can be seen as a critical resource which affects the relationship between headquarters and the focal subsidiary (Ghoshal and Bartlett, 1990; Pfeffer and Salancik, 1978). Interdependence between firms in a MNE increases the need for coordination, not only at the focal relationship level but also at the overall MNE level. This overall coordinating function is the responsibility of headquarters as the orchestrator of the MNE network. In the MNE, headquarters perform a variety of functions, amongst others, to (a) locate or recognize needs existing in the organization, (b) fill these needs by matching resources to the needs identified, and (c) facilitate the process of resource allocation in the MNE network. Thus, there is a broad spectrum of reasons for headquarters to get involved in innovation transfer activities, as a broker filling needs throughout the MNE.

Hypotheses development

Dependent development and adaptation by the developing subsidiary

Subsidiaries that have cooperated over a long period of time have a great deal of interdependence in the relationship as implied by the relational embeddedness perspective (Andersson, Blankenburg Holm, and Johanson, 2007; Dacin et al. 1999). One way of capturing the embeddedness of subsidiaries is by looking at whether the innovation development process has been dependent on other MNE units. Developing an innovation in cooperation with other units intra-MNE, both headquarters and sister subsidiaries, utilizes many different competences located throughout the MNE network. By having other units integrated into the innovation development process, the innovation draws upon already existing knowledge and competences within the MNE, the corollary being an innovation that is better adapted to the needs and current technological configuration of the organization. This facilitates the search-transfer process in filling knowledge gaps in the MNE. Furthermore, by cooperating intra-MNE during the development gains organizational visibility, that is, many other units that are potential receivers are aware of the innovation (Gulati and Gargiulo, 1999). This reasoning leads to the following hypothesis being suggested:

Hypothesis 1: The more embedded the subsidiary is in relationships with other MNE units when developing innovations, the more headquarters involvement in the transfer process.

The argument leading to the previous hypothesis was focused on a general level of embeddedness. We now turn to dependence and adaptation, from the developing subsidiary's perspective, in relation to a specific counterpart which means that the actors are embedded in specific relationships. If the developing partners are important to each other and have adapted activities to each other they can be described as relationally embedded, that is, there is some sort of 'lock-in' effect owing to the embeddedness. The specificity of the relationship can trigger headquarters attention indicating a potentially arduous innovation transfer process. Due to the specificity of the focal relationship, headquarters may feel the need to coordinate and facilitate the transfer process. If the partners have collaborated for a long time and are 'locked-in', the relationship may be damaged by innovation transfer to someone outside this focal relationship, even if the transfer takes place intra-MNE. Hence, in this case headquarters can play the political game and leverage the burden of cooperating with other units in a transfer project. Additionally, they can exert their formal influence in such a transfer process. In other words, headquarters involves itself in order to facilitate a potentially arduous transfer process and ensures that the innovation becomes transferred. If the counterpart is important, the subsidiaries may not seek out new contacts, or be aware of many other actors owing to the fact that it takes a lot of resources, time and commitment to maintain a deeply embedded relationship. Hence, headquarters can increase visibility and facilitate contact with a receiver since it has many contacts intra-MNE and can add additional resources. This leads to the following hypothesis being postulated:

Hypothesis 2: The more the innovation subject to transfer has been developed in a dependent relationship, the more headquarters involvement in the transfer process.

Counterpart participation and adaptation in relation to the innovation

If the counterpart has participated in the development process of the innovation this signals specificity and relationship uniqueness. The innovation is then more likely to be adapted to the needs of the interacting counterparts and not to the overall needs of the entire MNE. This relationship-specific innovation can be sticky (Szulanski, 1996; von Hippel, 1988), both due to the characteristics of the knowledge, but also owing to the fact that such an innovation may be perceived as important and the motivational disposition towards transfer can be lower from the sending subsidiary's perspective. The receiver can also have a negative disposition towards receiving the innovation, that is, the 'not-invented-here' syndrome (Katz and Allen, 1982). In such a situation, in the hope of facilitating the process, headquarters will more actively involve itself in the transfer process and consequently the following hypothesis is suggested:

> *Hypothesis 3: The more a counterpart has participated in the development of an innovation, the more headquarters involve itself in the subsequent transfer process.*

If the counterpart has specifically adapted its activities in the technological or marketing dimensions, this is a sign of the specificity of the relationship in different activity structures that are connected to the innovation development process. There is a link between the specific innovation and change at the subsidiary level. As previously discussed, this should lead to a negative disposition towards transfer to other units in the MNE, and stickiness. Hence, headquarters will tend to involve itself. However, the activity dimensions should work in different directions since the technological side relates more to the characteristics of the knowledge. This should influence headquarters involvement positively whereas the marketing dimension has less to do with the transfer process and how arduous it can be expected to be. Thus, the following two hypotheses are postulated:

> *Hypothesis 4: The more the subsidiary is embedded in technology-related activities in terms of the counterpart's adaptation, the more headquarters involve itself in the innovation transfer process.*

> *Hypothesis 5: The more the subsidiary is embedded in marketing-related activities in terms of the counterpart's adaptation, the less headquarters involve itself in the innovation transfer process.*

The model

The five hypotheses are summarized in Figure 8.1. In the next section the model is confronted with the empirical data.

Data and methods

The data used in this research was collected between 2002 and 2005 from 62 subsidiaries belonging to 23 MNEs. This study uses data from 169 specific

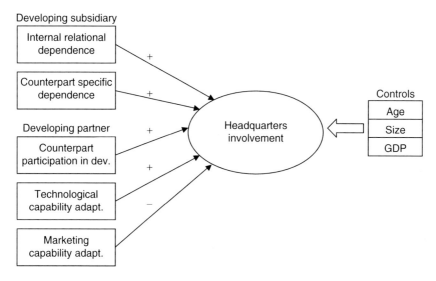

Figure 8.1   The model

intra-MNE transfer projects containing detailed information about the innovation, the development process, the developing subsidiary, the sender-receiver relationship and the transfer process. Different industries are represented, for example, manufacturing, telecommunications, transportation, and the steel industry. The subsidiaries are located across 14 countries in Europe, Asia, and the United States. The number of employees in the subsidiaries ranged from 9 to 6000, with a mean of 589. Innovations in subsidiaries were identified through snowball sampling. The selection criterion for the innovations studied was based on the novelty and value of the specific innovation to the organization, which is similar to the definition of an innovation as 'an idea, practice, or object that is perceived as new by an individual' (Rogers, 1983, p. 11). This selection was done by the innovating/developing subsidiary. The innovations had to have the potential of being transferred. Moreover, they had to have been completed 1 to 10 years prior to the interview. This means that all the innovations were considered as developed at the time of the interview. One potential bias with the sample is that it only contains successful innovations. However, given the question at hand – what role does embeddedness play for headquarters involvement in the innovation transfer process – this bias is almost intrinsic since the transfer of unsuccessful innovations is highly unlikely to occur and would not add anything substantial to the MNE's competitive advantage. The incentive for headquarters to involve itself during such circumstances would be marginal.

The data was collected through face-to-face interviews on site at the subsidiaries. The person deemed most appropriate to answer the questionnaire was interviewed for approximately two hours. The respondents had been involved in the development of the innovation and usually had the role of R&D manager, project manager or subsidiary CEO. Typically, more than one interviewer was involved in the interview process. The questionnaire used had been pretested in two pilot interviews and minor changes were made in order to eliminate ambiguous questions and phrasings as well as to exclude erroneous indicators. By having access to specific managers with detailed knowledge of the innovations investigated, a deeper understanding of the specific innovations could be gained as well as the possibility to discuss the questions with the respondents. This approach gives the opportunity to target the appropriate respondent and detect inconsistencies in the answers during the interview, hence increasing reliability.

Measures

In this study multiple indicators are used in both the dependent and independent variables. This approach minimizes measurement error, is parsimonious and offers a multifaceted representation of the underlying construct (Hair, Black, Babin, Anderson, and Tatham, 2006). As recommended by Cox (1980), 7-point Likert type scales were used in order to obtain the data on innovation transfer in MNEs. Besides estimations by the respondents, other measures such as GDP, size, and age are included as control variables. The constructs were identified in an iterative process where coefficient alphas as well as theoretical issues were considered (Churchill, 1979; Nunnally, 1978). Hence, the constructs developed can be claimed to be theoretically valid and empirically verified. Factor analysis was used in order to confirm the discriminant validity of the constructs.

Dependent variables

Headquarters involvement in the transfer of innovations is one way of giving attention and resources to activities at the subsidiary level. This is a specification and extension to the literature on attention (Bouquet and Birkinshaw, 2008; Ocasio, 1997). In order to capture this phenomenon a three item construct is used. The respondents were asked to indicate, on a scale from (1) totally disagree to (7) totally agree, to what extent:<The MNE HQ has formally instructed you to share this innovation with the counterpart>, <The MNE HQ has themselves been heavily involved in conducting the actual transfer process with the counterpart>, and finally <The MNE HQ has taken complete responsibility for the transfer of this innovation to this counterpart>. The items were summed and averaged to form the dependent variable. Internal reliability of the construct can be deemed as satisfactory with a coefficient alpha of 0.697.

Table 8.1 Factor analysis with varimax rotation

Variable	Components	Communality
Factor 1: Headquarter involvement in the innovation transfer		
The MNE HQ has formally instructed you to share this innovation with the counterpart	0.807	0.652
The MNE HQ has themselves been heavily involved in conducting the actual transfer process with the counterpart	0.874	0.764
The MNE HQ has taken complete responsibility for the transfer of this innovation to this counterpart	0.762	0.580

The indicators for headquarters involvement in the innovation transfer (see Table 8.1) were examined in a factor analysis (principal component with varimax rotation and Kaiser normalization). The factor analysis approach was appropriate since the Kaiser-Mayer-Olkin (KMO) measure of sampling adequacy exceeded the acceptable level (0.6) with a value of 0.648 (Tabachnick and Fidell, 2001). Sufficient correlations existed between the indicators as indicated by Bartlett's test of sphericity, which returned at a 0.001 significance level. The eigen value for the extracted factor was 1.996, and the value for the second factor was 0.627 indicating that only one factor could be extracted from the items used in the dependent variable. This construct explains 66.519% of the variance in relation to the extraction of the sums of squared loadings.

Independent variables

The *internal relational dependence* of the subsidiary during the innovation development is captured with a four item construct where the respondents were asked to indicate on a scale ranging from (1) strongly disagree to (4) neither/nor up to (7) strongly agree, to what extent: <Developing the innovation has been highly dependent on your unit's relationship with other units within your division/business area>, <Developing the innovation has been highly dependent on your unit's relationship with the division/business area headquarters>, <Developing the innovation has been highly dependent on your unit's relationship with other MNE units external to your division/business area>, and finally <Developing the innovation has been highly dependent on your unit's relationship with the MNE headquarters>. These indicators were added up and divided by four to form the scale for the construct. Internal reliability exceeded the recommendations set by Nunnally (1978) with a coefficient alpha of 0.798. This construct is similar to the operationalization used by Holm, Holmström and Sharma (2005) where the relational embeddedness was measured as importance of relationships to specific network actors for the competence development of the subsidiary.

The *counterpart-specific dependence* construct employs three indicators. The respondents were asked to evaluate, on a scale from (1) totally disagree to (4) totally agree up to (7) totally agree whether: <You have adapted your resources and activities very much to this counterpart>, <This counterpart has been important for your business for a very long time>, and <It would be difficult for you to substitute this counterpart with some other company>. This builds on subsidiary adaptation (Andersson and Forsgren, 1996) and importance of the counterparts (Ambos and Reitsperger, 2004; Ambos and Schlegelmilch, 2007). The items were summed and averaged to form the construct. Internal reliability of the construct did not meet the criteria set by Nunnally (1978), with a coefficient alpha of 0.642. However, it is not uncommon to find low alphas when dealing with few indicators and it is in those instances appropriate to check for the mean interitem correlation (MIC). Given the same mean inter-item correlation, the inclusion of additional items will lead to an increase of the cronbach alpha (Carmines and Zeller, 1979). The optimal range for the MIC is 0.2 to 0.4 (Briggs and Cheek, 1986). This construct has a MIC of 0.374 and falls out as distinct from the other in the principal component analysis; see Table 8.2. Consequently, this indicates that counterpart dependence can be included in the subsequent analysis despite having a somewhat low coefficient alpha.

The *counterpart participation in the development* construct is captured using four indicators. This construct builds on the notion that the counterpart has added value to the development process, instead of on how difficult it would be to substitute the counterpart as in the previous construct. The respondents were asked to evaluate the following statements on a scale from (1) totally disagree to (4) neither/nor up to (7) totally agree: <This counterpart has participated closely in developing this innovation>, <This counterpart has brought competence of use for the development of this innovation>, <This counterpart has been important through specifying requests>, and finally <This counterpart has taken important initiatives for developing this innovation>. The four indicators were summed and averaged to form the construct. Internal reliability was under the recommended limit with a coefficient alpha of 0.662 but met the MIC the criteria with a value of 0.332 and was distinct from other constructs in the factor analysis. Hence, this construct is included in the model despite the marginally low coefficient alpha.

Subsidiaries can become relationally embedded in many different dimensions in terms of what kind of activities the embeddedness relates to. In order to capture the *technological capability adaptation* three items are used to form a construct. The respondents were asked to indicate, on a scale ranging from (1) not at all to (7) very much, to what extent:<With regard to the innovation

has the counterparts made specific adaptations in their activities to fit your organization's a. basic research, b. technical development and c. production>. The items were summed and averaged to form the construct. The internal reliability was satisfactory with a coefficient alpha of 0.749. This construct draws inspiration from the conceptualization of a technological embeddedness dimension (Andersson et al. 2002).

Another relational embeddedness dimension connected to subsidiary activities is the *marketing capability adaptation* which is similar to the technological embeddedness dimension, but in the marketing dimension. Three indicators were used to form this construct where the respondents were asked to indicate, on a scale ranging from (1) not at all to (7) very much to what extent:<With regard to the innovation has the counterparts made specific adaptations in their activities to fit your organization's a. marketing and sales, b. purchasing and c. service>. An average was calculated to form the construct and the internal reliability was above the stipulated recommendations with a coefficient alpha of 0.730.

Control variables

In order to control for unobserved heterogeneity, three variables were introduced as control variables in the model. The *size* of the subsidiary is a good proxy for many characteristics, that is, how important the subsidiary is within the MNE but also for the external environment. A large subsidiary may be able to exert influence over other units in the business network (Mudambi and Navarra, 2004). Here, the natural log of the number of employees in the subsidiary is used to capture size. *Age*, measured as the natural log of the number of years the subsidiary has existed is used as a control. Age can be seen as a proxy for the potential of being embedded in different relationships and older subsidiaries may have evolved in the MNE value chain performing different activities compared to younger subsidiaries. The *GDP* of the developing subsidiary's home country as measured in the total GDP in 2005 dollars captures the munificence of the local technological and business environment. This data was gathered from the GGDC Total Economy Database.

Common method bias and multicollinearity

In this study self-reported data is used in many variables and consequently the risk of having augmented relationships due to common method bias is present. In order to control for this, Harman's one-factor test was employed (Podsakoff and Organ, 1986). All independent variables were examined in a factor analysis (principal component with varimax rotation and Kaiser normalization) (see Table 8.2). The KMO-measure of sampling adequacy was used to test if it was appropriate to conduct a factor analysis. The KMO-value exceeded the

Table 8.2 Factor analysis with varimax rotation

Variable	Factor loadings		Communality
Factor 1: Internal relational dependence			
Developing the innovation has been highly dependent on your unit's relationship with other units within your division/business area	0.660		0.455
Developing the innovation has been highly dependent on your unit's relationship with the division/business area headquarters	0.796		0.714
Developing the innovation has been highly dependent on your unit's relationship with other MNE units external to your division/business area	0.769		0.606
Developing the innovation has been highly dependent on your unit's relationship with the MNE headquarters	0.753		0.735
Eigenvalue		2.251	
% Variance		13.240	
Factor 2: Counterpart specific dependence			
You have adapted your resources and activities very much to this counterpart	0.611		0.423
This counterpart has been important for your business for a very long time	0.811		0.668
It would be difficult for you to substitute this counterpart with some other company	0.740		0.585
Eigenvalue		1.802	
% Variance		10.600	
Factor 3: Counterpart participation in development			
This counterpart has participated closely in developing this innovation	0.719		0.539
This counterpart has brought competence of use for the development of this innovation	0.831		0.694
This counterpart has been important through specifying requests	0.550		0.531
This counterpart has taken important initiatives for developing this innovation	0.544		0.427
Eigenvalue		1.881	
Variance		11.063	
Factor 4: Technology capability adaptation and marketing capability adaptation			
With regard to the innovation has the counterparts made specific adaptations in their activities to fit your organizations basic research	0.642		0.726

Continued

Table 8.2 Continued

Variable	Factor loadings	Communality
With regard to the innovation has the counterparts made specific adaptations in their activities to fit your organizations technical development	0.671	0.616
With regard to the innovation has the counterparts made specific adaptations in their activities to fit your organizations production	0.716	0.657
With regard to the innovation has the counterparts made specific adaptations in their activities to fit your organizations marketing and sales	0.820	0.749
With regard to the innovation has the counterparts made specific adaptations in their activities to fit your organizations purchasing	0.770	0.646
With regard to the innovation has the counterparts made specific adaptations in their activities to fit your organizations service	0.577	0.428
Eigenvalue	4.265	
% Variance	25.089	
Total variance explained	59.992	

recommended level of 0.6 with a KMO-value of 0.656 (Tabachnick and Fidell, 2001). In addition to this, Bartlett's test of sphericity returned at a $p < 0.001$ significance level indicating that sufficient correlations exists between the items (Hair et al. 2006). The factor analysis indicated validity of the data and reported good properties. However, in the factor analysis only four factors could be extracted with an eigen value above 1, not five factors as expected. These four factors explained 59.992% of the total variance. In the rotated factor solution, no significant cross-loadings appeared. Following Comrey and Lee (1992), factor loadings below 0.32 can be considered poor since the overlapping variance then is below 10% and a factor loading of 0.45, representing 20% overlapping variance, can be seen as fair. Only one item cross-loaded with a value exceeding 0.45. This was one of the indicators for technological capability adaptation that loaded with a value of 0.528 on counterpart participation in development. Still, this does not exceed 30% of overlapping variance, that is, a factor loading of 0.55 (Comrey and Lee, 1992). Hence, this fact can not be considered to raise any major concerns. However the presence of common method bias can not be excluded, but is not likely to cause any major issues when interpreting the data.

Despite extracting only four factors in the factor analysis, five factors were used in the following statistical analysis owing to theoretical and statistical considerations. Technological adaptation and marketing adaptation were split in different dimensions due to the fact that these are two distinct activities and functions performed by the subsidiaries. Also, the cronbach alpha for the two constructs were satisfactory indicating good internal reliability of the measures.

The variance inflation factor (VIF) was calculated for all the predictor variables in order to check for potential problems of multicollinearity. If multicollinearity exists, this indicates a correlation between two or more of the predictor variables and the dataset may then be biased and the estimated model can show a high R^2 value. No consensus exists in the literature regarding what threshold should be applied for multicollinearity. Common cut-off points for VIF-values are usually set around 5 (Stedenmund, 1992) or 10 (Hair et al. 2006; Marquardt, 1970). All VIF-values were well below five in the analysis. Consequently, there is no reason for multicollinearity to cause any misinterpretation of the predictive ability of the regression model results.

Results

The mean values, standard deviations and the correlation matrix for all the variables are presented in Table 8.3 and the results from the regression analysis are presented in Table 8.4. The current chapter examines the effect of relational embeddedness on headquarters decision and willingness to involve itself in innovation transfer projects between a sending and receiving subsidiary intra-MNE. In order to estimate the models, Ordinary Least Squares (OLS) regressions were used, first with only the control variables and, in the second model, specifications for all the variables were entered. Model 1 did not return as significant with an F-value of 1.373. Neither did this model explain much of the variance with an adjusted R^2 of 0.008. The control variables did not return as significant in this model specification. In the second model specification, the adjusted R^2 was high with a value of 0.466 and this model was highly significant with an F-value of 11.574 ($p < 0.001$) lending support to the overall model specifications.

Hypothesis 1 posited that internal relational dependence would influence headquarters involvement positively. In Model 2, a significant ($p < 0.001$) and positive relationship was found. Therefore, support can be claimed to be found for the first hypothesis. Consistent with Hypothesis 2, the counterpart specific dependence is positively and significantly ($p < 0.01$) related to headquarters involvement in the innovation transfer process. Consequently, Hypothesis 2 is supported. No support is found for Hypothesis 3 since an almost unrelated

Table 8.3 Correlations and descriptive statistics

	Mean	S.D	1.	2.	3.	4.	5.	6.	7.	8.	9.
1. Headquarter involvement in transfer	1.924	1.446	1.000								
2. Size	5.518	1.588	0.013	1.000							
3. Age	3.528	0.903	0.079	0.121	1.000						
4. GDP	9.914	0.144	0.121	0.162*	-0.032	1.000					
5. Internal relational dependence	3.374	1.767	0.633**	-0.081	-0.282**	-0.103	1.000				
6. Counterpart specific dependence	4.208	1.245	0.258**	0.136	-0.191**	0.157*	0.024	1.000			
7. Counterpart participation in development	4.037	0.939	0.126	0.018	-0.042	0.012	0.287**	0.067	1.000		
8. Technological capability adaptation	2.878	1.372	0.095	0.032	0.086	-0.085	0.132	0.302*	0.475**	1.000	
9. Marketing capability adaptation	2.210	1.189	-0.004	-0.078	-0.155*	-0.218**	0.322**	0.124	0.191*	0.627*	1.000

Spearman's correlation

**Correlation is significant at the 0.01 level (2-tailed).

*Correlation is significant at the 0.05 level (2-tailed).

Table 8.4   Results from the regression analysis[a]

Regressor	Model 1		Model 2	
	B	s.e.	β	s.e.
Size	0.064	0.078	0.046	0.072
Age	0.046	0.137	0.274*	0.137
GDP	0.142	0.871	0.180**	0.813
Internal relational dependence	–	–	0.677***	0.071
Counterpart specific dependence	–	–	0.261**	0.102
Counterpart participation in development	–	–	−0.002	0.157
Technological capability adaptation	–	–	0.084	0.156
Marketing capability adaptation	–	–	−0.144	0.150
Diagnostics				
N	169		169	
R^2	0.029		0.510	
Adj.R^2	0.008		0.466	
ΔR^2	0.029		0.481	
F-statistics	1.373		11.574***	

[a] Standardized parameter estimates reported.
$^\dagger p < 0.1$, $^*p < 0.05$, $^{**}p < 0.01$, $^{***}p < 0.001$

and insignificant relationship is found between counterpart participation in the development and the dependent variable. No support can be found for the postulated relationships in Hypothesis 4 and 5. The relationships go in the hypothesized direction, but no significant effects are derived from the statistical analysis. These results will be commented on in the following section.

Discussion

This study set out to investigate headquarters involvement in innovation transfer projects between a sending and receiving subsidiary intra-MNE. Factors related to the sending subsidiary's embeddedness during the innovation development process were assumed to influence headquarters involvement. If a developing subsidiary is dependent on other units within the MNE this will lead to headquarters involvement in the transfer process that the sending subsidiary subsequently gets involved in. Headquarters will get involved if the developing subsidiary has adapted its processes and is dependent on specific actors involved in the development process. These actors can be both internal or external relationship partners, all part of the focal subsidiary's business network. This effect is not as strong as the more general dependence intra-MNE.

Important to be aware of is that this embeddedness is related to the developing subsidiary. These results, that is, Hypotheses 1 and 2, indicates that subsidiaries, by actively participating and adapting their business activities, can trigger an embeddedness configuration in their business network in order to either get, or not get, headquarters involved in subsidiary level activities. These findings can be related to the literature on subsidiary evolution (Birkinshaw and Hood, 1998) which in turn is connected to mandates (Birkinshaw, 1996; Roth and Morrison, 1992) and Centres of Excellence (Holm and Pedersen, 2000). Embeddedness is a driver behind subsidiary level activities and capability development and headquarters involvement can lead to change in the subsidiary mandate, perceived legitimacy by other units' intra-MNE, and consequently enhance the focal subsidiary's power base. Additionally, a subsidiary that is recognized by headquarters as important through its direct involvement can either directly, by headquarters recognition, or indirectly be allocated the role of a Centre of Excellence. Furthermore, headquarters involvement can be perceived as a critical resource that subsidiaries compete for internally. Thus, the embeddedness of subsidiaries is one of the factors that helps them to compete intra-MNE, where the MNE is conceptualized as an internal market for capital and other types of resources (Mudambi, 1999).

No significant effects were found for what the counterpart did in any dimension during the development of an innovation, that is, Hypotheses 3–5. Here, the perspective has moved from what the developing subsidiary actively has done in terms of adaptation and dependence to what the counterpart involved in the development has done. That no significant effect of headquarters involvement was found may be due to the fact that headquarters do not have knowledge of the entire business network, that is, to the relationship partners of a subsidiary, but instead primarily are interested in what the developing subsidiary is doing and what its network configuration looks like. Headquarters may not be able to handle all the information needed, or they may not have access to the entire business network. This makes it more difficult for them to obtain knowledge about both sides of the embeddedness dimension in a dyadic relationship. Put differently, headquarters will find information related to what a subsidiary belonging to the MNE has done more accessible compared to information about what another actor connected to that subsidiary has done. These results are related to both internal and external counterparts. Headquarters knowledge about internal MNE actors is likely to be as high as for the developing subsidiary. However, more features such as the innovation in itself and its underlying characteristics are also likely to drive headquarters involvement in the innovation transfer process. These are interesting issues, not covered by the present study.

The control variables yielded interesting results. It was found that the GDP of the sending subsidiary's home country matters. This can be an indication that headquarters assess the value of the knowledge sent from the developing subsidiary (Björkman, Barner-Rasumussen, and Li, 2004; Gupta and Govindarajan, 2000) where a higher GDP indicates more valuable knowledge from headquarters perspective. Older subsidiaries tend to get headquarters support. This can potentially be explained in that older subsidiaries have had time to develop relationships and become embedded in a business network that provides them with knowledge, ideas and opportunities of value for the entire MNE.

Concluding remarks

This study indicates that subsidiary embeddedness matters for strategic development and power positioning within the MNE. It adds insights into the importance of how to configure the embedded relationships in a business network as well as the importance of communicating this to headquarters, if their support is sought. The study presents managers with an understanding of what type of activities to focus on if headquarters involvement is desired. It does not say anything about what type of relationships should be maintained and stimulated for the development process of an innovation and for how specific innovations add to the competitive advantage of the MNE. It only speaks about what dimensions drive headquarters involvement in subsidiary level activities. By doing so, the study adds to the understanding of intra-MNE resource allocation as well as theories connected to subsidiary evolution.

This study suffers from a number of limitations. First, the data is collected at the developing subsidiary where respondents have estimated the embeddedness of counterparts. Hence, adaptation from the counterpart's perspective is estimated by the developing subsidiary and not by the actual counterpart. However, the respondents should be able to give a fair estimation of the functioning of the focal dyadic relationship. The same limitation is applicable to headquarters involvement. The sending/developing subsidiary has estimated how much headquarters involves itself in the transfer process. However, it could be argued that the estimation regarding headquarters involvement made by the responding subsidiary is a restrictive one and that the estimation concerning embeddedness stems from the network actor with the best knowledge about the focal relationship in connection to the innovation development process, that is, the developing subsidiary. Finally, many of the measurements consist of estimations made by the respondents. The use of perceptual measurements may be problematic due to self-assessment bias and social desirability. This is mediated by the fact that the data is collected from key informants through face-to-face interviews.

Future studies should focus on a better operationalization and distinction between the internal and external network. Embeddedness is a reciprocal concept which entails interdependencies from both sides of the dyadic relationship.

Few studies have captured this reciprocity of embeddedness. Another intriguing question is how network structures can be designed and what factors affects this design process. Furthermore, this study has mainly been concerned with the relational aspects of embeddedness. Future studies could focus on the structural aspects of embeddedness and how this relates to subsidiary power and evolution. One way of approaching the question of embeddedness and headquarters involvement would be through case study research.

Acknowledgements

I would like to express my gratitude to my colleagues within the TIME research group at the Department of Business Studies, Uppsala University, for data collection. I would like to thank Ian Woozley at the Centre for International Business University of Leeds, for comments on earlier versions of this chapter. All errors and omissions are the responsibility of the author.

References

Ambos, B. and Reitsperger, W.D. (2004) 'Offshore centres of excellence: Social control and success', *Management International Review*, 44(2), 51–65.

Ambos, B. and Schlegelmilch, B.B. (2007) 'Innovation and control in the multinational firm: A comparison of political and contingency approaches', *Strategic Management Journal*, 28(5), 473–86.

Andersson, U., Blankenburg Holm, D. and Johanson, M. (2007) 'Moving or doing? Knowledge flow, problem solving, and change in industrial networks', *Journal of Business Research*, 60(1), 32–40.

Andersson, U., Björkman, I. and Forsgren, M. (2005) 'Managing subsidiary knowledge creation: the effect of control mechanisms on subsidiary local embeddedness', *International Business Review*, 14(5), 521–38.

Andersson, U. and Forsgren, M. (1996) 'Subsidiary embeddedness and control in the multinational corporation', *International Business Review*, 5(5), 487–508.

Andersson, U., Forsgren, M. and Holm, U. (2002) 'The strategic impact of external networks: Subsidiary performance and competence development in the multinational corporation', *Strategic Management Journal*, 23(11), 979–96.

Argote, L. and Ingram, P. (2000) 'Knowledge transfer: A basis for competitive advantage', *Organizational Behaviour and Human Decision Processes*, 82(1), 150–69.

Birkinshaw, J. (1996) 'How multinational subsidiary mandates are gained and lost', *Journal of International Business Studies*, 27(3), 467–95.

Birkinshaw, J. and Hood, N. (1998) 'Multinational subsidiary evolution: Capability and charter change in foreign-owned subsidiary companies', *Academy of Management Review*, 23(4), 773–95.

Björkman, I., Barner-Rasmussen, W. and Li, L. (2004) 'Managing knowledge transfers in MNCs: The impact of headquarters control mechanisms', *Journal of International Business Studies*, 35(5), 443–55.

Bouquet, C. and Birkinshaw, J. (2008) 'Weight versus voice: How foreign subsidiaries capture the attention of corporate headquarters', *Academy of Management Journal*, 51(3), 577–601.

Bouquet, C., Morrison, A. and Birkinshaw, J. (2009) 'International attention and multinational enterprise performance', *Journal of International Business Studies*, 40(1), 108–31.

Briggs, S.R. and Cheek, J.M. (1986) 'The role of factor analysis in the development and evaluation of personality scales', *Journal of Personality*, 54(1), 106–48.

Carmines, E.G. and Zeller, R.A. (1979) *Reliability and Validity Assessment* (Beverly Hills, Calif.: Sage).

Churchill, G.A.J. (1979) 'A paradigm for developing better measures of marketing constructs', *Journal of Marketing Research*, 16(1), 64–73.

Comrey, A.L. and Lee, H.B. (1992) *A First Course in Factor Analysis*, 2nd ed. (Hillsdale, N.J.: Lawrence Earlbaum Associates).

Cox, E.P. (1980) 'The optimal number of response alternatives for a scale: A review', *Journal of Marketing Research*, 17(4), 407–22.

Dacin, T.M., Ventresca, M.J. and Beal, B.D. (1999) 'The embeddedness of organizations: dialogue & directions', *Journal of Management*, 25(3), 317–56.

Forsgren, M., Holm, U. and Johanson, J. (2005) *Managing the Embedded Multinational* (Cheltenham, U.K.: Edward Elgar Publishing).

Ghoshal, S. and Bartlett, C. (1990) 'The multinational corporation as an interorganizational Network', *Academy of Management Review*, 15(4), 603–25.

Grabher, G. (1993) *The Embedded Firm: On the Socioeconomics of Industrial Relations* (London: Routledge).

Grandori, A. and Soda, G. (1995) 'Inter-firm networks: Antecedents, mechanisms and forms', *Organization Studies*, 16(2), 183–214.

Granovetter, M.S. (1985) 'Economic action and social structure: The problem of embeddedness', *American Journal of Sociology*, 91(3), 481–510.

Granovetter, M.S. (1992) 'Problems of explanation in economic sociology', in N. Nohria, and R.G. Eccels, (eds), *Networks and Organizations* (Boston, Mass.: Harvard Business School Press).

Gulati, R. and Gargiulo, M. (1999) 'Where do interorganizational networks come from?', *The American Journal of Sociology*, 104(5), 1439–93.

Gulati, R., Nohria, N. and Zaheer, A. (2000) 'Strategic networks', *Strategic Management Journal*, 21(3), 203–15.

Gupta, A.K. and Govindarajan, V. (2000) 'Knowledge flows within multinational corporations', *Strategic Management Journal*, 21(4), 473–96.

Hair, J.F., Black, W.C., Babin, B.J., Anderson, R.E. and Tatham, R.L. (2006) *Multivariate Data Analysis*, 6th ed. (Upper Saddle River, N.J.: Prentice Hall).

Holm, U., Holmström, C. and Sharma, D.D. (2005) 'Competence development through business relationships or competitive environment? Subsidiary impact on MNC competitive advantage', *Management International Review*, 45(2), 197–218.

Holm, U. and Pedersen, T. (2000) *The Emergence and Impact of MNC Centres of Excellence: A Subsidiary Perspective* (London: Macmillan).

Katz, R. and Allen, T.J. (1982) 'Investigating the not Invented Here (NIH) syndrome: A look at the performance tenure, and communication patterns of 50 R&D project groups', *R&D Management*, 12(1), 7–19.

Kogut, B. (2000) 'The network as knowledge: Generative rules and the emergence of structure', *Strategic Management Journal*, 21(3), 405–25.

Kogut, B. and Zander, U. (1992) 'Knowledge of the firm, combinative capabilities, and the replication of technology', *Organization Science*, 3(3), 383–97.

Kogut, B. and Zander, U. (1993) 'Knowledge of the firm and the evolutionary theory of the multinational corporation', *Journal of International Business Studies*, 24(4), 625–45.

Marquardt, D.W. (1970) 'Generalized inverses, ridge regression, biased linear estimation and non-linear estimation', *Technometrics*, 12(3), 591–612.

Mudambi, R. (1999) 'MNE internal capital markets and subsidiary strategic independence', *International Business Review*, 8(2), 197–211.

Mudambi, R. and Navarra, P. (2004) 'Is knowledge power? Knowledge flows, subsidiary power and rent-seeking within MNCs', *Journal of International Business Studies*, 35(5), 385–406.

Nunnally, J. (1978) *Psychometric theory*, 2nd ed. (New York: Mc-Graw Hill).

Ocasio, W. (1997) 'Towards an attention-based view of the firm', *Strategic Management Journal*, 18(Summer Special Issue), 187–206.

Pfeffer, J. and Salancik, G.R. (1978) *The External Control of Organizations: A Resource Dependency Perspective* (New York: Harper & Row, Stanford Business Books).

Podsakoff, P.M. and Organ, D. (1986) 'Self-reports in organizational research: Problems and Prospects', *Journal of Management* 12(4), 531–44.

Polanyi, K. (1944) *The Great Transformation: The political and economic origins of our time.* (Boston, Mass.: Beacon Press).

Rogers, E. (1983) *Diffusion of Innovations*, 3rd ed. (New York: Free Press).

Roth, K. and Morrison, A. (1992) 'Implementing global strategy: Characteristics of global subsidiary mandates', *Journal of International Business Studies*, 23(4), 715–35.

Rugman, A.M. and Verbeke, A. (2001) 'Subsidiary-specific advantages in multinational enterprises', *Strategic Management Journal*, 22(3), 237–50.

Stedenmund, A.H. (1992) *Using economics. A practical guide*, 2nd ed. (New York: HarperCollins).

Szulanski, G. (1996) 'Exploring internal stickiness: Impediments to the transfer of best practice within the firm', *Strategic Management Journal*, 17(Winter Special Issue), 27–43.

Tabachnick, B.G. and Fidell, L.S. (2001) *Using multivariate statistics*, 4th ed. (New York: HarperCollins).

Tsai, W. and Ghoshal, S. (1998) 'Social capital and value creation: The role of intrafirm networks', *Academy of Management Journal*, 41(4), 464–76.

Uzzi, B. (1996) 'The sources and consequences of embeddedness for the economic Performance of organizations: The network effect', *American Sociological Review*, 61(4), 674–98.

Uzzi, B. and Gillespie, J.J. (1999) 'Interfirm ties and the organization of the firm's capital structure in the middle financial market', in, D. Knoke and S. Grabbay (eds), *Corporate Social Capital* (Dordrecht, The Netherlands: Kluwer Press).

Von Hippel, E. (1988) *The sources of innovation* (Oxford: Oxford University Press).

Zukin, S. and DiMaggio, P. (1990) *Structures of Capital: The Social Organization of the Economy* (Cambridge: Cambridge University Press).

Part IV

Internationalized SMEs, Strategies, and Efficiency

9
Hybrid Competitive Strategies for Achieving Superior Performance During Global Expansion: Small and Medium-Sized Enterprises Originating in SMOPECs

Mika Gabrielsson, Tomi Seppälä, and Peter Gabrielsson

Introduction

The ongoing almost three decade's lasting debate around whether a firm should rely on a 'single' (or pure) generic competitive strategy of either differentiation or cost leadership, or whether a combined 'hybrid' (or dual) competitive strategy should be used is far from being resolved. Porter (1980, 1985) originally postulated that a firm must make a choice between the two or it will become stuck in the middle (Porter, 1985, p. 16). With stuck in the middle he refers to a firm that attempts to achieve both cost leadership and differentiation advantage and as an end result fails in achieving any competitive advantage leading to below-average performance. Researchers have been heavily divided with respect to this issue (Campbell-Hunt, 2000). Researchers that support Porter's view have in fact found empirical evidence of firms applying a hybrid strategy to underperform their rivals that follow either a cost leadership or a differentiation strategy (Kim and Lim, 1988; Aulakh and Teegen, 2000). In contrast, the opposing researchers claim that a combination of differentiation and low-cost position may lead to superior performance (Hill, 1988; Murray, 1988; Miller and Dess, 1993; Spanos et al. 2004). The interest in the SMOPECs can be understood from the view point that tentative qualitative research from leading Finnish and Greek firms indicate that use of hybrid strategy can be highly profitable (Salonen et al. 2007; Spanos et al. 2004). The study, however, suggest that the results of this chapter are particularly relevant for SMEs originating in Finland, Sweden, Denmark, Norway, Greece, New Zealand, Israel and other SMOPEC countries. Hence, in this research we strived to understand better the conditions when hybrid strategies are preferable and what performance implications they may have when compared to single approach emphasizing either cost leadership or differentiation advantage.

Porter (1985, pp. 19–20) recognizes that firms can simultaneously pursue cost leadership and differentiation advantage only under certain specific conditions: (1) when all competitors are stuck in the middle, (2) cost is strongly affected by share or interrelationships, or (3) a firm is pioneering a major innovation. The first condition would refer to an instant when the competitors are not well enough positioned to cost or differentiation advantage and hence the firms can all be stuck in the middle without the risk of someone overperforming the others. This condition hardly holds in the usually highly competitive markets, such as for example the ICT-field, in which SMEs from SMOPECs often compete. The second condition which may explain the use of hybrid strategies of such leading firms refers to a circumstance in which the market leader can afford the 'additional cost' of differentiation due to economies of large market shares or synergies across different business units. The third condition refers to those firms that have recently introduced a new innovation and this condition disappears if not constantly remaining a pioneer.

Other researchers have suggested that this list is not necessarily comprehensive and in fact other factors such as firm size (Wright, 1987), level of market homogeneity (Murray, 1988), and concentration (Li and Li, 2008) may be more important. It is postulated that earlier research has neglected three important factors which may be important in explaining when hybrid strategies are suitable for the SMEs originating in SMOPECs, namely globalization of industry environment, global expansion phase and the resources of the firm. These factors may be assumed to be particularly important for firms originating from SMOPEC due their high reliance on international business. It is anticipated that these undiscovered factors may partly provide an answer to the debate lasting over three decades. Hence, the main research question of this study is as follows: Is hybrid competitive strategy a means of achieving superior performance during global expansion of an SME originating in a SMOPEC country. This can be broken down to two more specific research questions:

1. What is the impact of globalization pressure, global expansion phase and the resources of the SMEs originating in SMOPECs on the selection of hybrid versus single competitive strategies?
2. What are the performance implications of the use of hybrid versus single competitive advantages?

The research is of conceptual-analytical nature taking the perspective of SMEs originating from SMOPEC countries.

Literature review

Globalization pressure

Morrison (1990) characterized a global industry as 'having intense levels of international competition, competitors marketing a standardized product worldwide, industry competitors that have a presence in all key international markets, and high levels of international trade'. Yip (2003) has presented a grouping of industry globalization drivers including (1) market drivers (e.g., customer segments with common needs, global customers, global channels and marketing practices, lead countries), (2) cost drivers (scale, sourcing and logistics efficiencies, differences in country costs, high level of product development costs and change of technology), (3) competitive drivers (globalized competitors, transferability of the competitive advantage, interdependence of trade), and (4) government drivers (global trade environment versus protected markets). Moreover, for many technology- and knowledge-intensive products increasing technological standardization at the beginning of 1990s has been an important trigger for globalization (see, e.g., Gabrielsson and Gabrielsson, 2004). This comprehensive list of factors has been used as the basis for analyzing industry globalization pressure in line with some other recent research that has also found these useful (Hult et al. 2006; Solberg, 1997). In order to achieve sustainable competitive advantage, it is important for firms to assess the degree of their industry globalization pressure, expand their global phase to match this potential, however, within the limits of their resources (Yip, 1989, 2003).

Global expansion of firms

Craig and Douglas (1996) have described global market expansion as an evolution in three phases from the initial entry phase to the local market expansion phase, and further to the global rationalization phase. In this chapter, the term international penetrations is used for the second phase as it illustrates better the penetration within the countries that is important at that phase. Moreover, although the term global rationalization well describes the phenomena in this work, the term global market alignment is used as the name of the last phase, in order to avoid the possible association that the previous international phases have been irrational. The market strategy is expected to change from international to global when entering the global alignment phase and when the company starts to see the target markets as global instead of separate country markets, which leads to alignment of activities across countries. Therefore, as the company globalizes, the market strategy is expected to develop from (1) international market entries and (2) international market penetrations phases towards (3) a global market alignment phase. These three stages have been found to be particularly relevant for the SMOPEC originating firms in several qualitative studies (see e.g. Gabrielsson et al. 2006).

Resources

The resource-based view originating from Penrose (1959) and Wernerfelt (1984) is useful when analyzing the ability of firms to implement a global strategy. According to Barney (1991), firms obtain sustained competitive advantage by implementing strategies that utilize their internal strengths through responding to environmental opportunities, while at the same time neutralizing external threats and avoiding internal weaknesses. The organization's ability to implement the formulated global strategy depends on its resources and capabilities (Yip, 2003, p. 6).

Resources can be defined as the tangible and intangible assets that are tied to the firm. Examples of resources are brand names, in-house knowledge of technology, employment of skilled personnel, trade contacts, machinery, efficient processes, and capital (Wernerfelt, 1984, p. 172). Not all resources are potential sources of sustained competitive advantage. The requirement is that these resources are not available freely within the industry and they are not easy to copy, in other words, they are heterogeneous and immobile. Therefore, to have the potential for a sustained competitive advantage, the resource must fulfil four attributes. It must be valuable for exploiting opportunities or neutralizing threats, it must be rare among the firm's current and potential competition, it must be imperfectly imitable, and cannot be substituted (Barney, 1991).

Resources by themselves are not sufficient. Firms must have the capabilities needed to deploy them. The difference between resources and capabilities is that capabilities aim at deploying and coordinating different resources (Verona, 1999). Some more recent research highlights the importance of dynamic capabilities in achieving competitive advantage (see, e.g., Teece et al. 1997; Teece, 1998). The dynamic capabilities can be seen as the firm's ability to integrate, build, and reconfigure internal and external resources to address rapidly changing environments. Moreover, this approach emphasizes the importance of a firm's internal processes as bases for competitive advantage. (Teece et al. 1997) The extent to which resources may be deployed for alternative uses at low cost, that is, resource fungibility, is important when the company is changing its strategy (Sapienza et al. 2006). Besides the spatial configuration of the entire value chain, including the firm's assets, capabilities and resources, the ability to manage and use these resources effectively is important (Craig and Douglas, 2000). The resources are seen as critical when analyzing the capability of a firm to implement a chosen global strategy and selected competitive strategy.

Competitive advantage and performance

The debate around the implications of the selection of hybrid over single competitive advantage on performance has been inconclusive (Campbell-Hunt, 2000; Li and Li, 2008). Porter (1980, 1985) originally emphasized that the firm has to make a choice between the types of competitive advantage it seeks.

According to him a firm that can achieve and sustain differentiation enjoys above industry performance if its price premium exceeds the extra cost incurred in being unique. The differentiation can be based on the product, the supply system, marketing approach or some other factors. Alternatively, above-industry performance can be achieved if the firm gains overall cost leadership and sells at equivalent or lower prices than its rivals. A firm pursuing this strategy must find and exploit all sources of cost advantages such as economies of scale, access to raw material, proprietary technology or some other factors. Further, Porter warns that a hybrid position is 'a recipe for below average performance' as these firms will compete at the disadvantage compared to the ones that have selected a single generic strategy (Porter, 1985, pp. 12–14). This view has been supported by empirical evidence (see, e.g., Aulakh and Teegen, 2000).

However, other researchers have argued that a combination of differentiation and low cost may be needed for firms to achieve sustained competitive advantage in certain environmental context (Hill, 1988; Murray, 1988; Li and Li, 2008), and this type of a hybrid strategy may lead to success (Li and Li, 2008; Spanos et al. 2004). A study investigating means for achieving superior financial performance in China found that impacts of hybrid strategies and cost leadership strategies on financial performance were higher for foreign firms than domestic firms and this could be explained by the better resource situation of the foreign firms (Li and Li, 2008). The increasing global competition (Yip, 2003) can be expected to require globalizing companies to achieve simultaneously both cost and differentiation advantages to enjoy above industry performance.

In line with earlier research on success in global markets the performance is divided in this research into strategic and financial performance (Zou and Cavusgil, 2002). Strategic performance concerns strategic position, market share and rate of new product introductions of the firm while financial performance includes sales and profitability related components of firm performance.

Theoretical framework and proposition development

The examination of the research question originally inspired by Porter (1985) and later studied by many others (Campbell-Hunt, 2000) of whether hybrid versus single competitive strategies may result in superior performance has lead to the assumption that competitive strategies depend on the contextual environment in which they are implemented. Factors such as industry/market structure (Hill, 1988), home country environment (Brouthers et al. 2000), and differences of domestic versus foreign firms (Li and Li, 2008) have been offered as explanations impacting towards use of hybrid strategies. In this research it is expected that the industry globalization pressure is an important determinant of firms' choice of competitive strategies. The achievement of sustainable competitive advantage requires the firm to develop its geographic scope and diversity of operations and their inter-linkage to match the global market potential within the particular industry (Craig and Douglas, 2000). Typically research has encountered for this by comparing the firms that have only domestic business with those that also have foreign business (cf. Roth and Morrison, 1992). This may not be enough, but instead the earlier examined globalization phases must be encountered for. Moreover, firm resources and capabilities are expected to be critical for achieving a sustainable competitive advantage (Barney 1991) and implementing the chosen strategy (Yip, 2003; Li and Li, 2008). More specifically the building blocks of the developed framework include the globalization pressure (Yip, 2003), firm level global expansion phase (Craig and Douglas, 1996) and resources (Barney, 1991). These are expected to influence on the selection of a single or hybrid competitive strategy. Moreover, it is expected that there is a relationship between competitive strategy and performance of the firm (Porter, 1985, pp. 12–14; Hill, 1988, Murray, 1988; Li and Li, 2008). See below Figure 9.1.

First, the influence of increased globalization pressure on the development of competitive strategy is analyzed. It can be noted that the local environment in which a firm is based also affects its competitive advantage (Marshall, 1981). Porter (1990, 1991) in his diamond model emphasizes that success in distinct businesses is dependent on the country in which they originate from. The source of competitiveness must be found in the firm's home market for companies to sustain competitiveness in the long run. In SMOPEC and other developed countries, this historically has been innovation and differentiated offering. However, companies should selectively tap into sources of advantage in other nations' diamonds to enhance their competitive position.

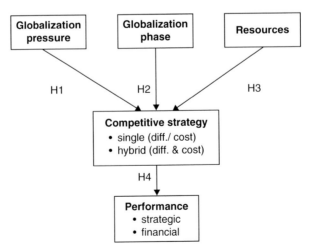

Figure 9.1 Framework: Antecedents of competitive strategy and performance implications

Globalization will have a growing effect on the way firms configure their value chains. According to Dunning (1998, p. 12) it is now generally accepted that 'the different parts of the value chain may be distributed between countries, or regions within countries, according to their knowledge, capital, natural resource and labour content, and to the geography of these inputs'. The multinational corporations increasingly are in the position to use their location choice in enhancing their global competitive advantage (cf. Flores and Aguilera, 2007; Dunning, 2009). This inevitably will mean that firms wherever located will be able to benefit from the location specific benefits available from other countries (cf. Dunning, 2000). For example, Finnish and Swedish firms can benefit from the lower cost level in China, India, and other low-cost countries. The fit between the firm and its environment has been suggested to lead to superior performance (Hofer and Schendel, 1978). Under high globalization pressures in an industry the MNCs have no other option that to match the global cost level, or other locations specific advantage such as innovation capability for that matter. Using this contingency-based reasoning, businesses may be expected to adapt their competitive strategy to the impact of globalization pressure (Roth and Morrison, 1992). This will, under high globalization pressure, eventually lead to increased use of hybrid strategies in which both differentiation advantage and cost leadership are used. Hence, it is postulated as follows:

Hypothesis 1: Companies that have chosen the hybrid strategy have, in average, a higher globalization pressure than the ones that have chosen a single strategy (cost or differentiation).

During the global expansion of firms, they ideally match the globalization potential of the industry (Yip, 2003, p. 21). A business in an industry with low global pressure should have a strategy that is not very global, and a business in a global industry should have a global strategy. In fact, Yip (2003) is claiming that other positions may lead to a strategic disadvantage, because the business either fails to exploit potential global benefits or to respond to local market requirements. Hence, it is expected that the global expansion phase is critical factor when competitive advantages are sought for. In the international entry phase, the attention is on leveraging the domestic competitive position (Douglas and Craig, 1989), be that cost leadership or differentiation advantage (Porter, 1985). However, when engaging in the penetration phase (local market expansion) it becomes paramount to adapt to the needs of particular markets resulting in possibly country adapted competitive strategies, based on either differentiation or cost leadership. However, when entering the global alignment (rationalization) phase the efficiency concerns will become central but also marketing strategies that meet the specific needs of the global target segments must be established (Douglas and Craig, 1989). At the global phase the requirements of an MNC is to be both globally integrative and locally adaptive (Bartlett and Ghoshal, 1987; Doz, 1986; Heenan and Perlmutter, 1979, Yip, 2003). Global integration brings scale, synergy and other cost benefits, whereas local adaptation is required for enhanced differentiation. Based on the above examination we postulate that Porter's (1985) warning of the use of hybrid competitive strategy may at most be valid for the purely domestically operating firm. But, during the advancement of global expansion and latest at the global alignment phase a necessity to apply a hybrid competitive strategy will arise. Hence, it is proposed as follows:

Hypothesis 2: Companies that have chosen the hybrid strategy are, in average, in a more advanced global phase than the ones that have chosen a single strategy (cost or differentiation).

The resource-based view originating from Penrose (1959) and Wernerfelt (1984) is useful when the firm competitive strategies are considered. The resource-based view argues that there is a connection between firm resources, capabilities, and competitive advantage (Grant, 1991; Gabrielsson et al. 2008). Resources can be defined as tangible and intangible assets that are tied to the firm. These include such as (A) physical resources consisting of plants and equipment, (B) financial resources, or (C) intangible assets such as brands (cf. Chatterjee and Wernerfelt 1991). However, the key requirements of resources for sustained competitiveness are that they are valuable, rare, nonimitable, and nonsubstitutable (Barney, 1991). Implementing a single or hybrid competitive strategy by a firm operating in foreign markets requires sufficient resources and competences (Li and Li, 2008). However, since both cost leadership and differentiation advantages require distinctive resources it may be postulated that a hybrid competitive strategy is resource wise the most demanding one. Hence, the following hypothesis:

Hypothesis 3: Companies that have chosen the hybrid strategy have, in average, more key resources than the ones that have chosen a single strategy (cost or differentiation).

Next we turn into discussing the influence of competitiveness on performance. As discussed the effectiveness of a single or hybrid competitive strategy is dependent on the contextual environment in which they are implemented (Campbell-Hunt, 2000; Murray, 1988; Li and Li, 2008). Here, it is emphasized that when Porter (1985, p. 16) concluded that attainment of hybrid approach is 'a recipe for below average performance', he was basing it on examples of mostly U.S. firms with limited exposure to foreign business. When considering the small and medium-sized firms originating from a SMOPEC country, the conditions are very different. The firms are often highly international and often global. Based on the discussion above about the globalization pressure (Yip, 2003), global expansion (Douglas and Craig, 1989) and the key resources for sustained performance (Barney, 1991) it becomes evident that hybrid competitive strategies are actually not expected to underperform as Porter (1985) claimed, but as matter of fact be the only recipe for performing well. The SMOPEC originated firms are operating in a highly competitive global market, in which hybrid strategy is often required to win the competition. Differentiation strategy enables charging higher prices, while cost leadership provides lowest cost structure in the industry. Thus, if the firm successfully achieves both differentiation and cost advantage a higher performance can be expected. This is of course a strong statement that is subject to empirical verification. The examination is suggested to be divided into two separate hypotheses in order to examine whether this holds for both strategic performance and financial performance (Cavusgil and Zou, 1994).

Hypothesis 4a: Companies that have chosen the hybrid strategy have, in average, a better strategic performance than the ones that have chosen a single strategy (cost or differentiation).

Hypothesis 4b: Companies that have chosen the hybrid strategy have, in average, a better financial performance than the ones that have chosen a single strategy (cost or differentiation).

Conclusions

A long-lasting debate has been ongoing whether it is preferable to select a single competitive advantage based on either differentiation or cost leadership (Porter, 1980; 1985; Aulakh et al. 2000) or a hybrid competitive strategy (Hill, 1988; Murray, 1988; Li and Li, 2008). Earlier research has indicated that contextual factors may influence the selection of strategy (Hill, 1988). This research has argued that the global industry pressure (Yip, 2003), global expansion phase of the firm (Craig and Douglas, 1996) and the key resources (Barney, 1991) influence the selection of single versus hybrid competitive strategy. Moreover, it was asserted that hybrid strategy may have better strategic and financial performance than a single strategy, which is contrary to Porter's (1980, 1985) argument of being 'stuck in the middle'.

This chapter has suggested four hypotheses, which are asserted to be particularly important for SMEs originating in SMOPEC countries. It would be interesting to study to what extent these hypotheses hold in different industries and country settings. Based on this chapter, the managers must carefully analyze globalization pressure in the environment, the phase of the global development of the company and the resource situation of the company, and based on that select the competitive strategy.

References

Aulakh, P.S., Kotabe, M. and Teegen, H. (2000) 'Export strategies and performance of firms from emerging economies: evidence from Brazil, Chile, and Mexico', *Academy of Management Journal*, 43(3), 342–61.

Barney, J.B. (1991) 'Firm resources and sustained competitive advantage', *Journal of Management*, 17(1), 99–120.

Bartlett, C.A. and Ghoshal, S. (1987) 'Managing across borders: New strategic requirements', *Sloan Management Review*, Summer, 7–17.

Brouthers, L.E., Werner, S. and Matulich, E. (2000) 'The influence of Triad Nations' environments on price-quality product strategies and MNC performance', *Journal of international Business Studies*, 31(1), 39–62.

Campbell-Hunt, C. (2000) 'What have we learned about generic competitive strategy? A meta-analysis', *Strategic Management Journal*, 21, 127–54.

Cavusgil, T.S. and Zou, S. (1994) 'Marketing strategy-performance relationship: An investigation of the empirical link in export market ventures', *Journal of Marketing*, 58(1), 1–21.

Chatterjee, S. and Wernerfelt, B. (1991), 'The link between resources and type of diversification: Theory and evidence', *Strategic Management Journal*, 12, 33–48.

Craig, C.S. and Douglas, S.P. (1996) 'Developing strategies for global markets: An Evolutionary Perspective', *The Columbia Journal of World Business*, 31(1), 71–81.

Craig, C.S. and Douglas, S.P. (2000) 'Configural advantage in global markets', *Journal of International Marketing*, 8(1), 6–26.

Douglas, S.P. and Craig, C.S. (1989) 'Evolution of global marketing strategy: Scale, scope and synergy', *Columbia Journal of World Business*, Fall, 47–59.

Doz, Y.L. (1986) *Strategic Management in Multinational Companies* (Oxford: Pergamon Press).

Dunning, J.H. (1998) 'Location and the multinational enterprise: A neglected factor?', *Journal of International Business Studies*, 29(1), 45–66.

Dunning, J.H. (2000) 'The eclectic paradigm as an envelope for economic and business theories of MNE activity', *International Business Review*, 9, 163–90.

Dunning, J.H. (2009) 'Location and the multinational enterprise: John Dunning's thoughts on receiving the *Journal of International Business Studies* 2008 Decade Award', *Journal of International Business Studies*, 40(1), 20–34.

Flores, R.G. and Aguilera, R.V. (2007) 'Globalization and location choice: an analysis of US multinational firms in 1980 and 2000', *Journal of International Business Studies*, 38(7), 1187–1210.

Gabrielsson, P. and Gabrielsson, M. (2004) 'Globalising internationals: Business portfolio and marketing strategies in the ICT field', *International Business Review*, 13 (6), 661–84.

Gabrielsson, P., Gabrielsson, M., Darling, J. and Luostarinen, R. (2006) 'Globalizing internationals: Product strategies of ICT manufacturers', *International Marketing Review*, 23 (6), 650–71.

Gabrielsson, M., Gabrielsson, P., Al-Obaidi, Z. and Salimäki, M. (2008) 'Firm response strategies under globalization impact in high-tech and knowledge intensive fields', *The Finnish Journal of Business Economics*, 1/2008, 9–32.

Grant, R.M. (1991) 'The resource-based theory of competitive advantage: Implications for strategy formulations', *California Management Review*, 33(3), 114–35.

Heenan, D.A. and Perlmutter, H.V. (1979) *Multinational Organization Development* (USA : Addison-Wesley Publishing Company, Inc.).

Hill, C.W.L. (1988) 'Differentiation versus low cost or differentiation and low cost: a contingency framework', *Academy of Management Review*, 13(3), 401–12.

Hofer, C.W. and Schendel, D. (1978) *Strategy Formulation: Analytical Concepts* (St Paul, Minn.: West Publishing Co).

Hult, G.T.M., Cavusgil, S.T., Deligonul, S., Kiyak, T. and Lagerström, K. (2006) 'What drives performance in globally focused marketing organizations? A three-country study', *Journal of International Marketing*, 15(2), 58–85.

Kim, L. and Lim, Y. (1988) 'Environment, generic strategies, and performance in a rapidly developing country: a taxonomic approach', *Academy of Management Journal*, 31(4), 802–27.

Li, C.B. and Li, J.J. (2008) 'Achieving superior financial performance in China: Differentiation, cost leadership, or both?', *Journal of International Marketing*, 16(3), 1–22.

Marshall, A. (1981) *Principles of Economics* (London: Macmillan).

Miller, A. and Dess, G.G. (1993) 'Assessing Porter's (1980) model in terms of its generalizability, accuracy and simplicity', *Journal of Management Studies*, 30(4), 553–85.

Morrison, A.J. (1990) *Strategies in Global Industries: How U.S. Business Compete* (Westpoint, Conn.: Quorum Books).

Murray, A.I. (1988) 'A contingency view of Porter's generic strategies', *The Academy of Management Review*, 13(3), 390–99.

Penrose, E.T. (1959) *The Theory of the Growth of The Firm* (Oxford: Basil Blackwell).

Porter, M.E. (1980) *Competitive strategy* (New York: Free Press).

Porter, M.E. (1985) *Competitive Advantage: Creating and Sustaining Superior Performance* (New York: The Free Press).

Roth, K. and Morrison, A.J. (1992) 'Business-level competitive strategy: S Contingency link to Internationalization', *Journal of Management*, 18(3), 473–87.

Salonen, A., Gabrielsson, M., Kilpinen, P., Paukku, M. and Wren, J. (2007) 'The impact of globalization on firm generic competitive strategy', Academy of International Business (AIB) UKI Conference, London 13–14 April.

Sapienza, H.J., Autio, E., George, G. and Zahra, S. (2006) 'A capabilities perspective on the effects of early internationalization on firm survival and growth', *Academy of Management Review*, 31(4), 914–33.

Solberg, C.A. (1997) 'A framework for analysis of strategy development in globalizing markets', *Journal of International Marketing*, 5(1), 9–30.

Spanos, Y.E., Zaralis, G. and Lioukas, S. (2004) 'Strategy and industry effects on profitability: evidence from Greece', *Strategic Management Journal*, 25, 139–65.

Teece, D.J., Pisano, G. and Shuen, A. (1997) 'Dynamic capabilities and strategic management', *Strategic Management Journal*, 18(7), 509–33.

Teece, D.J. (1998) 'Capturing value from knowledge assets: The new economy, markets for know-how, and intangible assets', *California Management Review*, 40(3), 55–79.

Verona, G. (1999) 'A resource-based view of product development', *Academy of Management Review*, 24(1), 132–42.

Wernerfelt, B. (1984) 'A resource-based view of the firm', *Strategic Management Journal*, 5, 171–80.

Wright, P. (1987) 'Research notes and communications, a refinement of Porter's strategies', *Strategic Management Journal*, 8, 93–101.

Yip, G.S. (1989) 'Global strategy...in an world of nations?', *Sloan Management Review*, 29 (Fall), 29–41.

Yip, G.S. (2003) *Total Global Strategy II* (Upper Saddle River, N.J.: Pearson Education).

Zou, S. and Cavusgil, S.T. (2002) 'The GMS: A broader conceptualization of global marketing strategy and its effect on firm performance', *Journal of Marketing*, 66(4), 40–56.

10
Standardization versus Adaptation of the Marketing Mix Strategy in SME Exports

Jorma Larimo and Minnie Kontkanen

Introduction

The role of foreign sales in the operations of companies has long attracted interest, and there is an increasing interest in the strategies used by companies in their foreign marketing. One of the key focus areas has been the interest in the degree of standardization versus adaptation of various international marketing mix elements. During the past 40 years, there have been numerous studies focussing on the general question of whether to standardize or adapt in international marketing strategy (Ryans, Griffith, and White 2003). The more specific questions of what would be the antecedents for the degree of standardization against adaptation, and whether a standardized or an adapted international marketing strategy leads to better performance, have also attracted research. However, this research is still criticized for lacking a strong underlying theoretical framework (Ryans et al. 2003). Thus, earlier literature has not contributed a clear theoretical approach explaining the basis on which the various antecedents for the degree of standardization or adaptation are developed.

Even though the latest studies have used a multidimensional construct rather than a generalized construct 'standardized / adapted marketing strategy', the main interest has so far focussed on the communication and product dimensions of the marketing mix. Although recently other marketing mix dimensions have also received increasing attention, the number of studies exploring the degree of standardization of all four marketing mix elements at the same time is still limited. However, in order to increase our understanding of the relative 'importance' of each key marketing mix element, studies incorporating all the four elements into a single study are needed.

Another feature of the research so far has been that it has largely focused on the strategies used by multinational corporations (MNCs) in their international marketing. Research focusing on the marketing strategies of small and medium-sized companies (SMEs) has been far more limited, even though a significant number of SMEs have commenced foreign sales during the past 30 years, and several of them are highly dependent on the success of their foreign marketing strategies. Finally, most studies have so far focussed on the strategies used by firms from the United States or from big Western European economies, and strategies used by firms from smaller countries have received much less attention.

The goal of this study is to use the resource-based view (RBV) as a basis to analyze the impact of certain firm, management, product, market, and customer factors on the extent to which standardization or adaptation is applied to the marketing mix elements by SMEs in their foreign sales. Specifically, the relationship between antecedents and the degree of standardization and/or adaptation is based on arguments for the transferability of competitive advantage. In its most common definition, SMEs are considered to be those firms which employ fewer than 250 staff and have an annual turnover not exceeding 50 million euros (Commission 2003).

The contribution of this piece is in incorporating RBV in international marketing mix strategy, and thus offering arguments for the impact of antecedents on the degree of standardization or adaptation. In addition, the study contributes new insights into the influence of firm-, managerial-, and customer-related antecedents on the degree of standardization or adaptation of the marketing mix strategy, and also in the strategies used by SMEs from a small, developed market economy. The empirical part of the study will focus on the strategies used by 188 Finnish SMEs.

The structure of the paper is as follows: In the second section, we will conduct a general overview of the literature related to the antecedents of standardization and adaptation of the marketing mix and the resource-based view. In the third section, we develop the conceptual framework, and in the fourth section, the key methodological and sample related issues are discussed. The fifth section presents the key results of the study. Finally, The sixth section presents a discussion and that is followed by the conclusions of the study.

General literature review

The review by Theodisou and Leonidou (2003: 148) indicated that the role of various antecedents in international marketing standardization and adaptation had been explored in 25 studies, of which 15 provided evidence of a direct link between antecedents and international marketing standardization and adaptation. The number of factors examined varied significantly across the studies, ranging from 1 to 22, with most focusing on up to 3. Altogether, 50 factors were identified, which were subsequently reduced to 22, based on their substantive conceptual meaning. These can be broadly categorized into seven groups, namely, environmental (four factors), market (four factors), customer (three factors), competition (two factors), product/industry (three factors), organizational (four factors), and managerial (two factors). However, most of the studies lacked a clear theoretical approach explaining why the relationships between various antecedents and standardization or adaptation would exist.

RBV has become one of the most influential frameworks in several research disciplines (Barney, Wright, and Ketchen 2001). Marketing is one of the research fields to which RBV has been applied, but marketing scholars have applied it to only a limited extent. However, applying RBV can refine and extend the traditional frames of analysis in marketing (Srivastava, Fahey, and Christensen 2001). In RBV, strategy is understood as a way of exploiting a firm's resources and developing or acquiring new resources for the firm to generate economic success (Wong and Merrilees 2007). Because of its focus on developing strategy, RBV offers a theoretical approach to explain why certain factors may affect the degree of standardization and/or adaptation employed in marketing mix strategy. RBV sees resources as sources of competitive advantage. However, in order to maintain the potential of competitive advantage, a firm's resources must be valuable, rare, imperfectly imitable, and not having strategically equivalent substitutes (Barney 1991). Competitive advantage, on the other hand, may be defined as 'the strengths of a firm relative to the competition in a specific arena or in a particular context' (Viswanathan and Dickson 2007: 52). However, for the decision whether to standardize or adapt the international marketing mix strategy instead of just identifying the potential sources of competitive advantage, it is even more important to consider whether the competitive advantage can be transferred from one market to another. Viswanathan and Dickson (2007) argue that similarity in the nature of competitive advantage in different markets would mean that competitive advantage is transferable and thus would encourage a higher degree of standardization of marketing mix strategies. They identify three conditions that are prerequisites for competitive advantage to be transferable. These are (1) core competence, (2) market power, and (3) similarity of market. Thus, if a firm possesses core competences, has high degree of market power and is entering into markets which are similar to its existing ones, it should be encouraged to use a standardized marketing mix strategy.

Antecedents of the degree of standardization and adaptation of the marketing mix strategy

The following section addresses the impact of five groups of potential antecedents on the degree of standardization or adaptation in the marketing mix strategy. The five groups are factors relating to the firm, to managerial issues, to product, to target market, and to the customer.

Firm-related

Export dependence: There are a limited number of studies exploring the role of export dependence as an antecedent for the marketing mix adaptation level. Calantone, Kim, Schmidt, and Cavusgil (2006) studied the influence of export dependence on product adaptation and found that the more dependent the firm was on exports, the more product adaptation was used. However, other marketing mix elements were not included in the study. Export dependence may play an important role in influencing the decisions to adapt and standardize marketing mix elements. It might be expected that the more critical the role of exporting, the less market power the firm has, due to its dependence on those foreign sales. A low level of market power makes competitive advantage nontransferable and, therefore, firms try to satisfy their customers by adapting the marketing mix elements to fit the potential differences in various target countries. Thus, we suggest that:

> *Hypothesis 1: Firms with a high dependence on export use more adapted marketing mix strategies than do firms with a low export dependence.*

Speed of internationalization: During the past 15 years, one of the key research focus areas in the analysis of exports and internationalization of SMEs has been the impact of the speed of internationalization on the behaviour of firms and the strategies they use (see, e.g., Rialp, Rialp, and Knight 2005). Rapidly internationalized companies – companies making foreign sales within three years of establishment and where export sales rapidly reach an important level (forming at least 25% of the total sales), are often known as International New Ventures, Born Globals, or Born Internationals (ibid.). Some of the key features of these types of companies include: they expand rapidly into several foreign markets; they often use more networking and strategic alliances in their operations than slowly internationalizing firms; and they often operate in high-tech sectors. The reason why firms are able to rapidly expand into several foreign markets is related to the possession of some core competencies. These include tacit knowledge of global opportunities and the capacity to leverage that knowledge in a way unmatched by competitors, as was identified by Peng (2001) in his review of the role of the RBV in international entrepreneurship. Possession of these core competencies makes it possible to transfer their competitive advantage across markets and supports the use of highly standardized marketing mix strategies. Cases in which firms internationalize more slowly and do not possess these core competencies would tend to support the use of more adapted strategies. Thus, we suggest that:

> *Hypothesis 2: Slowly internationalized companies use more adapted marketing mix strategies than rapidly internationalized companies do.*

Number of target countries: Cavusgil, Zou, and Naidu (1993) found that adaptation of positioning and the use of a promotional approach was greater when a product was exported simultaneously to multiple markets, but the opposite result was noted for product elements, in which adaptation was higher when the product was exported to a single market. In addition, no significant differences in terms of adaptation were found for the packaging and labelling elements. Sousa and Bradley (2008), on the other hand, find a negative relationship with the adaptation level of a pricing strategy. Earlier results thus do not provide a clear indication of the relationship between the number of target countries and the degree of standardization. However, we can assume that the more concentrated the sales effort of the company is on a few markets, the less market power the firm has, and thus the conditions under which competitive advantage is transferable would not be met. This leads to the assumption that the lower the number of target countries the more adapted the marketing mix elements will be – because of the lack of transferability of the competitive advantage – leading to the suggestion that:

Hypothesis 3: Firms with a low number of target countries use more adapted marketing mix strategies than firms with a high number of target countries.

Managerially related

Managers' international experience

There are apparently no prior empirical studies directly analyzing the influence of managers' international experience on the adaptation level of marketing mix strategies. On the other hand, there have been some studies exploring the role of firm level international experience, using various measures, in marketing mix strategies. Cavusgil et al. (1993) found a positive influence on a firm's international experience on the adaptation level of product marketing after entry and Leonidou (1996) found, based on descriptive data, that Japanese firms with a longer market presence in the host country used adaptation more extensively in their product strategy than those that were relatively new. On the other hand, the results relating to the influence of experience on product standardization or adaptation were not as clear in a study focusing on small U.S. industrial goods manufacturers by Seifert and Ford (1989). In a study of pricing strategy, Sousa and Bradley (2008), surprisingly, found a negative relationship while Seifert and Ford (1989) found no significant influence. Thus, the results have been contradictory. However, it can be argued that managers' international experience is a potential source of competitive advantage and contributes to the core competence of the firm. In this case, the possession of these core competencies makes it possible to transfer their competitive advantage across markets and supports the use of highly standardized marketing mix strategies. Thus, we suggest that:

Hypothesis 4: Firms with a low level of international managerial experience favour the use of an adapted marketing mix strategy more than firms with a high level of international managerial experience.

Management commitment to international operations

Although there do not seem to be any empirical studies exploring the role of management commitment to international operations in marketing mix adaptations, a study by Koh (1991) gives some indication of the potential influence. Koh explored the relationship between marketing strategy and management motivation in exporting, using *reactive, sustaining,* and *proactive* labels to classify it, and found that motivation was related to the level of export pricing but not to the other components studied in the pricing or in the product areas. In cases in which management was more proactive and committed to exporting, export prices were higher, and so were adapted to foreign markets. However, we can assume that management commitment to international operations plays an important role in marketing strategy through increasing the availability of resources and in terms of the willingness to be involved in an international venture (Wong and Merrilees 2007). Nevertheless, even though management's commitment to international operations can be regarded as a valuable resource, it can hardly be regarded as a rare and hard to imitate type of resource, and therefore cannot be a source of competitive advantage. Thus, it is not related to the core competence of the firm and therefore supports the use of more adapted marketing mix strategies. Thus, we suggest that:

Hypothesis 5: Firms with a higher level of managerial commitment to international operations use more adapted marketing mix strategies than firms with a lower level of managerial commitment to international operations.

Product-related

Quality of the product

In the review by Theodisou and Leonidou (2003), no prior studies exploring the relationship between product quality and the level of adaptation in marketing strategies was found. However, high-quality product can be a source of competitive advantage that may lead to perceived customer benefits and act as an entry barrier to competition; therefore, it would have the characteristics of a core competence as proposed by Viswanathan and Dickson (2007: 53). This would mean conditions under which competitive advantage is transferable are met and support the use of a standardized marketing mix strategy. Thus, it is suggested that:

> *Hypothesis 6: For low-quality products, more adapted marketing mix strategies are used than for higher-quality products.*

Target market characteristics

There are several studies exploring the role export market environment similarity plays in the adaptation of different elements of the marketing mix. Many of them treat the market environment as one variable and do not separate out the influence of individual elements of the environment like political, legal, economic, culture, competition, and customer characteristics (see, e.g., Mengüc 1997; Alashban, Hayes, Zinkhan, and Balazs 2002; O'Cass and Julian 2003; Calantone et al. 2006). However, it is important to understand the role of specific environmental elements in the level of adaptation introduced into the marketing mix strategy. In the following section, we will focus on the potential role of the economic and cultural environments.

Economic size

Leonidou (1996) found that target country-related factors had only a moderate impact on the adaptation of product strategy, with demographic and political-legal factors having the greatest influence and sociocultural and economic factors having the least influence. However, the differences between the scores were very small and the study employs no statistical testing. Michell, Lynch, and Alabdali (1998) studied, among other things, the influence of GNP similarity of target and parent countries on the degree of adaptation and found no influence. Theodosiou and Katsikeas (2001) found support for a positive relationship between similarity in the economic conditions of home and host countries and the degree of standardization in pricing strategy. Thus, earlier empirical results have been contradictory. However, we assume that the more similar the market size and level of development between key target countries and the home market of the firm, the more standardized the marketing mix elements would be, because of the transferability of the competitive advantage. Thus, it is suggested that:

> *Hypothesis 7: Differences in economic size between the target and parent countries lead to more adapted marketing mix strategies.*

Cultural distance

Johnson and Arunthanes (1995) found no significant relationship between cultural differences and actual or ideal product adaptation. Roth (1995), on the other hand, found that the greater the extent of differences in cultural uncertainty avoidance and individualism, the higher was the level of brand image adaptation. However, cultural power distance had no significant influence. Thus, the results have so far been somewhat mixed and quite limited. However, the above-mentioned arguments on economic size also is concerned with the impact of cultural distance between the target countries and home country of the firm. The shorter the distance, the more similar the customer and buyer preferences, media availability, and reactions to communication, amongst other things, and the easier it is to transfer the competitive advantage and use standardized marketing mix elements. The greater the cultural distance the greater the differences, for example, in buyer preferences and buying habits, reactions to communication, and availability and efficiency of various distribution channels. Therefore, the more difficult it is to transfer the competitive advantage, the greater the need for adaptation of the various marketing mix elements. Thus, it is suggested that:

Hypothesis 8: Greater cultural distance between target and parent country leads to more adapted marketing mix strategies than with lesser cultural distance.

Customer-related

Number and type of customers

A limited number of studies has focused on exploring the role of customer related factors on the adaptation level in marketing mix strategies (see, e.g., Cavusgil et al. 1993; Cavusgil and Zou 1994; Theodesiou and Katsikeas 2001). These studies have focussed on studying the influence of product or brand familiarity of export customers or similarity of customer preferences, perceptions, and purchasing behaviour. However, the influence of the number and type of customers has not been studied. As the number of customers in the target country increases, the sales levels also increase, making the target market more important. We might assume that the more important the target market is, the lower is the firm's level of market power and thus competitive advantages are not transferable. This would then lead to adapting marketing mix strategies to fit the specific characteristics in the target country. In addition, the relative adaptation costs are lower when the number of customers in a specific target country is higher. Thus, it is suggested that:

Hypothesis 9: A greater number of customers in the target country leads to a preference for more adapted marketing mix strategies than in target countries with fewer customers.

Usually it is thought that the customers are local (other industrial buyers or local consumers). In consumer goods sectors, the customers are usually totally or mainly local customers – although there are some exceptions, such as the

Standardization versus Adaptation 201

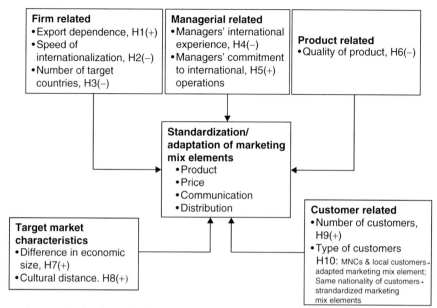

+ = increase in the dependent factor, increases the probability to use more
adapted marketing mix elements

Figure 10.1   A summary of the conceptual framework

mobile phone sector. However, in the industrial product sectors, there may be
a greater variation in customer types. Companies may follow their customers
from the domestic market to the foreign markets. In these cases, one could
expect that the level of adaptation in the various marketing mix elements
would be lower than in cases in which the buyers are totally or mainly target
country–based customers or third-country multinationals that are not customers of the exporting firm in their home markets, making it more difficult
to transfer the competitive advantage. Thus, it is suggested that:

> *Hypothesis 10: Where target customers are mainly MNCs or locals, firms will opt
> for more adapted marketing mix strategies than when the customers are mainly of
> the same nationality as in the firm's home country.*

In Figure 10.1, a summary of the conceptual framework, is presented.

Methodology, data collection, and sample

The empirical part of the study is based on a two-step mail survey complemented with a telephone survey, the process being completed between June and
November 2006. The survey focused on the motives for exporting, development

of the export business, export strategies including standardization versus adaptation, export performance, and future export prospects. The target group derives from two sources: a Finnish company register (the Blue Book company register) and also the respondents to an earlier survey focussing on the export and internationalization behaviour of Finnish SMEs, conducted by the leading author of the article some years earlier (in 2002).

The selection from both sources was based on five criteria, in that the firm: (a) had 10–249 employees, (b) had an annual turnover of less than 50 million euros (c) demonstrated regular export activity, (d) operated in the manufacturing or ICT sectors, and (e) had been established between 1980 and 2000, or between 1960 and 1999 if the firm had contributed to the earlier survey. These criteria produced the target group of 1481 firms that were sent a four-page-long questionnaire. In firms having fewer than 50 employees, the survey was sent to the managing director of the firm, and in bigger companies to the person in charge of international operations.

Fifty-two of the questionnaires were returned due to the company ceasing to exist or being otherwise untraceable, reducing the number of target firms to 1429. A total of 269 firms responded to the questionnaire, indicating an effective response rate of 18.8%. The rate is relatively low but clearly higher than in several large-scale surveys where response rates of 10% or even less have been reported (see, e.g., Menon, Bharadwaj, and Howell 1996).

For this study, two additional criteria were set: the share of export had to have been 10% or more in 2005, and the company should have had two or more export target countries in 2005. These additional conditions reduced the sample size to 188 companies. As discussed in the second section, the average sample size in standardization versus adaptation studies has been below 100. Thus, the sample size in this study is clearly above the average. The statistical methods used in the study are the *t*-test and ANOVA test. The operationalization of the key variables and descriptive sample statistics is presented in Table 10.1.

The mean number of employees was 55 (median 38), the mean total sales around 12 million euros (median 7.0), and the mean share of exports was 60% of total sales (median 60.0). Companies had on average 16.7 target countries (median 12.0) for exports in 2005. The exports were relatively concentrated because the share taken by the three main target countries – Sweden, Germany, and Russia – was on average 44% (median 40.0) of the total exports.

Results of the study

Before going through the results related to the hypotheses, it is worth considering how the four marketing mix elements differ in their degree of standardization and/or adaptation. Based on the means, presented in Table 10.2, the extent to which standardization is used in the product, communication,

Table 10.1 Operationalization of the variables and descriptive statistics of the sample (Number of firms/%)

FIRM SIZE: Total number of employees in 2005								
Mean 55.3	10–49:	115	61.1%		50–249:	73	38.9%	
EXPORT AGE: 2005 minus the year of starting exports								
Mean 14.23	1–5 years:	23 12.4%	6–14 years:	89 48.1%	15-years:	73 39.5%		
SPEED OF INTERNATIONALIZATION: Starting and share of exports within three years from establishment								
Classification 1	No exports:	69 (38.1%)	Exports:	112 (61.9%)				
Classification 2	No exports or share below 25%	114 (63.0%)	Exports at least 25%	67 (38.1%)				
EXPORT DEPENDENCE: Share of exports from total sales in 2005								
Mean 60.2	10–24:	12 (6.4%)	25–49:	55 (29.4%)				
	50–74	57 (30.5%)	75–99:	63 (33.7%)				
INTERNATIONAL MANAGERIAL EXPERIENCE: International experience of the management (scale 1=very low 5=very high)								
Mean 3.79	Very low – Medium	50 (22.2%)	High – Very High	112 (77.8%)				
INTERNATIONAL MANAGERIAL COMMITMENT: Managements commitment to the foreign business (scale 1=very low – 5=very high)								
Very Low – Medium	24 (14.6%)	High – Very High	140 (85.4%)					
PRODUCT QUALITY: Rate how well the following statement describes your company: Customers regard our products as a of higher quality than our competitors product (scale 1=very poorly ... 5=very well)								
Mean 3.95	Describes very poorly – medium	39 (19.8%)	Describes well– very well	138 (80.2%)				

TYPE OF CUSTOMERS:	
Same important customer or your main customers are Finnish companies	7 (3.7%)
Mainly multinational companies	27 (14.4%)
Mainly local companies	108 (57.4%)
Different types of customers	46 (24.5%)

NUMBERS OF CUSTOMERS IN THE MAIN MARKETS:								
One	38 (20.2%)	2–5	50 (226.6%)	6–19	27 (14.4%)	20–	18 (9.6%)	Variation between countries	55 (29.3%)

NUMBER OF TARGET COUNTRIES: Number of target countries in 2005						
Mean 16.7	2–9:	85 (45.9%)	10–19:	56 (30.3%)	20–:	44 (23.8%)

MAIN TARGET COUNTRIES OF EXPORTS: Both two main target countries belong to these groups				
Economic size G6 countries (Canada, USA, UK, France, Germany, Italy):	Yes	23	No	165
Region	Yes	18	No	170
Nordic countries (Sweden, Denmark, Norway) CEE (Central-Eastern and Eastern Europe):	Yes	13	No	175
Non-European (exe. Canada, USA & Australia):	Yes	2	No	186
Cultural distance (Cultural distance from Finland based on Hofstede's four dimensions and score values (Hofstede 1980 & 2001) and Kogut and Singh index) (1998)				
Culturally close (Distance value < 1.0 from Finland); Nordic countries + Canada, Estonia, Germany, the Netherlands	Yes	41	No	147
Culturally more distant (Distance value ≥ 1.0); other countries	Yes	25	No	163
DEGREE OF STANDARDIZATION VS. ADAPTATION: Total degree of standardization of product/price/communication/distribution activities in the main target countries of exports (scale 1=fully standardized ... 5=fully adapted)				

and distribution strategies is very evenly matched. Pricing strategy, however, is more often adapted than the other marketing mix elements. Nevertheless, analyzing those firms that have fully standardized or fully adapted the marketing mix elements, we can observe more differences. For product and communication elements, a fully standardized strategy (14.5% and 13.9%) has been more commonly employed than a fully adapted strategy (8.9% and 7.5%). On the other hand, for the pricing element, full adaptation has been more common (16.9%) than full standardization (7.9%). For distribution, there is not a great difference in the use of full standardization (9.8%) and full adaptation (11.6%). Thus, the results indicate that product strategy is the most standardized and pricing strategy the most adapted marketing mix element.

The following section considers the test results of the firm-, managerial-, product-, market-, and customer-related factors on the adaptation level of marketing mix elements. *T*-test results are presented in Table 10.3, and the ANOVA test results in Table 10.4. The relationships are considered statistically significant when $p \leq 0.10$.

We hypothesized that there would be differences in the level of adaptation employed with the various marketing mix elements based on the following firm-related antecedents: export dependence (H1), speed of internationalization (H2), and number of target countries (H3). However, there were no statistically significant differences, and, thus, the results did not confirm the hypotheses. With the management-related antecedents, we suggested that the level of managers' international experience (H4) and commitment to international operations (H5) would have an influence on the level of adaptation employed in the marketing mix elements. Based on the results, those hypotheses are not supported.

Even though the results are not statistically significant, it is interesting that the use of adaptation in all four marketing mix constituents is highest when the managers have a moderate level of international experience. This may indicate that the relationship is U-shaped instead of linear.

In the case of product-related antecedents, we suggested through Hypothesis 6 that firms use more adapted marketing strategies for low-quality products than for high-quality products. However, the hypothesis was not confirmed. For target market–related antecedents, we hypothesized that differences between target countries and parent country, based on the economic size (H7) and culture (H8), would support the use of more adapted marketing mix elements. The empirical results did not confirm the hypothesis.

Table 10.2 Means and degree of standardization/adaptation of marketing mix elements

Mean and level of standardization / adaptation	Product strategy	Pricing strategy	Communication strategy	Distribution strategy
Mean	3.08	3.42	3.07	3.09
Fully standardized(%)	**14.5**	7.9	**13.9**	9.8
Quite standardized(%)	13.4	12.4	14.5	20.8
Neutral(%)	30.7	26.0	30.1	31.2
Quite adapted(%)	32.4	36.7	34.1	26.6
Fully adapted(%)	8.9	**16.9**	7.5	**11.6**

Table 10.3 Results of t-Tests

	Product strategy			Price strategy			Communication strategy			Distribution strategy		
	N	Mean	t-Value (p)	N	Mean	t-Value (p)	N	Mean	t-Value (p)	N	Mean	t-Value (p)
Product quality:												
Low	37	3,11	0,045	38	3,39	−0,229	38	3,18	0,086	36	3,28	0,610
High	132	3,10	(0,964)	129	3,44	(0,819)	126	3,17	(0,932)	127	3,15	(0,543)
Speed of internationalization Definition 1: loose												
Traditional	66	3,17	0,788	66	3,59	1,540	64	3,23	1,469	64	3,17	0,876
Born global	106	3,02	(0,432)	104	3,33	(0,125)	103	2,96	(0,144)	103	3,02	(0,382)
Speed of internationalization Definition 2: strict												
Traditional	109	3,01	−0,922	109	3,48	0,672	106	3,14	1,039	106	3,07	−0,159
Born Global	63	3,19	(0,359)	61	3,34	(0,503)	61	2,93	(0,301)	61	3,10	(0,874)
Economic size												
G6	94	3,06	0,171	91	3,45	−0,319	87	2,99	0,922	87	3,06	0,401
Others	85	3,09	(0,865)	86	3,40	(0,750)	86	3,15	(0,358)	86	3,13	(0,689)
Cultural distance												
Close	155	3,08	−0,022	153	3,42	0,032	149	3,07	0,126	150	3,07	−0,751
More distant	24	3,08	(0,982)	24	3,42	(0,974)	24	3,04	(0,900)	23	3,26	(0,453)

Table 10.4 Results of ANOVA tests

	Product strategy				Price strategy				Communication strategy				Distribution strategy			
	N	Mean	Std Dev.	F Sig.	N	Mean	Std Dev.	F Sig.	N	Mean	Std Dev.	F Sig.	N	Mean	Std Dev.	F Sig.
No of customers:																
1	36	3.36	1.018	2.861	37	3.59	1.142	2.027	36	3.14	0.188	0.394	36	3.08	0.184	0.378
2–5	49	3.20	1.190	(0.025)	49	3.16	1.161	(0.093)	45	3.16	0.171	(0.813)	45	3.16	0.182	(0.824)
6–19	26	3.00	1.166		25	3.88	0.927		26	3.15	0.227		25	3.24	0.247	
>20	15	3.53	1.125		15	3.20	1.521		16	2.81	0.319		16	2.81	0.292	
Varies	53	2.68	1.221		51	3.39	1.060		50	2.98	0.168		51	3.06	1.103	
Type of customers																
Same or Finnish company	7	2.57	1.272	0.729	6	2.83	1.722	0.560	5	2.33	1.211	0.858	5	2.60	0.548	0.395
MNC	27	3.04	1.224	(0.536)	25	3.40	1.225	(0.642)	25	3.04	1.098	(0.464)	24	3.21	1.215	(0.756)
Local	105	3.06	1.223		104	3.45	1.148		100	3.10	1.267		103	3.08	1.266	
Different types	40	3.25	1.032		42	3.45	1.017		42	3.12	0.889		41	3.12	0.842	
Export dependence																
10–49	65	2.98	1.166	0.358	64	3.47	1.140	0.133	62	3.08	1.191	0.026	60	3.12	1.121	0.047
50–74	53	3.17	1.189	(0.700)	53	3.36	1.162	(0.876)	53	3.08	1.190	(0.974)	54	3.09	1.103	(0.954)
75–	60	3.08	1.211		59	3.42	1.163		57	3.04	1.117		58	3.05	1.248	
No of traget countries																
2–9	64	3.20	1.157	0.629	61	3.21	1.156	1.902	61	3.03	1.183	0.120	60	3.20	1.162	1.814
10–19	54	2.96	1.165	(0.534)	54	3.44	1.144	(0.152)	52	3.13	1.121	(0.887)	51	3.24	1.069	(0.166)
20–	61	3.05	1.231		62	3.61	1.121		60	3.05	1.185		62	2.87	1.194	
Management int. Experience																
Low	13	2.92	0.954	1.016	13	3.38	1.193	0.054	13	2.92	0.862	0.745	13	3.00	0.913	0.422
Medium	36	3.36	0.833	(0.365)	34	3.50	1.080	(0.947)	35	3.34	0.938	(0.476)	34	3.32	0.976	(0.656)
High	106	3.10	1.203		107	3.49	1.119		102	3.18	1.155		102	3.19	1.183	
Managerial commitment to int. Operations																
Low	5	3.40	0.548	0.123	4	3.75	0.957	0.479	4	3.75	1.258	(0.847)	4	3.50	1.291	0.229
Medium	18	3.17	0.924	(0.885)	19	3.26	1.098	(0.621)	19	3.00	0.943	(0.431)	19	3.26	1.046	(0.796)
High	134	3.15	1.147		132	3.49	1.122		129	3.21	1.095		128	3.16	1.121	

Concerning the customer-related antecedents, we suggested in Hypotheses 9 and 10 that the level of adaptation would differ based on the number (H9) and type of customers (H10) in the target countries. As can be seen in Table 10.4, the level of product and pricing adaptation differs significantly ($p = 0.025$; $p = 0.093$) according to the number of customers. When a firm has more than 20 customers in the target country, the product strategy is the most adapted. However, the relationship is not linear. In the communication and distribution strategy, no differences were found. It is interesting to find out that the standard deviation is lowest in these marketing mix elements when the number of customers is taken into account. The results of the level of adaptation of different marketing mix elements based on the type of customers do not support Hypothesis 10, thus indicating that the type of customer does not influence the level of adaptation in any of the marketing mix elements.

Additional tests

The nonsignificant results related to the number of target countries (TCs) and level of export dependence were surprising. However, the results may be explained by the fact that it is not their individual but rather their interactive effect which influences the level of adaptation. In order to analyze the potential interaction effects, we conducted some additional tests. We found that the number of TCs and level of export dependence had a significant interaction effect on product ($p = 0.082$) and pricing strategy ($p = 0.081$). Where there are few TCs (2–9) both product and pricing strategies were more adapted when the level of export dependence increased. However, when the number of TCs was between 10 and 19, the strategies were more standardized when the level of export dependence increased. On the other hand, when the number of TCs was over 20, there was no relationship with the level of increased export dependence.

Discussion

The goal of this study was to analyze the degree of standardization against that of adaptation of the marketing mix elements by SMEs in their foreign sales, especially the degree of standardization versus adaptation of the four key marketing mix elements – product, price, distribution, and communication – and the impact of selected antecedents on the strategies selected. Five groups of antecedents – firm, managerial, product, market, and customer – and the effects on the choice and degree of standardization or adaptation were studied. Based on the RBV, 10 hypotheses were developed for the empirical part of the study, which was based on survey results from 188 Finnish SMEs (10–249 employees) with exports constituting at least 10% of total sales and at least two export target countries in 2005.

The study found that the marketing mix element most adapted by Finnish firms was pricing. On the other hand, no differences were found in the degree of adaptation of product, communication and distribution elements, based on the mean scores. However, when comparing the group of firms which have fully standardized or fully adapted the marketing mix elements more differences were noted. Those figures show the most fully standardized marketing mix element to be product, and that it is more often fully standardized than fully adapted. In addition, in the case of communication, too, Finnish firms have more often adopted a fully standardized strategy than a fully adapted strategy.

Regarding the impact of the 10 firm-, managerial-, product-, market-, and customer-specific variables on the degree of adaptation in the marketing mix strategies, the results are surprising. Only one customer-specific factor was found to have a significant influence on the degree of adaptation. The results indicate that the extent to which Finnish firms standardize or adapt their product and pricing strategy depends on the number of customers.

Regarding the influence of the number of customers on product and pricing strategy, it is interesting to notice that the relationship is not linear. In the case of Finnish firms, pricing strategy is most adapted when the number of customers is 6–9, but when the number of customers is less or more than that, the level of adaptation in pricing strategy declines. However, the degree of product adaptation is lowest when the number of customers is 6–9, but when the number of customers is less or more, the degree of product adaptation increases. The results imply that the number of customers in the target country is an important antecedent, and deserves more attention. In addition, the results indicate that there is a turning point in the number of customers, before and after which the degree of adaptation changes and that the impact on these two elements is reversed.

The nonsignificant results of several antecedents did not confirm prior findings on the impact of export dependence (Calantone et al. 2006), number of target countries (Cavusgil et al. 1993), managers' international experience (e.g., Seifert and Ford 1989; Cavusgil et al. 1993; Leonidou 1996) and managers' international commitment (Koh 1990). None of the target market characteristics – economic size and cultural distance – have an influence on the degree of adaptation. Results in earlier studies of these target market characteristics have been quite contradictory, some of them finding a positive relationship and some no relationship at all. Thus, the results of this study support the findings by Michell et al. (1998) and Johnson and Arunthanes (1995).

The additional tests on the interaction effect of the number of target countries and the level of export dependence do however provide some interesting results. The results support the idea that it is not just the number of target countries or the level of export dependence in general which influence the level of adaptation strategy but, rather, their interaction effect. In other words, the more a firm is dependent on its exports (and particularly when the exports are limited to a small number of countries) increases the probability of the firm using more adapted product and pricing strategies.

Conclusions

The contribution of the paper lies in using the RBV as a base from which to analyze the impact of firm, management, market, and customer factors on the degree of adaptation of the marketing mix elements. It also provides new insights into firm and customer strategies. Furthermore, the focus was on the strategies used by SMEs from a small, developed market economy. The influence of the number of customers on the degree of marketing mix elements has not been studied earlier and thus the study contributes to identifying one relevant customer related factor which should be taken into account.

Although several of the expected relationships did not receive support, this study was the first step in analyzing these relationships, and thus the study contributed by opening the doors for new research avenues. The study also contributes by showing that the relationship between potential contingency factors and the level of adaptation is quite complex, which has not been properly taken into account in prior studies.

By complexity, firstly, we mean that the relationship may not always be linear but curve linear instead. Secondly, the influence of specific antecedents on the adaptation level may differ depending on the marketing mix element. In some cases, the antecedents may indicate an increasing level of adaptation in some of the marketing mix elements, but a decreasing level in some others or indeed may have no influence at all on some elements. This requires managers to consider carefully the potential trade-off implication of different antecedents. Thirdly, the results imply that even though specific antecedents would not have an individual effect on the level of adaptation, they may have important interaction effects, which should be studied more directly.

It is also important to take into account that the results of this study are valid only in the main export countries exploited by the Finnish firms polled. It is noteworthy that the number of target countries was quite high for most of the firms (see Table 10.1); thus, the results should be interpreted with caution. In the future, it would be important to assess the marketing mix adaptation for each country separately.

This study focussed only on the analysis of degree of standardization versus adaptation of the four key marketing mix elements, not on the more specific analysis of various specific elements related to the four key elements. Thus, in the future, one key avenue to explore would be the more detailed analysis of the degree of standardization versus adaptation in various specific elements like branding, design, warranties, advertising, and sales methods, and thus whether it would be possible to apply a multi-item scale for each of the marketing mix elements. The focus only on the total degree of standardization versus adaptation may partly explain the unexpected results. Furthermore, this study did not analyze the relationship between the degree of standardization or adaptation and the export performance. Thus, a third main avenue to explore would be to analyze in which specific situations a higher degree of standardization or of adaptation leads to better performance. As the study applied the RBV, the arguments for the relationships between antecedents and the degree of standardization or adaptation are based on the transferability of competitive advantage and thus also on efficiency considerations. Linking performance to the model, too, would show whether the firms which determine the strategy for the degree of standardization or adaptation according to the hypothesis performed better than those firms in which decisions were not made according to the model. A fourth interesting research avenue would be to compare the degree of standardization versus adaptation over time. Do companies change the degree of standardization versus adaptation over the years and is there any relationship between these possible changes and the export performance of the companies? Finally, the reasons given by the managers for the choice of the standardization or adaptation strategies used were not analyzed. Thus, a more detailed analysis of the reasons for the strategies used would be of interest.

References

Barney, J. (1991) 'Firm resources and sustained competitive advantage', *Journal of Management*, 17(1), 99–120.

Barney, J., Wright, M. and Ketchen, D. (2001) 'The resource-based view of the firm: Then years after 1991', *Journal of Management*, 27(6), 625–41.

Calantone, R.J., Kim, D., Schmidt, J.B. and Cavusgil, T.S. (2006) 'The influence of internal and external firm factors on international product adaptation strategy and export performance: A three country comparison', *Journal of Business Research*, 59(2), 176–85.

Cavusgil, T.S. and Zou, S. (1994) 'Marketing strategy-performance relationship: an investigation of the empirical link in export market ventures', *Journal of Marketing*, 58, 1–21.

Cavusgil, T.S., Zou, S. and Naidu, G.M. (1993) 'Product and promotion adaptation in export ventures: an empirical investigation', *Journal of International Business Studies*, 24(3), 479–506.

Commission (2003) *Official Journal of the European Union*, http://europa.eu/eur-lex/pri/en/oj/dat/2003/l_124/l_12420030520en00360041.pdf.

Johnson, J.L. and Arunthanes, W. (1995) 'Ideal and actual product adaptation in US exporting firms: market related determinants and impact on performance', *International Marketing Review*, 12(3), 31–46.

Koh, A.C. (1990) 'Relationship among organizational characteristics, marketing strategy and export performance', *International Marketing Review*, 8(3), 46–60.

Leonidou, L.C. (1996) 'Product standardization or adaptation: the Japanese approach', *Journal of Marketing Practice: Applied Marketing Science*, 2(4), 53–71.

Mengüc, B. (1997) 'Product adaptation practices in the context of export activity: An empirical study of Turkish manufacturing firms', *Journal of Euromarketing*, 6(2), 25–66.

Menon, A., Bharadwaj, S.G. and Howell, R. (1996) 'The quality and effectiveness of marketing strategy: Effects of functional and dysfunctional conflict in intraorganizational relationships', *Journal of Academy of Marketing Science*, 24, 299–313.

Michell, P., Lynch, J. and Alabdali, O. (1998) 'New perspective on marketing mix program standardization', *International Business Review*, 7, 617–34.

O'Cass, A. and Julian, C. (2003) 'Examining firm and environmental influences on export marketing mix strategy and export performance of Australian Exporters', *European Journal of Marketing*, 37 3(4), 366–84.

Peng, M.W. (2001) 'The resource-based view and international business', *Journal of Management*, 27(6), 803–29.

Rialp, A., Rialp, J. and Knight, G.A. (2005) 'The phenomenon of early internationalizing firms. What do we know after a decade (1993–2003) of scientific inquiry?', *International Business Review*, 14(2), 147–66.

Roth, M.S. (1995) 'Effects of global market conditions on brand image customization and brand performance', *Journal of Advertising*, 14(4), 55–75.

Ryans, J.K., Griffith, D.A. and White, D.S. (2003) 'Standardization/adaptation of international marketing strategy. Necessary conditions for the advancement of knowledge', *International Marketing Review*, 20(6), 588–603.

Seifert, B. and Ford, J. (1989) 'Are exporting firms modifying their product, pricing and promotion policies?', *International Marketing Review*, 6(6), 53–68.

Srivastava, R., Fahey, L. and Christensen, K.(2001) 'The resource-based view and marketing: The role of market-based assets in gaining competitive advantage', *Journal of Management* 27(6), 777–802.

Sousa, C. and Bradley, F. (2008) 'Antecedents of international pricing adaptation and export performance', *Journal of World Business*, 43, 307–20.

Theodosiou, M. and Katsikeas, C.S. (2001) 'Factors influencing the degree of international pricing strategy standardization of multinational corporations', *Journal of International Marketing*, 9(3), 1–18.

Theodosiou, M. and Leonidou, L. (2003) 'Standardization versus adaptation of international marketing strategy: an integrative assessment of the empirical research', *International Business Review*, 12(2), 141–71.

Viswanathan, N.K. and Dickson, P.R. (2007) 'The fundamentals of standardizing global marketing strategy', *International Marketing Review*, 24(1), 46–63.

Wong, H.Y. and Merrilees, B. (2007) 'Multiple roles for branding in international marketing', *International Marketing Review*, 24(4), 384–408.

11
Knowledge Management and Growth Strategies: Evidence from Chinese Knowledge-Intensive New Ventures

Huan Zou and Pervez Ghauri

Introduction

Entrepreneurial studies have paid significant attention to the importance of knowledge on the internationalization and performance of knowledge-intensive (K-I) firms, although considerably less attention has been carried out so far to find the impact of the knowledge management practices on different growth strategies of K-I firms. Presutti and his colleagues (2007) recently suggest that knowledge acquired from external relationships play an important role in reinforcing the foreign operations by K-I firms. Further, acquired knowledge needs to be absorbed and translated inside the business for technology, production and even management development (Grant and Baden-Fuller, 2004). Effective intrafirm knowledge transfer by leveraging of knowledge resources through the transfer and reuse of existing knowledge acts another important role in firm's knowledge management and growth (Watson and Hewett, 2006). However, so far most existing work focuses on one aspect of knowledge transfer instead of developing an integrated perspective on both the mechanisms in knowledge management on firm growth strategies. It is probably due to the fact that traditional studies neglect the importance of growth orientation in K-I firm growth and especially of its potential role in reinforcing the knowledge learning (Gilbert, McDougall, and Audretsch, 2006).

According to the idea that knowledge is the key element in driving international growth of a K-I firm, this study integrates the knowledge-based view, learning perspective, and social capital approach to identify the mechanisms useful in reinforcing the sharing and learning of profitable knowledge of K-I firms from their domestic and international relationships. International-oriented growth strategy indicates the strategic direction and focus on international markets with more commitment in the geographical markets. We argue that firms involving international joint ventures and acquisitions do have a strong commitment and strategic mind-set in venturing in international markets. Such firms are more likely to engage in knowledge learning for acquiring and leveraging knowledge than domestic-oriented firms are. Our idea is based on the merging knowledge-based view of K-I firms from international new venture literature, which reckons that a K-I firm knowledge pool and the effectiveness knowledge management determines its strategic direction and operation focus on whether to internationalize and how to internationalize. Rather than defining knowledge management as a broad concept in terms of knowledge exploitation and exploration (Argote, McEvily, and Reagans, 2003). Specifically, we refer knowledge management in this study to the behaviour of knowledge sharing and learning by a K-I firm (Collins and Smith, 2006) from emerging markets. These concerns raise important research questions: 'How do interfirm and intrafirm knowledge management influence new venture growth strategy? Are interfirm and intrafirm knowledge management associated with an international-oriented growth strategy?'

This paper concentrates on knowledge-intensive new ventures in China to analyze the impact of internal and external knowledge management, and international experience on different growth strategies. The reason for focussing on Chinese high-tech new ventures is two-fold. First, high-tech new ventures from China have an increasing tendency to engage in international activities and to establish their global presence. As reported by Deloitte Touche Tohmatsu (2008), of the top 100 fast-growing Asia-Pacific firms in technology-intensive industry, 29 firms are from China and over half of these have established their international presences. This new phenomenon represents an important but underexplored topic. Entrepreneurial managers have to develop effective knowledge management if they are about to compete in international markets. Second, whether theoretical or empirical, limited research focusses on firm internationalization from emerging economies. Within the limited studies, most focus on the internationalization of high-profile companies from China, such as Lenova, Haier, and Huawei. Despite the increasing expansion of small and new firms entering foreign markets, including developed economies, research on the internationalization strategies of such ventures from emerging economies, such as China, remains an unfilled gap (Yamakawa, Peng, and Deeds, 2008).

This study takes a step towards empirically demonstrating the significance of knowledge management on the internationalization strategies of Chinese companies. The study contributes to new venture growth literature by making a link between knowledge learning process and growth strategies. This study further provides new insights into the issue how knowledge is shared and leveraged through the interfirm and intrafirm mechanisms affects the growth path of new ventures. The findings from this study also help to advance knowledge of the hidden 'process black box' (Priem and Bulter, 2001, p.33) in understanding the entrepreneurial behaviour and generating important managerial implications.

Literature review and conceptual framework

International-oriented strategy

In terms of their domestic and international focus, growth strategies are complex choices for new ventures because of resource constraints (Penrose, 1959), environmental uncertainty (Ensley, Pearce, and Hmieleski, 2006; Zahra and Garvis, 2000) and the different perceptions of entrepreneurs (Begley and Boyd, 1987). Earlier studies adopt the Uppsala model to explain the internationalization strategy of firms; however, some recent studies argue explicitly that the emergence of born global firms or international new ventures contradicts the Uppsala model (Crick and Spence, 2005; Fillis, 2001; Knight and Cavusgil, 1996; McDougall, Shane, and Oviatt, 1994). Internally, international new ventures face constraints to international growth in terms of limited capital, management, time, experience, and information resources (Bruton and Rubanik, 2002; Freeman, Carroll, and Hanan, 1983). Externally, the dynamic environment due to technological, social, and economic changes, (McDougall and Oviatt, 2000) as well as the fast obsolescence of products or limited domestic demand (Crick and Spence, 2005), urge new ventures to have an international focus from their inception. Following this reasoning, these firms do not follow a systematic and sequential internationalization process as suggested by the Uppsala model.

Compared with domestic-oriented growth strategy, international expansion is a very complicated endeavour that requires good planning and management but can also require vast knowledge of international cultures and practices from those engaging in the process (Gilbert et al., 2006). Although past research establishes that both domestic and international expansion are affected by entrepreneur's knowledge and capabilities to guide the firm in identifying market opportunities, localizing and ultimately distributing products within the newly targeted market, how knowledge and capabilities are utilized and leveraged in the two growth paths is not fully answered. In particular, the question of why and what firms may adopt international-oriented growth strategy is still underresearched except for early work done by McDougall and her colleagues (McDougall, 1989; McDougall, Robinson, and DeNisi, 1992; McDougall et al. 1994), and requires more empirical investigation. This study therefore endeavours to contribute to the literature by dealing with the determinants of an international-oriented growth strategy adopted by a K-I firm from the perspective of the Chinese high-tech industry. The conceptual framework is presented in Figure 11.1.

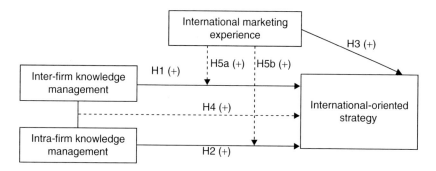

Figure 11.1   A framework of international-oriented strategy

Interfirm and intrafirm knowledge management

The knowledge-based analysis focusses on the exploitation of existing knowledge bases and the exploration of new knowledge bases, thus establishing a link between firms' knowledge process and their likely path of international growth (Meyer, Wright, and Pruthi, 2009; Peng, 2001b). Knowledge, particular tacit knowledge is embedded in individual professionals and is extremely difficult to replicate and imitate by competitors (Grant, 1996). The transfer of such knowledge is more likely to take place within the firm through direct interactions between individuals (Kogut and Zander, 1993). An international-oriented strategy additionally provides a means to explore a firm's knowledge base in two interacted ways. Internally, firms can explore existing knowledge through organizational learning while externally they are able to access to complementary knowledge through interactions with external partners in host countries. Interfirm learning is an important vehicle for knowledge acquisition(Zander and Kogut, 1995) while intrafirm learning develops, controls, and protects firm-specific advantages inside the firm (Easterby-Smith, Lyles, and Tsang, 2008). Both the two mechanisms are extensively influenced by social capital that a K-I firm holds.

Interfirm knowledge management refers to the learning process that relies upon significant external relationships, such as with customers or ties with business or social network (Yli-Renko, Autio, and Sapienza, 2001). Social capital in the form of such extensive networks is a powerful tool for K-I firms enabling them to gain access to resources and identify growth opportunities (Alvarez and Barney, 2001; Burt, 1997; Hitt and Ireland, 2000). Being embedded in social networks helps ventures establish credibility and access critical resources, including knowledge and technology (McDougall et al. 1994). Studies have reported that supports from a range of external relationships such as government initiatives (Li and Zhang, 2007), supportive customers (Yeoh, 2004), cooperating constellations of firms and professional and specialist networks

(Baucus, Baucus, and Human, 1996)facilitate the transfer of business management knowledge to entrepreneur and contribute to firm growth. In addition, knowledge spillovers may occur through formal and informal contacts with business partners which provide resource advantages for enhanced technical and business skills to be further applied for growth opportunities. Establishing and consolidating business network ties, both at home and at abroad helps foster international venturing (Child and Rodrigues, 2005; Yiu, Lau, and Bruton, 2007). Guillén (2002) explains that firms belonging to the same business network can gain precious information and experience from peer members who have undertaken international expansion, thereby overcoming the liability of foreignness. Thus, we expect:

Hypothesis 1: An international-oriented strategy of a K-I firm is positively associated with interfirm knowledge management.

Intrafirm knowledge management based on the internal knowledge transfer, reuse, and leveraging is important for building a venture's competencies and achieving high performance. The development of new technological knowledge, in most cases, takes place within the organization and drive firm to succeed in markets (McCann, 1991). K-I firms usually have organic structures that permits speedy and effective flow of knowledge and its subsequent use in new product development activities. The internal structures encourage the exchange of information and experiences which promotes learning by managers and employees (Zahra, Ireland, and Hitt, 2000). Further, intrafirm knowledge management encourages managers to recognize and rapidly internalize the technological knowledge gained externally. This mechanism promotes communication and discussions among managers, between managers and employees, thereby facilitating the quick recognition, inventory, synthesis, and use of the knowledge in international markets (Johanson and Vahlne, 1977).

Hypothesis 2: An international-oriented strategy of a K-I firm is positively associated with intrafirm knowledge management.

International marketing practices

A substantial body of research has examined the role of accumulated knowledge and experience in the context of internationalization, including the stages and paths of internationalization (Johanson and Vahlne, 1977), the implementation of entry modes (Zahra et al. 2000) and firm performance in international markets (Yeoh, 2004). The repeated exposure to different business environments alongside the internationalization process compels the small firm to expand both its set of organizing processes and its awareness of the cause-effect relationships among these processes. Therefore, internationalization not only presents growth opportunities for the entrepreneurial firm but also creates a need to develop organizational knowledge and other dimensions of these capabilities (Zahra et al. 2000).

Further, while market-specific knowledge develops through international marketing practices at organizational level, it consequently becomes a part of general knowledge which function as a driving force to take steps in directions which are new to the firm (Forsgren, 2002). Case study evidence also confirms that international new ventures often seek to transfer market-based practices and advantages to foreign markets. K-I firms with experiential market practices therefore are capable of searching for information about potential new alternatives, identifying recognizing and exploiting new market opportunities (Johanson and Vahlne, 1990). Therefore, we expect:

Hypothesis 3: An international-oriented strategy is positively associated with the international marketing practices.

These hypotheses emphasize separately the importance of knowledge management and international marketing practices in international-oriented growth strategy. However, they may be interrelated in the sense that the factors may complement or reinforce others in terms of knowledge learning and strategic decision making. Therefore, in addition to the proposed three individual hypotheses, we further consider interactions between interfirm knowledge management and intrafirm knowledge management, as well as international marketing practices and the two mechanisms of knowledge management.

While interfirm and intrafirm knowledge management respectively contributes to international venturing, Cohen (1990) further address that the most responsive and competitive organizations have a balance between the external knowledge acquisition and internal knowledge distribution. Together, the two mechanisms of organizational learning create new substantive capabilities and the organization's knowledge base (Zahra, Sapienza, and Davidsson, 2006). This argument is supported by the study by Kogut and Zander (1993), which suggests that both the internal and external aspects of knowledge accumulation, its application and its recombinining enhance the growth prospects of the firm. Acquired knowledge from external partners and internalized knowledge enable a K-I firm to augment its existing knowledge bases and direct its growth path (Liesch and Knight, 1999; Meyer et al. 2009). Therefore:

Hypothesis 4: The combination of interfirm and intrafirm knowledge management is positively related to the international-oriented strategy of a K-I firm.

Market-specific knowledge is important for firms' internationalization. Market-specific knowledge is gained by conducting existing activities in the market and can be transferred from one market to the other depending on the nature of operations. Simultaneously, learning directed at increasing the effectiveness in current business take places within the firm and strategic actions are taken in order to seize the growth opportunities. Thus, firms that engage in international markets previously are capable of accumulate market knowledge and experience for further learning and sharing (Yeoh, 2004). In other words, internationalization not only presents growth opportunities for the K-I firms but also creates a need to develop organizational knowledge and other dimensions of these capabilities continuously.

Moreover, in the case of China, as latecomers, Chinese K-I firms share and augment knowledge and experience during the process of unifying and building trust with local partners. Acquired market knowledge relating to specific product-market combinations and across market over time provides a platform and a capability for future international expansion of the firm. In so doing, K-I firms acquire knowledge relating to specific product-market combinations and across market over time(Kogut and Zander, 1993; Lamb and Liesch, 2002), providing a platform and a capability for recognizing their strategic needs and understanding what particular kinds of asset in other countries are required in obtaining a competitive advantage. Knowledge learning therefore fosters a set of knowledge-questioning and knowledge-enhancing values that lead to the development of breakthrough products, services and technologies and the exploration of new markets (Keskin, 2006). The higher the level of market-specific knowledge a K-I firm possesses, the greater the driving force for firms to learn about how and where to fill strategic needs. Therefore, we expect:

Hypothesis 5a: An international-oriented strategy is positively associated with the interaction between international marketing practices and interfirm knowledge management.

Hypothesis 5b: An international-oriented strategy is positively associated with the interaction between international marketing practices and intrafirm knowledge management.

Research method

Sampling and data collection

The study sample consists of knowledge-intensive firms operating in high-tech sectors in Shanghai, China. As the most advanced region for technology development, Shanghai has approximately 35 high-technology science parks and incubators, with a total of more than 2300 high-tech ventures and a total industrial output of $4,197 billion RMB by 2005 (STCSM, 2006). Administrative offices of high-tech zones and incubators as well as industrial associations were contacted initially to obtain firm lists, and then 400 firms were randomly selected. Formal and informal sources of information provided the names of senior managers from the firm list. Telephone calls and e-mails were used to explain the purpose of the study and invite their participation. Of the 400 firms contacted, 306 agreed to participate in the survey. A good key informant, mostly from within the founding team, or top management team, with sufficient knowledge and rich information about strategy decision making and company performance was identified and contacted to secure an interview.

Many previous studies recognize the difficulties in collecting primary data from firms in China (Park and Luo, 2001; Zhou, Wu, and Luo, 2007). In order to overcome the problems of low response rate, distrust and managers' unwillingness to respond, local research assistants were employed to conduct interview-based questionnaire surveys, which is similar to a method used by Zhou et al. (2007). Four final-year postgraduate students at the School of Economics and Management of Tongji University, one of the leading universities in China, underwent training to conduct face-to-face field visits from April to August 2007. These selected research assistants were provided with financial support to conduct interviews and collect data. With adequate knowledge about the research project, they were instructed to take, in person, an official letter to the senior managers of the selected firms. These actions were taken in order to ensure good response rates and data reliability (Gao, Zhou, and Yim, 2007; Ghauri and Gronhaug, 2005; Hoskisson, Eden, Lau, and Wright, 2000).

An initial screening of the questionnaires ensured that the respondents had sufficient knowledge to respond to the questionnaire. All respondents were informed of the confidentiality of their responses in advance. The average time for each interview was 45 minutes. A total of 306 responses were collected. Eighty-nine responses were excluded from the analysis because they failed to meet the age criteria (six years old or younger) of international new ventures (Brush, 1995). Thus, this study has a final sample of 217 high-tech new ventures, with a response rate of 54% of the total sample (217 out of 400 firms). Within these new ventures, 76 ventures had implemented international operations while the remaining 141 ventures were regarded as domestic new ventures.

The annual sales of the sample firms range from $20,000 RMB to $15 million RMB, with a mean value of $160,000 RMB. All of the ventures that operate in international markets have been in business for up to six years. These ventures operate in knowledge-intensive sectors, such as information technology, software development, biotechnology, and electronics product development. Most of the managers (98%) are between 24 and 45 years of age. Over 40% of the respondents have a Master's or a Ph.D. degree. All respondents are involved in strategic decision-making processes, as defined by their position or responsibilities.

Measures

This study mainly adopts the measures from established studies in entrepreneurship, with modifications to represent the research context of Chinese high-tech industries. The measures were translated into Chinese, followed by a back-translation procedure, in accordance with common standards to verify the equivalence between the English and Chinese versions (Peng, 2001a; Sinkovics, Penz, and Ghauri, 2008). In addition, marketing and economics professors of Chinese origin as well as mangers who have at least three years business experience in high-tech industries were consulted to ensure the validity and accuracy of the measures (Atuahene-Gima, 1995), before finalizing the questionnaire.

Dependent variable: strategic orientation

Unlike previous studies which classify new ventures according to the percentage of their sales in the international market (McDougall, 1989), this study asked respondents to indicate whether or not their firms implemented international operations through equity modes such as joint ventures and acquisitions. Specifically, ventures without such international engagement were considered as 'domestic' K-I new ventures (coded as 0) and ventures with international operations as 'international K-I new ventures' (coded as 1).

Independent variables

Interfirm knowledge management

According to prior research, interfirm knowledge management is a process based on the relationship between the firm and external partners (Becerra, Lunnan, and Huemer, 2008; Kogut and Zander, 1993; Miles, Snow, Mathews, Miles, and Coleman Jr, 1997). Following prior research, this study uses five questions in the questionnaire to measure the interfirm knowledge-sharing variable. These questions on a 5-point Likert scale, focus on the behaviour of knowledge management with external partners: (1) we appoint coordinators who are responsible for the relationships with our partners; (2) we analyze what we would like to and desire to achieve with which partner; (3) we can deal flexibly with our partners; (4) we have the ability to build good personal relationships with business partners; (5) we judge in advance which possible partners to talk to about building up relationships; and (6) we discuss regularly with our partners how we can support each other in our success. The six items load on to a single factor, with high loadings and Eigen values exceeding 1.0, and the cumulative variance explained was 50%.

Intrafirm Knowledge Management

Existing literature acknowledges the internal mechanism as one of the key platforms on how knowledge in transferred and internalized inside the business. We use intrafirm knowledge management variable in this study to capture the knowledge management within the business. This variable was constructed on the basis on four questions that managers were asked to judge (on a 5-point Likert scale): (1) within the firm, information is often spontaneously exchanged; (2) within the firm, we develop informal contacts and discussion channels among employees; (3) within the firm, managers and employees do give intensive feedback on each other; and (4) within the firm, we have regular meetings for every project. Factor analysis confirmed that these four questions loaded on to one factor, with Eigen value exceeding 1.0, and the cumulative variance explained was 60%.

International marketing practices

We adopted the concepts from Johanson (1990) and Shrader (2001). Market-specific advantage variable, measured by three items, assesses a firm's experience and knowledge in international market. Three questions were asked to the respondents on a 5-point Likert scale: (1) we expand to other geographical markets independently by having our own overseas experiences and knowledge; (2) we expand our products/services to other geographical markets by utilizing relationship with our partners; and (3) we engage in promotional activities, advertising to promote our products/services and differentiate from our competitors in different markets. Factor analysis confirmed that these three questions loaded on to one factor, with Eigen value exceeding 1.0, and the cumulative variance explained was 65%.

Control variables

Four control variables – firm size, firm age, firm life cycle, and the industry life cycle – were used to account for the effects of extraneous variables. Firm age is measured as the logarithm of the number of years that a firm has operated in the industry and firm size is the logarithm of the number of employees in the company (Lee, Lee, and Johannes, 2001). Prior studies suggest that firm stage and industry stage, from the life-cycle perspective, can influence strategic decisions (Bantel, 1998; McCann, 1991; Robinson, 1999). The firm life-cycle and industry life-cycle variables were computed by using dummy variables denoting infancy (very early growth stage), early growth stage (rapid, still increasing rate of growth), late growth stage (growing, but at a slowing rate), mature (about as fast as it will get), and decline (decreasing growth rate), as operationalized by McCann (1991).

Results

Descriptive statistics and correlations

Table 11.1 reports the means, standard deviations, and correlations for the variables used in the present study. No correlation between the variables was deemed large enough to raise serious concerns about multicollinearity.

Table 11.1   Means, standard deviations, and correlations

	1	2	3	4	5	6	7	8
1. Strategic orientation	1.000							
2. Firm age[a]	−0.183**	1.000						
3. Firm size[a]	−0.032	−0.22	1.000					
4. Industry life-cycle	−0.204**	0.485**	−0.142*	1.000				
5. Firm life-cycle	0.113	−0.305**	0.110	0.408**	1.000			
6. Interfirm knowledge management	0.108	−0.145*	0.185**	−0.162*	−0.046	1.000		
7. Intrafirm knowledge management	0.133	−0.142*	0.124	−0.198**	−0.060	0.574**	1.000	
8. International marketing practice	0.327**	−0.176*	0.101	−0.200**	0.061	0.460**	0.416**	1.000
Mean	0.350	0.612	1.488	3.19	2.74	0.01	0.01	0.01
Standard deviation	0.478	0.255	0.342	0.730	0.681	1.00	1.00	1.00

Note:
N = 217.
Significant at the 0.05 level (two-tailed test) when Pearson correlations > 0.140 or < −0.140.
[a] Logarithmic transformation.

Hypothesis tests

The hypotheses related to strategic orientation were tested using a binomial logistic model in which the regression coefficients estimated the impact of the independent variables on a new venture's choice of internationalization strategy or a domestic strategy. A positive/negative coefficient means that the independent variable tended to increase the probability that a new venture would choose international-oriented/domestic-oriented strategy. A total of three logistic regression models were estimated. As shown in Table 11.2, one model includes control variables only; one further incorporates the main explanatory variables, interfirm, intrafirm knowledge management, and international marketing practices, and the third model includes the hypothesized interaction terms between interfirm and intrafirm knowledge management, and the interaction effect of international marketing practices.

Model 1 in Table 11.2 reports the results from the base model with the control variables only. Firm size is not a significant determinant of a venture's selection of international-oriented strategy while firm age is marginally significant. Nevertheless, industry life cycle and firm life cycle are all statistically significant. The results suggest that industry factors and firm life cycle play an important role in new ventures' internationalization strategies. K-I new ventures that have established their growth routine tend to seek growth opportunities in international markets. In addition, it is quite likely that the product market is in an emerging stage while an international-oriented strategy will be pursued. This can be explained by the first-mover advantages in firm internationalization process (Low and Abrahamson, 1997). The explanatory power of this model is low.

Table 11.2 Results of binomial logit analyses on strategic orientation

	Model 1	Model 2	Model 3
Firm age	−1.212 †	−0.985	−0.781
	(0.650)	(0.679)	(0.688)
Firm size	−0.646	−0.752	−0.855†
	(0.459)	(0.471)	(0.481)
Industry life cycle	−0.870**	−0.738**	−0.671*
	(0.268)	(0.277)	(0.304)
Firm life cycle	0.981***	0.836***	0.740**
	(0.272)	(0.282)	(0.292)
Interfirm knowledge sharing	–	−0.150	−0.202
		(0.216)	(0.237)
Intrafirm knowledge sharing	–	0.077	0.144
		(0.210)	(0.233)
International marketing practice	–	0.713***	0.979***
		(0.203)	(0.249)
Interfirm knowledge sharing × Intrafirm knowledge sharing	–	–	0.421*
			(0.195)
Interfirm knowledge sharing × International marketing practice	–	–	0.286†
			(0.188)
Intrafirm knowledge sharing × International marketing practice	–	–	−0.793**
			(0.290)
-2 Log-likelihood	254.979	252.367	219.531
Chi-sq. (d.f.)	26.075***	42.757***	51.936***
	(4)	(7)	(10)
Cox and Snell R^2	0.11	0.18	0.21
ΔR^2		0.07	0.03
N	217	217	217

Note: *** $p < 0.001$, ** $p < 0.01$, *$p < 0.05$, † $p < 0.10$

Model 2 tests the effects of the independent variables on new ventures' growth strategies. Interfirm knowledge management is negatively and insignificantly associated with the probability of an international-oriented strategy, and our Hypothesis 1 is not supported. The activities of intrafirm knowledge management is positively but insignificantly associated with the probability of an international-oriented strategy, thus does not support Hypothesis 2. The presence of international marketing practice is positively and significantly associated with the probability of an international-oriented strategy, as predicted in Hypothesis 3. As Model 2 shows, adding the regressors improves the explanatory power of the regression.

Finally, Model 3 tests for potential complementaries among the effects of knowledge management and prior international marketing experience. In Model 3, we introduced interaction effects between the *Interfirm Knowledge Management* variables and *Intrafirm Knowledge Management* variables, and between the *International Marketing Practices* and two types of *Knowledge Management* variables. As this model clearly shows, the *Interfirm Knowledge Management* and *Intrafirm Knowledge Management* variables complement each other: firms capable of both internal and external knowledge sharing and learning are more likely to go abroad in search of new markets. Further, relationship between *International Marketing Practices* and *Interfirm Knowledge Management* variables is positive and significant, suggesting that the previous international market knowledge and experience do reinforce the knowledge sharing and learning between a K-I firm and external partners and thus impact on an international-oriented strategic choice. However, relationship between *International Marketing Practices* and *Intrafirm Knowledge Management* is statistically significant with a negative coefficient. This result indicates that the internalization of international market experience and knowledge does not lead to an international-oriented strategy. Instead, these firms are more likely to be domestic-focussed players.

Discussion

The results show that the international marketing practices (H3), combination of the two knowledge management mechanisms (H4), and the interaction between international marketing practices and knowledge management (H5a, 5b) are significantly associated with international-oriented growth strategy. The result in relation to knowledge and how knowledge is shared and transferred is central to our study. International market practices, especially the experience that K-I new ventures accumulate from their previous international market practices such as export adds advantages for understanding and exploiting new market opportunities in other geographical markets. Moreover, the way how such knowledge is transferred and learnt by K-I firms impacts greatly on their decision to go abroad with more commitment. The results strongly support the KBV analysis and learning perspective of entrepreneurial firms, and emphasize the important role of knowledge management in the internationalization of their firms.

By focussing on knowledge management behaviour, this study examines how knowledge is shared and transferred. The results are interesting and important. Broadly, they confirm prior findings on the importance of international market experience. Internationalization experience can be valuable, as it contributes to a firm's capabilities to manage international operations (Eriksson, Johanson, Majkgård, and Sharma, 2000) select among diverse market opportunities (Johanson and Vahlne, 1977), and operate in new international markets with similar institutional configurations as encountered in the past (Delios and Henisz, 2003). In addition to previous findings on the role of entrepreneur's international experience on internationalization of new ventures (Peng, 2001a;

Westhead, Wright, and Ucbasaran, 2001), we provide evidence that firm-level international experience also contribute the internationalization strategies. Going further, the analysis shows that firms that manage knowledge learning effectively both in external and internal platforms tend to choose international-oriented growth strategy. However, the results are inconclusive on the impacts of how K-I firms share and learn market knowledge in each knowledge management mechanism, showing differentiated impacts of knowledge management on international-oriented strategic choices.

The data support our arguments that knowledge management based on external network relationships motivates international-oriented strategies when firms are with previous international marketing experience. External relationships enables the sharing of knowledge (including technology, know-how, and organizational capability) between K-I firms and business or social partners. Further, such partnership allows young and small K-I firms to exploit complementaries by accessing its partner's stock of knowledge (Stieglitz and Heine, 2007). By examining the K-I new ventures from an emerging economy perspective, the results confirm that interfirm knowledge learning adds value to Chinese K-I firms (Li and Catherine, 2001). Meanwhile, it indicates that the K-I new ventures from emerging economies with capabilities in dealing with knowledge transfer and learning from external partners are likely to go abroad through joint ventures or acquisitions. Such international entry strategies often require high levels of knowledge and capabilities and market commitment (Meyer et al. 2009). By acquiring knowledge and advantages from partners, together with firm-specific market experience, K-I new ventures from emerging markets are capable of handling the integration and cooperation with partners and subsidiaries.

Interfirm knowledge sharing and learning may expand a K-I firm's knowledge bases, yet the acquired knowledge itself does not automatically become useful for K-I firms. The ability to internalize acquired knowledge and utilize these assets to their full capacity represents a key challenge to the firm (Grant and Baden-Fuller, 2004). Collins and Smith (2006) suggest the ability to use existing knowledge and create new knowledge, which enables firm both to innovate and to outperform their rivals in dynamic environments, results from the collective ability of employees to exchange and combine knowledge. We predict the benefits of intrafirm knowledge management that enables the exchange of knowledge inside the business. However, we are somewhat surprised that the results show the opposite way. We find that the intrafirm knowledge sharing and learning, combined with international market experience, decreases the possibility of an international-oriented strategy. It is likely that such intrafirm mechanisms overemphasize and protect the internal knowledge development without paying attention to the external knowledge stocks which may provide business opportunities outside the business (Fu, Tsui, and Dess, 2006). It further hampers the exchange and communication between the firm and the external partners. In addition, internal platform may harm efforts to leverage and utilize knowledge in an effective manner because they rely heavily on the organizational autonomy and flexible structure, thereby may disrupt strategic directions and decisions in a systematic way. Further, the likelihood of knowledge exchange and combination among employees is dependent upon employee motivation and ability (Argote et al. 2003). Tsai further (2001) reckons that even within a small K-I firm, organizational units differ in their internal knowledge, practices and capabilities. Thus, intrafirm knowledge sharing and learning may increase their cost efficiency through dissemination of knowledge within the organization. In addition, knowledge learning and utilization is not static but dynamic.

Conclusions

This study investigates the determinants of new ventures' growth strategies and how internal and external knowledge management combined with international market experiences affects the strategic orientation of new ventures. The results suggest that firms need to utilize both internal and external platforms for acquiring and internalizing complementary knowledge stocks and thus to identify and grasp growth opportunities. Additionally, market experience complements the two knowledge sharing and learning routines. The study advances existing knowledge of the hidden 'process black box' (Priem and Bulter, 2001: 33) in understanding the knowledge management and its impact on international-oriented growth strategy. Furthermore, we argue that the study extends the learning and international entrepreneurship literature in two main ways.

First, it adds to the few studies of internationalization in an emerging economy context, providing evidence that emphasizes the need to consider the particular knowledge learning process in understanding the drivers of internationalization activity. This study therefore confirms that early findings by Kogut and Zander (1993) is also applicable in emerging economies.

Second, both international business and entrepreneurship scholars and policy makers have paid much attention to the speed and paths of international new ventures or born-globals. In particular, the phenomenon of these new types of organizations is largely driven by knowledge as one of the focusses in previous studies. However, the dynamic knowledge-learning process and the integrated-learning mechanism represent key channels for international knowledge transfer and international venturing. Therefore, the study develops entrepreneurship research by reinforcing its traditional focus on knowledge and furthering the focus towards the different platforms on how knowledge is acquired, utilized, and leveraged for firm growth opportunities in emerging economies.

Finally, the findings have some important implications for high-tech new ventures in China. New ventures should highlight the importance of knowledge management, especially when they position themselves in global markets. It is critical for these firms to understand how to augment and utilize knowledge assets through a combination of internal resources and capabilities with those of network partners (Elg, Ghauri, and Tarnovskaya, 2008; Ghauri, Hadjikhani, and Johanson, 2005). Therefore, new ventures should be aware of the effective mechanisms and processes through which knowledge can be created, acquired and utilized in order to exploit valuable resources and capabilities for sustainable growth. While interfirm knowledge sharing and transfer provides opportunities for young K-I firms from emerging economies to expand knowledge stocks and growth directions, managers should be cautious about the possible risks of knowledge sharing and learning based on this channel (Hagedoorn and Duysters, 2002). Gomes-Casseres (1997) suggest that cooperative agreements, which always involve some knowledge sharing may undermine the firm's competitive edge if a firm based on very specific knowledge, is a leading player in a market niche. Therefore, how to manage knowledge learning and transfer through interfirm relationships can be a challenge for K-I firms. Meanwhile, overemphasis on intrafirm knowledge management may be harmful for firm to keep up market trend and seize market opportunities. Therefore, managers may develop effective internal communication system, organized corporate governance in order to respond to any growth opportunities quickly.

Like all research, this paper has limitations and hence may provide a number of future research directions. First, the study is cross-sectional and hence is constrained in the analysis of the effectiveness of international-oriented strategies. The nature of cross-sectional data makes it difficult to detect the potential endogeneity between knowledge management and growth strategy. Further research should be conducted on this issue using longitudinal datasets to better mitigate the endogeneity concern.

Second, this study uses a single informant approach in our data collection, as Kumar et al. (1993) recommends to choose appropriate respondents who are well informed about their own organization to alleviate some potential problems. Though it is a common practice in new venture research, the use of multiple informants represents a more rigorous test (Dess, Lumpkin, and Covin, 1997; Zahra, 1993). Third, this study made an attempt to explore how these high-tech new ventures in China choose either domestic or international-oriented strategy based on their knowledge management behaviour, to respond to Gilbert (2006)'s call to address the strategic decision that causes ventures to grow in different ways. The results show that in fast-growing economies such as China, K-I new ventures that are more capable of knowledge sharing and learning through combining market knowledge are more likely to internationalize.

However, whether those international new ventures from emerging markets such as China perform better than their domestic counterparts remains a question for future research.

Finally, by exploring the resource and knowledge aspects of international entrepreneurship our analysis examines the two mechanisms: interfirm and intrafirm knowledge learning on international orientation. Yet, Lumpkin (2001) argues that knowledge is continually being created, refined, discarded, and reconfigured into new products and opportunities and that this dynamic process can be impacted by the uncertainties and risks surrounding the organizations. Therefore, important research is awaited on assessing the mediating effect of business environment in the relationship between knowledge management and strategic decisions.

References

Alvarez, S. and Barney, J. (2001) 'How entrepreneurial firms can benefit from alliances with large partners?', *Academy of Management Executive*, 15, 139–48.

Argote, L., McEvily, B. and Reagans, R. (2003) 'Managing knowledge in organizations: An integrative framework and review of emerging themes', *Management Science*, 49, 571–82.

Atuahene-Gima, K. (1995) 'An exploratory analysis of the impact of market orientation on new product performance a contingency approach', *Journal of Product Innovation Management*, 12, 275–93.

Bantel, K.A. (1998) 'Technology-based, "Adolescent" firm configurations: Strategy identification, context, and performance', *Journal of Business Venturing*, 13, 205–30.

Baucus, D.A., Baucus, M.S. and Human, S.E. (1996) 'Consensus in franchise organizations: A cooperative arrangement among entrepreneurs', *Journal of Business Venturing*, 11, 359–78.

Becerra, M., Lunnan, R. and Huemer, L. (2008) 'Trustworthiness, risk, and the transfer of tacit and explicit knowledge between alliance partners' *Journal of Management Studies*, 45, 691–713.

Begley, T.M. and Boyd, D.P. (1987) 'Psychological characteristics associated with performance in entrepreneurial firms and smaller businesses', *Journal of Business Venturing*, 2, 79–93.

Brush, C.G. (1995) *International Entrepreneurship: The Effects of Firm Age on Motives of Internationalization* (New York: Garland).

Bruton, G.D. and Rubanik, Y. (2002) 'Resources of the firm, russian high-technology startups, and firm growth', *Journal of Business Venturing*, 17, 553–76.

Burt, R.S. (1997) 'The contingent value of social capital ', *Administrative Science Quarterly*, 42, 339–65.

Child, J. and Rodrigues, S.B. (2005) 'The Internationalization of chinese firms: A case for Theoretical Extension?', *Management and Organization Review*, 1, 381–410.

Cohen, W.M. and Levinthal, D.A. (1990) 'Absorptive capacity: A new perspective on learning and innovation', *Administrative Science Quarterly*, 35, 128–52.

Collins, C.J and Smith, K.G. (2006) 'Knowledge exchange and combination: The role of human resource practices in the performance of high-technology firms', *Academy of Management Journal*, 49, 544–60.

Crick, D. and Spence, M. (2005) 'The internationalization of "High Performing" Uk High-Tech SMEs: A study of planned and unplanned strategies', *International Business Review*, 14, 167–85.

Delios, A. and Henisz, W. (2003) 'Political hazards, experience, and sequential entry Strategies: The international expansion of japanese firms, 1980–1998', *Strategic Management Journal*, 24, 1153–64.

Deloitte Touche Tohmatsu (2008) *Lighting the Way: Deloitte Technology Fast 500 Asia Pacific 2008 Ranking and CEO Survey.*

Dess, G.G, Lumpkin, G.T. and Covin, J.G. (1997) 'Entrepreneurial strategy making and firm performance: Tests of contingency and configurational models', *Strategic Management Journal*, 18, 677–95.

Easterby-Smith, M., Lyles, M.A. and Tsang, E.W.K. (2008) 'Inter-organizational knowledge transfer: Current themes and future prospects', *Journal of Management Studies*, 45, 677–90.

Elg, U., Ghauri, P.N. and Tarnovskaya, V. (2008) 'The role of networking and matching in market entry to emerging retail markets', *International Marketing Review*, 25, 674–99.

Ensley, M.D., Pearce, C.L. and Hmieleski, K.M. (2006) 'The moderating effect of environmental dynamism on the relationship between entrepreneur leadership behavior and new venture performance', *Journal of Business Venturing*, 21, 243–63.

Eriksson, K., Johanson, J., Majkgård, A. and Sharma, D. (2000) 'Variation in the internationalization process', *International Studies in Management and Organization*, 30, 26–44.

Fillis, I. (2001) 'Small firm internationalization: An investigative survey and future research Directions', *Management Decision*, 39, 767.

Forsgren, M. (2002) 'The concept of learning in the Uppsala internationalization process model: A critical review', *International Business Review*, 11, 257–77.

Freeman, J., Carroll, G.R. and Hanan, M.T. (1983) 'The liability of newness: Age dependence in organizational death rates', *American Sociological Review*, 48, 692–710.

Fu, P.P., Tsui, A.S. and Dess, G.G. (2006) 'The dynamics of guanxi in chinese high-tech firms: implications for knowledge management and decision making', *Management International Review*, 46, 277–305.

Gao, G.Y., Zhou, K.Z. and Yim, C.K. (2007) 'On what should firms focus in transitional economies? A study of the contingent value of strategic orientations in China', *International Journal of Research in Marketing*, 24, 3–15.

Ghauri, P.N. and Gronhaug, K. (2005) *Research Methods in Business Studies: A Practical Guide,* 3rd edn (London: FT-Prentice Hall).

Ghauri, P.N., Hadjikhani, A. and Johanson, J. (2005) *Managing Opportunity Development in Business Networks* (London: Palgrave).

Gilbert, B.A., McDougall, P.P. and Audretsch, D.B. (2006) 'New venture growth: A review and extension', *Journal of Management*, 32, 926–50.

Gomes-Casseres, B. (1997) 'Alliance strategies of small firms' *Small Business Economics*, 9, 33–44.

Grant, R.M. (1996) 'Prospering in dynamically-competitive environments: Organizational capability as knowledge integration', *Organization Science*, 7, 375–87.

Grant, R.M. and Baden-Fuller, C. (2004) 'A knowledge accessing theory of strategic alliance', *Journal of Management Studies*, 41, 61–84.

Guillén, M.F. (2002) 'Structural inertia, imitation, and foreign expansion: South Korea firms and business groups in China', *Academy of Management Journal*, 45, 509–25.

Hagedoorn, J. and Duysters, G. (2002) 'External sources of innovative capabilities: The preference for strategic alliances or mergers and acquisitions', *Journal of Management Studies*, 39, 167–88.

Hitt, M. and Ireland, D. (2000) 'The intersection of entrepreneurship and strategic management', in D. Sexton and H. Landstrom (eds), *Handbook of Entrepreneurship* (Oxford: Blackwell Publishing).

Hoskisson, R.E., Eden, L., Lau, C.M. and Wright, M. (2000) 'Strategy in emerging economies', *The Academy of Management Journal*, 43, 249–67.

Johanson, J. and Vahlne, J.-E. (1977) 'The internationalization process of the firm – a model of knowledge development and increasing foreign market commitments', *Journal of International Business Studies*, 8, 25–34.

Johanson, J. and Vahlne, J.-E (1990) 'The mechanism of internationalization', *International Marketing Review*, 7, 11–24.

Keskin, H. (2006) 'Market orientation, learning orientation, and innovation capabilities in SMEs: An extended model', *European Journal of Innovation Management*, 9, 396–417.

Knight, G. and Cavusgil, S.T. (1996) 'The born global firm: A challenge to traditional internationalization theory', *Advances in International Marketing*, 8, 11–26.

B. Kogut and U. Zander. (1993) 'Knowledge of the Firm and the Evolutionary Theory of the Multinational Corporation'. *Journal of International Business Studies*, 24, 625–45.

Kumar, N., Stern, L.W. and Anderson, J.C. (1993) 'Conducting interorganizational research using key informants', *Academy of Management Journal*, 36, 1633–51.

P. W. Lamb and P. W. Liesch. (2002) 'The internationalization process of the smaller firm: re-framing the relationships between market commitment, knowledge and involvement'. *Management International Review*, 42, 7.

Lee, C., Lee, K. and Johannes, M.P. (2001) 'Internal capabilities, external networks, and performance: A study on technology-based ventures', *Strategic Management Journal*, 22, 615.

Li, H. and Zhang, Y. (2007) 'The role of managers' political networking and functional experience in new venture performance: Evidence from china's transition economy', *Strategic Management Journal*, 28, 791–804.

Li, M. and Catherine, N.A. a. P.M. (2001) 'Firm internationalization and economic performance: A conceptual synthesis and an empirical assessment of the chinese Experience', *Advances in International Marketing*: JAI, 179–96.

Liesch, P.W. and Knight, G.A. (1999) 'Information internalization and hurdle rates in small and medium enterprise internationalization', *Journal of International Business Studies*, 30, 383–94.

Low, M.B. and Abrahamson, E. (1997) 'Movements, bandwagons, and clones: Industry evolution and the entrepreneurial process', *Journal of Business Venturing*, 12, 435–57.

Lumpkin, G.T. and Dess, G.G. (2001) 'Linking two dimensions of entrepreneurial orientation to firm performance: The moderating role of environment and industry life cycle', *Journal of Business Venturing*, 16, 429–51.

McCann, J.E. (1991) 'Patterns of growth, competitive technology, and financial strategies in young ventures'. *Journal of Business Venturing*, 6, 189–208.

McDougall, P.P. (1989) 'International versus domestic entrepreneurship: New venture strategic behavior and industry structure', *Journal of Business Venturing*, 4, 387–400.

McDougall, P.P. and Oviatt, B.M. (2000) 'International entrepreneurship: The intersection of two research paths', *Academy of Management Journal*, 43, 902.

McDougall, P.P., Robinson, R.B. and DeNisi, A.C. (1992) 'Modeling new venture Performance: An analysis of new venture strategy, industry structure, and venture origin', *Journal of Business Venturing*, 7, 267–89.

McDougall, P.P., Shane, S. and Oviatt, B.M. (1994) 'Explaining the formation of international new ventures: The limits of theories from international business research', *Journal of Business Venturing*, 9, 469–87.

Meyer, K.E., Wright, M. and Pruthi, S. (2009) 'Managing knowledge in foreign entry strategies: A resource-based analysis', *Strategic Management Journal*, 30, 557–74.

Miles, R.E., Snow, C.S., Mathews, J.A, Miles, G. and Coleman, Jr.H.J. (1997) 'Organizing in the knowledge age: Anticipating the cellular form', *Academy of Management Executive*, 11, 7–20.

Park, S.H. and Luo, Y. (2001) 'Guanxi and organizational dynamics: Organizational networking in chinese firms', *Strategic Management Journal*, 22, 455–77.

Peng, M.W. (2001a) 'How entrepreneurs create wealth in transition economies', *Academy of Management Executive*, 15, 95–108.

Peng, M.W. (2001b) 'The resource-based view and international business', *Journal of Management*, 27, 803–29.

Penrose, E. (1959) *The Theory of the Growth of the Firm* (New York: Oxford University Press).

Presutti, M., Boari, C. and Fratocchi, L. (2007) 'Knowledge acquisition and the foreign development of high-tech start-ups: A social capital approach', *International Business Review*, 16, 23–46.

Priem, R.L and Bulter, J.E. (2001) 'Is the resource-based 'view' a useful perspective for strategic management research?', *Academy of Management Review*, 26, 22–40.

Robinson, K.C. (1999) 'An examination of the influence of industry structure on eight alternative measures of new venture performance for high potential independent new ventures', *Journal of Business Venturing*, 14, 165–87.

Shrader, R.C. (2001) 'Collaboration and performance in foreign markets: The case of young high-technology manufacturing firms', *The Academy of Management Journal*, 44, 45–60.

Sinkovics, R.R., Penz, E. and Ghauri, P.N. (2008) 'Enhancing the trustworthiness of qualitative research in international business', *Management International Review*, 48, 689–714.

STCSM *2006 Shang Hai Ke Ji Jin Bu Bao Gao* (2006). Shanghai: Science and Technology Commission of Shanghai Municipality.

Stieglitz, N. and Heine, K. (2007) 'Innovations and the role of complementarities in a strategic theory of the firm', *Strategic Management Journal*, 28, 15.

Tsai, W. (2001) 'Knowledge transfer in intraorganizational networks: Effects of network position and absorptive gapacity on business unit innovation and performance', *Academy of Management Journal*, 44, 996–1004.

Watson, S. and Hewett, K. (2006) 'A multi-theoretical model of knowledge transfer in organizations: Determinants of knowledge contribution and knowledge reuse', *Journal of Management Studies*, 43, 141–73.

Westhead, P., Wright, M. and Ucbasaran, D. (2001) 'The internationalization of new and small firms: A resource-based view', *Journal of Business Venturing*, 16, 333–58.

Yamakawa, Y., Peng, M.W. and Deeds, D.L. (2008) 'What drives new ventures to internationalize from emerging to developed economies?', *Entrepreneurship: Theory & Practice*, 32, 59–82.

Yeoh, P.-L. (2004) 'International learning: Antecedents and performance implications among newly internationalizing companies in an exporting context', *International Marketing Review*, 21, 511–35.

Yiu, D.W., Lau, C. and Bruton,G.D. (2007) 'International venturing by emerging economy firms: The effects of firm capabilities, home country networks, and corporate entrepreneurship', *Journal of International Business Studies*, 38, 519–40.

Yli-Renko, H., Autio, E. and Sapienza, H.J. (2001) 'Social capital, knowledge acquisitions, and knowledge exploitation in young technology-based firms', *Strategic Management Journal*, 22, 587.

Zahra, S.A. (1993) 'Environment, corporate entrepreneurship, and financial perform-ance: A taxonomic approach', *Journal of Business Venturing*, 8, 319–40.

Zahra, S.A. and Garvis, D.M. (2000) 'International corporate entrepreneurship and firm performance: The moderating effect of international environmental hostility', *Journal of Business Venturing*, 15, 469–92.

Zahra, S.A., Ireland, R.D. and Hitt, M.A. (2000) 'International expansion by new venture firms: International diversity, mode of market entry, technological learning, and per-formance', *The Academy of Management Journal*, 43, 925–50.

Zahra, S.A., Sapienza, H.J. and Davidsson, P. (2006) 'Entrepreneurship and dynamic capabilities: A review, model and research agenda', *Journal of Management Studies*, 43, 917–55.

Zander, U. and Kogut, B. (1995) 'Knowledge and the speed of the transfer and imitation of organizational capabilities: An empirical test', *Organization Science*, 6, 76–92.

Zhou, L., Wu, W.-P. and Luo, X. (2007) 'Internationalization and the performance of born-global SMEs: The mediating role of social networks', *Journal of International Business Studies*, 38, 673–90.

12
A Conceptualization of e-Risk Perceptions and the Offline-Online Risk Trade-Off for Small Firm Internationalization

Noemi Pezderka and Rudolf R. Sinkovics

Introduction

With growing competitive pressures, companies are increasingly deploying the Internet (Porter, 2001) as strategic option of performance enhancement. With the Internet representing a potentially fluid and boundary-less medium (Lim et al. 2004), this deployment takes place not only in domestic but also in international markets. The adoption of the Internet appears to be particularly important for smaller firms. They are naturally poorer in terms of resource-endowment than large MNEs (Welsh and White, 1981) and the Internet promises a fast-track and time-compressed option for international expansion (Sinkovics and Penz, 2005; Yamin and Sinkovics, 2006). However, as international business deals with a multitude of contingencies in its environment progressive expansion comes at a price and is increasingly risky (Shrader, Oviatt, and Phillips McDougall, 2000). Internet reliance and the deployment of information and communication technologies (ICT) may implicate 'ambiguous' effects (Jean, 2007). The virtual analogue to traditional physical exchange is not risk-free but exposes firms to an array of related risks (Scott, 2004; Viehland, 2001; Wat, Ngai, and Cheng, 2005). While some of these risks are only relevant in the online context, others have their origins in the traditional international business environment. Even though many risks belonging to the latter category are deemed less relevant for companies predominantly doing business in cyberspace, they need to be carefully examined as they might still affect these companies in a different and/or in a less visible way. Understanding international risk in both its traditional and virtual form is thus crucial. While the conscious and controlled handling of risks may represent an important source of sustainable competitive advantage in terms of the resource based view (Barney, 1991), the lack of a thorough risk assessment and of the weighing of the offline-online risk trade-off can not only deprive a business of future profits but might also lead to complete business failure. However, the development of an international e-risk framework is not only relevant from a small firm survival and prosperity perspective, it also contributes to conceptual and theoretical development of international business and international entrepreneurship thinking, as the concept of risk occupies a pivotal theoretical position in both domains.

Thus, this chapter pursues two objectives. First, it aims at investigating how traditional international risks take effect in the online context based on Brouthers's (1995) empirically tested risk dimensions taking a first step towards the construction of an international e-risk framework. Second, it endeavours to explain the risk trade-off between offline and online internationalization for small firms that give preference to a more virtualized market entrysolution rather than to traditional market entry. The structure of the chapter is as follows: The first section introduces the international e-risk framework. The second section discusses the role of risk perceptions in online market entry mode decisions by proposing a simple model based on the internalization constituent of Dunning's eclectic (OLI) framework. The section concludes by considering limitations and implications for future research.

An international e-business risk framework

The international business literature lacks a generally accepted definition of international risk (Ahmed et al. 2002; Miller, 1992). In this chapter, Ahmed et al.'s (2002) definition of international risk is adopted, pointing at *'dangers firms face in terms of limitations, restrictions, or even losses when engaging in international business'*. In the early international trade literature scholars generally concentrated only on a limited number of risks. Even though gradually attempts had been made to classify international risks, Miller (1992) was the first to develop a framework for categorizing uncertainties confronting firms in international operations. At this point, the difference between the notion of risk and uncertainty needs to be delineated despite their occasional interchangeable use throughout the literature. In his paper Garratt (2007) cites Knight's definitions of risk and uncertainty. According to Knight, *'risk is where the probabilities of different outcomes are known, but not the outcome itself'* and *'uncertainty is where the probabilities themselves are unknown'* (Garratt, 2007, p. 11). Risk is thus the probability of loss in outcome variables (Flowerday and von Solms, 2005; Miller, 1992). Brouthers (1995) extended Miller's framework, creating the most comprehensive and empirically tested framework of international risks to date (Figure 12.1). Before embarking on the discussion how these traditional risk dimensions may

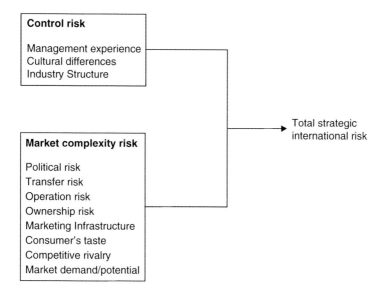

Figure 12.1   Strategic international risk (adopted from Brouthers, 1995)

still take effect in the online context despite their expected full or partial elimination, a short reference to the factors leading to these discrepancies is deemed important. Essentially, the degree of online market entry is contingent on the nature of the goods. Physical products, by their very nature, expose businesses to offline international risks. Products with high online transferability such as software, on the other hand, introduce international risks on a less visible level.

Control risk

Control risk is a function of management's (perceived) ability to reduce certain types of risks by directly managing foreign operations (Brouthers, 1995; Cyert and March, 1963). In particular, three factors are expected to have an effect on the perception of control risk. Management's control ambitions, their knowledge about the target market and the existence, awareness of, and access to alternative control mechanisms will influence risk perceptions at different cognitive levels (Brouthers, 1995). Generally, when total control risk, consisting of (1) management experience, (2) cultural differences, and (3) the industry structure is perceived as too high, management is expected to be more inclined to sacrifice certain aspects of their controlling power in order to share responsibility (Brouthers, 1995). The advancement of ICT, however, may offer a viable alternative to traditional ways of exerting control.

Management experience

Management's experience is built step by step in the course of conducting business operations internationally. Since this knowledge is mainly classified as tacit and implicit its externalization and communication to others is rather difficult. Consequently, mere virtual interaction with foreign markets does not result in the same learning experience given the externalized knowledge character of the information displayed on the Internet (Petersen, Welch, and Liesch, 2002). As low levels of experience not only affect managements' strategic decision making but also their level of risk perception, the lower the level of management's experience the higher the level of perceived international risk (Brouthers, 1995). A high perception and incorrect assessment of risks due to insufficient experience may result in taking unsuitable strategic decisions (Scott, 2004). At this point a discussion of the nature of managerial experience is required. While international business experience is important for strategic decisions regarding internationalization, it has been found to have no significant impact on the choice of using online media as a means of international expansion. For that latter purpose previous Internet experience has proved to be a key factor (Berry and Brock, 2004). Consequently, it seems that for making sound strategic decisions for online internationalization, both international business experience and Internet experience are needed. Nevertheless, management's experience and expertise has been often undervalued which repeatedly led to the collapse of many Internet firms (Vahlne and Johanson, 2002).

Cultural risk

A study conducted by (Bennett, 1997) among 358 exporting companies (148 Web users and 210 nonusers) showed that those using the Internet for internationalization purposes regard psychic distance as less relevant than nonusers. Psychic distance is defined by (O' Grady and Lane, 1996) as '[...] *a firm's degree of uncertainty about a foreign market resulting from cultural differences and other business difficulties that present barriers to learning about the market and operating there'*. The underestimation of differences across (Internet-)markets represents a major risk for e-companies, as cultural distance has a detrimental effect on Internet shopping rates (Lim et al. 2004). Yamin and Sinkovics (2006) also find that the possibility of 'virtuality trap' may emerge in online internationalization, when companies mistakenly assume that they understand the environmental basis of different consumer behaviour and inappropriately generalize business conditions as similar. Thus not adequately adapting the company's Web site and products to national preferences can lead to a negative impact on company performance (Reeves, 2000; Scott, 2004).

Industry structure risk

Industry structure risk can be defined as the risk of not correctly assessing the nature and intensity of competition in a market (Brouthers, 1995). Companies in highly concentrated industries have the ability to maintain high barriers to entry and to inflict greater damage on their competitors due to a better knowledge of one another's strengths and weaknesses than companies in more fragmented industries (Brouthers, 1995). The spread of the Internet, however, effectuates a reduction in entry and exit barriers entailing a *'flood of new entrants into many industries'* (Porter, 2001, p. 67). Due to the expansion of geographic markets companies increasingly face competition not only from within the global industry but also from firms offering substitute products (Porter, 2001). Thus, while the Internet mitigates the power of established companies of (formerly) concentrated markets, it also impedes the assessment and identification of actual competition (Porter, 2001; Quelch and Klein, 1996).

Market complexity risk

Market complexity risks include market-specific variables related to a firm's market entry, distribution and profitability. Similarly to control risks, market complexity risks are based on how management perceives similarities and differences between their home market and the foreign market. From a traditional market entry perspective, perception of similarities with the home market is expected to result in higher resource commitment (Brouthers, 1995). Online market entry, although bearing the potential to reduce resource commitment while maintaining tight control over foreign operations (Yamin and Sinkovics, 2007), not only presupposes certain conditions such as the existence of a compatible ICT infrastructure in the host country (Jean, Sinkovics, and Kim, 2008; Yamin and Sinkovics, 2006, 2007), it also re-introduces the market complexity risk in a different form.

Political risk

The risk of political changes in a host country, due to, for example, war or revolution, affecting a company's business is one of the most researched traditional risks in the international business literature (Bannister and Bawcutt, 1981; Brouthers, 1995; Miller, 1992; Root, 1987). Yet, it is underresearched and often ignored in the evolving e-commerce literature (Frynas, 2002; Lynne, 2000). Although it might be expected that political risk will have a less dramatic impact on virtual enterprises than on their physical counterparts, when it comes to destructive turmoils e-companies may be harmed more immediately than by a mere slump in sales. Since all networks have a physical infrastructure (Malecki, 2002) these may be severely damaged in the event of military encounters. Furthermore, large cities not only tend to dominate in network connections (Malecki, 2002); they also happen to be the most likely targets for attacks. As soon as physical products are involved, political risks regain in importance in their traditional sense, as the delivery process takes place offline.

Transfer risk

The risk of not adequately adapting to institutional restrictions regarding product and/or information flows in a country belongs to the relatively well-researched dimensions of the international trade literature (Brouthers, 1995; Miller, 1992; Root, 1987). Root (1987) refers to it as future government action that might restrict foreign companies' payment and/or capital transfers out of the country. He also includes inconvertibility or depreciation of currency into his definition. However, these dimensions are mostly dealt with under the heading of exchange risk in the literature. Brouthers (1995) extended this definition to government policies restricting the free flow of goods and services. While the Internet is reducing certain traditional trade barriers (Hamill, 1997; Porter, 2001) and is regarded as an alternative/complement to physical market entry (e.g., Bennett, 1997, Berry and Brock, 2004; Stockdale and Standing, 2004) the intercountry regulatory competition inter alia to set ICT standards (Winn, 2007) may still lead to government measures affecting the undisturbed flow of products and/or information (Braga, 2005; Frynas, 2002; Kobrin, 2001). Furthermore, it appears that countries tend to regulate e-commerce in a similar fashion in which they regulate other domestic issues (Winn, 2007). Consequently, there is a probability that with growing online internationalization less democratic countries may take action of protectionist nature which might impair on foreign e-companies' business (Andonova, 2006; Braga, 2005).

Operation risk

This risk dimension has been used by several authors. While Root (1987) applied the term similar to the transfer risk dimension, Miller (1992) subsumed under operation risk firm-level risks occurring in the course of business conduct such as employee unrest, raw materials shortages, machine failure, and so on. Depending on the nature of the business, for example, manufacturing or service, different operation risks may be relevant. The nature of the goods produced, for example, tangible-dominant, intangible-dominant, is a further contingency factor for operation risk. In the online context, there is an array of risks which have only been rudimentarily investigated in the literature. With increasing product digitizability risks such as privacy, intellectual property, reliability, identification, security, and identity theft come to the fore (Scott 2004). While these risks are specific to the online context, others such as physical security, logistics, dependency, reputation, credit, and legal dimensions can also be found in the offline context. Thus operation risk is, rather, an umbrella term subsuming two streams of risks. However, given the focus on international aspects, the elaborate analysis of operation risks is left to future investigation.

Ownership risk

Even though owing to their predominant virtuality e-companies are generally not expected to be affected by the risk of losing company assets due to expropriation, confiscation or domestication in a foreign country (Frynas, 2002), there are certain aspects to e-commerce to which ownership risk still applies. E-companies are highly dependent on Internet infrastructure which is manifested in the physical world through telecommunications companies, Internet service providers (ISP), backbone carriers, and so on (Malecki, 2002). Companies with the means to invest in private networks (Malecki, 2002) for higher security and speed may be by implication subject to expropriation. Furthermore, international e-commerce firms need servers to host their virtual assets such as Web sites and other applications (Ossi, 2001). Since these servers may be located in several countries, depending on whether the enterprise chooses to directly own and operate the servers or to outsource this task to third-party ISPs (Ossi, 2001), there may be a certain exposure to ownership risk.

Marketing infrastructure risk

In Brouthers's (1995, p. 17) international risk framework, marketing infrastructure risk refers to the lack of a *'structured and secure infrastructure'*. When it comes to physical distribution of goods the existence and state of a country's road, rail, air, and water networks maintain their traditional relevance. Furthermore, the distribution of intangible and digital products is affected by a country's poor infrastructure in its traditional sense when factors such as electricity are concerned (Brouthers, 1995). Pure online infrastructure risks, however, stem from differences across countries in bandwidth affecting the speed of information flows (Kannan, 2001), in telecommunications infrastructure, for example, phone lines, fibre trunks, and so on (Javalgi et al. 2005), in the Internet access method used by customers such as computers, mobile phones, TV sets, and so on. (Guillen, 2002), in the cost of Internet use (Guillen, 2002; Javalgi et al. 2005) and in the number of Internet hosts (Javalgi et al. 2005).

Consumers' taste and market demand risk

While consumers' taste refers to the risk of not adequately understanding how consumers use the firm's products, market demand risk is defined as the risk of not adequately gauging the market. As consumers may use the same product in different ways across countries or even not use them at all, identification, assessment of, and adaptation to those differences is crucial to a company's profitability. The geographic separation between a firm and their international customers, will add to the problem by disengaging or disconnecting the firm from the business and institutional environment and expose them to the 'virtuality trap' (Yamin and Sinkovics 2006). Hence, assessing the current and/or future demand for a firm's products is essential for effective strategy creation (Brouthers, 1995).

Competitive risk

Despite expectations for an increase in competitiveness (Nittana, Terrence Clifford, and Antonia, 2008), when substituting traditional channels with online media without sufficient strategic considerations, companies may be confronted with a decrease thereof stemming from (1) low switching costs negating the positive effects of network externalities (Porter, 2001); (2) the incorrect choice of online product offerings (de Figueiredo, 2000); (3) the existence of product comparison platforms (Scott, 2004; Porter, 2001); as well as (4) from ignoring the potential benefits of complementary offline presence (Amit and Zott, 2001; Porter, 2001).

The role of risk perceptions in SMEs' entry mode decisions

As already accentuated in the introduction section, engaging in virtual internationalization makes it necessary to understand the risks it involves. Whereas some of these risks can be paralleled with traditional business risks, others stem from the uniqueness of Information and Communication Technologies. For that reason a classification in three main categories may be of practical importance, that is, traditional IB, operational, and online media risks. This differentiation is required as risks belonging to the respective categories may be perceived differently by managers. However, as the focus of this chapter was set on the traditional IB-risk stream, the two latter categories will not be considered in the following discussion. For the purpose of this paper online internationalization is defined as a form of foreign market entry which takes place *'in the virtual rather than the real or spatial domain'* (Yamin and Sinkovics, 2006, p. 340). Even though depending on the nature of the goods, the special domain cannot be completely ignored, companies opting for this mode of entry do not have an equity based market presence in the host country. While there are studies speculating on the potential advantages and disadvantages of e-commerce adoption as well as on the Internet's impact on the internationalization process and existing export marketing theories (e.g., Gregory, Karavdic, and Zou, 2007; Karavdic and Gregory, 2005) the literature lacks a conceptual framework that explicitly details the reasons for online market entry choice over more traditional entry modes. In this section, a simple model is proposed in an attempt to explain the role of risk perceptions, both traditional and electronic, in SMEs' decision to engage in virtual market expansion (see Figure 12.2).

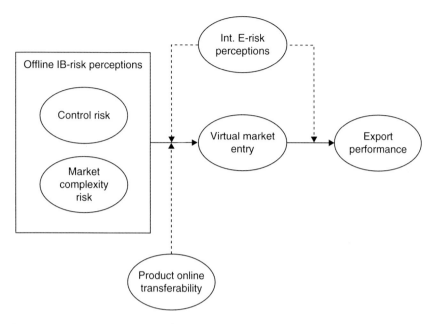

Figure 12.2 Conceptualization of risk trade-offs and impacts on export performance

Perception is a learned mental process used to reduce the complexity of information and/or misinformation about the environment. Generally, decisions are based on *'perceptions of the environment,* [and] *not on environmental reality'* (Johnston and Wright, 2004, p. 235). Applying this definition to managerial risk perceptions, from the actual risk level predominantly differing perceptions of traditional international business risks and of their virtual counterparts are expected to affect decision making. The existence of international risk trade-offs among country risk, resource commitment, and market revenue exposure is already documented in the international business literature (Miller, 1992; Shrader et al. 2000). Previous research also showed that perceiving high traditional international risks in a target market may lead to less committed market entry modes in terms of resources and control (Brouthers 1995). Since ICT seem to offer a low-resource-commitment-high-control alternative, the following proposition can be derived:

P1: SMEs are more likely to prefer online market entry when perceived offline control risks in a target country are high than when perceived offline control risks are low.

P2: SMEs are more likely to prefer online market entry when perceived offline market complexity risks in a target country are high than when perceived offline market complexity risks are low.

Based on the above argumentation, it may appear that online market entry has the potential to counterbalance the risk-resource-commitment-control trade-off. Yet, as delineated in the second section, this entry form exhibits its own set of risks. Consequently, the perception of international e-risks entails a different kind of managerial trade-off decision. In this scenario traditional international business risks are traded off against international e-risks.

P3: High perceptions of total international e-risks have a moderating effect on SMEs' online market entry decision.

Informational, intangible-dominant and digitizable products are more suitable for online commerce than tangible-dominant goods because of their increased online transferability (Karavdic and Gregory, 2005). Gregory et al. (2007) found empirical evidence for product online transferability to have a positive, direct effect on export marketing strategy as it facilitates product adaptation to customers' needs leading to increased efficiency, enhanced distribution support, and under certain circumstances to a more competitive price. Since tangible products often require 'tactile feedback' and cannot be directly distributed through ICT the level of reliance on online media for dealing in these products is likely to be lower than that for intangible-dominant or digitizable goods (Peterson, Balasubramanian, and Bronnenberg, 1997; Varadarajan and Yadav, 2002). Even though many companies offer both physical and digital/digitizable products since supplementary services (e.g., after-sales services) increasingly tend to be provided online (Petersen and Welch, 2003), when opting for pure online market entry firms are expected to predominantly carry product offerings with high product online transferability. Thus, Proposition 4 suggests that:

P4: Product online transferability has a moderating effect on SMEs' online market entry decision.

The impact of risk perceptions on entry mode decisions have been empirically tested and confirmed using Dunning's eclectic paradigm (Brouthers, 1995; Nakos and Brouthers, 2002). Since the OLI framework builds on a number of economic and behavioural theories including transaction-cost economics theory (Dunning, 2001), Brouthers and Nakos (2004) investigated SME entry mode choice from a TCE perspective. They found support for small firms exhibiting a significantly better performance when selecting transaction-cost predicted entry modes as opposed to other modes of entry (Brouthers and Nakos, 2004). In this paper, we are only concerned with the 'internalization' component of the OLI framework, as the empirically supported risk concepts were subsumed under that dimension (Nakos and Brouthers, 2002). Nevertheless, in analogy with previous findings on the framework's entry-mode-predicting-ability firms can be expected to demonstrate better export performance when choosing an 'internalization' predicted internationalization strategy than when opting for a different alternative.

> *P5: Given a compliance with the strategy prediction of the OLI framework's internalization component, there is a positive relationship between online market entry strategy and export performance.*

In addition to their moderating function on online market entry selection, risk perceptions may also play an important role after an online market entry decision has been made. International e-risks are in many cases difficult to anticipate. Their existence is believed to have a negative effect on company profitability (Braga, 2005; Porter, 2001; Reeves, 2000). Even though Miller's (1992) suggestion of risk management applying a financial approach (e.g., by insurance) is also appealing in the online context, this presupposes the existence of such instruments in the host country. While in countries such as Germany a relatively advanced insurance infrastructure in the form of 'traditional' and 'special' e-insurance offers is already in place (Grzebiela, 2002), this may not be the case in other countries to the same extent. Consequently, when the occurrence probability of online risks is perceived as high after an online market entry strategy has already been implemented, it can be expected that SMEs' export sales and export performance as a whole will be affected (Acedo and Florin, 2007; Andrijcic and Horowitz, 2006; Bromiley, 1991). Therefore, it is proposed that:

> *P6: High perceptions of international e-risks after the implementation of an online market entry strategy has a negative impact on SMEs export performance.*

Conclusions

This paper attempted to investigate how Brouthers's (1995) empirically tested international risk framework takes effect in the online context. It is suggested that despite its potential to offset certain aspects of the risk–resource–commitment–control trade-off, online market entry requires trade-off decisions of a different kind, that is, trading off traditional international risks against international e-risks. Since the risk dimensions under scrutiny tend to be considered under the internalization constituent of Dunning's OLI framework, a model is proposed how offline and online risk perceptions may influence SMEs' decision to select online market entry over more traditional entry forms.

The main limitation of the above model is its simplicity. Factors affecting risk perceptions such as culture, the current government's transaction governance capability, the owner-manager's entrepreneurial orientation, and so on, have not been considered. Future research may not only wish to include supplementary variables, but may also consider to expand the risk framework by introducing additional risk dimensions which complement the operational and online media risk streams, and integrate them into a more elaborate contingency model explaining online entry mode decisions. Since this paper only considered the internalization dimension, an investigation of how the other two OLI components (ownership and location) impact on online internationalization strategy may be of future research interest. Furthermore, work is also required to operationalize the proposed international e-risk dimensions empirically and test their viability and relevance for international e-commerce.

References

Acedo, F.J. and Florin, J. (2007) 'Understanding the risk perception of strategic opportunities: A tripartite model', *Strategic Change*, 16(3), 97–116.

Ahmed, Z.U., Mohamad, O., Tan, B. and Johnson, J.P. (2002) 'International risk perceptions and mode of entry: A case study of Malaysian multinational firms', *Journal of Business Research* 55(10), 805–13.

Amit, R. and Zott, C. (2001) 'Value creation in e-business', *Strategic Management Journal*, 22(6/7), 493–520.

Andonova, V. (2006) 'Mobile phones, the internet and the institutional environment', *Telecommunications Policy*, 30(1), 29–45.

Andrijcic, E. and Horowitz, B. (2006) 'A macro-economic framework for evaluation of cyber security risks related to protection of intellectual property', *Risk Analysis: An International Journal*, 26(4), 907–23.

Bannister, J.E. and Bawcutt, P.A. (1981) *Practical Risk Management* (London: Witherby & Co. Ltd).

Barney, J.B. (1991) 'Firm resources and sustained competitive advantage', *Journal of Management*, 17(1), 99–121.

Bennett, R. (1997) 'Export marketing and the internet: Experiences of web site use and perceptions of export barriers among UK businesses', *International Marketing Review*, 14(5), 324–44.

Berry, M.M.J. and Brock, J.K.-U. (2004) 'Marketspace and the internationalisation process of the small firm', *Journal of International Entrepreneurship*, 2(3), 187–216.

Braga, C. A P. (2005) 'E-commerce regulation: New game, new rules?', *Quarterly Review of Economics and Finance*, 45(2,3), 541–58.

Bromiley, P. (1991) 'Testing a causal model of corporate risk taking and performance', *Academy of Management Journal*, 34(1), 37–59.

Brouthers, K.D. (1995) 'The influence of international risk on entry mode strategy in the computer software industry', *Management International Review*, 35(1), 7–28.

Brouthers, K.D. and Nakos, G.D. (2004) 'SME entry mode choice and performance: A transaction cost perspective', *Entrepreneurship Theory and Practice*, 28(3), 229–47.

Cyert, R.M. and March, J.G. (1963) *A Behavioral Theory of the Firm*, Prentice-Hall Behavioral Sciences in Business Series (Englewood Cliffs, N.J.: Prentice Hall).

de Figueiredo, J.M. (2000) 'Finding sustainable profitability in electronic commerce', *MIT Sloan Management Review*, 41(4), 41–52.

Dunning, J.H. (2001) 'The eclectic (oli) paradigm of international production: Past, present and future', *International Journal of the Economics of Business*, 8(2), 173–90.

Flowerday, S. and von Solms, R. (2005) 'Real-time information integrity = system integrity + data integrity + continuous assurances', *Computers & Security*, 24(8), 604–13.

Frynas, J.G. (2002) 'The limits of globalization-legal and political issues in e-commerce', *Management Decision*, 40(9), 871–80.

Garratt, B. (2007) 'Dilemmas, uncertainty, risks, and board performance', *BT Technology Journal*, 25(1), 11–18.

Gregory, G, Karavdic, M. and Zou, S. (2007) 'The effects of e-commerce drivers on export marketing strategy', *Journal of International Marketing*, 15(2), 30–57.

Grzebiela, T. (2002) 'Insurability of electronic commerce risks', Proceedings of the 35th Hawaii International Conference on System Sciences – 2002, IEEE Computer Society, Hawaii.

Guillen, M.F. (2002) 'What is the best global strategy for the internet?', *Business Horizons*, 45(3), 39–46.

Hamill, J. (1997) 'The internet and international marketing', *International Marketing Review*, 14(5), 300–23.

Javalgi, R.G., Wickramasinghe, N., Scherer, R. F. and Sharma, S.K. (2005) 'An assessment and strategic guidelines for developing e-commerce in the asia-pacific region', *International Journal of Management*, 22(4), 523–31.

Jean, R.-J. "Bryan" (2007) 'The ambiguous relationship of ICT and organizational performance: A literature review', *Critical Perspectives on International Business*, 3(4), 306–21.

Jean, R.-J. "Bryan", Sinkovics, R.R. and Kim, D. (2008) 'Information technology and organizational performance within international business to business relationships: A review and an integrated conceptual framework', *International Marketing Review*, 25(5), 563–83.

Johnston, D.A. and Wright, L. (2004) 'The e-business capability of small and medium sized firms in international supply chains', *Information Systems and EBusiness Management*, 2(2–3), 223–40.

Kannan, P.K. (2001) 'Introduction to the special issue: Marketing in the e-channel', *International Journal of Electronic Commerce*, 5(3), 3–6.

Karavdic, M. and Gregory, G. (2005) 'Integrating e-commerce into existing export marketing theories: A contingency model', *Marketing Theory*, 5(1), 75–104.

Kobrin, S.J. (2001) 'Territoriality and the governance of cyberspace', *Journal of International Business Studies*, 32(4), 687–705.

Lim, K.H, Leung, K., Sia, C.L. and Lee, M. KO (2004) 'Is ecommerce boundary-less? Effects of individualism-collectivism and uncertainty avoidance on internet shopping', *Journal of International Business Studies*, 35(6), 545–59.

Lynne, M. (2000) 'Toward an integrative theory of risk control', in, R. Baskerville, J. Stage and J.I. DeGross, (eds), *Organizational and Social Perspectives on Information Technology*, 167–174 (Boston, Mass.: Kluywer Academic Publishers).

Malecki, E.J. (2002) 'The economic geography of the internet's infrastructure', *Economic Geography*, 78(4), 399–424.

Miller, K.D. (1992) 'A framework for integrated risk management in international business', *Journal of International Business Studies*, 23(2), 311–31.

Nakos, G. and Brouthers, K.D. (2002) 'Entry mode choice of SMEs in Central and Eastern Europe', *Entrepreneurship: Theory & Practice*, 27(1), 47–63.

Nittana, S., Terrence Clifford, S. and Antonia, M.-S. (2008) 'E-commerce entrepreneurship as a national priority: The case of Thailand', *The Service Industries Journal*, 28(7), 1.

O' Grady, S. and Lane, H.W. (1996) 'The psychic distance paradox', *Journal of International Business Studies*, 27(2), 309–33.

Ossi, G. (2001) 'Web servers', *International Tax Review*, (4), 19–29.

Petersen, B., Welch, Lawrence S. and Liesch, P.W. (2002) 'The internet and foreign market expansion by firms', *Management International Review*, 42(2), 207–21.

Petersen, B. and Welch, L.S. (2003) 'International business development and the internet, post-hype', *Management International Review*, 43(1), 7–29.

Peterson, R.A., Balasubramanian, S. and Bronnenberg, B. J. (1997) 'Exploring the implications of the internet for consumer marketing', *Journal of the Academy of Marketing Science*, 25(4), 329–46.

Porter, M.E. (2001) 'Strategy and the internet', *Harvard Business Review*, 79(3), 62–78.

Quelch, J.A. and Klein, L.R. (1996) 'The internet and international marketing', *Sloan Management Review*, 37(3), 60–75.

Reeves, J.Ed. (2000) *Business risk* (London: Caspian Publishing Ltd).

Root, F.R. (1987) *Entry Strategies for International Markets* (Boston, Mass.: D.C. Heath and Company).

Scott, J.E. (2004) 'Measuring dimensions of perceived e-business risks', *Information Systems and E-business Management*, 2(1), 31–55.

Shrader, R.C., Oviatt, B.M. and Phillips McDougall, P. (2000) 'How new ventures exploit trade-offs among international risk factors: Lessons for the accelerated internationalization of the 21st century', *Academy of Management Journal*, 43(6), 1227–47.

Sinkovics, R. and Penz, E. (2005) 'Empowerment of SME websites: Development of a web-empowerment scale and preliminary evidence', *Journal of International Entrepreneurship*, 3(4), 303–15.

Stockdale, R. and Standing, C. (2004) 'Benefits and barriers of electronic marketplace participation: An SME perspective', *Journal of Enterprise Information Management*, 17(4), 301–11.

Vahlne, J-E and Johanson, J. (2002) 'New technology, new companies, new business environments and new internationalisation processes?' in V. Havila, M. Forsgren, and H. Håkansson (eds), *Critical Perspectives on Internationalisation*, 209–27 (Amsterdam, NL: Pergamon).

Varadarajan, P.R.and Yadav, M.S. (2002) 'Marketing strategy and the internet: An organizing framework', *Journal of the Academy of Marketing Science*, 30(4), 296–312.

Viehland, D.W. (2001) 'Managing business risk in electronic commerce', Americas Conference on Information Systems.

Wat, F.K.T., Ngai, E.W.T and Cheng, T.C.E. (2005) 'Potential risks to e-commerce development using exploratory factor analysis', *International Journal of Services Technology and Management*, 6(1), 55–71.

Welsh, J.A. and White, J.F. (1981) 'A small business is not a little big business', *Harvard Business Review*, 59(4), 18–27.

Winn, J.K. (2007) 'U.S. And EU regulatory competition and authentication standards in electronic commerce', *International Journal of IT Standards and Standardization Research*, 5(1), 84–102.

Yamin, M. and Sinkovics, R. R. (2007) 'ICT and MNE reorganisation: The paradox of control', *Critical Perspectives on International Business*, 3(4), 322–36.

Yamin, M. and Sinkovics, R. R. (2006) 'Online internationalisation, psychic distance reduction and the virtuality trap', *International Business Review*, 15(4), 339–60.

Part V

Internationalized SMEs, Resources, and Entrepreneurship

13

Resources and Performance in Foreign Markets: The Case of High-Technology SMEs in Portugal

Luis Bernardino, Marian V. Jones, and Anna Morgan-Thomas

Introduction

The current generally accepted understanding of internationalization is that it is a process of growth and development of the firm in which various aspects of the firm's activities are extended across national borders (Bell, Crick, and Young 2004; Jones 2001). Ultimately, this may involve the transfer of products/services across national boundaries from which international revenue is generated. The challenge for SMEs is that the process of internationalization relies on the firm having, or acquiring sufficient resources to support its entry into and development of foreign markets (Sapienza et al. 2006; Rodríguez and Rodríguez 2005) and specific types of resources are associated with the early and rapid internationalization of small firms, particularly those in high technology sectors. These include for example; unique resources (Oviatt and McDougall 1994), human capital on which networks are built (Chetty and Campbell-Hunt 2003), the prior experience of the management team (Reuber and Fischer 1997), and international orientation (Johanson and Vahlne 1997). While there has been significant interest in the effect of resources or resource limitations on early internationalization, less attention has been paid to the relationship between firm resources and performance once internationalization has been established.

This aim of this chapter is to present some preliminary findings from a study of high-technology SMEs in Portugal which examined the relationship between resource types and performance as measured by international intensity and contribute in three ways to extant knowledge. Firstly, although several authors have focused on the firm's resource-base in internationalization, only a few studies concern exclusively technology-intensive sectors, and their potential effects of resources on international performance (Sapienza et al. 2006).

Secondly, the advent of the international new venture approach (McDougall and Oviatt 2000) has stimulated interest in the means by which small firms internationalize and calls for a closer look at the resources underpinning internationalization. Thirdly, this chapter extends quantitative research in international entrepreneurship by developing and testing measures on key firm resources, thus contributing to the methodological advancement of the field. In sum, this study attempts to enhance the current knowledge on internationalization of the SMEs.

This study examines the influence of firm resources on the international performance of high-tech SMEs through the theoretical lens of the resource-based view (RBV). Using primary data from 106 firms, it empirically tests for the effects of marketing resources, technological resources, financial resources, international orientation, human capital of the entrepreneur, entrepreneur/management team international experience, and entrepreneurial orientation on international performance, as measured by international intensity, in the main export market.

Theoretical background

According to the RBV, each firm is characterized by its distinctive resource profile, which induces or reinforces heterogeneity among firms. Thus firms' business strategies may depend upon their resource base (Barney, 1991). When an SME expands into a foreign market due to its limited resource base, it is more likely to rely on its current resources to compete in that market rather than developing new ones from scratch. Madhok (1997) suggested that internationalization can be viewed as a means to transfer resources from the domestic to the target market (Madhok, 1997).

However, a firm's resources can be difficult to identify and separate (Barney 1991; Teece, Pisano, and Shuen 1997) and what shows up in the firm's formal information system may be only a partial and fragmented representation of firm's resources, since many are tacit and knowledge based. To overcome this problem, Miller and Shamsie (1996) consider both property and knowledge-based resources specific to high-technology SMEs operating in very dynamic, unpredictable, and uncertain environments. Drawing on those arguments, we suggest that the following resources may be considered as potential sources of competitive advantage and most likely to influence firm's international performance:

- Discrete knowledge-based resources: marketing and technological resources
- Systemic knowledge-based resources: entrepreneurial orientation
- Discrete proprietary-based resources: financial resources

In addition, empirical evidence suggests that in small high-technology firms the entrepreneur or CEO plays, at an individual level, a critical role in firm's long-term success (Bruderl and Preisendorfer 2000; Bruderl, Preisendorfer, and Ziegler 1992; Lee, Lee and Pennings 2001).

High technology SMEs often internationalize on the basis of a technological advantage – a resource that gives them a head start in international markets especially where their products/services are unique, or at least innovative and differentiated (Coviello and Munro 1995; McDougall et al. 1994). At the same time, such firms may be at a financial disadvantage and internationalization may be driven, at least in part, by the need to recoup investments in R&D, and to pursue global niche markets where the domestic market is too small and/or specialized to recover the costs of product development (Bell, Crick, and Young 2004). In order to maintain competitive advantage such firms need to make continuous investments in R&D and internationalization may provide welcome revenue through the licensing of proprietary and knowledge-based resources, gained from R&D, can be transferred to partners against the payment of royalties or other fees. This transfer of resources to a foreign partner may not always be desirable or possible because knowledge-based resources are idiosyncratic by nature, sometimes ill-codified, complex, and characterized by uncertainty (Barney 1991). Very often, this knowledge may be so complex that even firm's personnel do not comprehend it, and consequently it cannot be communicated to an external partner (Buckley and Casson 1996). High-technology SMEs may miss important foreign market opportunities if they do not move quickly into foreign markets or if they lack the necessary resources to internationalize. There is also the additional risk of losing a key advantage to a partner through collaboration.

High-technology SMEs may not possess all the required resources to establish business activities overseas and consequently face the paradox of trying to protect their core competencies (e.g., technology knowledge, trade secrets, manufacturing skills), whilst simultaneously trying to establish linkages with other firms to get access to external resources. Furthermore, the higher the endowment of firm resources is, the more likely it will look for potential partners, mainly in downstream value chain activities, in order to expand abroad quicker and to more locations (Shrader 2001); thus, the more likely the firm will be seen as a suitable partner by other firms.

Given this background, the purpose of this study is to examine the influence of marketing resources, technological resources, financial resources, international orientation, human capital of the entrepreneur, entrepreneur/management team international experience, and entrepreneurial orientation on the international performance in the main export market.

Key resources of high-technology SMES

Marketing resources

Marketing resources reflect how the firm targets customers both in domestic and/or foreign markets and positions or differentiates its offering in relation to its competitors. At the operating level, marketing resources consist of firms' effective performance on product, price, distribution, promotion, and market research activities. In other words, marketing resources refer to firm's ability to build a strong awareness and reputation for its products and services. Firms with greater reputation can successfully exploit market niches, charging premium prices and increasing profitability. Thus, a firm to be successful should be market-oriented, staying close to its customers and ahead of its competitors (Day 1994).

For example, market research analysis is fundamental to the development of the marketing strategy of the high-technology firm since it is the foundation to market segmentation and targeting decisions. In high-technology sectors, important issues relative to firm's products are their innovativeness that is the assessment as to whether, in recent years, the firm has launched new product lines and whether changes in product lines have been dramatic or of a minor nature (Covin and Slevin 1989). Overall, marketing resources leverage firm competitiveness by anticipating customers' needs ahead of competition and creating long lasting relationships with customers, suppliers, distribution channels, and other potential partners (Day 1994). Thus, high technology firms should be market-oriented organizations focussing on collecting, analyzing, and using market information in a more systematic and rigorous way before current and potential competitors do it. This market information may include the following behavioural components: firstly, customer orientation that is firm's understanding of customers' needs and expectations in the target market; secondly, competitor orientation that is firm's understanding of long-term distinctive capabilities of current and potential competitors in the target market and finally the long-lasting cooperative relationships both within the organization and with other external partners, such as distributors and suppliers (Narver and Slater 1990).

H1: Marketing resources positively influence international performance of high-tech SMEs

Technological resources

Technological resources may represent sources of sustainable competitive advantage since they are currently valuable and difficult to imitate by competitors (Dhanaraj and Beamish 2003; Rodríguez and Rodríguez 2005). Technological resources include technological knowledge generated by R&D

activities, product and process innovations and other technology-specific intellectual capital, patents protected by law and intellectual property rights. In addition, if these skills are tacit and complex, as is often the case with technological resources, they become hard to imitate knowing and may remain embedded in a firm's organizational routines (Barney 1991; Kogut and Zander 1995; Winter 1987). Furthermore, they have a high degree of specificity; that is, they are idiosyncratic, making them more valuable to the firm than for other organizations. Thus, they are imperfectly mobile and complex in the sense that is difficult to identify the sources that generate this type of capabilities (Kogut and Zander 1993). In this context, each firm is heterogeneous in terms of its endowment of technological resources (Rodríguez and Rodríguez 2005). Therefore, firms possessing superior technological resources may gain competitive advantage vis-à-vis their competitors, mainly in foreign markets (Rodríguez and Rodríguez 2005). In fact, competitive advantage may be achieved either through cost reductions via the development of new and more efficient production processes or through differentiation by means of product innovations, which address the needs of firm's target customers, or even by developing products with a higher quality content. Indeed, a high quality product characterized by differentiation in relation to its competitors may be a key element in terms of firm's international success (Cavusgil, Zou, and Naidu 1993; Styles and Ambler 1994).

H2: Technological resources positively influence international performance of high-tech SMEs

Financial resources

Financial resources represent resources used as a medium of exchange for other productive resources (Chatterjee 1990). Firm with larger financial resources can accumulate larger stocks of strategic assets, tangible and intangible, compared with other firms lacking financial resources for the development of their business (Dierickx and Cool 1989). For example, high-technology SMEs may invest a high proportion of their available financial capital in product and market development (Lee, Lee, and Pennings 2001). Firms with higher endowments of financial resources could expand more quickly and to more geographical areas (Elango 2000). In fact, the increasing market globalization drives forward high-technology firms to develop products/services to suit global markets often through massive financial investments in R&D while increasing the technological base of the firm. In fact, high-technology ventures with sufficient financial capital can afford to hire very skilful personnel in key areas such as in R&D, marketing, and international sales, which may be critical to firm's future development.

H3: Financial resources positively influence international performance of high-tech SMEs

Firm international orientation

International orientation refers to firm's increasing knowledge gained from international operations associated with the subsequent reduction of market uncertainty, which may lead to firm's higher commitment to foreign markets and, therefore, to the firm's better performance. Thus, it is reasonable to expect that a firm's international orientation may be an important predictor of firm's scope of international activities and, therefore, of the firm's international intensity. International orientation is related to a firm's efforts to expand business activities into foreign markets. Internationalization may allow the high-technology SME to have access to new and potentially more profitable markets, new product ideas, innovation in products/processes, and brand new technologies, while increasing its overall competitiveness (Cavusgil and Zou 1994).

H4: Firm's international orientation positively influences the international performance of high-tech SMEs

Human capital of the entrepreneur/chief executive

The entrepreneur/chief executive is the cornerstone in small business internationalization (Miesenbock 1988). In fact, the skills and competencies of the entrepreneur/chief executive, that is, his/her human capital are generally acknowledged as key factors for business survival and future growth irrespective of being in domestic or foreign markets (Storey 1994). Indeed, he/she can be considered the most valuable resource within the firm (Bruderl and Preisendorfer 2000; Bruderl, Preisendorfer, and Ziegler 1992). The role of the entrepreneur/chief executive is even more critical in the case of small firms since he/she may simultaneously create and develop the vision, strategy, and leadership for the firm, whilst also often performing some functional and administrative tasks towards venture success. At a personal level, he/she must have a sense of achievement with high motivation, high skills, and capabilities and possessing a network of personal contacts based on his/her own previous experience (Kuznetsov, McDonald, and Kuznetsova 2000). Very often, this network of contacts represent firm's initial customer base (Smith and Fleck 1987). People with higher human capital have the knowledge on how to start and run a business successfully through the assessment of all relevant information and, consequently, all opportunities and threats and this leads to better performance.

H5: Human capital of the entrepreneur/chief executive positively influences international performance of high-tech SMEs

Entrepreneur/management team international experience

Entrepreneur international experience suggested by human capital theory, and to a certain extent, by pre-export development models (Wiedersheim-Paul, Olson, and Welch 1978; Olson and Wiedersheim-Paul 1978) emphasis's the role of the entrepreneur/other founders as the decision makers within the organization. In fact, depending on his/her cognitive style, previous experience of living and/or working abroad associated with his or her perceptions and vision about the business may be highly influential in terms of firm's further internationalization. Thus, international experience of the entrepreneur/management team is viewed as a characteristic of the entrepreneur or management team of the high-technology SME rather than a characteristic of the firm itself (Reuber and Fischer 1997).

H6: Entrepreneur/management team's international experience positively influences the international performance of high-tech SMEs

Entrepreneurial orientation

The concept of entrepreneurship has been extended from individual level, the entrepreneur, to firm-level and is called entrepreneurial orientation (EO) (Covin and Slevin 1991; Lumpkin and Dess 1996). For Timmons (1994, p. 7) *'entrepreneurship is the process of creating or seizing an opportunity, by the entrepreneur, and pursuing it regardless of the resources currently controlled'*. As suggested by Miller (1983) and further developed in other studies (Lee, Lee, and Pennings 2001; Lumpkin and Dess 1996; Covin and Slevin 1989), EO is characterized by three dimensions: *innovativeness, risk-taking propensity, and proactiveness.* *Innovativeness* refers to a firm's propensity to engage in the generation and development of new ideas, in the introduction of new products/services and/ or technological processes. More particularly, innovation is very important for high technology small firms since otherwise they would rely on traditional ways of doing business and, consequently, they would have less chance to be successful on the market (Lumpkin and Dess 1996; Covin and Slevin 1989). Indeed, without innovation, high-technology SMEs would deliver traditional products and services through traditional distribution channels. Under these circumstances, high-technology SMEs would be disadvantaged, in relation to established competitors, due to their characteristic resource limitations, limited awareness, and brand reputation coupled with less competitive cost structures. Another dimension of EO is *risk-taking behaviour,* which is characterized by the willingness to commit resources to high-risk or uncertain business opportunities in order to achieve high returns. Examples of high-risk actions include: borrowing heavily, investing in new technologies, or launching new products in new markets (Lee, Lee, and Pennings 2001; Lumpkin and Dess 1996). In this context, internationalization may be considered part of the risk-taking behaviour of the entrepreneur since it represents new and innovative activities, which have the goal of value creation across national boundaries, to the firm (McDougall and Oviatt 1997). Finally, another dimension of EO is *proactiveness*. *Proactiveness* refers to the seeking of market opportunities, both domestic and international, which may or may not be related with firm's current activities. Examples include the introduction of new products, systems, and services ahead of the competition, and the streamlining of operations/processes which are in mature or declining life cycles. Proactive firms may be considered pioneers in their domain of activities by their first mover actions, influencing market trends, creating new market segments, or replacing existing firms by the introduction of new products and services.

> *H7: Entrepreneurial orientation positively influences the international performance of high-tech SMEs*

Methodology

Focussing on a sample of high-technology Portuguese SMEs, two sampling frames were used to identify the target firms. Firstly, "PORTUGAL HIGH TECH" database provided listing of all the Portuguese "technology-based" firms in the areas of information, and communication technologies and electronics (ICTs). Secondly, due to the importance of the mould industry to Portuguese exports, this study a sample of R&D-intensive-mould firms was selected from the comprehensive database of CEFAMOL 'Associação Nacional da Indústria de Moldes'.

Overall, the research sample included 197 ICT firms and 43 mould manufacturers. A total of 106 usable questionnaires were returned including 69 from the ICT sample frame and 36 from the mould industry. A drop and collect technique enabled verification that all replies came from the entrepreneur/chief executive or a member of the senior management team/board of directors generating a response rate of 44%.

Because of the potentially paradoxical role of partners in relation to the way the accumulation and exploitation of resources in high-technology firms, we distinguished the mode of entry into two categories: independent and collaborative (contractual) modes. Overall, 38 firms (55%) in the ICT sample have independent entry modes in the main foreign market; they are firms that export directly to end customers as well as those firms which establish sales and production and sales subsidiaries. By contrast, 31 firms (45%) have contractual arrangement modes in the main foreign market: they are those firms, which export through distributors as well as establishing other cooperative contractual modes such as contract R&D (six firms), contractual joint ventures (five firms), licensing (one firm), and piggybacking (two firms). On the other hand, for the mould sample 27 firms (73%) have independent entry modes in the main foreign market: they are those firms which export directly to end customers as well as those firms which establish sales and wholly owned subsidiaries. By contrast, only 10 firms (27%) of the sample have contractual modes in the main foreign market; they are those firms, which export through foreign agents/distributors or indirectly through domestic distributors.

Measures

This study employs existing scales from previous research and proposes several new scales. The latter were developed through a multistage procedure including the review of theoretical literature and qualitative interviews with key informants. The following scales were used for the study's dependent and independent variables:

International performance

Following other authors, in particular Aaby and Slater (1989), this study used international intensity as a proxy measure international performance. The measure captures the percentage of firm sales in the main foreign market.

Marketing resources

The scale is new and based on the insights of the exploratory interviews and on the existing scale of Spanos and Lioukas (2001). Marketing resources were measured by 11 variables, on a rating scale from 1 (much weaker compared to your major international competitors) to 7 (much stronger compared to your major international competitors) including: having a highly skilled sales force, promotion expenditures, market research activities, access to international distribution channels, or external links to social or business networks.

Technological resources

Based on the insights of the exploratory interviews, and Burgel and Murray (2000), four variables were used to measure technological resources. There are two 'input' measures of technological resources measured on ratio scales. These are R&D intensity measured by the percentage of R&D expenditures to turnover; and by the percentage of R&D full-time employees to total employees. The two 'output' measures included are: the innovativeness of the technology, and whether the main product/service was developed within the firm. These latter variables were measured on 1–7 ordinal opposite statement scales.

Financial resources

Based on previous research, two variables were used to measure financial resources. One indicator assesses the availability of capital for firm's development over the last three years using a 1–7 semantic differential scale from Wiklund (1999). The other indicator captures the current endowment of firms' financial resources for future development. Using 1–7 rating scale, the item assesses the availability of capital that can be considered as a flow; the endowment of capital is a stock.

Firm international orientation

Firm international orientation was measured by asking respondents to assess the importance, in that year, to their firms' *'international experience', 'knowledge about foreign markets',* and *'commitment to international markets'* on a 7-point rating scale (where 1= 'none' and 7= 'very substantial'), building on Johanson and Vahlne (1977) and on the results of the exploratory interviews.

Entrepreneur/chief executive international experience

Following Reuber and Fischer (1997), chief executives were asked to indicate either their level of the international experience on a 7-point rating scale (where 1= 'very low' and 7= 'very high').

Entrepreneur/chief executive human capital

Chief executives were asked to indicate both their number of years of working experience and their number of years of experience within the industry in which their firms operate.

Entrepreneurial orientation

As suggested by Miller (1983), entrepreneurial orientation is a composite construct characterized by three dimensions that are innovativeness, risk-taking, and proactiveness. The study uses Covin and Slevin (1989) scale.

Control variables

Using dummy variables, the study controls for the effects of industry sector and the use of contractual/noncontractual entry mode where noncontractual entry modes were coded 1 and contractual modes as 0. The former refers to direct exports to end customers, sales subsidiaries, and wholly owned subsidiaries, while the latter includes indirect exports via domestic intermediary, direct exports via foreign intermediary/sales agent, contract R&D, and contractual joint ventures.

All multi-item scales meet the reliability and validity criteria suggested by Anderson and Gerbing (1988). For example, the scale of *entrepreneurial orientation* (Covin and Slevin 1989) has a Cronbach's alpha of 0.773, which is comparable to other studies such as 0.79 in Knight (2000), 0.75 in Zahra and Covin (1995), 0.74 in Miller (1983), and 0.64 in Wiklund (1999).

Results

Moderated multiple regression was used to examine the relationship between the firm's resources and performance in the main foreign market. In addition

Appendix 13.1: Correlations matrix

	1	2	3	4	5	6	7	8	9
1. International intensity	1	–	–	–	–	–	–	–	–
2. Cooperation use / non use	−0.15	1	–	–	–	–	–	–	–
3. Marketing resources	0.23*	−0.11	1	–	–	–	–	–	–
4. Technological resources	0.36**	0.17	0.00	1	–	–	–	–	–
5. Financial resources	0.02	−0.09	0.00	0.00	1	–	–	–	–
6. Firm international orientation	0.33**	−0.12	0.00	0.00	0.00	1	–	–	–
7. Entrepreneur human capital	0.60**	−0.09	0.15	−0.41**	−0.06	0.20*	1	–	–
8. Man. international experience	0.12	−0.03	0.55**	0.07	0.04	0.35**	0.00	1	–
9. Entrepreneurial orientation	−0.10	0.06	0.08	0.46**	0.05	−0.07	0.00	0.00	1

N = 106; $p^* \leq 0.05$; $p^{**} \leq 0.01$

to the main effects, the regression includes interaction effects. Four regression equations were tested. The first contained only the control variable industry sector. The use/nonuse of contractual cooperation in the main foreign market was introduced in the second. Resources of high-technology SMEs were added in model 3, so that variables main effects could be assessed. Finally, interaction terms are presented in the fourth and complete model. Appendix 13.1 provides variable correlations. No correlation is greater than 0.55 and further tests confirm that multicollinearity between independent variables does not seem to be a problem (Hair et al. 1998; Field 2002). Table 13.1 presents the results of those four models for international intensity in the main foreign market.

All these four models are highly significant ($p < 0.001$) with adjusted R^2 ranging from 0.63 to 0.70. According to model 4, the data seems to confirm a significant positive association between international performance and firm's technological resources, firm international orientation and entrepreneur/chief executive human capital. These results provide support for hypotheses H_2, H_4, and H_5. The remaining hypotheses, including the influence of marketing resources H_1, financial resources H_3, entrepreneur international experience H_6, and entrepreneurial orientation H_7 were not supported.

Discussion

This research investigates the impact of firm's resources on international performance of high-technology SMEs. The results suggest that *technological resources, firm international orientation, and entrepreneur/chief executive human capital* are significant and positive predictors of international intensity in the main foreign market. That is among the sample of Portuguese high-technology SMEs international intensity was positively associated with *technological resources, firm international orientation, and entrepreneur/chief executive human capital.* For example, technological resources,

Table 13.1   Results of multiple regression for international intensity in the main foreign market

	Model 1	Model 2	Model 3	Model 4
Intercept	***	***	***	***
Industry	0.80***	0.80***	0.77***	0.83***
Contractual cooperation	–	–0.01	–0.01	0.01
Marketing resources	–	–	0.06	–0.05
Technological resources	–	–	0.19*	0.18*
Financial resources	–	–	–0.01	–0.02
Firm international orientation	–	–	0.14*	0.16*
Entrepreneur human capital	–	–	0.19**	0.16*
Entrepreneur international experience	–	–	–0.02	0.11
Entrepreneurial orientation	–	–	0.02	0.05
Marketing resources X contractual cooperation	–	–	–	0.19*
Technological resources X contractual cooperation	–	–	–	–
Financial resources X contractual cooperation	–	–	–	0.51
Firm international orientation X contractual cooperation	–	–	–	–
Entrepreneur human capital X contractual cooperation	–	–	–	–
Entrepreneur int. experience X contractual cooperation	–	–	–	–0.23*
Entrepreneurial orientation X contractual cooperation	–	–	–	–0.05
F	191.10***	94.72***	28.52***	20.93***
Adjusted R^2	0.63	0.63	0.69	0.70
Change in Adjusted R^2	–	–	0.06	0.01

embedded in tacit knowledge are difficult, and characterized by high risk of appropriation, and costly to transfer to external partners. In this context, and in line with previous research (Shrader 2001), conclusions from this study may suggest that high-technology SMEs with higher endowment of technological resources should avoid transferring technological knowledge to external partners in foreign operations. Given these results, technological resources enhance firm international performance that is its international intensity.

It would be expected that high-technology SMEs showing a stronger *international orientation* would privilege cooperation with partners in the target markets in order to move more quickly and into more locations since often these firms may lack the resources to do so through internalization. Therefore, those firms can achieve higher international intensity, with reduced costs and market uncertainty. Moreover, high-technology SMEs could leverage in foreign markets on partners resources rather than committing their own assets to the international venture. However, this study only found *international orientation* as a strong predictor of international intensity for the entire sample of Portuguese high-technology SMEs including firms that establish independent entry modes and those that establish contractual arrangements entry modes in that same market and not that the *international orientation* was stronger among firms that choose contractual cooperation in relation to firms that choose independent entry modes.

In the same vein, this study found *entrepreneur/chief executive human capital* as also an independent predictor of international intensity in the main foreign market. Finally, it can also be concluded that *financial resources and entrepreneurial orientation* are not significant in influencing international performance. In fact, the great majority of Portuguese high technology SMEs in this study seem to lack *financial resources*. This fact may limit their foreign market strategies and consequently their international intensity even though managers of Portuguese NTBFs stress that the Portuguese market is too small to recover from the high R&D investments. They need to make those investments if their firms want to stay technology intensive (Fontes and Combs 1997).

Moreover, the availability of capital for firms' development fell below the scale central value, which basically represents that for the majority of high-technology SMEs in this study, financial resources, over the last three years, were insufficient and, to some extent, a significant impediment for firm's development. In this context, just over 60% among the firms in this sample indicate insufficient financial resources, irrespective of using contractual cooperating or not in the main foreign market, and there may be not enough variation to provide explanatory power to financial resources or its interaction with contractual cooperation.

In the same vein, results did not find *entrepreneurial orientation* as a significant predictor and/or moderator of international intensity for the firms in this sample. This might be explained by time lags. For example, assuming that new product development may take some time; entrepreneurial behaviour may manifest itself in international intensity with a significant time lag.

Interestingly, the effect of marketing resources was insignificant. It is possible that firms seeking to expand more quickly and differentiate from competitors in foreign markets can benefit by accessing the market knowledge from partners in the host country. In addition, marketing resources may be less complex than technological resources and may be subject to fewer risks of erosion and more manageable transaction costs when transferred to local partners.

Contributions, limitations, and suggestions

A primary contribution of this study lies in advancing an understanding of the extent to which SMEs are involved in foreign operations considering their limited internal resource base. This study contributes to the SME internationalization, entrepreneurship and strategic management literatures. In the SME internationalization and entrepreneurship literature, few empirical studies have so far identified and examined resources, scarce, imperfectly imitable, and valuable in unpredictable and uncertain market environments where high-technology SMEs currently conduct business activities, which may impact upon their international intensity. For the strategic management literature this study may contribute by putting forward resources that can allow high technology SMEs to obtain sustainable competitive advantage, by suggesting to practitioners the resources that they need to develop/deploy or acquire in order to achieve superior performance, mainly in foreign markets.

The study provides important managerial implications. Faced with market globalization and economic integration and constrained by the internal resource base, high-technology SME often need to make decisions on the degree to which they should engage in foreign operations. Entrepreneurs/senior managers of high technology SMEs are advised to analyze carefully the resources identified as critical to the international performance of their firms and develop and implement business strategies building on those resources in order to enhance the likelihood of international success. Moreover, entrepreneurs/managers of high technology SMEs are encouraged to consider foreign market activities from an early stage of their existence if they want to be successful (McDougall and Oviatt 1996). In so doing, they benefit from incorporating an international perspective in their plans and business activities.

The findings of this study suggest that high-technology SMEs with stronger international orientation currently achieve higher levels of international performance. In this context, although entrepreneurs/chief executives of high-technology SMEs can face numerous barriers and obstacles throughout international activities, the study has found that firms can overcome those obstacles and challenges through determination and commitment while going on to successfully marketing their products and services internationally. This involves the increasing knowledge of foreign markets by conducting on going market research activities in target markets about market demand, prospective customers, competitors, and potential partners in order to enhance firm's international competitiveness. Additionally, the firm as a whole should have an international goal driven behaviour in order to increase its penetration in foreign markets. In these circumstances entrepreneurs/chief executives of high-technology SMEs should direct their efforts to create and develop an entrepreneurial culture that will promote the firm's orientation towards the achievement of ambitious international goals, while encouraging complete employee participation and involvement in business activities, and rewarding them relative to their performance, along firm's success in foreign markets.

The empirical findings also suggest that entrepreneurs/chief executives with higher working and industry experiences increase the likelihood of success of their ventures. In fact, entrepreneurs/chief executives with higher working experience generally have a high sense of achievement, leadership, and motivation, although they may face strong barriers and obstacles while running the business. Similarly, entrepreneurs/chief executives with higher industry experience normally possess extensive innovation and technological skills, a network of business contacts with prospective customers and partners associated with a deep knowledge about the industry sector and its market trends, business segments, customers, and competitors, which might allow the reduction of market uncertainty for the high-technology SME.

This industry experience might also be relevant to the overall personnel of the high-technology SME in areas such as R&D, Marketing and Sales, and Business Administration, where either previous experience in the same industry sector before joining the firm or an extensive experience within the firm are also suitable.

The findings also recommend that higher levels of performance by the high technology SME can be achieved by building a stronger technological base through a greater emphasis on R&D activities, by hiring very skilled personnel as well as by capitalization on continuous innovation based on technologies that are new to the market. In this context, the high technology SME should be characterized by delivering innovative products/services, on an ongoing basis, while engaging in continuous innovation, due to the products/services short life cycles. Thus entrepreneurs/chief executives of high-technology SMEs need to take these facts into consideration and allocating resources in key areas while developing and implementing appropriate strategies.

Nevertheless, a focus only on technology development will be not enough to business survival and future prospects. In this context, entrepreneurs/chief executives of high-technology SMEs should direct efforts towards international rather domestic products and services and developing awareness that geographical diversification may help recoup mainly from high R&D costs and building profits since high-technology SMEs compete in markets characterized by short and shortening life cycles, in which technologies become fast obsolete. In fact, often domestic markets may be too small to accommodate the technology-based niche strategies that they typically pursue.

It is acknowledged that this study has its own limitations. The main methodological limitation of this study refers to its cross-sectional nature which does not permit to accurately capture the causal effects between variables. Due to the static nature of the questionnaire, it is difficult to distinguish between cause and effect relationships between international performance and firm resources. For example, some empirical research suggests that the impact of firm's resource-base on international performance will take 2–3 years to materialize (Shrader 2001; Westhead et al. 2001). In this context, it would be preferable to collect the data regarding resources (the independent variables) and 2–3 years later the data concerned with outcomes (international intensity, international sales growth, degree of satisfaction of the CEO, etc.). In this situation, the time lag between collecting the explanatory variables and the corresponding outcome variables would make it possible to infer causality.

The other limitation concerns the research sample. In fact, this limitation relates to the small sample sizes for both populations ICT and, moulds even though the overall usable good response rates of 35% for the ICT sample and 84% for the mould sample. Nonetheless, the use of larger samples would be preferable and would strengthen the generalizability of findings.

Finally, the study uses data from a sample of Portuguese high-technology SMEs in ICT and moulds industry sectors only. It is not certain whether the results apply to other high technology sectors such as biotechnology, chemical (including pharmaceuticals), and mechanical engineering.

The limitations offer several avenues for future research. The study cross-sectional nature did not allow an assessment of firms' resource accumulation and capability development process and their impact on international performance, using, for example, different measures for this latter construct. Future studies can collect the data regarding resources at one point in time, and 2–3 years later the data concerned with international performance (international intensity, international sales growth, degree of satisfaction of the CEO, etc.). In this situation, the time lag existent in collecting the explanatory variables and the outcome variables allows to infer causality.

Another opportunity relates to the extending the target populations. Future studies could examine other industry sectors, such as biotechnology, chemical (including pharmaceuticals), and mechanical engineering, in order to achieve a deeper understanding of other high-tech industries. In addition, studies should seek a large sample of firms, with or without international activities. Lastly, further research could extend the scope of this study by focusing in factors, beyond firm resources, which may be important to the internationalization of high-technology SMEs such as industry dynamics, product/service characteristics, and specific country conditions where firms intend to establish foreign operations.

References

Aaby, N. and Slater, S.F. (1989) 'Management influences on export performance: A review of the empirical literature 1978–1988', *International Marketing Review*, 6(4), 7–23.

Anderson, J.C. and Gerbing, D.W. (1988) 'An updated paradigm for scale development incorporating unidimensionality and its assessment', *Journal of Marketing Research*, 25, 186–92.

Barney, J. (1991) 'Special theory forum. the resource-based model of the firm: Origins, implications and prospects', *Journal of Management*, 17(1), 97–98.

Bell, J., Crick, D. and Young, S. (2004) 'Small firm internationalization and business strategy', *International Small Business Journal*, 22(1), 23–56.

Bruderl, J. and Preisendorfer, P. (2000) 'Fast-growing businesses', *International Journal of Sociology*, 30, 45–70.

Bruderl, J., Preisendorfer, P. and Ziegler, R. (1992) 'Survival chances of newly funded business organizations', *American Sociological Review*, 57, 227–42.

Buckley, P. and Casson, M. (1996) 'An economic model of international joint venture strategy', *Journal of International Business Studies*, 27, 849–76.

Burgel, O. and Murray, G.C. (2000) 'The international market entry choices of start-up companies in high technology industries', *Journal of International Marketing*, 8(2), 33–62.

Cavusgil, S.T., Zou, S. and Naidu, G.M. (1993) 'Product and promotion adaptation in export ventures: An empirical investigation', *Journal of International Business Studies*, 24, 479–506.

Cavusgil, S.T. and Zou, S. (1994) 'Marketing strategy-performance relationship: An investigation of the empirical link in export market ventures', *Journal of Marketing*, 58(1), 1–21.

Chetty, S. and Campbell-Hunt, C. (2003) 'Explosive international growth and problems of success amongst small and medium sized firms', *International Small Business Journal*, 21(1), 5–27.

Chatterjee, S. (1990) 'Excess resources utilization costs and mode of entry', *Academy of Management Journal*, 33(4), 780–800.

Coviello, N.E. and Munro, H. (1995) 'Growing the entrepreneurial firm', *European Journal of Marketing*, 29(7), 49–61.

Covin, J.G. and Slevin, D.P. (1991) 'A conceptual model of entrepreneurship as firm behaviour', *Entrepreneurship Theory and Practice*, (Fall), 7–25.

Covin, J.G. and Slevin, D.P. (1989) 'Strategic management of small firms in hostile and benign environments', *Strategic Management Journal*, 10(1), 75–87.

Day, G.S. (1994) 'The resources of market-driven organizations', *Journal of Marketing*, 58, 37–52.

Dhanaraj, C. and Beamish, P.W. (2003) 'A resource-based approach to the study of export performance', *Journal of Small Business Management*, 41(3), 242–61.

Dierickx, I. and Cool, K. (1989) 'Asset stock accumulation and sustainability of competitive advantage', *Management Science*, 35, 1504–14.

Elango, B. (2000) 'An exploratory study into the linkages between corporate resources and the extent and form of internationalization of U.S. firms', *American Business Review*, 12–26.

Field, A. (2002) *Discovering Statistics Using SPSS for Windows* (London: Sage).

Fontes, M. and Combs, R. (1997) 'The coincidence of technology and market objectives in the internationalisation of new technology-based firms', *International Small Business Journal*, 15(4), 14–35.

Hair, Jr.J.F, Anderson, R.E., Tatham, R.L. and Black, W.C. (1998) *Multivariate Data Analysis*, 5th edn (Upper Saddle River, NJ: Prentice Hall).

Johanson, J. and Vahlne, J.-E. (1977) 'The internationalization process of the firm: z model of knowledge development and increasing foreign market commitments', *Journal of International Business Studies*, 8(1), 23–32.

Jones, M.V. (2001) 'A value chain analysis of small UK high technology based firms' internationalisation', in 4th McGill Conference on International Entrepreneurship, *Researching New Frontiers* (Glasgow: University of Strathclyde).

Knight, G. (2000) 'Entrepreneurship and marketing strategy: the SME under globalisation', *Journal of International Marketing*, 8(2), 12–32.

Kogut, B. and Zander, U. (1993) 'Knowledge of the firm and the evolutionary theory of the multinational corporation', *Journal of International Business Studies*, 24(4), 625–45.

Kogut, B. and Zander, U. (1995) 'What firms do? coordination, identity and learning', *Organization Science*, 7, 502–18.

Kuznetsov, A., McDonald, F. and Kuznetsova, O. (2000) 'Entrepreneurial qualities: A case from Russia', *Journal of Small Business Management*, (January), 101–107.

Lee, C., Lee, K. and Pennings, J.M. (2001) 'Internal resources, external networks, and performance: z study on technology-based ventures', *Strategic Management Journal*, 22, 615–40.

Lumpkin, G.T. and Dess, G. (1996) 'Clarifying the entrepreneurial orientation construct and linking it to performance', *Academy of Management Review*, 21(1), 135–72.

Madhok, A. (1997) 'Cost, value and foreign market entry mode: The transaction and the firm', *Strategic Management Journal*, 18(1), 39–61.

McDougall, P.P., Shane, S. and Oviatt, B.M. (1994) 'Explaining the formation of international new ventures: The limits of theories from international business research', *Journal of Business Venturing*, 9(6), 469–87.

McDougall, P.P. and Oviatt, B.M. (2000) 'International entrepreneurship: The intersection of two research paths', *Academy of Management Journal*, 43(5), 902–06.

McDougall, P.P. and Oviatt, B.M. (1997) 'International entrepreneurship literature in the 1990s and directions for future research', in D.L. Sexton and R.W. Smilor (eds), *Entrepreneurship 2000*, 291–320 (Chicago: Upstart Publishing).

McDougall, P.P. and Oviatt, B.M. (1996) 'New venture internationalization, strategic change, and performance: a follow-up study', *Journal of Business Venturing*, 11, 23–40.

Miesenbock, K.J. (1988) 'Small businesses and exporting: a literature review', *International Small Business Journal*, 6(2), 42–61.

Miller, D. (1983) 'The correlates of entrepreneurship in three types of firms', *Management Science*, 9(7), 770–91.

Miller, D. and Shamsie, J. (1996) 'The resource-based view of the firm in two environments: the Hollywood film studios from 1936 to 1965', *Academy of Management Journal*, 39(3), 519–43.

Narver, J.C. and Slater, S.F. (1990) 'The effect of marketing orientation on business profitability', *Journal of Marketing*, 54(October), 20–35.

Olson, H.C. and Wiedersheim-Paul, F. (1978) 'Factors affecting the pre-export behaviour of non-exporting firms: European research in international business', M. Ghertman and J. Leontiades (eds), 283–305 (Amsterdam: North-Holland).

Oviatt, B.M. and McDougall, P.P. (1994) 'Towards a theory of international new ventures', *Journal of International Business Studies*, 24(1), 45–64.

Reuber, R. and Fischer, E. (1997) 'The influence of the management team's international experience on the internationalization behaviours of SMEs', *Journal of International Business Studies*, 28, 807–25.

Rodríguez, J.L. and Rodríguez, R.M.G. (2005) 'Technology and export behaviour: a resource-based view approach', *International Business Review*, 14, 539–57.

Sapienza, H.J., Autio, E., George, G. and Zahra, S.A. (2006) 'A capabilities perspective on the effects of early internationalization on firm survival and growth', *Academy of Management Review*, 31(4), 914–33.

Shrader, R.C. (2001) 'Collaboration and performance in foreign markets: the case of young high technology manufacturing firms', *Academy of Management Journal*, 44(1), 45–60.

Smith, J.G. and Fleck, V. (1987) 'Business strategies in small high technology companies', *Long Range Planning*, 20(2), 61–68.

Spanos, Y.E. and Lioukas, S. (2001) 'An examination into the causal logic of rent generation: contrasting Porter's competitive strategy framework and the resource-based perspective', *Strategic Management Journal*, 22, 907–34.

Storey, D.J. (1994) *Understanding the Small Business Sector* (London: International Thomson Business Press).

Styles, C. and Ambler, T. (1994) 'Successful export practice: the UK experience', *International Marketing Review*, 11, 23–47.

Teece, D.J., Pisano, G. and Shuen, A. (1997) 'Dynamic resources and strategic management', *Strategic Management Journal*, 18(7), 509–33.

Timmons, J.A. (1994) *New Venture Creation* (Burr Ridge, IL: Irwin).

Westhead, P., Wright, M. and Ucbasaran, D. (2001) 'The internationalization of new and small firms: a resource-based view', *Journal of Business Venturing*, 16, 333–58.

Wiklund, J. (1999) 'The sustainability of the entrepreneurial orientation-performance Relationship', *Entrepreneurship: Theory & Practice*, 24(1), 37–48.

Wiedersheim-Paul F., Olson, H.C. and Welch, L. (1978) 'Pre-export activity: the first step in internationalization', *Journal of International Business Studies*, 9(Spring/Summer), 93–98.

Winter, S.G. (1987) 'Knowledge and competence as strategic assets', in D.J. Teece (ed), *The Competitive Challenge*, 159–84 (Cambridge, MA: Ballinger]

Zahra, S.A. and Covin, J.G. (1995) 'Contextual influences on the corporate entrepreneurship-performance relationship: a longitudinal analysis', *Journal of Business Venturing*, 10, 43–58.

14
The Internationalization of Knowledge-Based Small and Medium-Sized Enterprises from Syria

Laila Kasem and Kevin Ibeh

Introduction

The internationalization of small and medium-sized enterprises (SMEs) has been the focus of considerable academic and policy-oriented interest. However, most of this previous research has been focussed on developed economics (Leonidou and Katsikeas 1996; Bell 1997; Leonidou 2004). This situation has been slightly remedied by an increasing number of studies focussing on developing countries and economies in transition (Kuada and Sørensen 2000; Ibeh and Young 2001; Ibeh 2003, 2004; Rutashobya and Jaensson 2004; Aidis 2005; Lloyd-Reason et al. 2005; Chung, Chen, and Hsieh 2008; Crick and Kaganda 2008; Liu, Xiao, and Huang 2008). The relative scholarly neglect of developing country firms, nevertheless, remains. This is particularly true of the Middle East region where, apart from Turkey (e.g., Özkanlı, Benek and Akdeve 2006; Karadeniz and Göçer 2007), very few countries have been the focus of studies on SMEs' cross-border expansion (e.g., Lebanon: Ahmad et al. 2006; Saudi Arabia: Crick, Al Obaidi and Chaudhry 1998).

It is also the case that previous internationalization research undertaken in developing countries has tended to focus on SMEs in traditional sectors such as textiles and agro-business, which are considered to be 'suitable platforms for export development' (Ibeh and Young 2001, p.569). Studies of SMEs in high-tech sectors were few and far between (Zain and Ng 2006; Terjesen, O'Gorman, and Acs 2008; Thai and Chong 2008). There is, thus, a gap in the literature on the internationalization of knowledge-based SMEs from developing countries (Borchert and Ibeh 2008). Consequently, the aim of the present research is to redress this gap by investigating the internationalization process of six software SMEs in Syria, one of the developing Middle Eastern countries. In particular, the study aims to examine the extent to which the focal firms' internationalization can be explained by the major theoretical approaches available in the literature, specifically the 'stages' theory, the network perspective, the international new venture theory, and the resource-based viewpoint.

The remaining part of the chapter is structured as follows. The second section reviews the literature on firm internationalization theories. The third section provides an overview of the context of the study. Research methodology is explained in the fourth section. The findings of the primary research are presented in the fifth section, and discussed in the sixth section. We then end with some conclusions and future research implications.

Explaining firm internationalization

Internationalization can be defined as 'the process of increasing involvement in international operations' (Welch & Luostarinen, 1988, p. 36). A number of schools of thought have emerged to explain this process. These include the stages theory, the network approach to internationalization, the international new venture theory and the resource based view explanation of internationalization.

The stages theory

Early internationalization behaviour research dominantly suggests that firms take gradual steps in their international expansion (Johanson and Wiedersheim-Paul 1975). Conceptually rooted in previous evolutionary literature (Rogers 1962; Cyert and March 1963), this incremental approach was evident in the behavioural models developed during the 1970s and early 1980s to explain the international (Johanson and Vahlne 1977) and export development of firms (e.g., Bilkey and Tesar 1977; Cavusgil 1980; Reid 1981). The Uppsala model (Johanson and Wiedersheim-Paul 1975; Johanson and Vahlne 1977), named after the Swedish base of the key researchers, is the most prominent of this genre. Among the key assumptions of these models are that firms would have strong presence at the home market before initiating any international activities and that they tend to lack knowledge about foreign markets, which entails high uncertainty. Therefore, firms choose an incremental approach to internationalization to enable them learn more about the foreign market and consequently commit more resources to it.

The stages model identifies two patterns regarding firm internationalization behaviour. The first relates to the choice of markets and suggests that firms initially target psychologically close countries and successively enter markets with greater psychic distance. Psychic distance is defined as 'the sum of factors preventing the flow of information from and to the market, (including)...differences in language, education, business practices, culture, and industrial development' (Johanson and Vahlne 1977, p. 24). The second pattern is related to the type of engagement in the foreign country, which is suggested to be a step-wise extension of operations. Johanson and Wiedersheim-Paul (1975) call this process the 'establishment chain', which includes four stages: no regular export, export via agents, establishing overseas sales subsidiaries, and overseas production. Advancing to a subsequent stage reflects an increasing commitment to the foreign market and requires gradual acquisition, assimilation and use of knowledge about that market (Johanson and Vahlne 1977).

The stages theory has gained considerable support among researchers. Nevertheless, it has a number of shortcomings (Chetty 1999; Ibeh 2000, 2001). Melin (1992) argues that the model is too deterministic in proposing that the firm will pass through all the stages; this disregards the possibility of leapfrogging, which is not uncommon. In addition, its explanatory power is limited to the early stages of internationalization, making it less applicable to internationally experienced companies. The notion of psychic distance has also been found irrelevant in several empirical studies (e.g., Bell 1995). Leonidou and Katsikeas (1996) have further argued that the models essentially focus on export operations and exclude other forms of corporate international expansion – a viewpoint shared by several other scholars, including Chetty (1999), Jones (1999), and Fletcher (2001). As these researchers noted, companies do not only engage in 'outward' internationalization activities, but also conduct 'inward' internationalization activities such as importing, and that both sets of activities, inward and outward, directly reinforce each other. The foregoing may explain why the stages-based view of internationalization has largely been superseded by more holistic and integrative explanations of firm internationalization (Bell and Young 1998; Jones 2001; Ibeh 2001). Nevertheless, the model remains a useful framework for understanding the internationalization of SMEs, particularly those in traditional, rather than high-tech, industries (Bell, Crick and Young 2004).

The network approach to internationalization

The network perspective has received considerable support in internationalization research. According to this approach, companies are not isolated entities, but rather actors in markets, which are depicted as 'systems of social and industrial relationships encompassing, for example, customers, suppliers, competitors, family and friends' (Coviello and Munro 1997, p.365). These relationships are believed to significantly influence the strategic behaviour of firms, including their internationalization decisions, for example, pace of internationalization, foreign market selection and entry modes (Bell 1995; Coviello and Munro 1997; Moen, Gavlen, and Endresen 2004). In addition, they represent invaluable sources of information about foreign markets (Ellis 2000; Sharma and Blomstermo 2003), help to overcome export barriers (Ghauri, Lutzand, and

Tesfom 2003), facilitate the reduction of the cost and risk associated with cross-border activities, and assist in shoring up the credibility of firms from less developed countries (Zain and Ng 2006).

Much of the research in this area tended to focus on the role of business relationships in firms' internationalization (Bell 1995; Coviello and Munro 1997; Johanson and Mattsson 1988; Sharma and Blomstermo 2003; Moen, Gavlen, and Endresen 2004). However, social ties were also found to play a significant role in the internationalization process (Ellis 2000; Tyagi 2000; Ellis and Pecotich 2001; Rutashobya and Jaensson 2004; Harris and Wheeler 2005). Insights from the entrepreneurship literature also suggest that the networks of young entrepreneurial ventures start as socially embedded ties and then develop to economic ties (Larson and Starr 1993; Hite and Hesterly 2001). Although further research in the context of INVs provided contradictory evidence (Coviello 2006), these insights remain valuable when investigating the development of firms' networks.

It is important to highlight the fact that the network approach to internationalization does not contradict the incremental model of internationalization; however it suggests that the process is more complex than what is proposed in the stages theory (Bell 1995). Indeed, Coviello and Munro (1997) and Jansson and Sandberg (2008) suggested that integrating the stages model with the network approach would enhance our understanding of the internationalization process of SMEs. Furthermore, the network perspective is considered to be an integral part of the INV theory since established networks are vital for the early internationalization of new ventures (Coviello 2006). This again takes us back to the argument that the internationalization process is contingent on many factors and that no one single theory can fully explain the firm's internationalization. Thus, a more holistic approach, one that incorporates aspects from different theoretical approaches, should be adopted in studies examining this topic area (Bell and Young 1998; Bell, Crick and Young 2004; Crick and Jones 2000; Ibeh 2000, 2001; Jones and Coviello 2005; Spence and Crick 2006).

Theory of international new ventures

During the 1990s, evidence was uncovered regarding small firms that internationalize at inception or soon after that. These firms were given various names in the literature (Rialp, Rialp, and Knight 2005; Borchert and Ibeh 2008), the most prevalent of which are born-global firms (Rennie 1993) and international new ventures (Oviatt and McDougall 1994). Both terms will be used interchangeably in this chapter. Oviatt and McDougall (1994, p.49) define an international new venture (INV) as 'a business organization that, from inception, seeks to derive significant competitive advantage from the use of resources and the sale of outputs in multiple countries'.

Previous work by several researchers, including McDougall, Shane, and Oviatt (1994), Knight and Cavusgil (1996), Madsen and Servais (1997), Bell, Crick, and Young (2004), Chetty and Campbell-Hunt (2004), Rialp, Rialp, and Knight (2005) and Gabrielsson et al. (2008), has sought to characterize born-globals. These studies suggest that born-globals are small firms formed by entrepreneurs who view the world as one marketplace and do not confine their search for growth opportunities to their domestic market or a single country. Although their offerings are typically cutting edge technologies developed for a particular niche in international markets, the born-global phenomenon is not limited to high-tech industries (Bell 1995; Coviello and Munro 1997; Jones 1999; Crick and Jones 2000; Sharma and Blomstermo 2003). INVs may also come from traditional and low-tech industries (Madsen and Servais 1997; Rialp, Rialp, and Knight 2005; Vissak, Ibeh, and Paliwoda 2007). Furthermore, they tend to rely heavily on their networks to achieve rapid international growth and are often formed by people with extensive prior international experience that allows them to spot opportunities in the global marketplace.

Among the key forces associated with the emergence of this new breed of firms are developments in information and communication technologies; changing market conditions, particularly the increasing importance of niche markets; the ever-rising importance of international networks; the reduction of trade barriers; and the more sophisticated capabilities of new venture founders (Knight and Cavusgil 1996; Madsen and Servais 1997). Based on their understanding of the above triggering forces and the characteristics of born-globals, some researchers have argued that the traditional internationalization model and the born global phenomenon are not necessarily contradictory (Madsen and Servais 1997; Fan and Phan 2007). They contend that both approaches are valid but in different contexts, thus, reinforcing the view that the nature and pace of firm internationalization is conditioned by factors, including the experience and networks of the founders; the type of the product or industry, and other environmental variables (Bell and Young 1998; Ibeh 2000; Jones 2001).

The resource-based view

Conceptually rooted in strategic management research (Penrose 1959; Wernerfelt 1984; Barney 1991; Grant 1991), the resource-based view, including its recent refinements as the knowledge-based view (Kogut and Zander 1992; Nonaka and Takeuchi 1995; Grant 1996; Yli-Renko, Autio, and Tontti 2002; Acedo, Barroso, and Galan 2006) and the capability perspective (Weerawardena et al. 2007), has increasingly been adopted in explaining firm internationalization, international entrepreneurship, and international business performance. It suggests that the nature and relative uniqueness of the resource bundles, tangible and intangible, possessed by a firm or accessible to it, and the firm's ever renewing capacity to optimize benefits from resources, are the most enduring sources of sustainable competitive advantage (Barney 1991; Ibeh 2005) including in international markets (Bloodgood, Sapienza, and Almeida 1996). Advantage-generating resources, according to the RBV, have to be valuable, rare, imperfectly imitable, and non,substitutable (Barney 1991). They can also be categorized into managerial resources, physical resources, organizational resources and capabilities, and social capital and relational capabilities (Westhead, Wright and Ucbasaran 2001; Nummela, Saarenketo, and Puumalainen 2004; Ibeh 2005).

An increasing number of researchers have suggested that the resource-based view provides a better and more holistic explanation of firm internationalization (e.g., Bell and Young 1998; Ibeh 2001; Bell, Crick, and Young 2004; Jones and Coviello 2005; Spence and Crick 2006; Vissak, Ibeh, and Paliwoda 2007). Others, including Rialp, Rialp, and Knight (2005) have highlighted its potential to offer a more comprehensive explanation of the early internationalization phenomenon.

It would be interesting to explore, later in this chapter, *what the present study's findings might suggest in relation to the relative relevance of each of the above-reviewed theoretical perspectives in explaining the internationalization of Syrian software firms.*

The research context

The study took place in Syria, a lower-middle-class developing country with a population of approximately 19 million (World Bank 2008). Historically, Syrians were known as active international traders whose transactions were not only linked to the domestic market but may also include brokering deals across countries (Mills 1964). In the second half of the 20th century, however, Syria was virtually isolated from the world economy due to government ideology, which emphasized central planning and limited private sector activity. This remained the case until 1989, when the government initiated few economic reforms. In 1991, a new investment law was passed to encourage private sector investments and expand the scope of their economic participation (CCG 2002; CIA 2008). In 2000, Syria started moving towards a social market economy and undertook major reforms. These included developing strategies to attract foreign direct investment, liberalizing international trade and permitting private participation in the banking, insurance, and infrastructure sectors, after several decades of public sector monopoly (FCO 2008).

The Syrian IT sector is still in its infancy, even in comparison to its equivalent in neighbouring countries like Jordan and Egypt. It is estimated that there are around 120 companies operating in the software industry, the majority of which are small sized. Given that they operate in a non-demanding market, the offerings of these companies lag considerably behind international standards and are very limited in range; mostly financial management applications (Leão and Kabbani 2007). In addition, the Syrian ICT industry faces some major problems. The weak infrastructure, particularly in relation to internet access, represents a huge difficulty. The industry is also badly affected by brain drain as Syrian highly skilled IT graduates are attracted to foreign countries by higher salaries and potential exemption from compulsory military service (OBG 2008). However, the Syrian ICT market seems promising, as more and more governmental and private organizations are shifting to the electronic era.

Methodology

Reflecting the exploratory and inductive nature of the present study, and the absence of any previous work on the internationalization of Syrian SMEs, a qualitative research approach was employed. The specific method applied was qualitative interviewing, which typically gives free rein to the interviewees' viewpoints, stories, and perceptions, and whose characteristic flexibility allows pertinent areas to be investigated in greater depth (Bryman and Bell 2003). This, perhaps, explains why this approach (multiple-case study design; semistructured interviews) has been increasingly used in recent studies on the internationalization of software firms (Coviello and Munro 1997; Moen, Gavlen, and Endresen 2004) and other small firms (Spence and Crick 2006; Loane, Bell, and McNaughton 2007).

The interview questions were developed from the literature, and they comprised a variety of structured and open-ended questions. Structured questions were used to gather classification-type data such as organizational characteristics (age, number of employees and target markets) and management characteristics (age, education, experience and international exposure). Open-ended questions focussed mainly on the study firms' internationalization processes and motives. The interviewees were encouraged to share their views and experiences, to provide the researcher with a deeper understanding of the issues discussed.

The fieldwork was carried out over a three week period in the summer of 2008 in Damascus, the capital city and commercial centre of Syria. The selection of the case firms involved a series of steps. First an online search was undertaken to find a comprehensive list of Syrian software firms. No one suitable directory was, however, found. As a result, a few, notably the Software Industrial Forum (SIF) and Araboo online directories, were used to generate a list of target firms. Next, in line with best practice in case research, general parameters were set for selecting the case units. Cases needed to be Syrian software SMEs as defined by the Syrian authorities (firms with between 10 and 250 employees and 3 to 250 million Syrian pounds turnover – Syrian Enterprise Business Centre

2008). In the absence, however, of turnover data, only employee number was used in identifying SMEs for further screening. Another decision made was to eliminate companies located outside Damascus city from further consideration owing to logistical and time factors.

Further information about the companies was sought from their own Web sites, an approach previously used when there was little information available from other resources (Loane, Bell, and McNaughton 2007). More specifically, pertinent data was sought regarding the firms' inward or outward international activities, including obtaining distribution rights from foreign firms, providing subcontracting services to foreign firms, exporting and opening foreign sales subsidiaries (Crick and Jones 2000; Fletcher 2001). Although the search produced fourteen appropriate cases, it was thought that five to eight interviews would provide enough material to meet the research objectives. Therefore, eight companies were contacted for interviewing, first by e-mail to explain the research topic and what would be discussed during the interview, and then by a phone call directed to the key informant to request an appointment for the interview. In the event, only six interviews were conducted. The agreed key informants for the other two companies were either abroad or unavailable during the first named author's field trip to Syria.

The key informants were either founders/managing directors (MD) or managers responsible for international activities. Interviews were conducted in natural conditions at the interviewees' own offices. They ranged between 30 and 90 minutes in duration and were conducted in Arabic, the official language in Syria. Except for the 'get-to-know-you' phase, all interviews were voice-recorded and later transcribed and translated into English simultaneously.

The intra and cross-case analysis approach was employed in this study (Yin 2003). This allowed for each case to be treated independently and then compared with others to identify themes and patterns shared across cases.

Analysis and findings

Profiles of the case firms

Table 14.1 provides background information about the companies investigated, including their main activities, date of establishment, size, and ownership status. These case firms are represented by letters, ranging from A to F, in order to maintain their anonymity. As can be seen from the table, the firms' age ranged between 6 and 17 years at the time of the study. The number of full-time employees varied between 12 and 45, indicating that all firms are small in size. It is worth mentioning that all the case companies are privately owned enterprises that rely exclusively on their own funds. This is owing to the extreme difficulty that small businesses face in trying to secure loans from the banks,

Table 14.1   Profile of the case study firms

Name	Main activities	Founding year	Number of employees	Ownership status
A	Software development; computer networks; internet service provider (ISP); security solutions	1991	25	Private
B	Software for educational organizations	2002	20	Private
C	Accounting and HRM systems; management systems for restaurants, hospitals and schools	1993	12	Private
D	Enterprise Resources Planning (ERP) Systems; Enterprise Content Management (ECM) systems	2000	45 full-time + 15 part-time	Private
E	Outsourcing, billing and archiving systems	2000	15	Private
F	Outsourcing, Geo-graphic Information Systems (GIS), Customer Relationship Management solutions	1999	20	Private

as well as the fact that the notion of venture angels has only recently started being acknowledged in Syria.

Table 14.2 outlines the internationalization history and activities of each of the case firms, including their dates of founding and first cross-border activity and first overseas destination and entry mode. It also presents information regarding other market/s entered; changes, if any, in foreign market servicing mode; key influences on the study firms' internationalization; and their future internationalization plans. In line with best practice, intracase analysis of each of the case firms is now undertaken as a prelude to an appropriate cross-case analysis (Yin 2003).

Company A, the oldest of the case firms, was founded in 1991 by its current board chairman, an engineering graduate. It is now run by a young director with a business degree and local IT experience. It first internationalized in 1998 by exporting its products to United Arab Emirates (UAE) and later entered other Gulf Cooperation Council (GCC) countries through distribution agreements with local firms. However, overseas sales were rare and few. In its quest for internationally linked growth, the company, in

Table 14.2 Internationalization history and activities of the case firms

Name	Year established	Year of first int'l activity	First int'l market & mode used	Other markets & modes used	Mode changes	Key influences	Future plans
A	1991	1998	UAE / export distributors	GCC / export distributors; Russia / distribution agreement* & service exporting	UAE: from export distributors→sales subsidiary; Russia: from distribution agreement*→ service exporting	Relationship with Russian partner & management's commitment to international expansion	More regional & international growth
B	2002	2004	Saudi Arabia / export distributor	UAE / export distributor; Jordan / export distributor	'Forced' withdrawal from UAE and Jordan	Relationship with Saudi partner, management's international focus, & firm's resource limitations	Consolidate existing base & follow international growth plan
C	1994	1998	Kuwait / export distributor	Saudi Arabia / export distributor; Turkey, Iraq, Egypt, & Libya / export distributors	None. Export distributors are used in all current markets	Relationship with previous employees, management's international commitment & quality products	Searching for distributors in new overseas markets
D	2000	2004	France / licensing-in*	Jordan / partnership deal & JV; Yemen / exporting	Jordan: from partnership deal → JV	Relationship with business partners & background & contact networks of management team	to enter Saudi Arabia, UAE & Libya and secure subcontracting deal from UK
E	2000	2000	Germany / subcontracting	None	None	Relationships & networks, limited local demand & sanctions against Syria	Continuing focus on subcontracting opportunities
F	1999	1999	Italy / subcontracting	Kuwait, UAE & Saudi Arabia / export distributors; UAE / subcontracting; Belgium & France / Licensing-in*	None, but refocussed from particular product-markets	Relationships & networks, international commitment & learning orientation	Probable entry to Sudan & Yemen

* Inward internationalization

2004, signed a technical partnership and distribution agreement with a Russian firm, which enabled it to distribute this firm's product in Syria and the Middle East. This relationship evolved into a reciprocal deal in 2007, when Company A started providing software development services to the Russian firm.

Two factors greatly influenced Company A's initiation of a relationship with the Russian firm. First, the founder had obtained his higher education from Russia and was familiar with Russian products and language. The second factor pertains to the economic sanctions imposed by the United States on Syria in 2004, which banned all American imports into Syria, except for food and medicine (Marquis 2004). Although American software products sometimes enter the Syrian market unofficially, clients refrain from buying them because of lack of technical support. Entrenched in its position as the Middle Eastern representative of the Russian firm and driven by the goal of increasing overseas sales, A decided to open a sales subsidiary in Dubai, UAE in 2007 as its next major step in outward internationalization. Dubai was chosen because it is the Arabic world's business hub, and having an office there was considered critical to facilitating access to other Arabic, particularly GCC countries.

It would appear from the foregoing that after an initial seven year reliance on its local Syrian market, A commenced international activity by exporting to psychically close UAE market and subsequently other GCC countries. Its internationalization process was not uni-directional or linear, however, because the next step it took was to enter into an agreement to distribute Russian products in Syria, which was an inward internationalization move. Interestingly, this strategic relationship provided a platform for further outward international expansion for A, which involved setting up a sales subsidiary in the lucrative and strategically important Dubai market. As this company's managing director stated '*This [partnership] is making us able to expand, first locally then regionally and finally internationally. At this level we are trying to expand regionally in some of the Arabic countries'*.

Company B was founded by a young engineering graduate who had only one year of experience in a local IT firm. It internationalized soon after establishment mainly because of weak local demand, and its aim was to achieve 70 per cent of sales in foreign markets. After considering two internationalization routes – providing subcontracting services to Western companies and exporting offerings to the Arabic markets – the founder chose the latter as it was deemed more feasible and profitable. The subcontracting option was judged to be less feasible because Western companies require their outsourcing partners to hold CMMI certificates [1], a proxy for high standards. In addition, such contracts are typically facilitated by intermediaries and the founder did not know any.

This company's first export market was Saudi Arabia, a decision influenced chiefly by the size of the market and the founder's relationship with a Saudi based friend; they had agreed that this friend would start a company in Saudi Arabia that would be responsible for selling B's offerings there. The founder indicated during the interview that this partnership has been very successful and was continuing to flourish. B also expanded to a number of other Arabic markets. It entered UAE (described by the founder as '*the entrance to the gulf*') through a partner, but found the latter to be insufficiently committed to the partnership. The Emirati market was also found to be more complicated than the Saudi market. B also tried to enter Jordan, but found its resources (managerial and financial), overstretched. This resulted in a near collapse of the home office, and led the founder to restructure the firm, reducing the staff strength from 30 to 20, setting up procedures and standards, discontinuing expansion efforts and concentrating solely on the local and Saudi markets.

The company appears focussed on this strategy. Their aims, as explained by the founder, are to attain high quality work standards marked by zero tolerance for defects as well as devise a successful internationalization model that can be replicated in other countries, *albeit* with some localization. The founder also indicated his company's willingness to consider partnering proposals from distributors that may wish to sell B's products overseas, as long as such distributors are willing to pay a minimum guarantee to underline their credibility. The interview data suggests that many firms had approached B for partnering, but subsequently withdrew because of this minimum guarantee requirement. The founder, nevertheless, seemed very optimistic about achieving the company's international goals, particularly as they are now following a plan, which was not the case when they commenced their internationalization journey in 2004.

Taken together, the foregoing conveys a picture of a company that internationalized rapidly, driven largely by the commitment of its founder to leverage growth opportunities in regional and international markets, as a counter against the weak demand in its domestic market. There is also evidence of the effect of relational assets on this company's expansion, specifically to the Saudi market. This case also tells another important story regarding how significant limitations in resource base and partners' quality could check or sabotage an SME's international growth ambitions (B was only able to achieve 30% international sales ratio in 2007 as against its targeted 70 per cent), particularly where the company in question seems to be overreaching or overstretching itself. This raises an important point about born global failure, international market withdrawal or de-internationalization (Crick 2002, 2004), which will be discussed in the next section.

Company C, a provider of off-the-shelf accounting, HRM, and management systems to restaurants, hospitals and schools, started life as an IT department of a big conglomerate, offering software solutions to other departments. It later extended its services to other organizations and subsequently became an independent entity. The interviewed MD, an engineering degree holder, considered internationalization a normal step in the company growth path, and noted that the company internationalized about four years after establishment, 'once [the company] had ready products, built [its] name in the local market and became famous'. A key trigger for C's initial internationalization was a contact and unsolicited request from a previous employee to market the company's products in Kuwait. A broadly similar situation occurred in the Saudi Arabian market, where a previous employee also played an intermediary role between Company C and a local firm.

A distinctive feature of C's internationalization is that it is the only one among the case study firms that has generated sales revenue outside the Arabic region, specifically Turkey, which it serves through its distributor in Iraq. Although Turkey is a neighbouring country to Syria, the language difference creates a substantial barrier. Thus, Syrian companies tend to target Arabic countries only. C also went to Egypt and recently to Libya through distributors. Libya started liberalization recently and the interviewed MD considers it a very good market. This MD also indicated the company's continuing search for distribution partners in overseas markets where it is not currently present.

In addition to the relational factors above, the interviewed MD identified other influences on C's internationalization as including its reputable and high-quality products and participation in a number of important industry exhibitions. One example is the Gulf Information and Technology Exhibition [GITEX][2] in Dubai, which reportedly enabled the company to meet some of its subsequent distributors. The MD also indicated that the company has attracted many customers and partners through its quality reputation, personal networks, exhibitions and even the internet.

Company D, a provider of typically pricey Enterprise Resource Planning (ERP) systems, was established in 2000 by a five-person team, two of whom had IT experience in the United States; another two provided the financing and the last furnished local managerial experience. Its marketing and sales manager, the key informant for this study, has a degree in civil engineering, and Project Management Professional (PMI) and Executive Leadership certificates from the United States and Lebanon, respectively.

D started with a primary focus on the local market and a secondary attention on the Arabic markets. Its first cross-border activity, therefore, was a partnership agreement in 2004 with a French firm, a market leader in Enterprise Content Management (ECM) systems, to obtain access to software infrastructure (or tools) to be used in developing, implementing and supporting new applications for the Syrian market. This inward internationalization relationship commenced after a coincidental meeting between the D's CEO and the French company's regional manager in Lebanon and was apparently successful. The same cannot be said, however, of D's initial attempts to expand regionally, notably through participation in the 2005 GITEX-Dubai and the despatch of a sales team to Jordan with the remit to find new clients. These attempts reportedly foundered owing to the high price tag of the systems. A later partnership deal with a Jordanian firm in 2006 was, however, more successful, as it led to a joint venture arrangement between the two firms in 2007, to provide SMS and Internet-banking services. D's French partner played a role in facilitating this Jordanian expansion because it was keen to grow sales in Jordan through D. Further regional market entry was undertaken in 2008, when the company made its first sale of ERP systems in Yemen, a rapidly developing, software-hungry, market, which the interviewed sales manager found to be very similar to Syria. D learnt of this Yemeni opportunity through its Jordanian joint venture partner. It reportedly plans to expand in 2009 to the most important GCC countries, Saudi Arabia and UAE, in addition to Libya, where the CEO has some personal contacts. It is also trying to secure a subcontracting deal from the United Kingdom, which it learnt of, again, through the CEO's networks.

Overall, Company D's case demonstrates the critical importance of business networks in facilitating the internationalization process. This company's internationalization, indeed, seemed to have gained at every turn from the resource augmenting intervention of business networks and relational contacts.

Company E was established in 2000 to seize the opportunity of providing subcontracting services to a German firm specialized in security and time management systems. The contract was secured through contacts that E's founder had within the German firm. The interviewed MD, an engineer, emphasized the role of personal relationships in procuring subcontracting projects, noting that they are essential to ensuring trust, which is a key factor for such contracts. Although further attempts to obtain more subcontracting projects were not successful owing to sanctions on Syria and lack of similarly beneficial contacts, E still focusses on such projects and views them as having a greater potential for the company.

The company has also developed, in collaboration with a Syria-based German organization, archiving and billing systems for the local market. This reflects the management view of a strong home base as a platform to expanding internationally. Faced, however, with very limited local demand for its products and minimal success in building such a base, the company has not ruled out selling its products overseas. The interviewed MD perceived many obstacles to so doing but believes that the company's relationship with the above-mentioned German organization might give it the opportunity to develop systems for overseas markets.

Like the preceding case, *Company F* was set up in 1999 to provide subcontracting services to an Italian firm. The founder, a young engineering graduate, had met an Italian national of Syrian origins through his academic supervisor. This person was looking for a software developer to write a programme for his company in Italy, and F's founder did this job and gained the appreciation of the Italian businessman in the process. The latter subsequently outsourced all his computer firm's software development tasks to F. Even when this computer firm was acquired by a larger firm, F continued to provide subcontracting services to both firms, as well as a third Italian firm, though on a smaller scale.

Company F's software development tasks were in the area of Customer Relationship Management (CRM), and this knowledge led it to produce its own CRM systems and a few other products. However, these products did not meet with much success, either locally or regionally, because of the intense competition in such systems. The company appointed distributors in Kuwait, UAE, and Saudi Arabia, but was only able to make two sales in the latter country. This experience together with the decline of business with the Italian firms led F to pursue opportunities elsewhere. It subsequently got a subcontracting deal in Dubai, UAE, which it learnt of through a 'sister' firm. This project (a fleet management system) developed the company's expertise in providing space photos and made it realize the considerable local demand for such photos and related systems (Geographic Information Systems, GIS). Therefore, it attended GIT EX-Dubai 2005 to seek a foreign partner that can supply it with these systems, and later that year signed a partnership with a Belgian firm and French partner. Company F now provides customization, installation, implementation, and training for the above systems in the Syrian market.

The interviewed founder/CEO indicated thinking of overseas expansion using GIS systems in addition to his company's own products. GCC countries have been considered as targets, but the perceived intense competition in these 'open' markets has so far discouraged F's management. Sudan and Yemen are, however, being seriously considered for entry, after F's founder/manager was told by a business associate of these markets' great potential and similarity to the Syrian market.

Discussion

An aggregate look at the preceding case profiles suggests a number of important discussion points. The first is that whilst no one extant internationalization theory appears to fully explain the internationalization behaviour of the investigated Syrian knowledge-based SMEs, each seems partially relevant in explaining aspects of the observed internationalization behaviour. The second point is that certain commonalities observed among the case profiles seem to suggest the greater salience of particular theoretical perspectives in explaining the internationalization of Syrian SMEs. These discussion points are analyzed in the next several paragraphs, under the following subheadings: the 'stages' theory; the network perspective; the international new venture theory; and the resource-based view point.

The 'stages' theory (including the psychic distance notion)

Case study data suggests the limited salience of the incremental internationalization model in explaining the international expansion of Syrian software SMEs. Although the study firms generally commenced their internationalization journey with lower commitment modes (typically using export distributors, offering subcontracting services, or licensing-in), and although there were a few instances of shifts from lower to higher commitment modes within particular markets (A in UAE and D in Jordan), the balance of evidence weighs very much against the 'stages'-based explanation. For one, none of the study firms really waited to establish themselves in their home market before embarking on cross-border activities. Secondly, observed deviations from the unidirectional modal evolution thesis, including backward shifts and market withdrawals (Crick 2002, 2004), severally outstrip the few instances of agreement. Thirdly, rather than being guided by a risk minimizing mindset, the entry modes used by several of the case firms tend to be that required by network partners or needed to accomplish the internationalization task.

It is also correct to state that the 'stages' theory, with its essential focus on outward internationalization activities (Crick and Jones 2000; Fletcher 2001; Jones 2001) does not explain the impact of inward internationalization activities on export initiation as observed severally in the present study (for example, obtaining distribution rights for foreign firms motivated A to set up a sales subsidiary in UAE and allowed D to expand into Jordan. Also, providing subcontracting services enabled F to obtain the required expertise to produce its own software packages and explore opportunities in local and foreign markets).

The present study's evidence on the psychic distance notion is also weak, at best. Although the case firms' preponderant targeting of Arabic countries, particularly in their exporting activities, points to an uncertainty reducing regional approach, several aspects of their market selection decisions suggest that the psychic distance explanation does not tell the whole story. First, network relationships appear to have a major impact on the market entry decisions of these firms, which reinforce previous research findings (e.g., Moen, Gavlen, and Endresen 2004; Zain and Ng 2006). Second, market attractiveness factors, specifically potential market size and perceived level of competition, also seem very influential; this is suggested by the firms' observed emphasis on the relatively large, lucrative and strategic Saudi and Emirati markets and the less competitive Libyan, Sudanese, and Yemeni markets. Indeed, the latter markets appear to be virgin markets for technological products that are deemed very attractive by the Syrian software SMEs.

The network perspective

The network-based explanation seems relevant to a great deal of the internationalization behaviour observed among Syrian knowledge-based SMEs. The case firms either reacted to opportunities made available through their networks (C, E, F) or proactively pursued overseas opportunities that were facilitated by their existing networks (A, B, D). This is consistent with a considerable body of previous empirical literature (e.g., Coviello and Munro 1997; Moen, Gavlen, and Endresen 2004), which underline the critical importance of network relationships in promoting firm internationalization. Unlike Coviello and Munro (1997), however, we did not find any evidence regarding the constraining effect of network relationships. The present study's data also throws some light on the germane distinction between social relationships and business relationships. In half of the cases (B, E, F), initiation of cross-border activities was triggered or facilitated by social contacts, with business networks becoming more apparent in subsequent international expansion. This corresponds with previous research, which revealed the importance of social ties in firms' internationalization (Ellis 2000; Ellis and Pecotich 2001; Rutashobya and Jaensson 2004; Harris and Wheeler 2005). It also reflects arguments in the entrepreneurship literature that new ventures depend initially on socially embedded ties, while business relationships are more dominant in later stages of the venture life (Larson and Starr 1993; Hite and Hesterly 2001). This suggests the need for researchers to address both social and business relationships in their studies of small firm internationalization.

The international new venture theory

Case study data suggests that most of the investigated firms internationalized at an early stage in their lives. As Table 14.2 shows, two internationalized at inception and all remaining firms undertook their first cross-border activity within the first seven years. Thus, if we consider only the time to internationalization or the demographic dimension in defining born-global firms (within two years of inception – Knight and Cavusgil 1996; Chetty and Campbell-Hunt 2004; up to six years – Zahra, Ireland, and Hitt 2000; up to eight years – McDougall, Shane, and Oviatt 1994), virtually all of the case firms would qualify. However, born-global firms or INVs are not merely defined by the speed of internationalization, but also by a number of other key characteristics that seem to be lacking in the present study firms.

First, although the companies operate in a knowledge-based industry, they do not offer breakthrough technologies. They typically focus on simple products and tend to adapt existing technologies to local or regional markets' needs, which are much less sophisticated than the needs of advanced markets. In addition, most of the founders / managers (B, C, E, F) lacked global orientation and prior international experience (whether obtained by working abroad or for an international company in the home country – Loane, Bell, and McNaughton 2007), both attributes are considered fundamental for born-global firms (McDougall, Shane and Oviatt 1994; Gabrielsson et al. 2008). Whilst these limitations could be understood in the context of the relative newness of the software and IT sector in Syria, and the lack of foreign direct investment and concomitant spillovers (as in Ireland, for example – Heeks and Nicholson 2004), they nevertheless suggest that the study firms do not possess the threshold attributes and competencies typically linked with international new ventures (Chetty and Campbell-Hunt 2004; Gabrielsson et al. 2008; McDougall, Shane, and Oviatt 1994).

The resource-based viewpoint

Analysis of the case data appears to suggest a broad resource-based explanation for aspects of the internationalization outcomes reported by the investigated Syrian SMEs. As can be seen from Table 14.2, the case firms with more positive outcomes (A, C, D, F) tend to be those with relatively good resource indicators – managerial attributes, quality products, relationship making, and learning capabilities. The apparent 'strugglers', on the other hand, include a firm that lacks network access and another that admits of critical resource shortages. It must be noted, however, that the totality of evidence does not consistently favour a resource-based explanation, even in its broad form. Although Company B arguably belongs to the latter category, its managerial, entrepreneurial and relational attributes compare favourably with those of the firms with more positive internationalization outcomes. Indeed, B is among the four case firms (A, B, D, F) that suggest a fair amount of entrepreneurial orientation, in terms of their founders' / management's engagement in proactive search for international growth opportunities. This contrasts with C, which though a better performer, indicates a reactive rather than proactive attitude to internationalization.

Conclusions and implications

This study has employed a case-based approach to explore the relevance of the major theoretical perspectives available in the literature in explaining the observed internationalization behaviour of knowledge-based SMEs from Syria. It contributes by providing rare empirical insights on the internationalization behaviour of Middle-Eastern SMEs and redressing, *albeit* slightly, the apparent research gap on the internationalization of knowledge-based SMEs from developing countries.

Analysis results suggest the inadequacy of the extant theoretical approaches, on their individual basis, to fully explain the internationalization behaviour observed among Syrian software SMEs. This is particularly true for the born-global perspective which has gained considerable support in previous internationalization studies undertaken in economically advanced countries among knowledge-based SMEs. Although the knowledge-based SMEs from Syria initiated cross-border activities relatively early, they do not seem to possess the threshold attributes and typical characteristics of born-global firms, as suggested in the literature (McDougall, Shane, and Oviatt 1994; Chetty and Campbell-Hunt 2004; Gabrielsson et al. 2008). This is somewhat surprising, given that Syria's age-old history of active international trading and firms' knowledge-based orientation had led us to expect at least some born global firms. It also emerged that the study firms did not largely follow the evolutionary and unidirectional path described in the stages model, nor could their market selection decisions be comprehensively explained by the psychic distance notion. The network perspective, however, seems to offer relatively good explanatory insights, so is the resource-based view, *albeit* to a smaller extent. These summary findings reinforce previous calls in the literature for a more holistic approach or integrative platform for explaining firm internationalization (Bell and Young 1998; Crick and Jones 2000; Fletcher 2001; Ibeh 2001; Jones 2001).

Implications

The study has a number of implications for software SMEs' not only in the peripheral Middle East and North African countries but also in other developing countries. The first relates to the need for these SMEs and their management to become more actively aware of the feasibility of early internationalization and understand that it is not imperative to have a strong home market base in order to cross their borders. Second, the observed internationalization benefits of relational ties – social and business – should encourage managers to give priority attention to activating their repertoire of networks and building new ones to facilitate their international activities. This seems particularly sensible, given, for example, that the population of Syrian expatriates roughly equals the inhabitants in the homeland (MOEX 2006). SMEs should, therefore, view co-ethnics abroad as a valuable resource and actively seek to develop relationships with them as a means of furthering their internationalization. As the present study evidence also indicates, participation in international trade exhibitions and conferences can also be a good platform for new, potentially important, relationships. SMEs should, therefore, take advantage of such opportunities, particularly given the occasional availability of public sector support for attending such events. Additionally, software SMEs should consider all types of international activities, not only exporting, since providing outsourcing services and collaborative agreements with foreign companies can enhance the capabilities of the firm and enable it sense and take advantage of opportunities beyond its national borders.

This study also has some important policy implications. The first relates to the need for Syrian policy makers, and their counterparts in other developing countries, to acknowledge the reality that their knowledge-based SMEs may be internationalizing and, thus, extend available internationalization assistance beyond the traditional sector, as currently appears to be the case. This also applies to international bodies such as the World Bank, European Investment Bank and UNDP that aim to encourage export diversification within the Middle East and other developing countries.

Support should be given on various dimensions. First, any type of assistance should recognize the early internationalization behaviour exhibited by software SMEs and the various types of activities they engaged in. This suggests that support should go beyond promoting exporting. Given that software SMEs generally lack financial resources and do not typically have access to venture capital, innovative financial solutions should be put in place to enable these firms develop their technologies and adapt these to the needs of the international markets. In addition, the government must try to set up a vibrant venture capital and business angel community that can improve SMEs' access to much needed financial resources. Governmental efforts should also promote linkages and network relationships between local and international firms as well as support participation in international fairs. This would present SMEs with more opportunities to engage in international activities, not only exporting but also subcontracting projects and joint R&D activities. Furthermore, given the lack of international experience among SMEs managers, providing free training on international business could be very helpful to those managers.

Limitations and future research recommendations

This exploratory study is not without limitations. First, the small number of investigated firms (six internationalized software SMEs) and the nonprobability approach employed in case selection limit the potential for generalizing its findings (Saunders, Lewis, and Thornhill 1997). Additionally, the data generated were self-reported responses from interviewees; therefore, response bias cannot be ruled out (Yin 2003). Finally, the fact that interviews were recorded might have caused interviewees to hesitate or even avoid answering sensitive questions (Ghauri, Grønhaug, and Kristianslund 1995). Future researchers are, therefore, urged to revisit the issues explored in this work, using a more systematic quantitative approach. In addition, focussing on noninternationalized companies in future studies would be beneficial, since it may allow us to understand why these companies do not conduct international activities.

It would also be of great significance to examine the internationalization of software SMEs in other Middle Eastern countries in which the industry is more advanced, such as Egypt, as well as in countries that have had open economies for a longer period of time, such as Jordan and UAE. This could assist our understanding of the extent to which the present study's findings are limited to the Syrian context, where the software industry is still in its infancy and the economy has just been recently liberalized.

Notes

1. CMMI (Capability Maturity Model Integration) is a certification scheme that verifies the quality of the management of software writing process (Heeks and Nicholson, 2004).
2. The Gulf Information & Technology Exhibition (GITEX) is an annual exhibition held in Dubai, Cairo, Hyderabad, and Beirut. GITEX-Dubai is considered the most important IT exhibition in the Arabic region.

References

Acedo, F.J., Barroso, C. and Galan, L. (2006) 'The resource-based theory: Dissemination and main trends', *Strategic Management Journal*, 27(7), 621–36.

Ahmad, Z.U., Craig, C. J., Baalbaki, I. and Hadidian, T.V. (2006) 'Firm internationalisation and export incentives from a Middle Eastern perspective', *Journal of Small Business and Enterprise Development*, 13(4), 660–69.

Aidis, R. (2005) 'Institutional barriers to small and medium-sized enterprise operations in transition countries', *Small Business Economics*, 25(4), 305–18.

Barney, J.B. (1991) 'Firm resources and sustained competitive advantage', *Journal of Management*, 17(1), 99–120.

Bell, J. (1995) 'The internationalization of small computer software firms: a further challenge to stage theories', *European Journal of Marketing*, 29(8), 60–75.

Bell, J. (1997) 'A comparative study of the export problems of small computer software exporters in Finland, Ireland and Norway', *International Business Review*, 6(6), 585–604.

Bell, J., Crick, D. and Young, S. (2004) 'Small firm internationalisation and business strategy: an exploratory study of 'knowledge-intensive' and 'traditional' manufacturing firms in the UK', *International Small Business Journal*, 22(1), 23–56.

Bell, J. and Young, S. (1998) 'Toward an integrative framework on the internationalisation of the Firm', in G. Hooley, R. Loveridge and D. Wilson (eds), *Internationalisation: Process, Context and Markets*, 5–28 (London: Macmillan).

Bilkey, W.J. and Tesar, G. (1977) 'The export behaviour of smaller-sized Wisconsin manufacturing firms', *Journal of International Business Studies*, 8(1), 93–98.

Bloodgood, J.M., Sapienza, H.J. and Almeida, J.G. (1996) 'The internationalization of new high-potential US ventures: Antecedents and outcomes', *Entrepreneurship Theory and Practice*, 20(4), 61–76.

Borchert, O. and Ibeh, K.I.N. (2008) 'A quintessential 'Born Global'?: Case evidence from a rapidly internationalising Canadian small firm', in N.O. Ndubisi (ed.), *International Business: Theory and Strategy*, 49–64 (Selangor Darul Ehsan: Arah Publications).

Bryman, A. and Bell, E. (2003) *Business Research Methods* (Oxford: Oxford University Press).

Cavusgil, S.T. (1980) 'On the internationalisation process of the firm', *European Research*, 8(6), 273–81.

CCG (2002) 'Syria Country Commercial Guide FY2002', online available at http://www. buyusainfo.net/info.cfm?id=78495&keyx=5FCE5DA559C73E65E474492A24CDF5CF &dbf=ccg1&loadnav= [accessed 1 August 2008].

Chetty, S. (1999) 'Dimensions of internationalisation of manufacturing firms in the apparel industry', *European Journal of Marketing*, 33(1/2), 121–42.

Chetty, S. and Campbell-Hunt, C. (2004) 'A strategic approach to internationalization: A traditional versus a "Born-Global" approach', *Journal of International Marketing*, 12(1), 57–81.

Chung, H.-J., Chen, C.C. and Hsieh, T.-J. (2008) 'First geographic expansion of startup firms: Initial size and entry timing effects', *Journal of Business Research*, 60(4), 388–95.

CIA (Central Intelligence Agency) (2008) 'The World Factbook, Syria', online available at: https://www.cia.gov/library/publications/the-world-factbook/geos/sy.html [accessed 12 December 2008]

Coviello, N.E. (2006) 'The network dynamics of international new ventures', *Journal of International Business Studies*, 37(5), 713–31.

Coviello, N.E. and Munro, H. (1997) 'Network relationships and the internationalisation process of small software firms', *International Business Review*, 6(4), 361–86.

Crick, D. (2002) 'The decision to discontinue exporting: SMEs in two U.K. trade sectors', *Journal of Small Business Management*, 40(1), 66–77.

Crick, D. (2004) 'SMEs' decision to discontinue exporting: an exploratory investigation into practices within the clothing industry', *Journal of Business Venturing*, 19, 561–87.

Crick, D., Mansour Al Obaidi and Chaudhry, S. (1998) 'Perceived obstacles of Saudi-Arabian exporters of non-oil product', *Journal of Marketing Practice: Applied Marketing Science*, 4(7), 187–99.

Crick, D. and Kaganda, G. (2008) 'An Exploratory study of the international competitiveness of low and high intensity Tanzanian exporting SMEs', Proceedings of the Eleventh McGill International Entrepreneurship Conference, New Frontiers in International Entrepreneurship: Bridging the Gap between North & South and East & West.

Crick, D. and Jones, M.V. (2000) 'Small high-technology firms and international high-technology markets', *Journal of International Marketing*, 8(2), 63–85.

Cyret, R.M. and March, J.G. (1963) *A Behavioural Theory of the Firm* (Englewood Cliffs, NJ: Prentice Hall).

Ellis, P. (2000) 'Social ties and foreign market entry', *Journal of International Business Studies*, 31(3), 443–69.

Ellis, P. and Pecotich, A. (2001) 'Social factors influencing export initiation in small and medium-sized enterprises' *Journal of Marketing Research*, 38(1), 119–30.

Fan, T. and Phan, P. (2007) 'International new ventures: revisiting the influences behind the "born- global' firm', *Journal of International Business Studies*, 380(7), 1113–31.

FCO (Foreign and Commonwealth Office) (2008) 'Country Profile: Syria', online available at:http://www.fco.gov.uk/en/about-the-fco/country-profiles/middle-east-north-africa/syria?profile=economy&pg=2 [accessed 12 December 2008].

Fletcher, R. (2001) 'A holistic approach to internationalisation', *International Business Review*, 10(1), 25–49.

Gabrielsson, M., Kirpalani, V.H.M., Dimitratos, P., Solberg, C.A. and Zucchella, A. (2008) 'Born globals: Propositions to help advance the theory', *International Business Review*, 17(4), 385–401.

Ghauri, P., Grønhaug, K. and Kristianslund, I.(1995) *Research Methods in Business Studies: A practical Guide* (New York, London: Prentice Hall).

Ghauri, P., Lutz, C. and Tesfom, G. (2003) 'Using networks to solve export-marketing problems of small- and medium-sized firms from developing countries', *European Journal of Marketing*, 37(5/6), 728–52.

Grant, R.M. (1991) 'The resource-based view of competitive advantage: Implications for strategy formulation', *California Management Review*, 33(3), 114–35.

Grant, R.M. (1996) 'Toward a knowledge-based theory of the firm', *Strategic Management Journal*, 17, (Winter Special Issue), 109–22.

Harris, S. and Wheeler, C. (2005) 'Entrepreneurs' relationships for internationalization: functions, origins and strategies', *International Business Review*, 14(2), 187–207.

Heeks, R. and Nicholson, B. (2004) 'Software export success factors and strategies in 'Follower' nations', *Competition & Change*, 8(3), 267–303.

Hite, J.M. and Hesterly, W.S. (2001) 'The evolution of firm networks: from emergence to early growth of the firm', *Strategic Management Journal*, 22(3), 275–86.

Ibeh, K.I.N. (2000) 'Internationalisation and the small firm', in S. Carter and D. Jones-Evans (eds), *Enterprise and Small Business: Principles, Practice and Policy*, 434–52 (Harlow: Financial Times).

Ibeh, K.I.N. (2001) 'On the resource-based, integrative view of small firm internationalization: An exploratory study of Nigerian firms', in J.H. Taggart, M. Berry and M. McDermott, (eds), *Multinationals in the New Era* (London: Macmillan).

Ibeh, K.I.N. (2003) 'On the internal drivers of export performance among Nigerian firms: empirical findings and implications', *Management Decision*, 41 (3), 217–25.

Ibeh, K.I.N. (2004) 'Furthering export participation in less performing developing countries: The effects of entrepreneurial orientation and managerial capacity factors', *International Journal of Social Economics*, 31 (1/2), 94–110.

Ibeh, K.I.N. (2005) 'Toward greater firm-level international entrepreneurship within the UK agribusiness sector: Resource levers and strategic options', *Management International Review*, 45(3, Special Issue), 59–81.

Ibeh, K.I.N. and Young, S. (2001) 'Exporting as an entrepreneurial act: An empirical study of Nigerian firms', *European Journal of Marketing*, 35 (5/6), 566–86.

Jansson, H. and Sandberg, S. (2008) 'Internationalization of small and medium sized enterprises in the Baltic Sea Region', *Journal of International Management*, 14(1), 65–77.

Johanson, J. and Mattsson, L.-G. (1988) 'Interorganizational relations in industrial systems: A network approach compared with the transaction-cost approach', *International Studies of Management and Organization*, 18(1), 34–48.

Johanson, J. and Vahlne, J.-E. (1977) 'The internationalization process of the firm: a model of knowledge development and increasing foreign commitments', *Journal of International Business Studies*, 8(1), 23–32.

Johanson, J. and Wiedersheim-Paul, F. (1975) 'The internationalization of the firm: Four Swedish case studies', *Journal of Management Studies*, 12(3), 305–22.

Jones, M.V. (1999) 'The internationalization of small high-technology firms', *Journal of International Marketing*, 7(4), 15–41.

Jones, M.V. (2001) 'First steps in internationalisation: Concepts and evidence from a sample of small high-technology firms', *Journal of International Management*, 7(3), 191–210.

Jones, M.V. and Coviello, N.E. (2005) 'Internationalisation: conceptualising an entrepreneurial process of behaviour in time', *Journal of International Business Studies*, 36(3), 284–303.

Karadeniz, E.E. and Göçer, K. (2007) 'Internationalization of small firms: A case study of Turkish small- and medium-sized enterprises', *European Business Review*, 19(5), 387–403.

Knight, G.A. and Cavusgil, S.T. (1996) 'The born global firm: A challenge to traditional internationalization theory', in S.T. Cavusgil and T.K. Madsen (eds), *Advances in International Marketing*, 8, 11–26 (Greenwich: JAI Press).

Kogut, B. and Zander, U. (1992) 'Knowledge of the firm, combinative capabilities, and the replication of technology', *Organization Science*, 3(3), 383–97.

Kuada, J.E. and Sørensen, O.J. (2000) *Internationalization of Companies from Developing Countries* (New York; London: International Business Press).

Larson, A. and Starr, J.A. (1993) 'A network model of organization formation', *Entrepreneurship: Theory and Practice*, 17(2), 5–15.

Leão, C. and Kabbani, A. (2007) 'Design of a strategy and detailed action plan leading to the development of the software industry in Syria', Final Report, Damascus: Syrian Enterprise and Business Centre, SME Support Programme.

Leonidou, L.C. (2004) 'An analysis of the barriers hindering small business export Development', *Journal of Small Business Management*, 42(3), 279–302.

Leonidou, L.C. and Katsikeas, C.S. (1996) 'The export development process: an integrative review of empirical models', *Journal of International Business Studies*, 27(3), 517–51.

Liu, X., Xiao, W. and Huang, X. (2008) 'Bounded entrepreneurship and internationalisation of indigenous Chinese private-owned firms', *International Business Review*, Article in Press, Corrected Proof.

Lloyd-Reason, L., Damyanov, A., Nicolescu, O. and Wall, S. (2005) 'Internationalisation process, SMEs and transitional economies: a four-country perspective', *International Journal of Entrepreneurship & Innovation Management*, 5(3/4), 206–26.

Loane, S., Bell, J.D. and McNaughton, R. (2007) 'A cross-national study on the impact of management teams on the rapid internationalization of small firms', *Journal of World Business*, 42(4), 489–504.

Madsen, T.K. and Servais, P. (1997) 'The internationalisation of born globals: an evolutionary process?', *International Business Review*, 6(6), 561–83.

Marquis, C. (2004) 'Bush imposes sanctions on Syria, citing ties to terrorism', The New York Times, [online], 12 May 2004, available at: http://query.nytimes.com/gst/fullpage.html?res=9C0CEFDA103CF931A25756C0A9629C8B63 [accessed 31 July 2008].

McDougall, P.P., Shane, S. and Oviatt, B.M. (1994) 'Explaining the formation of international new ventures: the limits of theories from international business research', *Journal of Business Venturing*, 9(6), 469–87.

Melin, L. (1992) 'Internationalization as a strategy process', *Strategic Management Journal*, 13 (Winter, Special Issue: Fundamental Themes in Strategy Process Research), 99–118.

Mills, A.E. (1964) 'Environment and size of firm: A study of international trading in the Arab Middle East', *Journal of Management Studies*, 1(1), 67–80.

Moen, Ø., Gavlen, M. and Endresen, I. (2004) 'Internationalization of small, computer software firms: Entry forms and market selection', *European Journal of Marketing*, 38(9/10), 1236–51.

MOEX 2006, Ministry of Expatriates, About MOEX, [online] available at: http://ministryofexpatriates.gov.sy/cweb/MOEX_English/MOEX%20Pages_en/AboutMOEX_en.htm [accessed 20 January 2009].

Nonaka, I. and Takeuchi, H. (1995) *The knowledge-Creating Company: How Japanese Companies Create the Dynamics of Innovation* (New York: Oxford University Press).

Nummela, N., Saarenketo, S. and Puumalainen, K. (2004) 'A global mindset—a prerequisite for successful internationalization?', *Canadian Journal of Administrative Sciences*, 21(1), 51–64.

OBG, Oxford Business Group (2008), 'Emerging Syria 2008', [online] available at: http://www.oxfordbusinessgroup.com/publication.asp?country=6 [accessed 18 August 2008].

Oviatt, B.M. and McDougall, P.P. (1994) 'Toward a theory of international new ventures', *Journal of International Business Studies*, 25(1), 45–64.

Özkanlı, Ö., Benek, S. and Akdeve, E. (2006) 'Export barriers of small firms in Turkey: A study of Ankara-Ivedik industrial district', *Problems and Perspectives in Management*, 4(3), 78–90.

Penrose, E.T. (1959) *The Theory of the Growth of the Firm* (Oxford: Basil Blackwell).

Reid, S.D. (1981) 'The decision-maker and export entry and expansion' *Journal of International Business Studies*, 12(2), 101–12.

Rennie, M.W. (1993) 'Born Global', *The McKinsey Quarterly*, 4(4), 45–52.

Rialp, A., Rialp, J. and Knight, G.A. (2005) 'The phenomenon of early internationalizing firms: what do we know after a decade (1994–2003) of scientific inquiry?', *International Business Review*, 14(2), 147–66.

Rogers, e. (1962) *Diffusion of Innovations* (New York: The Free Press).

Rutashobya, L. and Jaensson J.-E. (2004) 'Small firms' internationalization for development in Tanzania: Exploring the network phenomenon', *International Journal of Social Economics*, 31(1/2), 159–72.

Saunders, M.N.K., Lewis, P. and Thornhill, A. (1997) *Research Methods for Business Students* (London: Pitman Publishing).

Sharma, D.D. and Blomstermo, A. (2003) 'The internationalization process of born globals: a network view', *International Business Review*, 12(6), 739–53.

Spence, M. and Crick, D. (2006) 'A comparative investigation into the internationalization of Canadian and UK high-tech SMEs', *International Marketing Review*, 23(5), 524–48.

Syrian Enterprise Business Centre (2008), SEBC discusses SME Strategy with Syrian government, [online] available at: http://www.sebcsyria.com/web2008/art.php?art_id=1338 [accessed 10 June 2008].

Terjesen, S., O'Gorman, C. and Acs, Z.J. (2008) 'Intermediated mode of internationalization: new software ventures in Ireland and India', *Entrepreneurship & Regional Development*, 20(1), 89–109.

Thai, M.T.T. and Chong, L.C. (2008) 'Born-global: The case of four Vietnamese SMEs', *Journal of International Entrepreneurship*, 6(2), 72–100.

Tyagi, P. (2000) 'Export behaviour of small business firms in developing economies: evidence from the Indian market', *Marketing Management Journal*, Fall/Winter, 12–20.

Weerawardena, J., Mort, G.S., Liesch, P.W. and Knight, G. (2007) 'Conceptualizing accelerated internationalization in the born global firm: A dynamic capabilities perspective', *Journal of World Business*, 42(3), 294–306.

Welch, L.S. and Luostarinen, R. (1988) 'Internationalisation: evolution of a concept', *Journal of General Management*, 14 (2), 34–55. Cited in Chetty, S.K. (1999), 'Dimensions of internationalisation of manufacturing firms in the apparel industry', *European Journal of Marketing*; 33 (1/2), 121–42.

Wernerfelt, B. (1984) 'A resource-based view of the firm', *Strategic Management Journal*, 5 (2), 171–80.

Westhead, P., Wright, M. and Ucbasaran, D. (2001), 'The internationalization of new and small firms: A resource-based view', *Journal of Business Venturing*, 16(4), 333–58.

Vissak, T., Ibeh, K. and Paliwoda, S. (2007) 'Internationalisation from the European Periphery: Triggers, processes and trajectories', *Journal of Euromarketing*, 17(1), 35–48.

World Bank (2008), *Syrian Arab Republic*, [online] available at: http://web.worldbank.org/
WBSITE/EXTERNAL/COUNTRIES/MENAEXT/SYRIANARABEXTN/0,,menuPK:31055
3~pagePK:141159~piPK:141110~theSitePK:310548,00.html [accessed 15 June 2008].
Yin, R.K. (2003) *Case Study Research: Design and Methods*, 3rd edn (Thousand Oaks, CA,
London: Sage).
Yli-Renko, H., Autio, E. and Tontti, V. (2002) 'Social capital, knowledge, and the international growth of technology-based new firms', *International Business Review*, 11(3),
279–304.
Zain, M. and Siew I. Ng (2006) 'The impacts of network relationships on SMEs' internationalization process', *Thunderbird International Business Review*, 48(2), 183–98.
Zahra, S., Ireland, D. and Hitt, M. (2000) 'International expansion by new technology
firms: International diversity, mode of entry, technological learning and performance', *Academy of Management Journal*, 43(5), 925–50.

15

Using the Resource-Based View to Advance International Entrepreneurship: An Empirical Review on How Far Have We Come since Peng's 2001 Predictions?

Alfredo D'Angelo and Karl S.R. Warner

Introduction

Overview

In the new global business environment, internationalization has become a primary driving force for competition (Hitt et al. 2001). Traditionally the competitive landscape in international markets was the realm of large companies (McDougall and Oviatt, 2000). However, in the last 20 years, we have witnessed not only an increasing presence of small and medium-sized firms (SMEs) on the international scene, but also an emergence of broader and more differentiated international business strategies among SMEs (European Commission, 2003). The advent of the rapid internationalization phenomenon has, furthermore, confirmed that SMEs are able to overcome resource constraints and the liabilities of smallness to compete in the global arena (Zahra and George, 2002). The emergence of the rapidly internationalizing small firms has challenged the evolutionary internationalization 'stage' model (Johanson and Valne, 1977) and the inherent disadvantage associated with the smallness (Liesch and Knight, 1999). Furthermore, it has paved the way for International Entrepreneurship (IE), a new and emerging field of study distinguishable from the traditional International Business (IB) perspective (Dimitratos and Jones, 2005). The most commonly accepted definition of IE is that: *'International entrepreneurship is a combination of innovative, proactive, and risk seeking behaviour that crosses national borders and is intended to create value in organizations'* (McDougall and Oviatt, 2000, p. 903). According to Jones and Coviello (2005) and Zucchella and Scabini (2007), the ontological roots of IE can be found at the interception of international business, entrepreneurship, and strategic management studies. With regard to the latter, while the Transaction Cost Theory has been largely associated with multinational firms (Brouthers and Nakos, 2004), the Resource-Based View (RBV) has been embraced by small business scholars and plays an important role behind the emergence of IE in explaining how smaller firms achieve a competitive advantage outside their domestic market (Peng, 2001).

Aims, objectives, and structure of the study

In this manuscript, we draw on the overall theme of this special edition book, by considering how the RBV (Wernerfelt, 1984; Barney, 1991; Grant, 1991) has advanced IE (Oviatt and McDouagll, 1994) literature since 2001. We set the parameters of our search from 2001 to the first semester of 2009, to question Peng's (2001, p.815) prediction whether the RBV-IE 'literature will grow more substantially in the new millennium'? The aims of this study are to determine whether RBV is informing thinking in IE research, and how the RBV has impacted on IE research. We, therefore, focus on reviewing empirical papers that apply the RBV framework in the field of IE during the selected timeframe. The paper is organized as follows. First, we report a general overview of the RBV literature. Second, we present a methodology section describing the review process undertaken to select the appropriate articles. The relevant papers will then be analyzed with particular emphasis on the following issues: (1) main research objectives; (2) application and conceptualization of the RBV; and the (3) key findings and conclusions. This will allow us to track the application of the RBV in IE literature, identify implications for theoretical, empirical, and practical development of IE, and suggest potential avenues for further research.

Literature review

The resource-based view

The mission of the strategic management research is to understand why some firms outperform others and therefore are more successful than their competitors (Rumelt, 1991; Mahoney and Pandian, 1992; Barney and Clark, 2007). The RBV deals with the problem of competition and profitability from the perspective of the resources controlled by the firm and its consequent market strategy rather than from product perspective. After all, 'for the firm, resources and products are two sides of the same coin' (Wernerfelt, 1984, p. 171). While not excluding the role of industry structure and the influence of the external environment (Amit and Schoemaker, 1993), the RBV stresses the importance of the firm's unique bundle of resources to explain the variation in firms' growth, success and performance (Wernerfelt, 1984; Barney, 1991; Peteraf, 1993).

The development of RBV has produced a variety of labels to describe the firm's resource set. The concepts of resources, capabilities, and competencies have been used interchangeably by different RBV scholars and sometimes they overlap (Fahy, 2002). Broad in scope *'resources* refer to stocks of available factors that are owned or controlled by the firm' (Amitt and Schoemaker, 1993, p. 35). More recently, Barney (2001) acknowledged the distinction between *resources* and *capabilities* after heavy criticism from Priem and Butler (2001) and revised his 1991 definition[1] specifying that 'resources are the tangible and intangible assets a firm uses to choose and implement its strategies' (p. 54). Tangible resources can be financial, organizational, physical, and technological, and they are identifiable when they are seen and quantified (Grant, 1991; Barney, 1991). Hall (1992) and Itami and Roehl (1987) both note that intangible assets are typically rooted deeply in the firm's history and have accumulated over time and are often tacit. Knowledge, trust between manager and employees, ldeas, the capacity for innovation, scientific capabilities, the firm's reputation, and its relationship with stakeholders are all examples of intangible assets (Grant, 1991; Branzei and Vertinsky, 2006).

Whatever their nature (i.e., resources, capabilities, competencies), the principals of the RBV suggest resources can be heterogeneous between firms and the rent obtained from such heterogeneity can be sustained (Wernerfelt, 1984; Barney, 1986). However, the condition of resources heterogeneity is necessary but not sufficient for a firm to generate a competitive advantage and earn economic rents (Peteraf, 1993). According to the RBV theorists (Amit and Schoemaker, 1991; Barney, 1991; Peteraf, 1993), not all resources are of equal importance or possess the potential to be a source of competitive advantage. Starting from the assumptions that firm's resources are heterogeneous, Barney (1991) proposed that resources must meet four conditions, namely, value, rareness, inimitability, and nonsubstitutability (VRIN) in order to create advantage for the firm. Put differently, in order for a resource to be a potential source of competitive advantage it has to be the result of an interplay of historical condition, casual ambiguity, and social complexity which enables a firm to implement unique strategies (Dierickx and Cool, 1989; Barney, 1991).

Despite some criticisms (Porter 1991; Foss, 1997; Priem and Butler, 2001; Hoopes et al. 2003), a mix of economic rigor and management reality has put the RBV at centre of strategy research (Barney, 1986; 1991; Dierickx and Cool, 1989; Amit and Schoemaker, 1993; Peteraf, 1993). The RBV has received large attention in diverse area of business and management studies and its conception has gained widespread acceptance within a multitude of writings (Cavusgil et al. 2007). However, although its conceptual advancements have been growing, empirical research testing the core premises of the theory has not kept the pace (Hoopes et al. 2003). In this study, we focus on reviewing a number of empirical papers that apply the RBV framework in the field of IE during the period 2001 through to the first semester of 2009 to determine whether the RBV is informing thinking in IE research, and how the RBV has impacted IE research.

Methodology

Setting a selection process criteria

This review focuses of the empirical contributions of the RBV on IE. Following a similar structure to Peng (2001), Coviello and Jones (2004) and Rialp et al. (2005), our task is to create a selection criteria that allow us to set realistic parameters for conducting this search. This led to us developing a five point selection criteria. First, to question Peng's (2001) prediction, we conducted our publication search over the time frame covering the period of 2001 to the first semester of 2009. Second, all articles had to be in English to facilitate comparison (Rialp et al. 2005). Third, for the sake of parsimony, we excluded conceptual and review papers from our sample to address the question of whether the RBV has empirically advanced IE.

Fourth, Coviello and Jones (2004) recommend the need to search 'international business', 'entrepreneurship', and 'strategy' journals to capture the multidisciplinary nature of IE. Our search supports their approach by reviewing the 2001 to 2009 volumes of *Journal of Business Venturing* (JBV), *Entrepreneurship Theory & Practice* (ETP), which are the leading entrepreneurship journals (Coviello and Jones, 2004). Next, we reviewed the *Journal of International Business Studies* (JIBS), *Management International Review* (MIR), and included *International Business Review* (IBR), *Journal of World Business* (JWB), and *International Small Business Journal* (ISBJ) which are considered the top rated IB journals (DuBois and Reeb, 2000). Finally, for strategy, we reviewed the *Academy of Management Journal* (AMJ) and *Strategic Management Journal* (SMJ).

Fifth, supporting Coviello and Jones (2004, p. 488) and Rialp et al. (2005, p. 149), in their contention of how to identify relevant IE articles, we prepared for a literature search including a range of keywords. These included 'international new venture(s)', 'born global(s)', 'global start-up(s)', 'international entrepreneurship' and 'Oviatt and McDougall'. In identifying RBV articles, our search comprised of the most common keywords referred to in resource-based papers. These included 'Barney', 'Wernerfelt', 'Grant', 'Penrose', 'RBV', 'resource-based view', 'capability (ies)', and 'competence (ies)'.

Conducting the literature search

Stage one: Determine use of RBV in IE articles

In conducting the literature search, we used the electronic bibliographic database *EBSCO-host* and the internet search engine *Google scholar*. As Rialp et al. (2005) contend, these tools offer a highly efficient method for conducting

Table 15.1   RBV Articles with Reference to IE

Year	International business					Entrepreneurship		Strategy		Totals
	JIBS	MIR	IBR	JWB	ISBJ	ETP	JBV	AMJ	SMJ	
2001	1	0	0	0	0	0	1	1	0	3
2002	0	0	0	0	1	1	2	0	1	5
2003	0	0	1	0	1	2	0	0	0	4
2004	1	0	0	0	2	1	2	0	0	6
2005	0	0	2	1	2	0	0	0	0	5
2006	2	0	1	0	0	0	3	0	0	6
2007	3	0	2	2	1	2	0	0	1	11
2008	3	0	3	1	1	2	0	0	0	10
2009	1	0	0	0	2	1	1	0	0	5
Total	11	0	9	4	10	9	9	1	2	55

a search and result in the most effective way in generating relevant articles. When conducting the keyword search, 146 potential articles emerged. After including all of the keywords in our search, we entered the details of each article into a *Microsoft Access* database for further assessment. We then omitted all of conceptual and review papers and ones that failed to reference Penrose (1959), Wernerfelt (1984), Barney (1991), Grant (1991), or the 'resource-based view'. This resulted in discarding 91 papers leaving a total of 55 papers. These results are listed in Table 15.1.

In assessing the table, it is clear JIBS, IBR, ISBJ, ETP, and JBV have been the core journals to publish articles that apply RBV as a theoretical lens. Surprisingly, MIR fail to publish any RBV related article with reference to IE. Similarly, it is clear the strategic management journals significantly lack RBV application when considering IE.

Stage two: Identifying relevant IE articles

In narrowing our results, we began to discard papers that explicitly fail to draw upon IE in the body of the text. This meant if authors did not position their work in the context of 'international new ventures', 'international entrepreneurship', 'born-globals', or 'international SMEs', we removed their contributions from our search. A common problem in the search process was many of the articles originally flagged in stage one only referred to IE keywords in the paper's reference list or as part of the author's bibliography. In this event, these papers were excluded. Finally, if each paper did not explicitly reference Oviatt and McDougall (1994), the paper was withdrawn from our list. This resulted in a final list of 18 relevant IE papers that have applied the RBV to support their empirical results. These articles are listed in Table 15.2.

Table 15.2   RBV Articles Applied to IE

Year	International business					Entrepreneurship		Strategy		Totals
	JIBS	MIR	IBR	JWB	ISBJ	ETP	JBV	AMJ	SMJ	
2001	0	0	0	0	0	0	1	0	0	1
2002	0	0	0	0	0	0	1	0	0	1
2003	0	0	1	0	1	0	0	0	0	2
2004	1	0	0	0	1	0	1	0	0	3
2005	0	0	2	1	0	0	0	0	0	3
2006	0	0	0	0	0	0	0	0	0	0
2007	0	0	1	2	0	0	0	0	1	4
2008	0	0	1	0	0	0	0	0	0	1
2009	2	0	0	0	0	1	0	0	0	3
Total	3	0	5	3	2	1	3	0	1	18

From this search, 13 relevant articles are positioned in IB journals, four articles are published in entrepreneurship journals and only one IE article has been published in the strategy journals. Inspecting the data chronologically, the entrepreneurship journals, specifically JBV have drawn upon the RBV in IE earlier on in the decade, but this trend has begun to fizzle out. While in IB, the very opposite has occurred as the RBV received no attention until 2003, which then resulted in a surge of attention from IBR and JWB. Finally, JIBS has recently published two articles in 2009 and it is anticipated these articles will have a significant impact in moving IE forward as we enter the new decade.

Analysis and discussion: reviewing the research results

In assessing the 18 selected articles, it is now very clear the RBV continues to be applied within IE since Peng's (2001, p. 815) predictions. However, what is not so clear are the trends surrounding publication of IE themes and the research findings that have had an impact on applying the RBV in the context IE. We therefore place focus on (1) main research aims and objectives; (2) application and conceptualization of the RBV; and (3) the key findings and conclusions to understand how IB, entrepreneurship and strategy journals have embraced the RBV to advance IE. The first two issues will be analyzed separating the international business journals from the entrepreneurship and strategic management journals and we will conclude by integrating both perspectives when analyzing the key findings and conclusions.

Applying RBV to advance IE: an international business journal perspective

Research aims and objectives

In addressing the main objectives and research questions, a common focus amongst the majority of papers revolves on the SMEs resource-base and the speed of internationalization (Knight and Cavusgil, 2004; Bell et al. 2004; Crick and Spence, 2005; Zucchella et al. 2007; Gassmann and Keupp, 2007; Tuppura et al. 2008). For example, Crick and Spence (2005) conduct a qualitative investigation with 'high-performing' U.K. high-tech SMEs to investigate the key influences on making internationalization decisions in response to changing environmental conditions. The authors apply the RBV to find that financial and managerial resources enable high-tech SMEs to prepare for internationalization when targeting growth markets (Crick and Spence, 2005, p. 180). Similarly, in a recent special edition of JWB (2007) the characteristics of the firms resource-base were empirically addressed revealing that specialized knowledge (Gassmann and Keupp, 2007) and the orientation of the international entrepreneur (Zucchella et al. 2007) to be resources that impact on the early and rapid internationalization of the firm. Surprisingly, no article in JIBS or ISBJ with exception from Knight and Cavusgil (2004) which specifically adopts an 'organizational capability' perspective, directly applies the RBV to address the early and rapid internationalization of SMEs.

The role of networks in facilitating international growth of SMEs is another area of the IB literature that is guided by the RBV framework (Chetty and Wilson, 2003; Boojihawon et al. 2007; Zucchella et al. 2007). In Chetty and Wilson's (2003), they use a mixed method approach to explore the role of networking relationships in the internationalization of SMEs by questioning whether various types of networks impact on resource acquisition. Indeed, one of Boojihawon et al. (2007) key research objectives considers 'entrepreneurial characteristics' and 'entrepreneurial culture' as a 'resource' within multinational subsidiaries to assess the management of multinational corporations (MNC) interorganizational networks. Finally, the value of business and social networks are positioned as valuable knowledge-based resources and it is conceptualized that sharing knowledge at interorganizational level will play a key role in early internationalization (Zucchella et al. 2007).

The final theme present in all four IB journals is the impact the RBV has on SME international performance (Majocchi and Zucchella, 2003; Majocchi et al. 2005; Haahti et al. 2005; Filatotchev et al. 2009; Knight and Kim, 2009). For example, Majocchi et al. (2005) utilizes the Transaction Cost Theory and RBV to test the effect of firm size and business experience on export performance. Advancing on export performance, Haahti et al. (2005) draw on the RBV to provide theoretical linkages between cooperative strategy and knowledge intensity to assess the relationship with SMEs export performance. This parallels Grant's (1996) knowledge based view (KBV) to examine factors that affect *export orientation* and *export performance* in high-technology SMEs in emerging markets, specifically China (Filatotchev et al. 2009). In contrast, Majocchi and Zucchella (2003) imply performance is not determined by export intensity (i.e., the traditional dependent variable) but by the impact of international expansion on SME profitability. This follows Knight and Kim's (2009) recent contribution in aiming to conceptualize a new construct called international business competence (IBC) which is expected to enhance *International SME performance* and empirically capture the international activity of today's contemporary firm.

Application and conceptualization of the RBV

Different methodological approaches have emerged between journals in the way research findings are conceptualized and constructed as empirical models (Bell et al. 2004; Crick and Spence, 2005, Tseng et al. 2007; Tuppura et al. 2008). In inspecting the 18 articles, it is clear that models have been common in demonstrating how business strategy impacts on internationalization. For example, in ISBJ, Bell et al. (2004) take a holistic approach through exploratory case studies. The authors develop a conceptual model of business strategy and internationalization interrelationships through the incorporation of *environmental influences* (internal resources and external international conditions) and application of functional strategies (finance, human resources, operations, and growth). Similarly, Gassmann and Keupp (2007, p.352) take a qualitative approach and are the only IE scholars in our search to explicitly question the basis of a born-globals competitive advantage and how this is generated, sustained and protected. Whereas in JIBS and IBR, all of the RBV articles follow a deductive hypothesis testing method developing precise models on how firm level resources impact on strategy and international growth (Knight and Cavusgil, 2004; Tseng et al. 2007; Tuppura et al. 2008; Knight and Kim, 2009).

Applying RBV to advance IE: an entrepreneurship and strategic management journal perspective

Research aims and objectives

In terms of research objectives, the vast majority of the studies aim to describe, understand and explain the early internationalization of new ventures (Westhead et al. 2001; Lévesque and Shepherd, 2004; Kuemmerle's (2002); Fernhaber and McDougall-Covin, 2009). Currently in IE, Westhead et al. (2001) contribution is the most referenced paper with a 194 citations as a result of the papers age and impact of their findings. In their JBV paper, the authors aim to position the founder(s) human capital as a 'resource', to 'explain' the measures of propensity and intensity of internationalization in SMEs. Taking a knowledge management perspective, Kuemmerle (2002) extends IE knowledge, by assessing the capability development of international new ventures (INV) from inspecting the entrepreneurial profile and the characteristics of a ventures 'home base', along with the resource accumulating activities that are carried out abroad. Finally, the venture capitalist has recently been identified as an outlet for acquiring resources, documenting that their international knowledge and reputation help promote strategies that facilitate new venture internationalization (Fernhaber and McDougall-Covin, 2009).

In the strategy and entrepreneurship journals, only two IE articles apply the RBV to international performance (Leblein and Reuer, 2004; Li and Zang, 2007). In Leblein and Reuer's paper (2004), they examine the linkages between the development of technological capabilities and international collaboration on the impact of foreign sales. Similarly, Li and Zhang (2007) give credence to value of international collaboration by drawing on the RBV to examine the impact of managerial resources (political networking and functional experience) on the performance of new ventures in China's high-technology industries. Both articles therefore use the RBV to demonstrate the value of networking resources on international performance.

Application and conceptualization of the RBV

Methodologically, it is clear that large-scale surveys have been most common (Westhead et al.; Leblein and Reuer, 2004; Li and Zhang, 2007 & Fernhaber and McDougall-Covin, 2009) in the entrepreneurship and strategic management journals. For example, Westhead et al. (2001) draws upon longitudinal data sample of 621 manufacturing, construction and services business located in the United Kingdom in 1990/91 and then reinterviewed them in 1997. However, from the six nominated papers, Kuemmerle (2002) is the only paper to offer a conceptual model. Furthermore, his study is the only paper to be qualitative and case-based and constructed in a way that supports empirical results. Therefore, it is clear the RBV has been conceptualized differently in the entrepreneurship and strategy in comparison to the earlier IB interpretations.

Applying RBV to advance IE: key findings and conclusions

In this final section, we aim to integrate discussion from the core journals to assess the impact the RBV has had on advancing IE research. In consulting Table 15.3, it is clear the RBV has had most application when researching the internationalization of the firm. Specifically, 15 of the 18 reviewed IE articles directly apply the RBV as theoretical tool to research the internationalization of SMEs. The core finding present in all of the journals is that the human capital of the international entrepreneur is a valuable, rare, nonimitable, and nonsubstitutable resource that inevitably impacts on the survival and growth of new ventures during internationalization (Westhead et al. 2001; Knight and Cavusgil, 2004; Bell et al. 2004; Crick and Spence, 2005; Zucchella et al. 2007; Li and Zang, 2007; Fernhaber and McDougall-Covin, 2009). In sum, it would be fair to contend that the RBV has been an effective framework in advancing knowledge on the internationalization process of small and new ventures.

Another common finding present in all of the journals apart from ETP is the impact of RBV on assessing international performance within IE (Majocchi and Zucchella, 2003; Leblein and Reuer, 2004; Haahti et al. 2005; Majocchi et al. 2005; Li and Zhang, 2007; Knight and Kim, 2009). For example, Majocchi and Zucchella (2003) found that Italian SMEs with high financial returns were common amongst firms that had entered North America, and internationalization had facilitated the capability to generate higher financial returns. Leblein and Reuer (2004, p.303) provide evidence of the relationship between 'externally forged relationships' and firm's foreign sales. The value of networking resources is similarly documented in the work of Li and Zhang (2007) and Chetty and Wilson (2003) who both find networks to have a positive relationship with international performance. Indeed, all of these findings correspond with Knight and Kim's (2009) recent contribution that international SMEs need to develop a unique and inimitable *international business competence* by developing (1) international market share; (2) international sales growth; (3) international profitability; and (4) export intensity to maximize *international SME performance*. As Table 15.3 indicates, the impact of the RBV-IE interface and performance has been embraced by the IB and strategy journals, while entrepreneurship journals typically fail to publish in this area.

Inspecting Table 15.3 chronologically, it appears the value of intangible resources, namely knowledge, has received increased IE scholarly attention over the past five years (Kuemmerle, 2002; Gassmann and Keupp, 2007; Tuppura et al. 2008; Filatotchev et al. 2009). However, since Kuemmerle's (2002) seminal work, no entrepreneurship or strategic management article directly applies the RBV or KBV to advance IE. Instead, articles in the IB journals such as Gassmann and Keupp (2007) apply the KBV to empirically find that the tangible resource constraints of born-global firms in high-technology environments can be overcome if there is a wealth of tacit and explicit product knowledge vested in the firm.

Indeed, the role of accumulated expertise is an additional knowledge asset that has been positively related to timing, entry and growth of internationalization (Tuppura et al. 2008). Our observation is that their is a movement from the RBV to the KBV and is further enhanced by Filatotchev et al. (2009) recent contention that international knowledge transfer is significantly associated with export orientation and export performance. Put simply, 'scientific

Table 15.3 Using the RBV to advance international entrepreneurship

Authors	Year	Journal	Method	Citations	Networks	Performance	Strategy	Knowledge	Internationalization
International Business Journals									
Chetty & Wilson	2003	IBR	Mixed Method	27	✓				✓
Majocchi & Zucchella	2003	ISBJ	Survey	42		✓			✓
Knight & Cavusgil	2004	JIBS	Survey	19		✓			✓
Bell, Crick & Young	2004	ISBJ	Case Study	81			✓		✓
Crick & Spence	2005	IBR	Case Study	8			✓		✓
Majocchi Bacchiocchi & Mayrhofer	2005	IBR	Survey	13		✓			
Haahti, Madupu, Yavas & Babakus	2005	JWB	Survey	42		✓	✓	✓	
Boojhawon, Dimitratos & Young	2007	IBR	Case Study	3	✓				✓
Zucchella, Palamara & Denicolai	2007	JWB	Survey	4			✓		✓
Gassmann & Keupp	2007	JWB	Case Study	11		✓	✓	✓	✓
Tuppura, Saarenketo & Puumalaninen	2008	IBR	Survey	1			✓	✓	✓
Filatotchev, Xiaohui, Buck & Wright	2009	JIBS	Survey	0		✓	✓	✓	✓
Knight & Kim	2009	JIBS	Mixed Method	0		✓	✓	✓	✓
Entrepreneurship / Strategy Journals									
Westhead, Wright & Ucbasaran	2001	JBV	Survey	194		✓			✓
Kuemmerle	2002	JBV	Case Study	64			✓	✓	✓
Leblein & Reuer	2004	JBV	Survey	21	✓	✓			
Li & Zhang	2007	SMJ	Survey	19	✓	✓			
Fernhaber & McDougall-Covin	2009	ETP	Survey	2				✓	

and technical human capital has become more mobile and more easily able to cross-national borders. The impact of mobile international entrepreneurs on internationalization and knowledge transfer has now become evident, adding a new dimension to IB theory' (Filatotchev et al. 2009, p. 13).

Conclusions and limitations: an integrative approach?

It is clear from this literature search that the RBV has advanced the discipline of IE since Peng's prediction in 2001. However, the fundamental purpose of this review was to question whether RBV theory has advanced IE identifying the core journals that have had most of impact within the RBV-IE interface. In short, there is an emerging widespread disparity between IB, entrepreneurship and strategic management journals in promoting RBV as a driving force in IE. Despite JBV having the top citation for IE-RBV contribution (Westhead et al. 2001), it is clear that JBV's impact is beginning to decrease over time as the majority of IE scholars are choosing to position their articles in JIBS, IBR, and JWB. Future research, begs to question, why is the RBV-IE interface more popular with IB scholars than it is with its entrepreneurship and strategy colleagues?

A major implication from this literature search is that only one article from the strategy literature which was published in SMJ (Li and Zhang, 2007) is relevant for the purpose of this review. Ironically, the ontological roots of the RBV are rooted in strategic management and it seems bemusing that scholars are either choosing to avoid the top strategic management journals or IE research fails to be accepted by a more widespread readership. We therefore send a stark warning to IE scholars that positioning resource-based research in only IB and entrepreneurship journals inevitably runs the risk of a movement to a more insular discipline and more effort should be placed in reaching publication within the top strategic management journals.

For the sake of parsimony, our search was confined to arguably the core IB, entrepreneurship and strategy journals. As a result, we are aware that excellent contributions in general management journals such as Dhanaraj and Beamish (2003), Sharma and Erramilli (2004), and Brouthers et al. (2008) have been excluded due to our criteria. Furthermore, the dynamic capabilities (Sapienza et al. 2006) literature was excluded as we agree with Whang and Ahmed (2007) that despite it evolving from the RBV, it is a separate theory and one that is beyond the boundaries of this study. We therefore call for extended literature research primarily in two areas. First, we acknowledge the need to broaden the RBV-IE search through a wider span of general and specific management journals (i.e., *Journal of Management* and *Journal of International Entrepreneurship*, to only name two). By doing this, we anticipate the results to differ significantly in respect to theoretical advancements in IB, entrepreneurship and strategic management readerships. Secondly, there is a need to track the application of the capabilities literature for advancing IE, as we particularly agree with Filatotchev et al. (2009) that the cross-border mobility of knowledge will have new research implications for the IE discipline as a whole. We believe these contributions will be of significant benefit for theoretical, empirical and practical development of IE as we move into this new decade with new, exciting, and unanswered questions to ask.

Note

1. Barney (1991) noted that resources were 'all assets, capabilities, organizational processes, firm attributes, information, knowledge, and so on controlled by the firm that enable the firm to conceive of and implement strategies that improve its efficiency and effectiveness' (p. 101).

References

Amit, R. and Schoemaker, P.J.H. (1993) 'Strategic assets and organizational rent', *Strategic Management Journal*, XIV, 33–46.

Barney, J.B. (1991) 'Firm resources and sustained competitive advantage', *Journal of Management*, XVII, 99–120.

Barney, J.B. (1986) 'Strategic factor markets: Expectations, luck, and business strategy', *Management Science*, XXXII, 1231–41.

Barney, J.B. (2001) 'Resource-based theories of competitive advantage: A ten-year retrospective on the resource-based view', *Journal of Management*, XXVII, 643–50.

Barney, J.B. and Clark, D.N. (2007) *Resource-Based Theory. Creating and Sustaining Competitive Advantage* (Oxford: Oxford University Press).

Bell, J., Crick, D. and Young, S. (2004) 'Small firm internationalisation and business strategy: An exploratory study of knowledge-intensive and traditional manufacturing firms in the UK', *International Small Business Journal*, XXII, 23–56.

Boojihawon, D.K., Dimitratos, P. and Young, S. (2007) 'Characteristics and influences of multinational subsidiary entrepreneurial culture: The case of the advertising sector', *International Business Review*, XVI, 549–72.

Branzei, O. and Vertinsky, I. (2006) 'Strategic pathways to product innovation capabilities in SMEs', *Journal of Business Venturing*, XXI, 75–105.

Brouthers, K.D. and Nakos, G. (2004) 'SME entry mode choice and performance: A transaction cost perspective', *Entrepreneurship: Theory & Practice*, XXVIII, 229–47.

Brouthers, K.D., Brouthers, L.E. and Werner, S. (2008) 'Resource-based advantages in an international context', *Journal of Management*, XXXIV, 189–217.

Cavusgil, E., Seggie, S.H. and Talay, M.B. (2007) 'Dynamic capabilities view: Foundations and research agenda', *Journal of Marketing Theory & Practice*, XV, 159–66.

Chetty, S.K. and Wilson, H.I.M. (2003) 'Collaborating with competitors to acquire resources', *International Business Review*, XII, 61–81.

Coviello, N.E. and Jones, M.V. (2004) 'Methodological issues in international entrepreneurship research', *Journal of Business Venturing*, XIX, 485–508.

Crick, D. and Spence, M. (2005) 'The internationalisation of 'high performing' UK high-tech SMEs: a study of planned and unplanned strategies', *International Business Review*, XIV, 167–85.

Dhanaraj, C. and Beamish, P.W. (2003) 'A resource-based approach to the study of export Performance', *Journal of Small Business Management*, XLI, 242–61.

Dierickx, I. and Cool, K. (1989) 'Asset stock accumulation and the sustainability of competitive advantage: Reply', *Management Science*, XXXV, 1231–41.

Dimitratos, P. and Jones, M.V. (2005) 'Future directions for international entrepreneurship research', *International Business Review*, XIV, 119–28.

DuBois, F.L. and Reeb, D. (2004) 'Ranking the international business journals', *Journal of International Business Studies*, XXXI, 689–704.

European Commission (2003) *SMEs in Europe 2003*, The Observatory of European SMEs, Luxemburg: European Communities, http://ec.europa.eu/enterprise/enterprise_policy/analysis/observatory_en.htm.

Fahy, J. (2002) 'A resource-based analysis of sustainable competitive advantage in a global environment', *International Business Review*, XI, 57–77.

Fernhaber, S.A. and McDougall-Covin, P.P. (2009) 'Venture capitalists as catalysts to new venture internationalization: The impact of their knowledge and reputation Resources', *Entrepreneurship Theory & Practice*, XXXIII, 277–95.

Filatotchev, I., Xiaohui, L., Buck, T. and Wright, M. (2009) 'The export orientation and export performance of high-technology SMEs in emerging markets: The effects of knowledge transfer by returnee entrepreneurs', *Journal of International Business Studies*, Online Publication, 1–17.

Foss, N. (1997) *Resource firms and Strategies. A Reader in the Resource-Based Perspective* (Oxford: Oxford University Press).

Gassmann, O. and Keupp, M.M. (2007) 'The competitive advantage of early and rapidly internationalising SMEs in the biotechnology industry: A knowledge-based view', *Journal of World Business*, XLII, 350–66.

Grant, R.M. (1991) 'The resource-based theory of competitive advantage: Implications for strategy formulation', *California Management Review*, XXXIII, 114–35.

Grant, R.M. (1996) 'Toward a knowledge-based theory of the firm', *Strategic Management Journal*, XVII, 109–122.

Haahti, A., Madupu, V., Yavas, U. and Babakus, E. (2005) 'Cooperative strategy, knowledge intensity and export performance of small and medium sized enterprises', *Journal of World Business*, XL, 124–38.

Hall, R. (1992) 'The strategic analysis of intangible resources', *Strategic Management Journal*, XIII, 135–44.

Hitt, M.A., Ireland, R.D., Camp, S.M. and Sexton, D.L.(2001) 'Guest editors' introduction to the special issue. Strategic entrepreneurship: Entrepreneurial strategies for wealth creation', *Strategic Management Journal*, XXII, 479–91.

Hoopes, D.G., Hadsen, T.L. and Walker, G. (2003) 'Guest editors' introduction to the special issue: Why is there a resource-based view? Toward a theory of competitive heterogeneity', *Strategic Management Journal*, XXIV, 889–902.

Itami, H.T. and Roehl, W. (1987) *Mobilizing Invisible Assets* (Cambridge, MA: Harvard University Press).

Johanson, J. and Vahlne, J.E. (1977) 'The internationalization process of the firm-a model of knowledge development and increasing foreign market commitments', *Journal of International Business Studies*, VIII, 23–32.

Jones, M.V. and Coviello, N.E. (2005) 'Internationalisation: Conceptualising an entrepreneurial process of behaviour in time', *Journal International Business Studies*, XXXVI, 284–303.

Knight, G.A. and Cavusgil, S.T. (2004) 'Innovation, organizational capabilities and the born-global firm', *Journal of International Business Studies*, XXXV, 124–41.

Knight, G.A. and Kim, D. (2009) 'International business competence and the contemporary firm', *Journal of International Business Studies*, XL, 255–73.

Kuemmerle, W. (2002) 'Home base and knowledge management in international ventures', *Journal of Business Venturing*, XVII, 99–122.

Leiblein, M.J. and Reuer, J.J. (2004) 'Building a foreign sales based: the roles of capabilities and alliances for entrepreneurial firms', *Journal of Business Venturing*, XIX, 285–307.

Lévesque, M. and Shepherd, D.A. (2004) 'Entrepreneurs' choice of entry strategy in emerging and developed markets', *Journal of Business Venturing*, XIX, 29–54.

Li, H. and Zhang, Y. (2007) 'The role of manager's political networking and functional experience in new venture performance', *Strategic Management Journal*, XXVIII, 791–804.

Liesch, P.W. and Knight, G.A. (1999) 'Information internalization and hurdle rates in small and medium enterprise internationalization', *Journal of International Business Studies*, XXX, 383–94.

Mahoney, J.T. and Pandian, J.R. (1992) 'The resource-based view within the conversation of strategic management', *Strategic Management Journal*, XIII, 363–80.

Majocchi, A. and Zucchella, A. (2003) 'Internationalization and performance: Findings from a set of italian SMEs', *International Small Business Journal*, XXI, 249–68.

Majocchi, A., Bacchiocchi, E. and Mayrhofer, U. (2005) 'Firm size, business experience and export intensity in SMEs: A longitudinal approach to complex relationships', *International Business Review*, XIV, 719–38.

McDougall, P.P. and Oviatt, B.M. (2000) 'International entrepreneurship: The intersection of two research paths', *Academy of Management Journal*, XLIII, 902–06.

Oviatt, B.M. and McDougall, P.P. (1994) 'Toward a theory of international new ventures', *Journal of International Business Studies*, XXV, 45–64.

Peng, M.W. (2001) 'The resource-based view and international business', *Journal of Management*, XXVII, 803–29.

Penrose, E.T. (1959) *The Theory of the Growth of the Firm* (New York: Wiley).

Peteraf, M.A. (1993) 'The cornerstones of competitive advantage: A resource-based view', *Strategic Management Journal*, XIV, 179–91.

Porter, M.E. (1991) 'Towards a dynamic theory of strategy', *Strategic Management Journal*, XII, 95–117.

Priem, R.L. and Butler, J.E. (2001) 'Is the resource-based 'View' a useful perspective for strategic management research?', *Academy of Management Review*, XXVI, 22–40.

Rialp, A., Rialp, J. and Knight, G.A. (2005) 'The phenomenon of early internationalizing firms: What do we know after a decade (1993–2003) of scientific inquiry?', *International Business Review*, XIV, 147–66.

Rumelt, R.P. (1991) 'How much does industry matter?', *Strategic Management Journal*, XII, 167–85.

Sapienza, H.J., Autio, E., George, G. and Zahra, S.A. (2006) 'A capabilities perspective on the effects of early internationalization on firm survival and growth', *Academy of Management Review*, XXXI, 914–33.

Sharma, V.M. and Erramilli, M.K. (2004) 'Resource-based explanation of entry mode choice', *Journal of Marketing Theory & Practice*, XII , 1–18.

Tseng, C.H., Tansuhaj, P., Hallagan, W. and McCullough, J. (2007) 'Effects of firm resources on growth in multinationality', *Journal of International Business Studies*, XXXVIII, 961–74.

Tuppura, A., Saarenketo, S., Puumalainen, K., Jantunen, A. and KylSheiko, K. (2008) 'Linking knowledge, entry timing and internationalization strategy', *International Business Review*, XVII, 473–87.

Wang, C.L. and Ahmed, P.K. (2007) 'Dynamic capabilities: A review and research agenda', *International Journal of Management Reviews*, IX , 31–51.

Wernerfelt, B. (1984) 'A resource-based view of the firm', *Strategic Management Journal*, V, 171–80.

Westhead, P., Wright, M. and Ucbasaran, D. (2001) 'The internationalization of new and small firms: A resource-based view', *Journal of Business Venturing*, XVI, 333–58.

Zhara, S.A. and George, G. (2002) 'International entrepreneurship: The current status of the field and future research agenda', in M.A. Hitt, R.D. Ireland, and D.L. Sexton (eds), *Strategic Entrepreneurship* (Oxford: Blackwell).

Zucchella, A., Palamara, G. and Denicolai, S. (2007) 'The drivers of the early internationalization of the firm', *Journal of World Business*, XLII, 268–80.

Zucchella, A. and Scabini, P. (2007) International Entrepreneurship. Theoretical Foundations and Empirical Analysis, 1st edn (London: Palgrave).

16
Barriers to the Internationalization of SMEs: An Analysis from the Perspective of Support Service Providers

Antonella Zucchella, Alberto Brugnoli, and Antonio Dal Bianco

Introduction

The internationalization process of small firms is subject to a number of constraints and bottlenecks. Academics and research institutions have devoted special attention to the issue of barriers to exporting for SMEs. Studies on export barriers for SMEs have been usually approached from the perspective of the firm, but they have rarely taken into consideration the perspective of support service providers. Studies on internationalization support programs have mostly focussed on export promotion programs (EPP) and export support services (ESS), and have taken the perspective of either the receiving firm in a micro-economic/business perspective or the institution involved in a macro-economic perspective. We find a research gap in the analysis of barriers to internationalization as seen by the service providers (both public and private), which could throw new light on the micro-foundations of these barriers and of the related policies and services to support the international growth of small firms, in particular, in the exporting field (Inkpen and Beamish, 1997; Brugnoli and Molteni, 2007).

The perspective adopted to approach the needs and problems of the small firms is the resource- and knowledge-based view. The literature available explains the role of internationalization service providers in terms of lack of the necessary resources and capabilities in small firms, in order to face the challenges of internationalization. Recent research (Leonidou, 2004; OECD, 2008) into barriers to internationalization (export, in particular) underlines the role of 'soft' barriers, such as information, knowledge, capabilities, if compared with 'hard' barriers (such as financial resources and technical equipment).

This analysis addresses the above-mentioned research gap, focussing on the following issues:

the types of barrier to the international growth of small firms and their relative importance in the perspective of service providers, which is complementary to the one of small firms and may throw new light on these issues

the role of support services in addressing these barriers

This chapter offers a theoretical analysis – based on extant literature – about the obstacles to an effective international growth for small firms and about the role of export promotion organizations, followed by an empirical section based on case studies and qualitative information from in-depth interviews to a group of private and public internationalization service providers.

The internationalization of small firms and the relationship with service providers

A theoretical framework

One of the most investigated fields of research in the internationalization of small firms is represented by the barriers to export activity (Bell, 1997). Attention to this issue is driven by the consideration that small firms are subject to relevant liabilities when challenged by internationalization opportunities. The role of the liability of newness and of foreignness have been highlighted together with the lack of resources which characterize these firms (Zaheer, 1995; Cuervo-Cazurra et al. 2007).

According to the resource-based view of the firm, resources are the primary determining factor of the competitive advantage of a firm (Barney, 1991; Penrose, 1959). The application of a resource-based framework to the analysis of the internationalization of firms has been considered appropriate by different authors (Dhanaraj and Beamish, 2003; Westhead et al. 2001), who highlight the role of a company's resources and capabilities in determining the propensity, the readiness, and the effectiveness of internationalization. Related to the RBV framework is the knowledge-based approach, which focusses in particular upon the role of 'soft' strategic resources such as information and knowledge (Liesch and Knight, 1999) to support (or constrain) the internationalization process within the firm.

New and small firms often lack some critically important complementary resources, usually possessed by larger and established companies (Teece, 1986). Support service providers may help small firms to access foreign markets (Inkpen and Beamish, 1997) and can contribute significantly in the access to information, business contacts, and in finding the needed managerial and financial resources for internationalization. The key issue is that the relationship building implies mutual understanding, alignment of objectives, expectations about the content of the exchange, shared vision of where to go, and how to reach it.

It is not the relationship with another subject which automatically provides access to opportunities and knowledge: the two parties have to 'meet', in the sense that the beneficiary of the knowledge transfer needs adequate absorptive capacity (Cohen and Levinthal, 1990). This issue is particularly important from the perspective of service providers, who cannot only take into consideration the traditional barriers to internationalization in designing their offer of services, but they also need to address the ability of the small firm to recognize the value of the information and to make it become part of the organizational knowledge. From this point of view, the opinions and feelings of services providers are particularly important and may permit a richer understanding of the nature of the barriers to internationalization for SMEs.

Barriers to the internationalization of small firms and the role of public and private service providers

The first studies regarding barriers to internationalization were mainly focussed on the issues of the lack of the necessary information to enter foreign markets and on transportation costs and trade barriers (Alexandrides, 1971; Pinney, 1971). Bilkey (1978) highlighted later on also the role of financial resources and distribution channels abroad. In the globalizing market space, we might expect that (due to the drop in transportation and communication costs and time, in a number of trade barriers among countries, and to a better access to information) small firms would internationalize much more easily. As a matter of fact, small firms still experience relevant barriers to international growth and there is general acceptance in literature that such barriers are mainly caused by internal constraints, among which the lack of information seems one of the most important ones (Bilkey and Tesar, 1977; Cavusgil, 1982; Czinkota and Johnson, 1983; Diamantopoulos and Inglis, 1988; Leonidou, 2004; OECD, 2008). Regarding the relative importance of the different barriers, those connected with material resources, such as capital, technology, and so on seem overshadowed by those related to lack of information, human capital and export capabilities. We call the latter ones 'soft barriers' as opposed to the 'hard' (tangible) ones. From this viewpoint, the literature which highlights the problem of lack of information by classifying these barriers among the internal ones, hinders the idea that small firms are constrained by lack of human resources and managerial capabilities (Dicht et al. 1990, Suárez-Ortega and Álamo-Vera, 2005; OECD, 1997 and 2008; Brugnoli and Molteni, 2007). The focussing on people and abilities enables us to identify more properly the nature of the problem, which is not information *per se* (which can be accessed at a cost or for free) but the existence in the organization of people who cannot only find the relevant information, but can also *recognize and use* the value of information for internationalization decisions. This involves two consequences, which are deeply interconnected: (1) at the level of entrepreneurial/managerial roles, the firm needs *knowledge gatekeepers*, that is, people who possess not just information but also know where to find it and how to use it (*know what* and *know how*); (2) at an organizational level, a certain level of absorptive capacity (Cohen and Levinthal, 1990) is needed, because this allows for the recognition and assimilation of new knowledge and enables organizational learning processes.

Here there clearly emerges a trade-off between what firms need to internationalize successfully and the constraints imposed by their size (which can be a proxy for the lack of resources). It is neither *per se* the small scale, nor the lack of adequate financial resources which represents a barrier to international markets, but their consequences when a firm needs skilled managers and dedicated human resources.

A number of micro-firms operates successfully in global markets, with high export intensity ratios and broad geographic scope – and there may also be new international ventures – but they are usually run by experienced entrepreneurs or management teams (Zucchella et al. 2007). In other cases similar outcomes are obtained by firms supported by people (business angels, consultants, distributors...) and organizations (venture capital companies, public and private service providers, multinationals...) who influence business decisions and managerial processes in foreign markets assuming part of the risks involved. The role of experienced entrepreneurs/managers and consultants is decidedly relevant when they support an increase in the entire organization's absorption capacity.

The upgrading in absorption capacity has two intertwined effects: on one hand, it improves the firm's readiness to face foreign markets (Tan et al. 2007) and, on the other hand, it establishes a fertile ground for the understanding, appreciation and use of specific support services (trade fairs and foreign missions, workshops on potential target countries, financing and export credit insurance...).

Export promotion organizations and their services: the issue of awareness and effectiveness for beneficiaries

Export promotion organizations (EPOs) have been created and developed in order to provide an answer to the above-mentioned barriers and difficulties in the international growth of small firms. EPOs may be either private (companies, associations and consortia, consultants or banks) or public organizations (local and national governments and their export promotion agencies).

Sometimes the distinction between public and private instruments is blurred, because some private services are partially subsidized by public funds, which may use this approach as complementary (or alternative) to the direct provision of services.

EPOs provide a variety of services, frequently classified into real and financial ones. This chapter addresses in particular the former category of services (which range from promoting participation to trade fairs, to supporting the selection of markets and partners abroad) because we think that the financial ones can be accessed only when the firm reaches an adequate readiness and awareness about foreign market opportunities.

The term EPOs usually addresses the export activity of the firm, even though also small firms are now confronted with a wider array of internationalization options (collaborations and joint ventures, international purchasing and production, off-shoring, ...). Many of these institutions have maintained the original focus on export assistance, while others have enlarged the spectrum of their services to the entire value chain of the firm and to the variety of entry modes.

Real services represent a complex and articulated reality where more research is needed in order to understand the effectiveness of single instruments in addressing specific needs and moreover in order to understand the complementary processes and synergies among different services. In the perspective of this analysis, some real services are addressed within a general upgrading of the firm's absorption capacity and prepare the ground for a better use and effectiveness of the more 'specific' ones, that is those aimed at providing information about opportunities in foreign countries and about potential partners or entry operations.

The findings concerning the effectiveness of export promotion services are controversial. Cavusgil and Jacob (1987) and Pointon (1978) found a positive relationship between these services and firm performance. The conduit of this effectiveness seems to be represented by managers, who – through such programmes – can swiftly access relevant information for decision making (Denis and Depeltau, 1985; Reid, 1985). On the other hand, Seringhaus (1986) concluded that the effectiveness of export promotion programs on the performance of exporting SMEs is doubtful. More recent studies find a positive impact when specific export support instruments are considered (Seringhaus and Rosson, 1991) and when specific performance indicators are used (Gençtürk and Kotabe, 2001; Lages and Montgomery, 2001).

Most analyses focus on the issue of awareness of public programs, while not much is written upon their specific content and alignment to the needs of the firms in question. Regarding the issue of program awareness, a crucial role is played by managers, who seem to be the effective knowledge gatekeepers of internationalization processes (Kumcu et al. 1995; Spence, 2003).

To sum up, the literature on export support services (both public and private) normally takes the perspective of the beneficiary; it seems more attentive to the issue of awareness, while the issue of effectiveness is less analyzed and relatively controversial. From the viewpoint of this analysis, two issues are mostly unexplored: the perspective of service providers on these matters and the SME learning failures. As a matter of fact, an analysis of these instruments not only on the basis of generic market failures but also on the basis of learning failures at the firm level is lacking. Finally, the debate about export support services is more driven by (partial) empirical evidence, rather than by theoretical developments and preliminary concept-building, with consequent scarce contributions on policy design issues. 'Like export research generally, the area of export promotion has also emphasized empirical results over theoretical development' (Wilkinson and Brouthers, 2006, p. 237).

In his survey on Chilean exporters, Alvarez (2004) finds out that one of the main significant drivers of export performance is represented by the training of employees in export operations. These results are consistent with those presented by Brugnoli and Molteni (2007) about Italian firms and encourage us to address the issue of human resources and organizational absorption capacity as key factors for awareness and effectiveness of services at the micro-level.

Empirical section

Research methodology

This study examines the role of resources and capabilities in the SME internationalization process from the point of view of export service provider organizations (EPOs). There is an abundant and fragmented range of literature on this issue and on the role of resource-based views of the firm (Barney, 1991) but a comprehensive research on the integration between internal resources and capabilities of SMEs and external information and knowledge provided by EPOs is lacking.

This is an intriguing issue as the shortage of internal resources and capabilities is almost recognized as a major difficulty in the SME internationalization process both by academics (Samiee and Walters, 1999) and practitioners (Esposito, 2003), while at the same time no attempt has been made to explain a feasible role of export support policies in helping SMEs to integrate resources and capabilities.

From the literature on the provision of public services (Bello and Williamson, 1985; Kotabe and Czinkota, 1993) it emerges that the transfer of exporting knowledge is a target for many EPOs. Understanding why this transfer may fail is of crucial relevance. Given the relevance of the resource-based view approach, it is surprising that little research has been carried out regarding how EPO services can meet the broad and specific capability requirements of exporters and potential exporters. Therefore, the main objective of the present study is to undertake an exploratory research with the aim of gaining further insight into the EPO's own perceptions about the role of resources and capabilities in the international performance of SMEs.

For this purpose, representatives of EPOs operating in an Italian region – Lombardy – were asked to discuss the perceived major barriers to the internationalization of small firms, about their readiness to face foreign markets and the main obstacles regarding both the start up of international operations and their management after the first entry decision. The second part of the interview focussed on the different services provided to address the above-mentioned perceived difficulties and how the different services offered by the interviewed EPO or by the others should/could be coordinated and integrated.

Face-to-face interviewing is the most suitable methodology in order to investigate in detail the EPO representatives' perception of the relevance of resources and capabilities with regard to international development of SMEs. A discourse analysis approach was used to analyze in-depth the interviews (Bryman, 2004). Results of this research cannot automatically be generalized because of the qualitative nature of the information collected. Yet this method brings a substantial advantage in order to investigate whether there is room for a resource and capabilities approach to the provision of support services from the other side of the coin, that is, from the point of view of EPOs. The interested parties consist of 10 organizations that offer facilitating services – promotion in export markets, sales intermediation, identification and selection of buyers, market analysis, recruiting export staff – to exporters as well as to potential exporters. The interviewed EPOs are the Milan Chamber of Commerce and its export promotion agency, an agency of the regional government which provides support to innovation and internationalization, three export consortia of enterprises, two banks offering also export assistance services (other than the financial ones) and two national government agencies (ICE, in charge of export promotion, SACE, in charge of insurance of export credits). All these organizations (five state owned or state-funded, five fully private) are localized or have a local department in Lombardy. The persons interviewed (one per each organization) are representative of the top management (CEO, director, or corresponding organizational roles).

A characteristic of the Lombard entrepreneurial system (and, more in general, of the Italian one) is a high fragmentation and the small average size of the enterprises: 97% of Lombard manufacturing firms is represented by small enterprises (fewer than 50 employees).

Lombardy represents an interesting regional case study to analyze, for two main reasons:

the region accounts for the greatest part of Italian exports (60%) and inward and outward FDIs (80%). It is a highly developed and internationally open system, with a diversified industrial base. On the other hand, it has common traits with the rest of the nation, that is the average small scale of firms and the presence of significant barriers to internationalization, confirmed by a number of studies, as we shall discuss further on

the need for the adoption of a regional scale of analysis has been advocated by recent literature on EPOs and barriers to international growth, in order to reach a better and deeper understanding of these issues. The regional scale of analysis is also coherent with a trend in recent years in favour of the partial 'regionalization' of internationalization policies in Italy as well as in other European countries. From this point of view, the regional government of Lombardy has been a forerunner and very active player in policy design for the internationalization of local firms

The perspective of service providers: main findings from the exploratory analysis

This section reports the main findings of 10 interviews with representatives of the above-mentioned EPOs located in Lombardy, conducted in 2007–2008. The interviews were carried out as part of a research project financed by regional government with the purpose of detecting the barriers to the internationalization of smaller firms.

The first issue refers to the way representatives of EPOs consider small firm potential and strategic orientations. They consider that there is much potential for their international growth, but this potential is not exploited and opportunities are overlooked, as well as threats, as it is demonstrated by statements as follows: '*Going international is no more an option for many small companies: it is simply where you have to go to survive. But many firms still look at foreign markets as the most dangerous of a set of growth options available...*' (CEO of an export consortium). The director of a national public organization declares, '*Many small enterprises are not even aware that they are taking part in a global value chain. They simply ignore it.*', while the top manager of a bank states: '*There is so much potential for international growth out there! Good products, good manufacturing abilities, innovative technology and design...and no global marketing vision.*'

Another problem is represented by the lack of adequate resources for international operations. The relationship between small scale and resources constraints is well documented by all interviews. In particular, human resources are considered by all interviewees as more important than financial ones for international growth: '*Our customers hardly ever have an employee dedicated to export operations. The firm's owner is directly engaged in international marketing activities as the dimension of the firm does not allow it to have a turnover compatible with specialized staff*' (CEO of an export consortium). According to the responsible of foreign trade services of a bank, '*The entrepreneur or someone from the top management team might have a good international plan in mind, but they do not have time and people just to write it down and submit it to us, not to mention implementing it...'* Another bank states: '*In some cases, entrepreneurs hesitate in committing themselves to an international venture. Apparently they fear more the organizational issues than the probability of commercial failure.'*

There is broad agreement on the relationship between the dimension of the firm and accessibility of resources and capabilities mobilized to undertake a foreign operation. EPOs representatives are aware of the low level of 'international skills' possessed by SME entrepreneurs and managers as well as an overall human capital deficiency that prevents firms from even seeking business opportunities with foreign partners. The director of a regional agency for export promotion declares: '*Our customers have a number of employees ranging from 20 to 25. In Lombardy, the companies are already considered to be well-staffed companies, when compared to the broad universe of micro-firms!'*

According to epo representatives, a viable remedy to the shortage of human resources and capabilities is to assign some extra staff to entrepreneurs or to train employees in order to help smaller firms in building their own ability in processing relevant information, developing networks, selecting market opportunities, and finding commercial partners.

The persons interviewed are aware that nowadays internationalization processes are for many firms 'compulsory' in order to maintain competitiveness in the long run and that they have to be realized faster than before, without waiting for an adequate consolidation in the home market. The representative of an export consortium says: '*International ventures most definitely require skilled personnel and greater efficiency even though I do not agree with those saying that it is necessary to outperform well in the home country in order to export in overseas markets.'*

According to the findings of a piece of analysis carried out upon export training programs (Brugnoli and Molteni, 2007), training costs are not a constraint *per se* when the firm needs to develop knowledge and capabilities. The real bottle-neck, especially for smaller firms, is the entrepreneur's cultural background. As Miesenböck (1988) asserted, the key variable in small business internationalization is the decision-maker in a firm. Entrepreneurs with more diverse levels of human capital are more able to tap into dense resources and information networks (Westhead et al. 2001). A public organization for export promotion declares: '*The real problem is a cultural one and this is related to entrepreneurs being or not being broad-minded. There are many difficulties that the entrepreneur has to overcome in order to enter into a foreign market. One of them is the ability to understand the foreign part. In one word, the knowledge of the foreign language has a major importance, as well the openness towards foreign contexts.'*

Similarly, a banker says: '*In my long international experience, I have noticed that Italian entrepreneurs are lacking a cultural approach when they start international ventures. In my opinion the main problem is the lack of knowledge of foreign markets.'*

In trying to identify more precisely the missing capabilities at the organizational level, the interviews focus on the role of the entrepreneur, who is seen – at the same time – as the strong and weak point of the small firm. *'I believe that the major barrier in the international expansion of the firm is the entrepreneur itself'* (according to a public organization). An export consortium representative says: *'Some small firms are actually outperforming in foreign growth, but they depend too much upon one person's vision and abilities:: we always wonder for how long.'*

In addition to this, the strategic orientation of entrepreneurs and top managers in small firms is mostly product-oriented, reflecting the background of the owners/founders and the origins of the firm. Many traditional Italian manufacturing firms commence as spin-offs by technical staff and blue collar workers, as the history of industrial districts suggests. However, the same holds for new high-tech companies, started by scientists and/or technicians. *'For sure entrepreneurs are very talented people with outstanding abilities to understand and organize manufacturing activities, but they are not good at marketing, regulatory matters and distribution channels regarding their business. Entrepreneurs alike do not realize that production and selling are integrated processes. They do not conceive that it is not enough just to make a good product'* (the CEO of an export consortium).

The idea that the main knowledge gap is in marketing activities and in marketing cultural orientation is shared in different interviews. This gap is transferred from the entrepreneur/top management team to the entire organization, which develops as a product-oriented firm, with inadequate sensibility concerning foreign market opportunities. *'In SMEs, managers and owners of the firm are in most cases the same. They have a great technical knowledge about the production process, and almost no abilities in marketing, in partner selection and management and foreign contexts understanding'* (a banker). According to a public organization, *'A distinctive feature of Italian firms is the ability to manufacture, but they do not have enough commercial and managing abilities. The problem has organizational consequences: the managers hire technical staff and do not see the need for marketing people.'*

The process of absorbing information and knowledge into the firm is affected by the entrepreneur's experiential learning as well as by her/his attitude towards internationalization. In this respect, EPO representatives agreed on the evidence that the process of gathering strategic information plays a key role for smaller enterprises, most of all in this globalization era with its spectacular increase of trade opportunities. Proof of the need for boosting the knowledge and capabilities of smaller firms is provided by the interviewers referring to their organization as a filter information mechanism for their customers. *'Well, there is of course a problem in accessing relevant information. The point here is not the scarcity of information – quite the reverse. There is a surplus of information and a lack of entrepreneurial ability mainly due to the cultural background to filter and transfer information inside the firm. Entrepreneurs cannot even distinguish between good information and bad information; they cannot separate what I call a relevant sound from the background noise'* (the director of a public agency).

At this stage, the integration and complementary processes between the firm's knowledge and support services as well as the organization of the tasks are discussed by EPO representatives. There is also room for more pro-active assistance by support services depending on the ability to understand the mentality of the entrepreneurs. According to a CEO of an export consortium: *'Our mission is to find commercial channels, to provide business contacts, to give information on international commercial regulations and on any other matters arising. However, first of all, we need a counterpart who listens and understands. It is important, in my opinion, to be familiar with entrepreneurs. The real difference is the similarity of the entrepreneurial approach, that is to say a service provider more oriented towards customer needs than to its own bureaucratic matters. Entrepreneurs perceive whether epos stand by their side or not.'*

A banker provides a very interesting comment regarding the evolution of supply and demand of export promotion services: *'In this world, where internationalization is more and more complex, in terms both of countries and entry modes, many service providers tend to specialize In some given business, while small firms are asking for a single counterpart to solve all their problems.'*

The relationship between the small firm and the EPO should be based on mutual understanding and trust. The latter takes time to be developed, but the first represents the first 'entry gate' for support service awareness and utilization. From this point of view, EPOs underline the difficulties in sharing a common language, which is a side effect of a low level of absorption capacity in the firm. Another side effect is the need for mentoring services in order to accompany the firm to access the other real and financial services, even though the coaching action is not explicitly foreseen by the EPO in its services menu and not rewarded by the small firm: *'For many smaller enterprises, the most important barrier to internationalization is the paucity of skills and abilities. Smes are forced to knock on the door of our organization as well as those of other epos in search of abilities. Another problem arises. There is a gap between the language of entrepreneurs and bureaucratic organizations and service providers or associations. In my opinion, this is a powerful barrier even for this organization (an entrepreneurial association) as far as we put all our energies into doing considerable business deals. The truth is that supporting SME internationalization is a behind-the-scenes job. 90 % of SMEs is not for value added services as we would expect. We are urged to give SMEs effective help with their business and not to merely give them technical solutions.'*

The CEO of an export consortium states: *'Small firms want us to be closer to them, less bureaucratic, providing tailor-made services...but they are not willing to pay for this! Furthermore, it is not just a matter of lack of money, they simply are not able to evaluate the value added concept in advanced services.'*

It is hard to conceive a more incisive role of EPOs in SME internationalization when that organizational structure rests entirely on the entrepreneur/s, especially in smaller firms, and on the traditional primacy of productive capabilities over other forms of knowledge (Grandinetti, 1992). Therefore, programs like vicarious entrepreneurship or temporary export managers, welcomed by EPOs, are more problematic in smaller firms because of hierarchical control over internationalization processes acting as a limit to the flow and speed of learning in smaller enterprises (Leonidou & Theodosiou, 2004). In the experience of temporary management we observe contrasting opinions. *'Indeed, only few firms have a representative in overseas markets with a full strategic mandate – to look after business dealings. A critical point is the assistance offered to the temporary export manager. I cannot even imagine that a micro-entrepreneur would accept someone teaching her/him how to do the work'* (a banker).

On the other hand, the representative of a regional agency which experienced temporary management programs declares: *'The temporary export management (TEM) programme is an effective policy instrument to bridge a gap in abilities and human resources. This experiment of the regional government of Lombardy is the proof that, upon a regional scale, it is easier to understand the needs of the firms and to test innovative policies.'*

There is a trade-off between the need for specialized staff – even temporary or shared with other companies – and the effective role they could play in small companies dominated by the founder/entrepreneur and more product-than market-oriented. The culture of the firm remains the key obstacle, and needs to be addressed with specific and innovative instruments.

A public support system, according to EPO representatives, should provide the entrepreneurial system with more export managers and other qualified workers in an effort to make it easier for smaller firms to access the resources essential for becoming successful international competitors. Whatever the policy suggested to bridge the gap in the firm's abilities, epo representatives ask for a fully integrated approach in the provision of resources and abilities from SMEs. A representative of regional government says: *'There is a generalized shortage of export managers and qualified professionals. The higher education system should be involved in this problem; it cannot be disconnected from what happens when people start their business. An increase in human capital is a necessary requirement for those SMEs willing to make the leap from the home market to the international market.'*

Discussion

The interviews with EPO representatives revealed that the perceived key obstacle to effective internationalization is represented by what we called soft barriers; that is barriers different from capital and technology (Leonidou, 2004; OECD, 2008), and represented by the lack of human resources, experience and knowledge, strategic orientation to foreign markets and, above all, culture. Many interviewed people use the word 'culture' to identify a lack of vision, orientation and absorption capacity. Without this particular element other export support services have few possibilities to be utilized effectively and even to be correctly understood.

Training people is a good instrument to enhance absorption capacity and export readiness, even though this needs to be complemented by instruments supporting vicarious learning such as the temporary export manager. The latter is coherent with the need for supporting experiential learning (Johasson and Vahlne, 1977), and enhancing its development. On the other hand, the contribution of the temporary export manager could vanish if there is no adequate preparation in the organization of the firm and also if the entrepreneur limits too much her/his autonomy. This consideration holds also for the other export support services.

EPOs need to develop close relationships with their customers because they are aware that small firms can benefit from these services only through relationships characterized by mutual trust and understanding which also support the exchange of tacit knowledge (Samiee and Walters, 1999; OECD, 1997). Close relationships favour the narrowing of the cultural gap between firms and EPOs, and facilitate the sharing of a common 'code'. Relationship building requires a long-term orientation in the provision of services and frequent interactions with the supported firms. Long-term relationships enable people to tailor support services to the single firms' needs and to develop a coaching function for the assisted company, which can be complementary or substitute the role of temporary management, and that could be assimilated within shared management services. A problem arises regarding the willingness/ability to pay for a coaching service and tailored instruments.

From this point of view, two main trade-offs emerge from the interviews, which need to be addressed by policy makers and service providers The first trade-off refers to the growing segmentation and sophistication of internationalization services (as an effect of more complex global markets and as an answer to differentiated needs of the firms) and the need for the small firm to have a stable counterpart to solve all its problems. A solution like a one-stop shop for different internationalization services would be worth being explored. The second trade-off deals with the request for tailor-made services, coaching, and assistance, for the selection of information and not just information provision, for partner selection and not just potential listing of partners. These firms need to contrast the difficulty/willingness to pay for value added services and – more notably – and need to recognize their value and consequently their pricing. Here, there could be market failure which public programs could address, for example, extending the use of the voucher, which has already been recently tested in Lombardy. The experimentation of new forms of public intervention based on vouchers seems to be an innovative response to all these issues: firms can dispose of a voucher which establishes the value of given services, and can choose the providers in a list of accredited private institutions, which are in competition. The voucher educates small firms about the understanding of the value of services obtained and creates a quasi-market of accredited service providers, stimulating competition.

Conclusions

This research adopts the point of view of service providers in order to highlight the barriers to international growth for SMEs from a different perspective.

The findings highlight some main issues which appear relevant for policy making. First, internal soft barriers are not only the most important obstacles to a firm's international commitment and performance, but they also influence the awareness and thus the capacity to access complementary resources and capabilities needed for foreign expansion, thus determining the probability of success. Secondly, internal soft barriers are linked more or less directly to the organizational absorption capacity (Cohen and Levinthal, 1990). To stimulate organizational learning the presence of knowledge gatekeepers in the internationalization process is fundamental, that is export managers or equivalent roles played by top management team members and/or entrepreneurs. When these roles are missing, the temporary export manager or shared management services could be an effective approach to cope with the small firms' barriers to internationalization but only if complemented by staff training, general training addressed to entrepreneurs to build an adequate cultural base, and training to enhance organizational learning processes. Thirdly, from the point of view of policy instruments, as suggested by Wilkinson and Brouthers (2000), the impact of each intervention may differ. Only a few studies try to throw some light on this complex matter, but it seems that the most effective instruments are those which allow for a better tailoring to individual companies or to homogeneous (small) groups of firms, on the one hand, and, on the other hand, those actions which support better learning processes, enhancing the organization's absorption capacity and the entrepreneurs' cultural orientation. The benefit of the latter is that improved learning has a positive impact on the organizational absorption capacity, thus opening the way to a better access to other services/instruments as well as in general to international opportunities (that is recognition and exploitation of the latter).

The findings suggest that more integration is needed not only between demand and offer of services, but also among different types of services and, finally – at a more general policy level – between the internationalization policies and the educational policies. The limitations of this study rest mainly on its exploratory nature, which does not permit to generalize findings. Moreover, the 10 interviewed organizations – while providing rich qualitative findings – may be somehow biased by the fact that they all reflect a regional experience (the region of Lombardy).

Future research directions are represented by the operationalization of the key variables and constructs developed through this study and in carrying out a quantitative survey on a sample of firms representative of different European regions.

References

Alexandrides, C.G. (1971) 'How the major obstacles to expansion can be overcome', *Atlanta Economic Review*, 21(5), 12–15.

Alvarez, R.E. (2004) 'Sources of export success in small-and medium-sized enterprises: The impact of public programs', *International Business Review*, 13(3), 383–402.

Barney, J. (1991) 'Firm resources and sustained competitive advantage', *Journal of Management*, 17(1), 99–120.

Bell, A. (1997) 'A comparative study of the export problems of small computer software exporters in Finland, Ireland and Norway', *International Business Review*, 6(6), 585–604.

Bello, D. and Williamson, N.C. (1985) 'The American export trading company: Designing a new international marketing institutions', *Journal of Marketing*, 49(4), 60–69.

Bilkey, W.J. and Tesar, G. (1977) 'The export behaviour of smaller wisconsin manufacturing firms', *Journal of International Business Studies*, 8(1), 93–98.

Bilkey, W.J. (1978) 'An attempted integration of the literature on the export behaviour of firms', *Journal of International Business Studies*, 9(1), 33–46.

Brugnoli, A. and Molteni, M. (2007) *Per un futuro nei mercati globali* (Milano: Guerini e Associati).

Bryman, A. (2004) *Social Research Method* (Oxford: Oxford University Press).

Cavusgil, S.T. and Jacob, N. (1987) 'Firm and management characteristics as discriminators of export marketing activity', *Journal of Business Research*, 15, 221–35.

Cavusgil, S.T. (1982) 'Some observations on the relevance of critical variables for internationalisation stages', in M. R. Czinkota and G. Tesar, (eds), *Export Management: An international Context* (New York: Praeger).

Cohen, W. and Levinthal, D. (1990) 'Absorptive capacity: a new perspective on learning and innovation', *Administration Science Quarterly*, 35, 128–52.

Cuervo-Cazurra, A., Maloney, M.M and Manrakhan, S. (2007) 'Causes of the difficulties in internationalisation', *Journal of International Business Studies*, 38(5), 709–25.

Czinkota, M.R. and Johnston, W.J. (1983) 'Exporting: Does sales volume make a difference?', *Journal of International Business Studies*, 14(1), 147-53.

Denis, J.E. and Depelteau, D. (1985) 'Market knowledge, diversification, and export expansion', *Journal of International Business Studies*, 16(3), 77–90.

Dhanaraj, C. and Beamish, P.W. (2003) 'A resource-based approach to the study of export performance' *Journal of Small Business Management*, 41(3), 242–61.

Diamantopoulos, A. and Inglis, K. (1988) 'Identifying differences between high- and low-involvement exporters', *International Marketing Review*, 5(2), 52–60.

Dicht, E., Koglmayr, H.G. and Muller, S. (1990) 'International orientation as a precondition for export success', *Journal of International Business Studies*, 21(1), 23–40.

Esposito, G.F. (2003) *La Globalizzazione dei piccoli. Fattori di competizione e promozione dell'internazionalizzazione per le pmi* (Milano: FrancoAngeli).

Gençtűrk, E.F. and Kotabe, M. (2001) 'The effect of export assistance program usage on export performance: A contingency explanation', *Journal of International Marketing*, 9(2), 51–72.

Grandinetti, R. (1992) 'Apprendimento ed evoluzione nei percorsi di internazionalizzazione delle piccole e medie imprese', *Piccola Impresa/Small Business*, 1, 79–123.

Inkpen, A.C. and Beamish, P.W. (1997) 'Knowledge, Bargaining Power, and the Instability of International Joint Ventures', *The Academy of Management Review*, 22(1), 177–202.

Johanson, J.and Vahlne, J.E. (1977) 'The internationalisation process of the firm. A model of knowledge development and increasing foreign market commitments', *Journal of International Business Studies*, 8, 23–32.

Kotabe, M. and Czinkota, M.R. (1993) 'State government promotion of manufacturing exports: A gap analysis', *Journal of International Business Studies*, 23(4), 637–58.

Kumcu, E., Harcar, T. and Kumcu, M.E., (1995) 'Managerial perceptions of the adequacy of Export Incentive Programs', *Journal of Business Research*, 32, 163–74.

Lages, L.F. and Montgomery, D.B. (2001) 'Export assistance, price adaptation to the foreign market, and annual export performance improvement: A structural model examination', Research paper, 1–20, Stanford University, Graduate School of Business.

Leonidou, L.C. (2004) 'An analysis of the barriers hindering small business export Development', *Journal of Small Business Management*, 40(3), 279–302.

Leonidou, L.C. and Theodosius, M. (2004) 'The export marketing information system: an integration of the extant literature', *Journal of World Business*, 39, 12–36.

Liesch, P.W. and Knight, G.A. (1999) 'Information internalisation and hurdle rates in small and medium enterprise internationalisation', *Journal of International Business Studies*, 30 (1), 383–94.

Miesenböck, K.J. (1988) 'Small business and exporting: a literature review', *International Small Business Journal*, 6(2), 42–61.

OECD (1997) *Globalisation and Small and Medium Enterprises (SMEs)* (Paris: OECD).

OECD (2008) *Removing Barriers to SME Access to International Markets* (Paris: OECD).

Penrose, E.T. (1959) *The Theory of the Growth of the Firm* (New York: John Wiley).

Pinney, J.K. (1971) 'Obstacles to foreign trade of 209 indiana manufacturers', Bulletin published by the Indiana Department of Commerce, Indianapolis.

Pointon, T. (1978) 'Measuring the gains from government export promotion', *European Journal of Marketing* 12(6), 451–62.

Reid,. S.D. (1985) 'Exporting: Does sales volume make a difference? A comment', *Journal of International Business Studies*, 16(2), 153–55.

Samiee, S. and Walters, P.G.P. (1999) 'Determinants of structured export knowledge acquisition', *International Business Review*, 8, 373–97.

Seringhaus, F.H.R. and Rosson, P.J. (1991) *Export development and promotion: The role of public organizations* (Boston: Kluwer).

Seringhaus, H.F.R. (1986) 'The impact of government export marketing assistance', *International Marketing Review*, 3(2), 55–66.

Spence, M.M. (2003) 'Evaluation export promotion programmes: UK overseas trade missions and export performance', *Small Business Economics*, 20, 83–103.

Suárez-Ortega, S.M. and Álamo-Vera, F.R. (2005) 'SMES' internationalisation: firms and managerial factors', *International Journal of Entrepreneurial Behaviour & Research*, 11(4), 258–79.

Tan, A., Brewer, P. and Liesch, P.W. (2007) 'Before the first export decision: Internationalisation readiness in the pre-export phase', *International Business Review*, 16, 294–309.

Teece, D.J.(1986) 'Profiting from Technological Innovation', *Research Policy*, 15, 285–305.

Westhead, P., Wright, M. and Ucbasaran, D. (2001) 'The Internationalisation of new and small firms: a resources-based view', *Journal of Business Venturing*, 16, 333–58.

Wilkinson, T.J. and Brouthers, L.E. (2000) 'An evaluation of state sponsored export promotion programs', *Journal of Business Research*, 47(3), 229–36.

Wilkinson, T.J. and Brouthers, L.E. (2006) 'Trade promotion and SME export performance', *International Business Review*, 15, 233–52.

Zaheer, S. (1995) 'Overcoming the liability of foreignness', *The Academy of Management Journal*, 38(2), 341–363.

Zucchella, A., Palamara, G. and Denicolai, S. (2007) 'The drivers of the early internationalisation of the firm', *Journal of World Business*, 42 (3), 268–80.

Index

QM LIBRARY
(MILE END)

WITHDRAWN
FROM STOCK
QMUL LIBRARY